# Citrix XenDesktop 5.6 Cookbook

Implement a fully featured XenDesktop 5.6 architecture in a rich and powerful VDI experience configuration

**Gaspare A. Silvestri**

BIRMINGHAM - MUMBAI

# Citrix XenDesktop 5.6 Cookbook



First published: January 2013

Production Reference: 1140113

Published by Packt Publishing Ltd.
Livery Place
35 Livery Street
Birmingham B3 2PB, UK.

ISBN 978-1-84968-504-7

www.packtpub.com

Cover Image by Artie Ng (artherng@yahoo.com.au)

# Credits

**Author**
Gaspare A. Silvestri

**Reviewers**
Aaron Black
Ferdinand Feenstra
Peter Nap
Juan Perez

**Acquisition Editor**
Grant Mizen

**Lead Technical Editor**
Arun Nadar

**Technical Editors**
Devdutt Kulkarni
Ankita Meshram

**Copy Editors**
Brandt D'Mello
Alfida Paiva
Laxmi Subramanian
Ruta Waghmare

**Project Coordinator**
Abhishek Kori

**Proofreader**
Stephen Swaney

**Indexer**
Hemangini Bari

**Production Coordinator**
Arvindkumar Gupta

**Cover Work**
Arvindkumar Gupta

# About the Author

**Gaspare A. Silvestri** is an IT Technical Director for an Italian Hosting Provider company with 10 years of experience in the Information Technology market. Being a Multicertified IT Director, he considers his job as the first of all his passions, with a particular preference for the virtualization and the Unix technology areas. He is always curious and in search of new IT projects on which he performs research activities. Gaspare has been involved in the design, tuning, and consolidation of physical and virtual infrastructures for important system integration companies based in Italy.

Thanks to Viola and Manuela, the shining stars of my life.

Thanks to all my family, for the strength and the support they have always given to me.

Thanks to Roberto, who gave me, some years ago, an opportunity to start working on the Citrix platforms.

Thanks to the coffee and Miles Davis, which have been my main fellowship during the working hours.

A special thanks to Stephanie Moss, Abhishek Kori, Arun Nadar, and the entire staff at Packt Publishing for the exceptional work they have done with me, and for all the work we have done together.

# About the Reviewers

**Aaron Black** is a Senior Product Manager at VMware® in the End User Computing business unit. He is currently responsible for ThinApp, ThinApp Factory, and the Horizon integration with ThinApp. At VMware he has worked at various positions in the field as a Systems Engineer, a stint in technical marketing, and now product management. His primary domain of knowledge revolves around all application-related things. At previous companies, he worked as a Systems Engineer with Citrix Systems, lead a technical corporate IT team at Sprint, and worked as a Solutions Designer for a platinum reseller of VMware and Citrix products.

**Ferdinand Feenstra** is a Citrix Certified Architect and Senior Specialist for Microsoft environments, based in the Netherlands. He is working in the IT branch since 1998, and he has experience in many complex environments with different customers in different functions.

His experience is in building and designing Citrix environments, implementation and migration projects, and consultancy projects. Since he discovered working with Citrix in 2004, a new world of solutions, working on any device combined with a great user experience, came his way. This makes IT more dynamic and easier to adapt for users. You can find his blog on `www.CitrixGuru.net`. You can also check his tweets on Twitter, `@f_feenstra`.

This is the second review for him. He has already reviewed the book *XenServer 6.0 Administration Essential Guide, Daniele Tosatto, Packt Publishing.*

Ferdinand works for Icento. Icento is a Citrix Partner Solution Advisor with the Silver status. Icento is also a V-Alliance member; the Virtualization collaboration between Microsoft and Citrix. Icento is located in Rotterdam, the Netherlands and delivers solutions for the desktop, unified communications, and virtualization and systems management. Icento delivers state-of-the-art ICT solutions for a broad set of international customers. You can find more information at `www.icento.nl`.

**Peter Nap** is a very experienced Server Based Computing consultant and Infrastructure Architect. He is 38 years old, lives in the Netherlands and is currently employed as an Infrastructure Architect for Logica (now part of CGI). He has 13 years of work experience in various large and small businesses, including the Ministry of Defense and the Ministry of Justice of the Netherlands.

In his latest project, Peter has created a VDI infrastructure with XenDesktop 5.6, Windows 7 x64, and Citrix Provisioning 6.1 on a VMware vSphere 5.1 hypervisor.

**Juan Perez** has been in the IT field for 12 years. He has been working with Citrix for just over 2 years and has thrived in it. He is looking forward to a newly accepted position with very highly regarded Citrix solutions Platinum Partner and attending Citrix Academy in January of 2013 in Santa Clara.

Juan is currently working for Stearns Lending, a fast growing company that has put the challenge on the IT team to help them grow to a world class company. Stearns is fully equipped with Citrix Xenap, Xendesktop, and Xenserver. Since being introduced to Citrix, Juan has learned the basics, and moved on to completely managing multiple Xenserver environments.

He has reviewed the book *XenServer 6.0 Administration Essential Guide, Daniele Tosatto, Packt Publishing*.

Simple thanks to all who have helped me in my career as an IT pro.

# Table of Contents


**Preface** 1

**Chapter 1: XenDesktop Installation and Configuration** 5

- Introduction 5
- Preparing the SQL Server database 7
- Installing and configuring the license server 10
- Installing XenDesktop components 15
- Installing and configuring Web Interface 18
- Installing and configuring Provisioning Services 26
- Chapter 1 XenDesktop lab 36

**Chapter 2: Deploying Virtual Machines for XenDesktop** 39

- Introduction 39
- Configuring the XenDesktop site 40
- Configuring XenDesktop to interact with Citrix XenServer 43
- Configuring XenDesktop to interact with VMware vSphere 49
- Configuring XenDesktop to interact with Microsoft Hyper-V 54
- Chapter 2 XenDesktop lab 71

**Chapter 3: Master Image Configuration and Tuning** 73

- Introduction 73
- Installing Citrix Profile Management 74
- Configuring virtual desktop policies 81
- Configuring Active Directory policies 89
- Optimizing the desktop experience 91
- Chapter 3 XenDesktop lab 97

**Chapter 4: User Experience – Planning and Configuring** 101

- Introduction 101
- Implementing profile architecture 102
- Installing Virtual Desktop Agent 108

Configuring advanced user experience – HDX 3D Pro 115
Configuring Citrix Receiver 119
Chapter 4 XenDesktop lab 124
**Chapter 5: Configuring Additional Architectural Components 127**
Introduction 127
Configuring the Merchandising Server 128
Configuring the Branch Repeater virtual appliance 140
Installing and configuring XenDesktop Collector 149
Chapter 5 XenDesktop lab 155
**Chapter 6: Creating and Configuring a Desktop Environment 159**
Introduction 159
Creating and configuring the machine catalog 160
Modifying an existing machine catalog 175
Using Citrix Desktop Director 184
Configuring printers 190
Configuring USB devices 198
Chapter 6 XenDesktop lab 202
**Chapter 7: Deploying Applications 205**
Introduction 205
Publishing the VM-hosted apps with XenDesktop 206
Publishing the streamed apps with XenApp 6.5 217
Publishing applications using Microsoft App-V 227
Chapter 7 XenDesktop lab 236
**Chapter 8: XenDesktop Tuning and Security 239**
Introduction 239
Configuring the XenDesktop policies 239
Configuring the Citrix Access Gateway virtual appliance 254
Configuring the XenDesktop logging 268
Chapter 8 XenDesktop lab 272
**Chapter 9: Working with XenDesktop PowerShell 273**
Introduction 273
Retrieving system information – configuration service cmdlets 274
Managing Active Directory accounts – AD identity cmdlets 278
Managing the Citrix Desktop Controller – broker cmdlets 283
Administering hosts and machines – host and machine creation cmdlets 292
Chapter 9 XenDesktop lab 297

**Chapter 10: Configuring the XenDesktop Advanced Logon** 299
Introduction 299
Implementing the XenDesktop smart card authentication 300
Implementing the XenDesktop strong authentication 309
Implementing the Citrix SSO platform 319
Chapter 10 XenDesktop lab 329
**Index** 331

# Preface

In the last few years, the way we work has changed and has evolved to the point that we now have the opportunity to access personal data not just when we are at our personal office desk. Thanks to new technologies such as smart phones and tablets, more and more users are now able to have the feeling of being able to work everywhere and anywhere. However, despite the advances, this feeling is not always supported by the real ability to operate this way.

In the current post-PC age, we need to change the approach.

Citrix is a market leader for end-user virtualization. In the range of products offered to IT customers, we are now able to implement a powerful solution such as XenDesktop 5.6, which allows users to have the published desktops and/or applications on platforms that can be Windows aware (for example, Android or Apple iOS), without losing agility and the rich user experience of the original.

With this book we'll cover the main implementation aspects, advanced features, and all the activities required to tune the infrastructure and enrich the final user impact.

At the end of this book, we're going to explain XenDesktop PowerShell, with real-case practical implementation; by this, any virtualization engineer will improve and consolidate his knowledge of XenDesktop.

## What this book covers

*Chapter 1, XenDesktop Installation and Configuration*, presents the prerequisites to install the platform, the differences between the two most important architectures, operations to perform during the installation phase, and the first configuration step for each component.

*Chapter 2, Deploying Virtual Machines for XenDesktop*, shows the way to interface XenDesktop with hypervisor hosts for farm and VM base image creation. This part will also include the second configuration phase for the XenDesktop components.

*Chapter 3, Master Image Configuration and Tuning*, is focused on configuration and optimization operations realized on the base desktop image for future deployments.

*Chapter 4, User Experience – Planning and Configuring*, helps the customers to implement all basic and advanced features of user experience (ICA and HDX).

*Chapter 5, Configuring Additional Architectural Components*, performs implementation and optimization activities for infrastructural satellite components such as Citrix Merchandising Server or the Citrix Branch Repeater virtual appliance.

*Chapter 6, Creating and Configuring a Desktop Environment*, explains administrative tasks for the desktop environment such as catalog creation, power management, resource allocation.

*Chapter 7, Deploying Applications*, shows the way to assign and publish applications only to specified users; we'll also explain interfacing with XenApp 6.5 and Microsoft App-V.

*Chapter 8, XenDesktop Tuning and Security*, performs optimization activities to enrich quality level for VDI. In this chapter, we'll also learn how to secure the XenDesktop system components.

*Chapter 9, Working with XenDesktop PowerShell*, will be an advanced guide to the XenDesktop PowerShell modules; with these, we'll realize high-level configurations by command line.

*Chapter 10, Configuring the XenDesktop Advanced Logon*, explains the operations to implement the secure and strong authentication for the Citrix XenDesktop architectures.

At the end of every chapter there will be a laboratory, a set of practical exercises used to test the comprehension of the chapter by the readers. Every laboratory will be a link to the exercises written in its next chapter, in order to implement a full functioning environment, without constraining the users in a predefined configuration, giving the ability to operate with a little bit more of a freedom regarding the operations to perform.

# What you need for this book

The prerequisites required to install the components are as follows:

- At least Windows 2008 with Service Pack 2 (32 or 64 bit); preferably Windows Server 2008 R2 (only 64 bit)
- Microsoft .NET Framework 3.5 SP1
- For Web Interface, IIS (7.0 for W2K8 SP2, 7.5 for W2K8 R2) web server and ASP.NET 2.0
- Visual J# 2.0 SE
- Visual C++ 2008 Service Pack 1

- 100 MB of disk space for each of these components – Web Interface, Controller, and SDK
- 50 MB of disk space for each of these components – Desktop Studio and Desktop Director
- 40 MB for licensing

# Who this book is for

This book is for system engineers who have just had an approach with previous Citrix XenDesktop releases. Some parts cover normal administration tasks, but the most of the book implements advanced features and techniques that require working knowledge about systems, servers, and desktop virtualization.

Because of its step-by-step method, users who approach virtualization for the first time can use this book as a practical integration of parallel theoretical studies.

# Conventions

In this book, you will find a number of styles of text that distinguish between different kinds of information. Here are some examples of these styles, and an explanation of their meaning.

Code words in text are shown as follows: "Once all the configurations are complete, under the temporary folder where we copied the JAR file, we will have a `.war` file and a `.xml` file."

Any command-line input or output is written as follows:

```
Set-ConfigDBConnection -DBConnection $null
Set-AcctDBConnection -DBConnection $null
Set-HypDBConnection -DBConnection $null
Set-BrokerDBConnection -DBConnection $null
```

**New terms** and **important words** are shown in bold. Words that you see on the screen, in menus or dialog boxes for example, appear in the text like this: "Click on the **Content...** button first, then click on **Add**, and select your language."

Warnings or important notes appear in a box like this.

Tips and tricks appear like this.

# Reader feedback

Feedback from our readers is always welcome. Let us know what you think about this book—what you liked or may have disliked. Reader feedback is important for us to develop titles that you really get the most out of.

To send us general feedback, simply send an e-mail to `feedback@packtpub.com`, and mention the book title via the subject of your message.

If there is a book that you need and would like to see us publish, please send us a note in the **SUGGEST A TITLE** form on `www.packtpub.com` or e-mail `suggest@packtpub.com`.

If there is a topic that you have expertise in and you are interested in either writing or contributing to a book, see our author guide on `www.packtpub.com/authors`.

# Customer support

Now that you are the proud owner of a Packt book, we have a number of things to help you to get the most from your purchase.

## Errata

Although we have taken every care to ensure the accuracy of our content, mistakes do happen. If you find a mistake in one of our books—maybe a mistake in the text or the code—we would be grateful if you would report this to us. By doing so, you can save other readers from frustration and help us improve subsequent versions of this book. If you find any errata, please report them by visiting `http://www.packtpub.com/support`, selecting your book, clicking on the **errata submission form** link, and entering the details of your errata. Once your errata are verified, your submission will be accepted and the errata will be uploaded on our website, or added to any list of existing errata, under the Errata section of that title. Any existing errata can be viewed by selecting your title from `http://www.packtpub.com/support`.

## Piracy

Piracy of copyright material on the Internet is an ongoing problem across all media. At Packt, we take the protection of our copyright and licenses very seriously. If you come across any illegal copies of our works, in any form, on the Internet, please provide us with the location address or website name immediately so that we can pursue a remedy.

Please contact us at `copyright@packtpub.com` with a link to the suspected pirated material.

We appreciate your help in protecting our authors, and our ability to bring you valuable content.

## Questions

You can contact us at `questions@packtpub.com` if you are having a problem with any aspect of the book, and we will do our best to address it.

# 1
# XenDesktop Installation and Configuration

In this chapter we will cover:

- Preparing the SQL Server database
- Installing and configuring the license server
- Installing XenDesktop components
- Installing and configuring Web Interface
- Installing and configuring Provisioning Services

## Introduction

XenDesktop 5.6 is the latest version of the Citrix end user virtualization platform. System engineers can choose between two architectural implementations – **Machine Creation Services** (**MCS**), which consist of hosted desktops and applications published to users based on given accessibility permissions, and **Provisioning Services** (**PVS**), which consist of a single desktop or a pool of them, booted over a network and streamed on demand to end users.

In both cases, information is stored in a Citrix database repository, based on Microsoft SQL Server (Standard or Express edition); it's used and populated with data coming from the main architectural components (Desktop Controller, Desktop Studio, Provisioning Services server). Configured resources, such as virtual desktops, can be accessed by end users through a web portal called Web Interface.

The MCS and PVS architectures can be combined together, and used within the same company for different desktop distribution areas; this is the implementation of the Citrix FlexCast technique.

For a number of delivered virtual desktops equal to or greater than 500, you should always consider using the PVS architecture.

The main goal of this chapter is for you to understand the differences between the two main kinds of architectures, MCS and PVS. Once you've understood this, you'll be able to better comprehend what and how to implement a consistent and coherent XenDesktop installation.

Starting from the database server and licensing configuration, we'll walk through the XenDesktop components, Web Interface, and the complex configuration of the PVS architecture.

The first implementable architecture type is MCS; its most important part is based on hosted virtual desktops.

How can we determine whether MCS is the better solution for us? We've got a set of main parameters to decide, as follows:

- MCS is the right solution if we only want to deploy the VDI infrastructure
- We should choose MCS when the number of deployed desktops is under 2,500
- MCS is preferable when we don't only want standardized machines, but we also want to give users the ability to install and customize their desktops
- It should be better to use MCS when we need to frequently upgrade base images; despite the complexity of the operations required with the use of the PVS architecture, this is a quite simple process for the machine creation platforms
- Consider implementing this architecture when you have a shared storage, such as **Network File System** (**NFS**) or **Storage Area Network** (**SAN**); especially in the second case, it's preferable to have the MCS architecture, thanks to its large IOPS capacity

To implement a pure MCS architecture, you need the following components:

- Desktop Director
- Desktop Controller
- Web Interface
- License server

The second kind of XenDesktop infrastructure is PVS, a Citrix implementation fully based on desktop streaming technology.

PVS is the right choice for the following cases:

- When we need to provide users with not only hosted desktops, but especially with streamed workstations.
- When we have more than one site with a number of desktops per location higher than 2,500.

- When we don't have a shared storage, or when we're in the situation of a low performance data area. In this case, we'll take advantage of PVS memory caching activity.
- When we have a lot of users logging on or logging off simultaneously; this is known as a **boot storm** phenomenon. Choosing PVS, we could avoid this problem by passing storage constraints.

To implement PVS instead of MCS, you must configure the following components in your architecture:

- Desktop Director
- Desktop Controller
- Web Interface
- License server
- Citrix Provisioning Services

You should consider combining MCS and PVS together, especially in cases where your architecture has the right balance of RAM quantity and storage performance. This is what Citrix calls the FlexCast approach - a way to combine different architectures to satisfy all the requirements for a set of different end users' topologies.

# Preparing the SQL Server database

XenDesktop 5.6 needs a repository to store all information about clients, users, permissions, and so on. The supported DBMS is Microsoft SQL Server. Depending on the specific application's requirements, we're able to choose between an integrated version of it, or a separate database installation, as discussed later in this chapter.

## Getting ready

Citrix XenDesktop 5.6 supports the following versions of Microsoft SQL Server:

- SQL Server 2008 Express Service Pack 1 (32 or 64 bit)
- SQL Server 2008 Service Pack 2 or 3 (32 or 64 bit)
- SQL Server 2008 R2 Express (64 bit only)
- SQL Server 2008 R2 (64 bit only)

How can we choose the correct database version? It depends on what level of performance and availability is needed. For standalone installations (integrated with the XenDesktop Controller server) within a small environment, the Express edition should be the right choice. In the presence of a huge number of clients and users, if you want to create a clustered database instance, you should implement the non-Express version of SQL Server.

If we have decided to implement an integrated version of the database, we only need to flag the **Install SQL Server Express** option when installing XenDesktop; all the components and the configuration parameters will automatically be created and configured.

For a separate database installation, we need to perform the installation operations, as explained in the following section.

## How to do it...

Perform the following steps to generate a SQL Server database, which will be used by XenDesktop:

1. From the SQL Server installation media, launch the executable setup file.
2. If you want, you can launch **System Configuration Checker** to perform a pre-installation test, and verify that all the requirements are met:

System Configuration Checker
Launch a tool to check for conditions

3. Click on the **Installation** tab, which you can see in the left-hand side menu and select **New installation or add features to an existing installation**. For the purpose of this book, we won't execute all the steps required to complete the database installation:

New installation or add features to an existing installation.
Launch a wizard to install SQL Server 2008 R2 in a non-clustered environment or to

New SQL Server failover cluster installation
Launch a wizard to install a single-node SQL Server 2008 R2 failover cluster.

Add node to a SQL Server failover cluster
Launch a wizard to add a node to an existing SQL Server 2008 R2 failover cluster.

Upgrade from SQL Server 2000, SQL Server 2005 or SQL Server 2008
Launch a wizard to upgrade SQL Server 2000, SQL Server 2005 or SQL Server 2008

Search for product updates
Search Microsoft Update for SQL Server 2008 R2 product updates.

4. If you've got available resources, you can select to create a new named instance, not using the default SQL Server instance (MSSQLSERVER).
5. On the database server, create a database on the desired instance (preferably having a dedicated instance for Citrix, as previously seen) with the following parameters:
    i. Create a new database instance on the database server, and set **Collation sequence** to **Latin1_General_CI_AS_KS**.
    ii. Configure the authentication method only as Windows authentication.
    iii. Configure the **Permissions** settings, as shown in the following table:

| Activity | Server role | Database role |
|---|---|---|
| Database creation | `dbcreator` | |
| Schema creation | `securityadmin` | `db_owner` |
| Controller addition | `securityadmin` | `db_owner` |
| Controller removal | | `db_owner` |
| Schema update | | `db_owner` |

6. This permission will be granted to the operating system user, who will perform configuration activities through the Desktop Studio console.

Using a separate instance is not mandatory, but it is better (more isolation, more security).

## How it works...

We've configured the most common format for the collation sequences (the same used by Citrix), and also restricted the way to log on to the database at Windows authentication, because XenDesktop does not support SQL or Mixed mode. For the collation, you are free to use not only the indicated version, but the most important thing is that you will choose one that is a member of the `*_CI_AS_KS` category (collation family is case and accent insensitive, but kanatype sensitive).

You must be careful when increasing the size of database logging. Despite the normal data component (you should expect to have a database size of 250 MB with some thousands of clients), logs could unexpectedly increase in 24 hours, in the presence of many thousands of desktops. Based on the following table for MCS architectures, we'll be able to calculate the database log and data files occupation:

| Component | Data/log | Occupation |
|---|---|---|
| Registration information | Data | 2.9 KB per desktop |
| Session state | Data | 5.1 KB per desktop |

| Component | Data/log | Occupation |
|---|---|---|
| Active Directory computer account info | Data | 1.8 KB per desktop |
| MCS machine info | Data | 1.94 KB per desktop |
| Transaction log for idle desktop | Log | 62 KB per hour |

For a more detailed SQL Server installation, please refer to the official Microsoft online documentation at `http://technet.microsoft.com/en-us/sqlserver/bb265254.aspx`.

## There's more...

In case of necessity to redeploy one or more Desktop Delivery Controller servers configured in your VDI infrastructure, the first action to perform is cleaning the Citrix XenDesktop configured database. To perform this task, you have to set all the Citrix components' database connection to null, using the custom Citrix PowerShell running the following commands:

```
Set-ConfigDBConnection -DBConnection $null
Set-AcctDBConnection -DBConnection $null
Set-HypDBConnection -DBConnection $null
Set-BrokerDBConnection -DBConnection $null
```

Once you've finished these operations, you can proceed with the manual deletion and the recreation of the SQL Server database.

Later in this book we will explain better how to use the Citrix PowerShell available with XenDesktop 5.6.

# Installing and configuring the license server

Citrix permits users to buy XenDesktop in different versions, as shown in the following list:

- Citrix XenDesktop Express Edition – a free edition that allows you to test the platform without any cost, with the ability to publish up to 10 desktops
- Citrix XenDesktop VDI Edition
- Citrix XenDesktop Enterprise Edition
- Citrix XenDesktop Platinum Edition

The choice is based on personal needs; in this book, when we refer to XenDesktop 5.6, it will be about Platinum Edition, which has the ability to show and implement the full functionality of the platform.

## Getting ready

The associated version of license server for XenDesktop 5.6 is Version 11.0. Starting from this release, we also have the ability to use a virtual appliance for XenServer (called License Server VPX). The system requirements for the usual setup (not VPX) are as follows:

- Windows Server 2003, 2008, or 2008 R2 version; or Windows 7 (32 or 64 bits)
- 50 MB for licensing components and 2 GB for user and/or device licenses
- .NET Framework 3.5
- A compatible browser

## How to do it...

In this section we are going to perform the required operations for the Citrix license server installation and configuration:

1. After downloading the software from your personal Citrix account, run the `CTX_Licensing.msi` installer.
2. Accept the Citrix license agreement.
3. Select a destination folder's path for the program, which is by default `C:\Program Files (x86)\Citrix\`.
4. Click on the **Finish** button when license server is successfully installed.
5. On the first configuration screen, you must assign port numbers for the **License Server Port**, **Vendor Daemon Port**, and **Management Console Web Port** fields, as shown in the following screenshot:

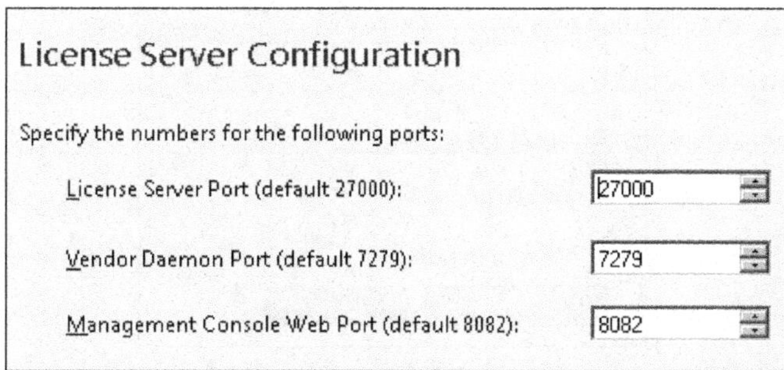


6. You can decide to leave default ports for these three options, or change them. In any case, the ports you'll decide to use must be opened on Windows Server's personal firewall.

7. To generate the license file for importing it to our license server, run a web browser installed on your client machine, connect to `www.citrix.com/MyCitrix`, and log in using your credentials.
8. Go to **Manage licenses**.
9. Click on **Allocate licenses**.
10. Insert the **Full Qualified Domain Name** (**FQDN**) of your license server, and select the number of licenses you want to allocate.
11. Generate the license file by clicking on the **Allocate** button.
12. Now you'll be able to save the file. When prompted for the location, select the path on which the license manager will read the file with the `.lic` extension, as `C:\Program Files (x86)\Citrix\Licensing\MyFiles`.

XenDesktop license server is case sensitive. Be careful when you insert server FQDN; you've got to respect all uppercase and lowercase characters.

13. Then, to configure the license server, click on **Start** | **All programs** | **Citrix** | **Management consoles**, and select **License Administration Console**.
14. You'll see the summary dashboard; click on the **Administration** button and insert the administrative credentials for your machine (domain or local admin account):

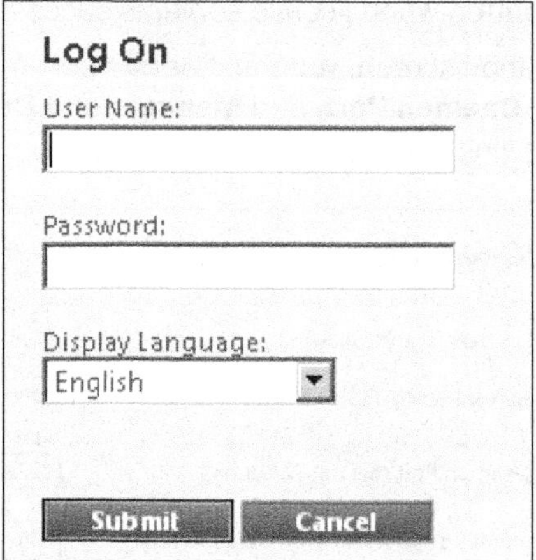

In case of a forgotten configured user and/or password, the default credentials for the license server console are both `admin`.

15. After a quick look in the **Summary** tab, click on the first button on the left-hand side menu, **User Configuration**.
16. Add a new user account to differentiate from standard administrative machine credentials; we can decide to create this account as locally managed or a domain admin. After this operation, click on **Save**.
17. Now it's time to configure alerting. Depending on our needs, we can set up critical and important alerts. It's preferable to leave them as default settings, and click on **Save** to archive the options.
18. In the **Server Configuration** menu, configure the port for the Web server (default is 8082) and session timeout period (default is 30 minutes, but if possible, you should reduce this value, so you can avoid inactive sessions locking unused resources). For security reasons, it's a good practice enabling SSL (port 443) and eventually using a personal certificate for strong authentication (as shown in the following screenshot).
19. For security reasons, you should change default license server port number, which is 27000. The default ports range is from 27000 to 27009:



20. At the end is the most important part, **Vendor Daemon Configuration**. After the license file has been generated, click on **Import License**, browse for the file location, and upload it.
21. If everything is ok, you'll receive a confirmation message about the success of the loading operation.

22. Click on **Vendor Daemon** in (in our case, the default daemon is called **Citrix**), and click on **Reread license file**, to make sure that everything's correct.

Never manually edit the license file! If vendor daemon configuration returns an error, probably you have to reallocate licenses and regenerate the file, but don't correct it with any text editor.

## How it works...

The XenDesktop license file is generated on the personal area on the MyCitrix Web portal. When you generate a `.lic` file, it must be generated and registered with the FQDN of the license server on which you're going to use the file. This means that, if for any reason you'll need to reinstall the server or change its name, you must deallocate the license currently assigned, and reassign it to the new server, always referring to its FQDN, regenerating a new file that must be reimported, as seen previously.

If you are using XenDesktop for test purposes, or in case of a license server's fault, Citrix gives you a grace period of 30 days.

## There's more...

It's also possible to install the license server from the command line, using the Windows command, `msiexec`, with the following parameters:

- `/I`: This is the installation option.
- `/qn`: This is for a silent installation.
- `INSTALLDIR`: This is used to specify the path of the installation folder (if not specified, default is `C:\Program files\Citrix\Licensing` for a 64-bit system, or `C:\Program files(x86)\Citrix\Licensing` for a 32-bit system).
- `LICSERVERPORT`: This is the port that the license server will listen to for connections (default is 27000).
- `ADMINPASS`: This is the administrative password for the user admin on the licensing console. In the presence of an active directory, you have to use administrative domain credentials.
- `VENDORDAEMONPORT`: This is the port of the vendor daemon component (default is 7279).
- `MNGMTCONSOLEWEBPORT`: This is the administrative license console port (default is 8082).

So, for example, if we would install Licensing in a silent way, using the `LICSERVER` folder on port 27004 and assigning `TestCase01` as the administrative password, the following will be the required string to run:

```
msiexec /I /qn INSTALLDIR=C:\LICSERVER  LICSERVERPORT=27004
ADMINPASS=TestCase01
```

# Installing XenDesktop components

We've implemented two fundamental components of a VDI infrastructure: database server and license server. Now we've got to implement the core of Citrix XenDesktop, which includes Desktop Director Controller, Desktop Director, and Desktop Studio.

In a Citrix environment, most of the activities are related to the **Desktop Director Controller**, also known as **DDC**; with this component we're able to interface with hypervisors, generate machine pools, and provision desktops and applications. This component is the engine of the VDI Citrix platform, also known as the broker. Combined with it there's Desktop Studio, a snap-in interface that allows administrators to manage desktop components. Last is Desktop Director, a centralized console management that gives us statistics about desktop usage and performance, allowing us to change machine assignments and user permissions.

## How to do it...

The following are the steps by which we will perform the installation of the core components of the XenDesktop platform:

1. After downloading the ISO file from your personal Citrix account, burn it or mount it as a virtual CD (for example, if performing the installation with a virtual machine).
2. Double-click on **Autoselect.exe**, and then launch the XenDesktop installation by clicking on **Install XenDesktop**, as shown in the following screenshot:

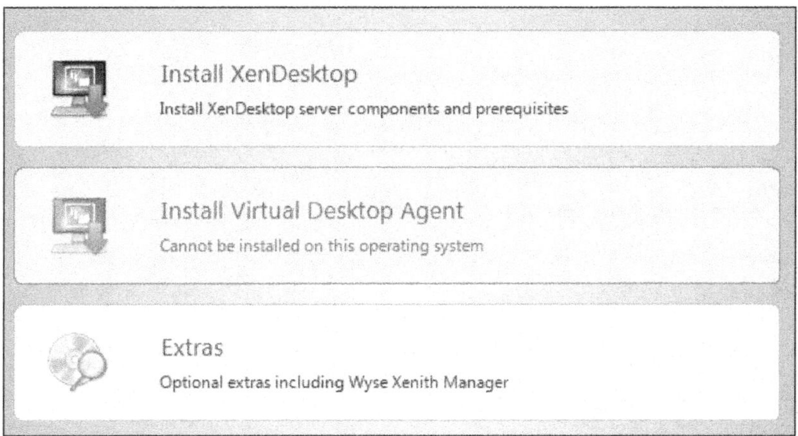

3. After the setup initialization, accept the licensing agreement.
4. At this point, select the components you want to install (Desktop Controller, Desktop Studio, and Desktop Director).
5. It's also possible to change the installation folder, by clicking on the **Change install location...** link.

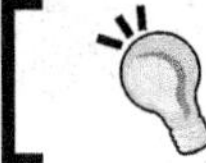

Don't check the **Web Access** installation checkbox, because we'll perform this operation in the next recipe.

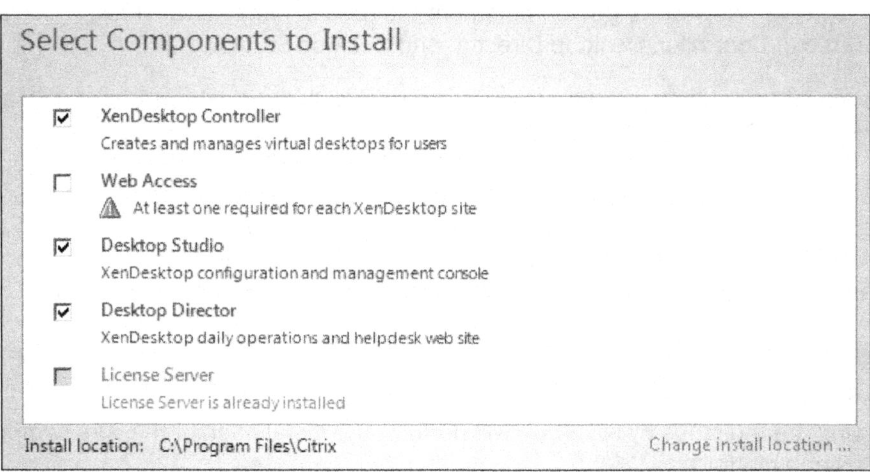


6. You'll be presented with the **Summary** window. If you agree with the summary details, click on the **Install** button to proceed.
7. At the end of the installation, leave the **Configure XenDesktop after closing** checkbox checked so that we can launch the XenDesktop MMC snap-in:

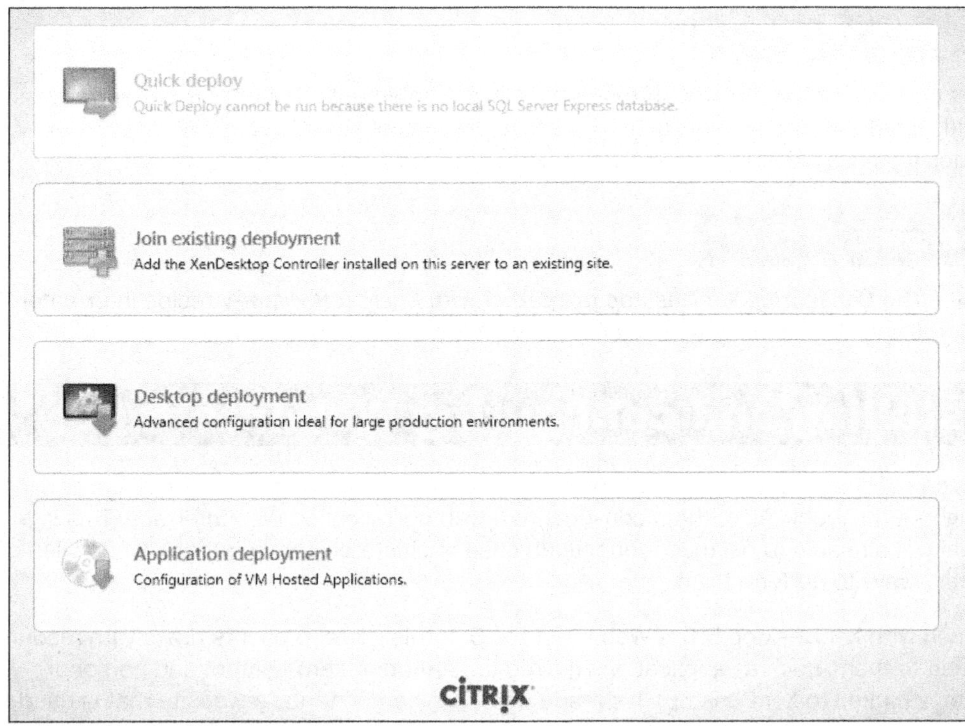

In the preceding screenshot, the **Quick deploy** option is grayed out, because we have not implemented the Express version of SQL Server; it's only available with this version of Microsoft DBMS.

8. Now that we've accomplished these installation tasks, in the **Program** menu we have a `Citrix` folder with two links: one for **Desktop Director** and another for **Desktop Studio**.

## How it works...

Desktop Controller is the component that allows one-to-one association between the user and the virtual desktop, and permits resource distribution based on what kind of desktop groups have been created; also known as a broker. It has the purpose of verifying and associating user accounts and assigned resources. Once this association is realized, the broker stops its intermediary channel activities and direct communication is established between the user's physical workstation and the delivered desktop.

## There's more...

A best practice for XenDesktop infrastructure is to implement components separately; you should install every single part of it on a single physical or virtual server. With Desktop Director, it's possible to implement a clustered broker infrastructure.

## See also

- The *Configuring XenDesktop to interact with Microsoft Hyper-V* recipe in *Chapter 2, Deploying Virtual Machines for XenDesktop*

# Installing and configuring Web Interface

Users can access their personal desktops in a set of different ways, which we'll cover throughout this book. All of them converge to a web portal called Web Interface. This is a special website able to balance requests (in case of clustered configuration), which also offers different ways to perform login.

Included with XenDesktop 5.6 is Web Interface 5.4; this portal presents users with resources mapped to them, such as applications (linked to XenApp or XenDesktop) and personal desktops (linked to XenDesktop). It's made up of two components: a website that is used to perform logon operations through a supported web browser, and a service site that is used by the Citrix online plugin to link to a XenDesktop/XenApp farm.

You can install the Web Interface site components under web servers, such as IIS 6.x/7.x and Java Application Servers (Apache Tomcat, Oracle Sun Glassfish, IBM WebSphere).

## How to do it...

The following are the steps required to install and configure the Citrix Web Interface platform:

1. On a separate server, launch the **XenDesktop Autoselect** setup, choose to install XenDesktop components, and flag the **Web Access** option.
2. Click on **Install** and continue; the Web Interface setup will automatically install **Microsoft Visual J# 2.0 SE**, as shown in the following screenshot:

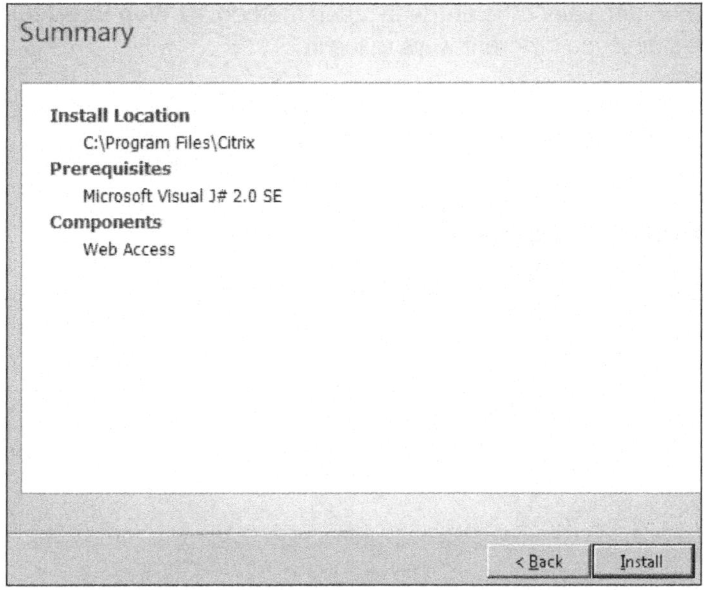


3. After the installation is complete, go to **Start** | **All Programs** | **Citrix** | **Management Consoles**, and click on **Citrix Web Interface Management**.
4. Click on the **Site** link on the left-hand side, then select the right-hand side link, **Site maintenance - Uninstall site**, and confirm the operation to remove both created websites. Now we can recreate them from scratch.
5. Select **XenApp Website** from the left-hand side menu, and click on **Create Site**.
6. Give a name to the site, leave the path with its default settings, and check the **Set as the default page for IIS site** checkbox; then click on **Next**:

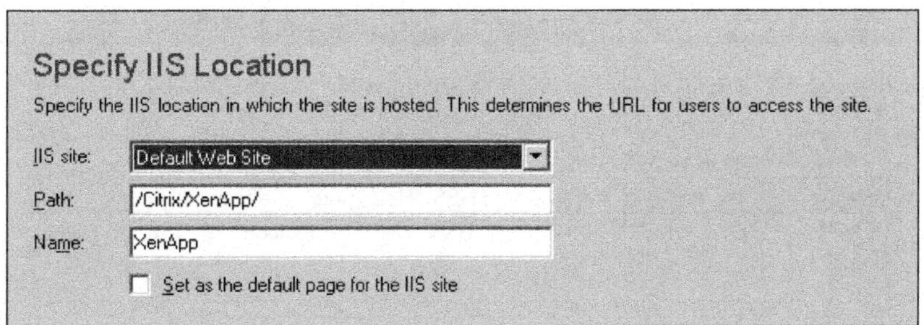

7. For the moment, select the authentication method, **At Web Interface**; throughout this book, we'll describe different ways to log in.

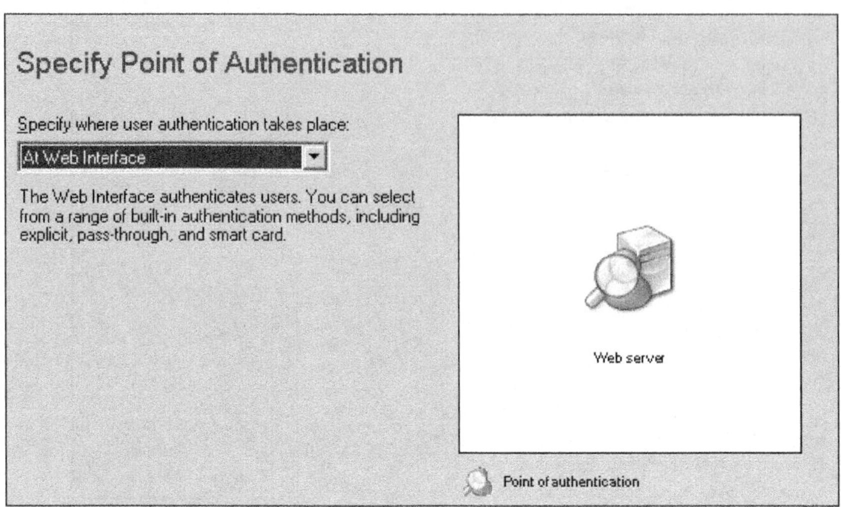


8. Click on **Next** and wait for the completion of the site creation. At the end, uncheck the **Configure this site now** checkbox.
9. Repeat the website creation operations for **XenApp Services Site**.
10. Select **Website** and click on the first configuration link, **Server Farms**; with this, we can do the following:
    - We can add any configured web farm to our infrastructure, for example, a separate XenApp Web Interface. In this way, it's possible to manage XenDesktop and XenApp farms from one centralized management console:

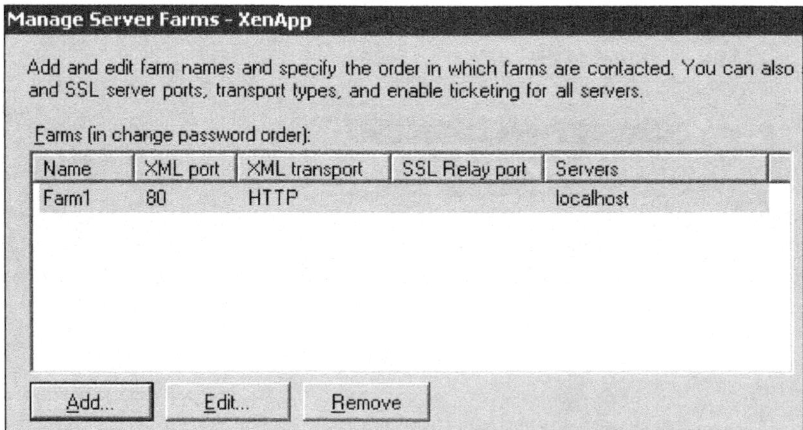

- We can insert the farm name and then add an alternative server that you want to configure:

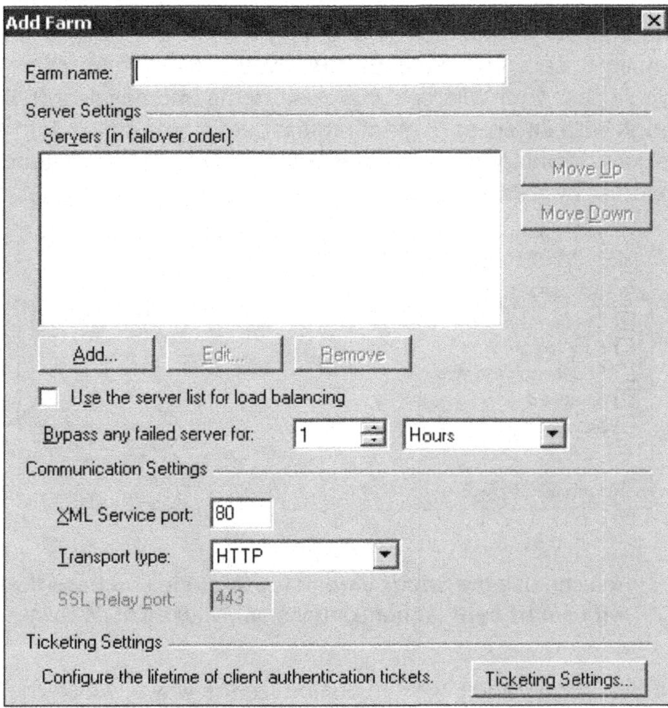


- We can add more servers to this website (for load-balancing); from the **Manage Server Farms** menu, highlight **XenDesktop farm**, click on **Edit**, and add one or more additional hosts:

11. Click on the **Authentication Methods** link in the right-hand side menu. We'll use only explicit authentication, so check the **Explicit** checkbox, as you can see in the next screenshot.

    Explicit authentication requires you to supply a username and a password. You also have the ability to select the **Pass-through** (you don't have to retype the credentials because you'll pass your Windows login username and password), **Smart card** and **Pass-through with smart card** (same thing, but using a smart card and not only a user/password combination), or **Anonymous** authentication methods; this last option is not supported by XenDesktop.

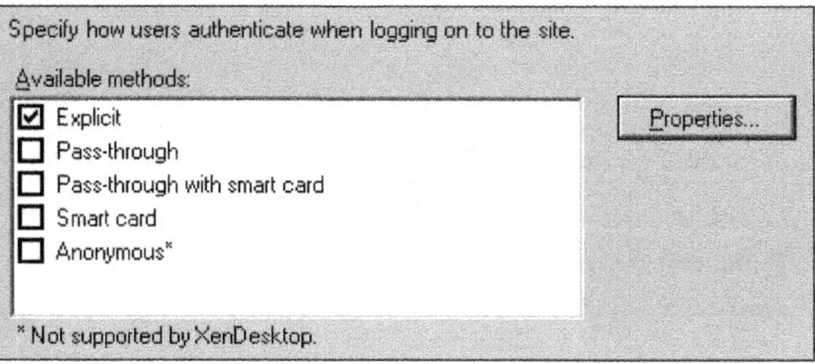

You can use the **Smart card**, **Pass-through**, and **Pass-through with smart card** authentications only with an IIS Web server.

12. Using Web Site Appearance, we can customize the way in which the Web Interface is presented to users. At this level, we can decide to present a full-appearance site, or a minimal and performing web portal:

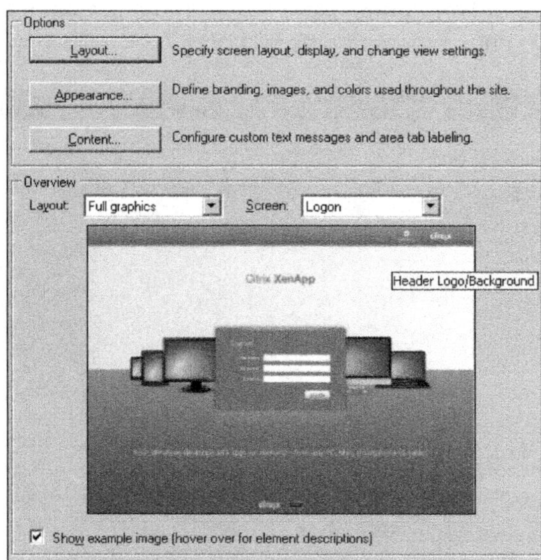

13. We could also insert customized elements, such as welcome text and national language. Click on the **Content...** button first, then click on **Add**, and select your language.
14. Select areas to customize, then enter the contents you want to visualize: 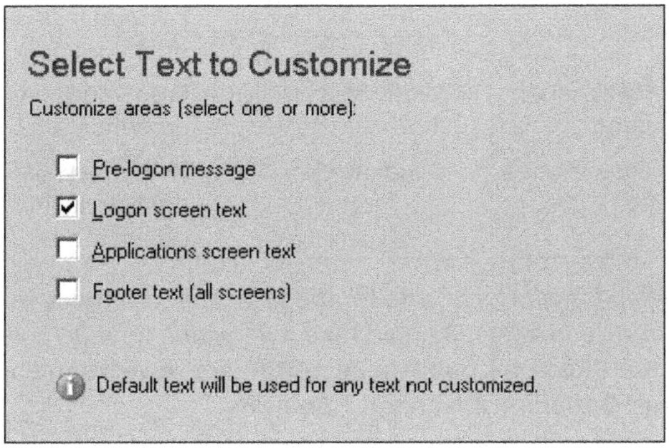
15. Type in a welcome message and a system message that you want to visualize on your Web Interface login screen, in the **Welcome message** and **System message** fields, respectively:

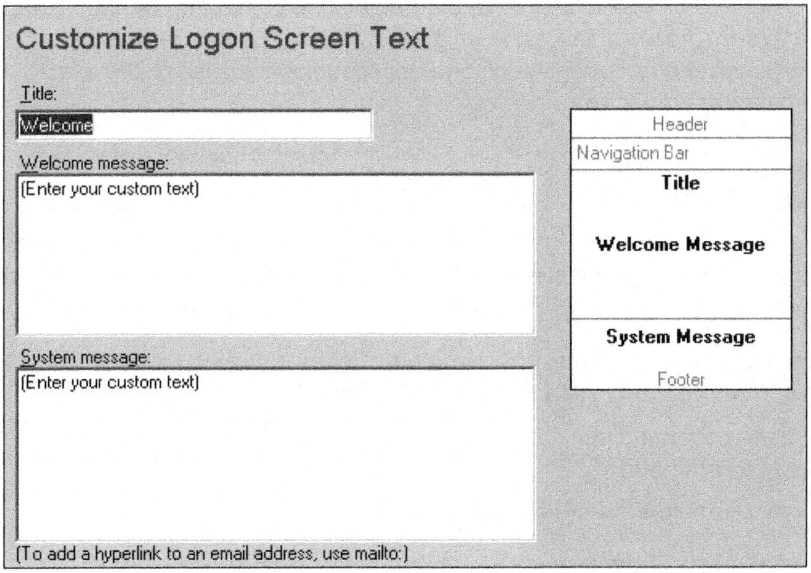

16. The following is a table with general configuration parameters of interest; leave all the parameters we haven't already discussed to their default values, for the moment.

| Area | Link | Parameters | Notes |
|---|---|---|---|
| Website | Resource types | Dual mode | In this way, users are able to perform login in both online and offline modes. |
| Services site | Authentication method | Prompt (default) | Web Interface will ask you for login credentials. |
| Services site | Resource types | Dual mode | In this way, users are able to perform login in both online and offline modes. |

When launching the Web Interface console for the first time, or after a web server's restart, using Internet Explorer as a browser, it could take a very long time; to solve this problem you have to uncheck the **Check for publisher's certificate revocation** checkbox in Internet Explorer under **Internet Options** | **Advanced** | **Security**.

## How it works...

Web Interface is a middleware component used as a connector for the interface between the end user and server broker; the user authenticates himself on this portal, and by the web server on which sites are configured, credentials are passed to the Citrix XML service (installed on a farm's server). This service retrieves information about the user, and passes it back to Citrix Receiver data for desktops and applications assigned to the user; XML is also able to load-balance a Citrix farm.

## There's more...

As described previously, it's possible to use different kinds of web servers to install the Web Interface's sites. In the following steps, we'll perform a Web Interface implementation under Apache Tomcat:

1. After you've started Tomcat from the Citrix installation media, copy the Java archive (`WebInteface.jar`) to a preferred location.
2. From the command line, launch the `.jar` installation by typing in the following command:

   ```
   java -jar <path>\WebInterface.jar
   ```

3. Read and accept the license agreement.

4. You will be prompted for the kind of site you want to install. As the first step, select option number **1**, **XenApp Web**, as shown in the following screenshot:

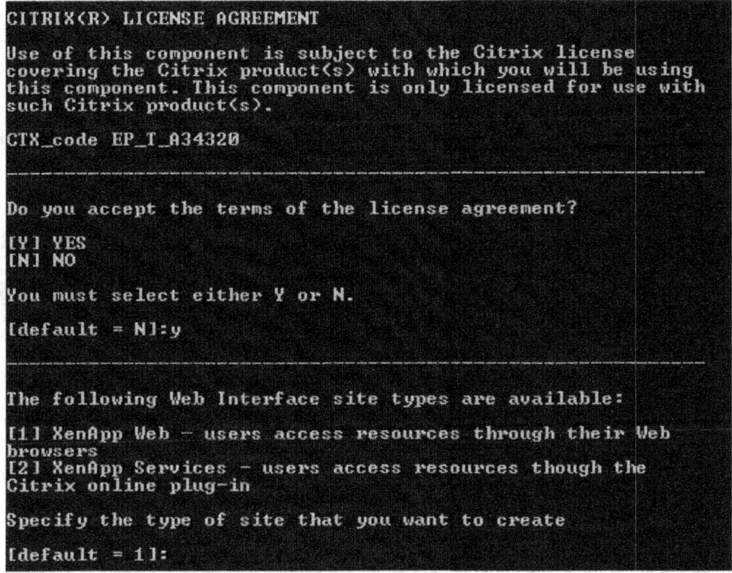


5. Provide the setup with the required information:
   - Hostname of Citrix XML service
   - Connection protocol (HTTP/HTTPs)
   - Connection port
   - User login appearance (Full/minimal)
   - Resources being delivered (Online/offline/dual)
   - Acceptance to copy client installation files, and specify the location where the setup can find installation files (you have to search for the `Citrix Receiver` and `Plug-ins` folders on installation media), then give the default `.war` name
   - If all the information is ok, accept to proceed by hitting the *Y* key
6. Repeat all the steps to configure a service website.

Once all the configurations are complete, under the temporary folder where we copied the JAR file, we will have a `.war` file and a `.xml` file. We have to copy them under `CATALINA_HOME\webapps`, and wait for Tomcat autodeploy operations. Now we're ready to use Web Interface running under Java Application Server.

For a higher level of functionality, install and use Apache Tomcat on a Linux distribution.

## See also

- The *Configuring the Citrix Access Gateway virtual appliance* recipe in *Chapter 8, XenDesktop Tuning and Security*

# Installing and configuring Provisioning Services

At this point, we've configured all the principal components to implement the MCS architecture. As described in the chapter's introduction, we've got the ability to implement two different kinds of infrastructures; the second of these is the Provisioning Services infrastructure. In this recipe, we're going to implement the last missing component, PVS.

## Getting ready

To implement Provisioning Services we need, together with Citrix software setup, to have the availability of a DHCP server and a TFTP server, to be able to perform network boot operations, in order to be able to deliver desktops via the network.

To avoid unexpected problems such as undelivered IP address from the DHCP server to the clients, you could consider the use of an IP Helper, also known as a DHCP relay, a way to use intermediate network devices (such as routers) used to forward DHCP client request to a DHCP server (for instance, located on a different network).

## How to do it...

In this recipe, we are going to execute all the steps required to install and configure the Citrix Provisioning Services platform, as follows:

1. Download the PVS ISO software from the Citrix website (log in using your credentials on `www.citrix.com/MyCitrix`, then click on the **Download** section, and search for Version **6.1**, the most current and bug-free version of this product).
2. It's necessary to install .NET Framework 3.5; if not present on your PVS server, you can install it from **Windows Server Features**.
3. Run `Autorun.exe` from the installation media.

4. From the **Installation** screen, select **Server installation**.
5. When requested for the installation type, select **Custom**, as shown in the following screenshot:

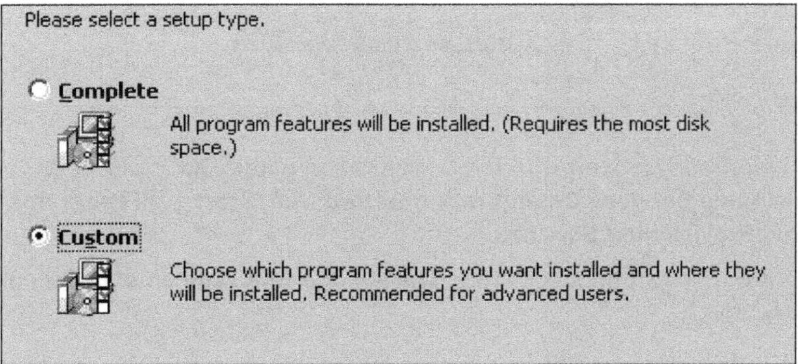


6. On the **Custom Setup** screen, select all the components from the installation objects' list, such as **Streaming Service**, **Network Boot Services**, **Documentation**, **Management API**, and **Image Update Service**, as shown in the following screenshot:

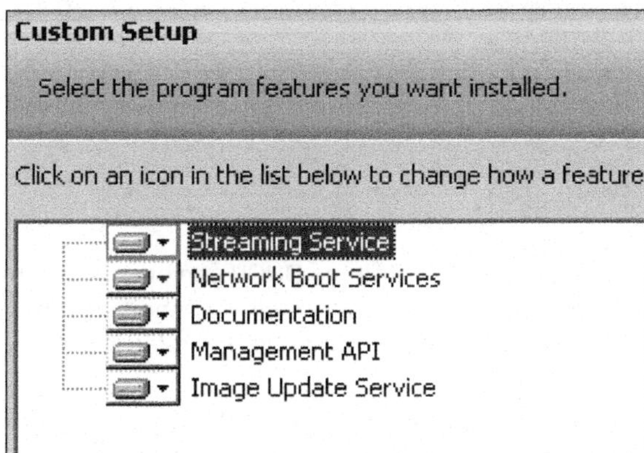


7. Wait until all the components' installations have been completed.
8. Then from the main installation menu, choose **Console installation**.

9. Again, select the **Custom** installation, and select all the components (**Provisioning Services Console** and **Boot Device Manager**), as shown in the following screenshot:

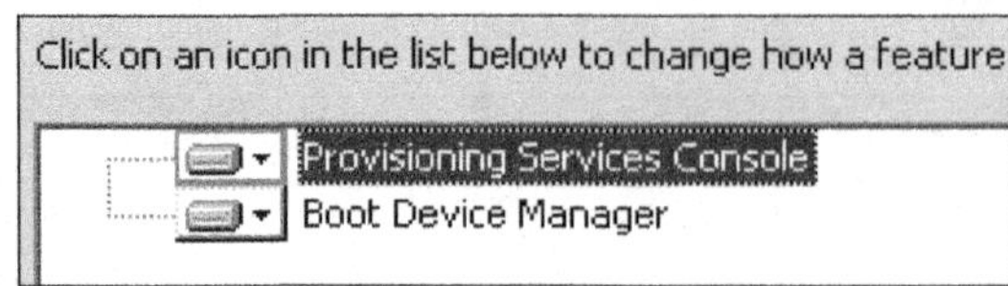


10. Now we're ready to start with the configuration of this Citrix role; select **Provisioning Services Configuration Wizard** from **Start** | **All Programs** | **Citrix** | **Provisioning Services**.
11. For DHCP configuration, select the **The service that runs on another computer** radio button:

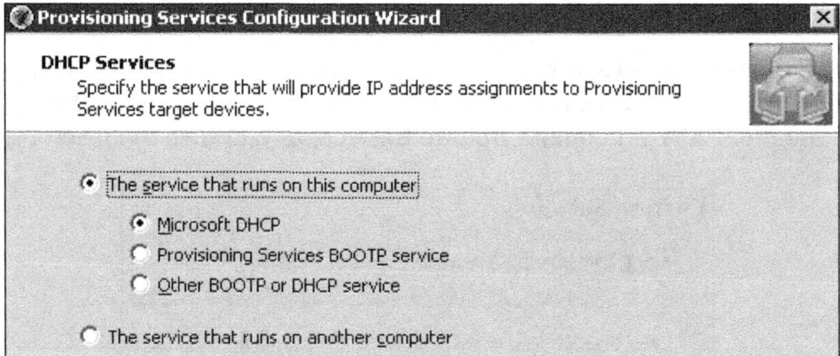

The best choice is to install the DHCP server on a machine different from the Provisioning Service server. You should always separate components for better performance and roles isolation.

12. For the **PXE Services** component, choose the local server as the provider by selecting the **The service that runs on this computer** radio button.

13. On the **Farm Configuration** screen, select **Create farm**, as shown in the following screenshot:

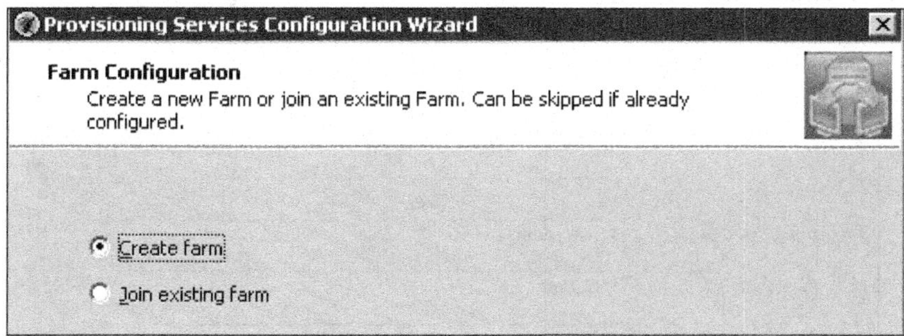

To better convey the differences between the MCS and PVS architectures, we'll always use two different farms to accomplish tasks for both architectures.

14. Enter the database's **Server name** on which we want to create an PVS DB instance, then type in **Instance name**, **Optional TCP port**, and in case of a failover architecture, specify the second database node in the cluster:

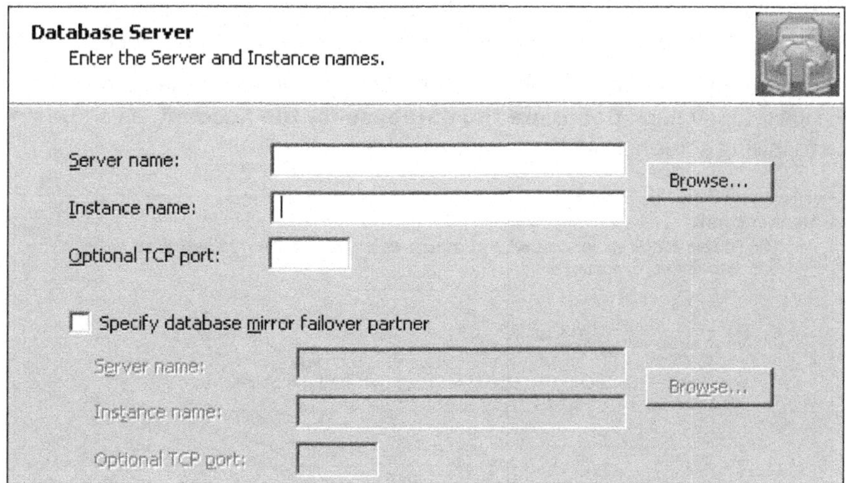

15. On the **New Farm** screen, configure the parameters for provisioning the farm (**Database name**, **Farm name**, **Site name**, and **Collection name**), then populate the **Farm Administrator group** field with an Active Directory group with a high elevated permission to manage the farm, as follows:

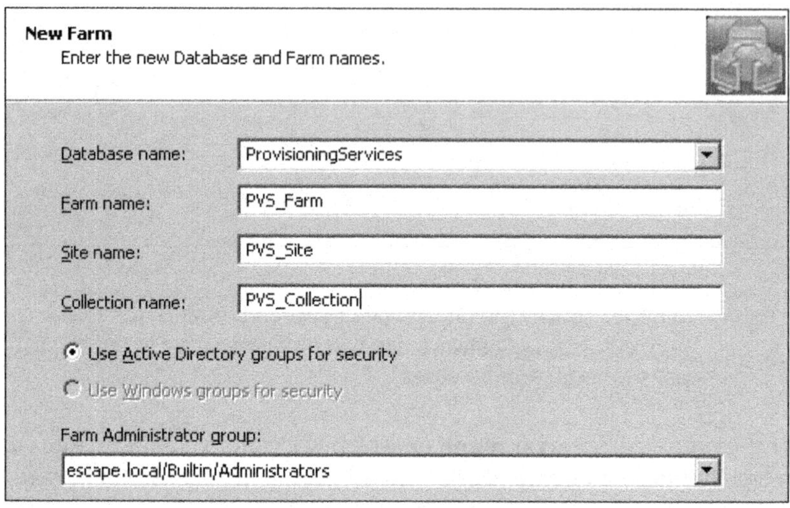


16. Select a name and the default path for the PVS store; then locate your license server name and port, to allow the PVS server to validate available licenses.
17. Select **Network service account** as the user account for stream and soap services, then check **Configure the database for the account**, as shown in the following screenshot:

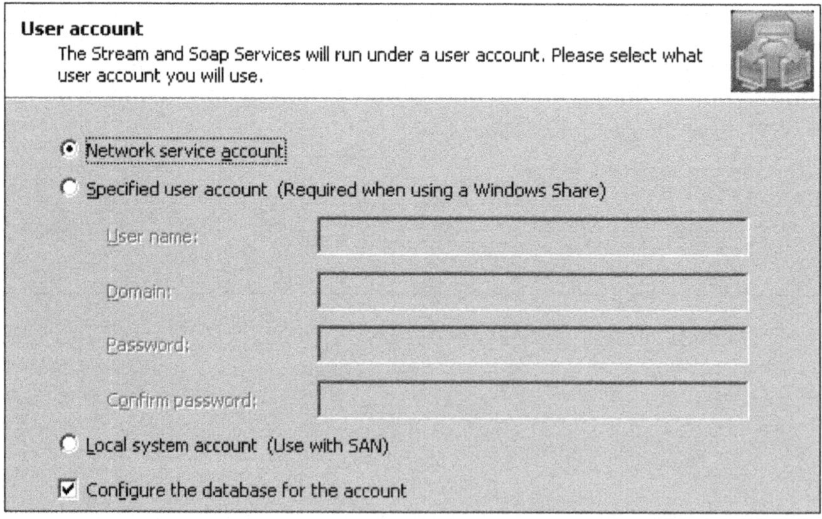

18. Select a value, in days, for the automation of computer account password updates (the default is seven days).
19. Select an available network card for streaming services, and choose a starting port number used to communicate (default is 6890), and also the console port number (default is 54321).
20. Check the **Use the Provisioning Services TFTP service** checkbox, and leave the default image boot path, as shown in the following screenshot:

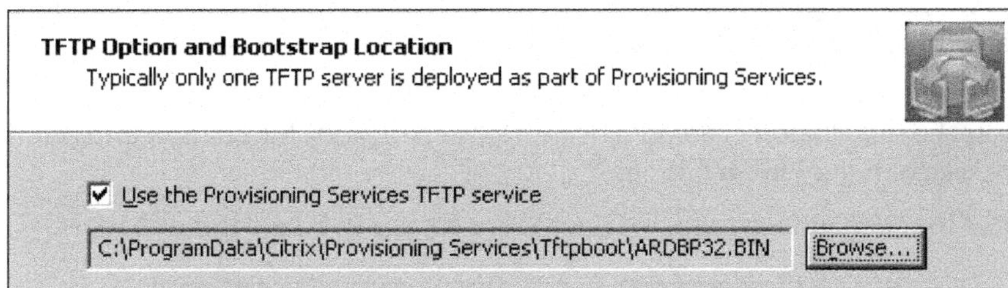


21. At the end, the wizard will perform service installation and it starts after all the operations have been completed.

> Remember that active Windows Firewall might be a problem for your installation process; you have to open the required ports, or turn it off. The ports are TCP 389 (LDAP), TCP 27000,7279 (license server traffic), TCP 1433 (SQL Server instance), TCP 54321-54322 (SOAP), UDP 67,4011 (PXE), UDP 69 (TFTP), and UDP 6509-6909 (internal server communication).

22. If everything is ok, you'll see the following screen:

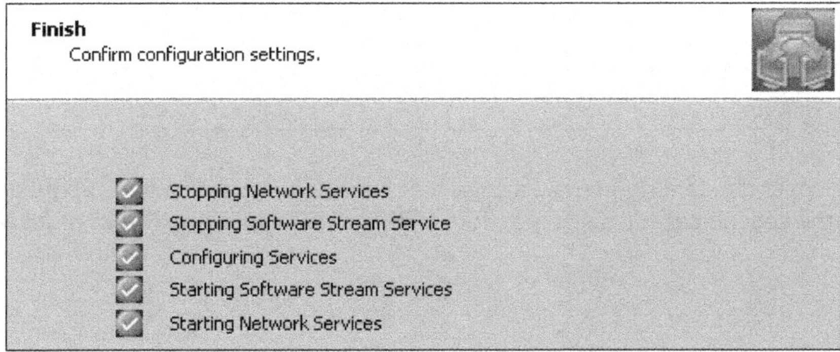


23. Now we're able to connect for the first time to our PVS farm. Go to **Start** | **All Programs** | **Citrix** | **Provisioning Services**, and click on **Provisioning Services Console**.

24. Then, type in `localhost` in the **Name** field as the farm location, insert the number of the configured listening port in the **Port** field, and check the radio button for **Use my Windows credentials** to log in.
25. Now we have to install the last PVS component, target device. To perform this operation, we first need to install a client Windows machine (virtual or physical with Windows XP, Windows Vista, or Windows 7 as the operating system).
26. After this, run **Target device setup** on the client machine.
27. Refer to the target device as the client machines that will use this prepared disk to perform a network boot. Accept the license agreement, insert information about your company, and then select a path for the installation.
28. After the installation is complete, check the checkbox for **Launch Imaging Wizard** and click on the **Finish** button.
29. After the **Welcome** screen, we have to insert the PVS server credentials:

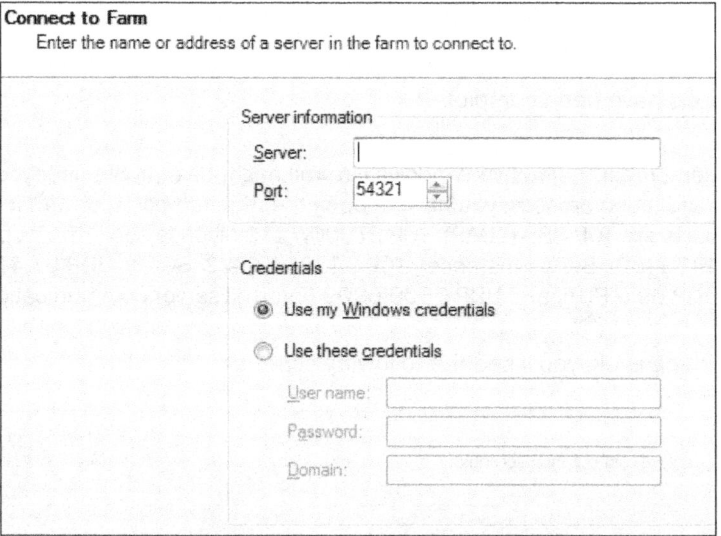


30. Select to create a new vDisk, assign it a name, a store, and a type, **Fixed** or **Dynamic**; in the second case, it's also possible to select disk block size (2 MB or 16 MB).

31. Select the kind of Microsoft Volume Licensing you need (MAK for cumulative licenses, KMS if an activation server is available):

Microsoft Volume Licensing
Choose if the vDisk is to be configured for Microsoft KMS or MAK volume license management.
None
Key Management Service (KMS)
Multiple Activation Key (MAK)

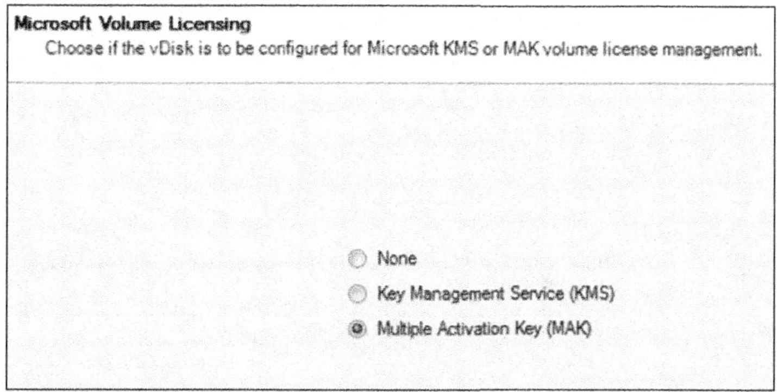

32. When possible, you should always consider the use of **Key Management Service (KMS)**, in order to avoid problems of depletion of licenses. Then, configure the disk image size, starting from the original disk; of course, the disk size must be at least the minimum original disk dimension:

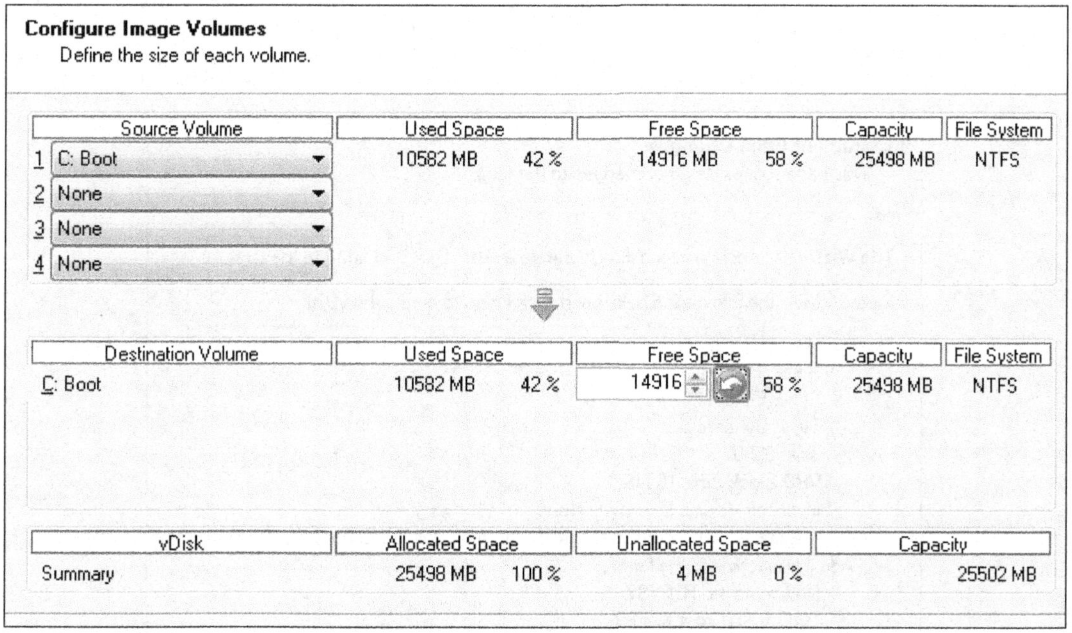

Configure Image Volumes
Define the size of each volume.
Source Volume
Used Space
Free Space
Capacity
File System
1 C: Boot
10582 MB 42 %
14916 MB 58 %
25498 MB
NTFS
2 None
3 None
4 None
Destination Volume
Used Space
Free Space
Capacity
File System
C: Boot
10582 MB 42 %
14916
58 %
25498 MB
NTFS
vDisk
Allocated Space
Unallocated Space
Capacity
Summary
25498 MB 100 %
4 MB 0 %
25502 MB

33. Configure **Target device name** (a different name from the Active Directory computer account), **MAC** (network card) from the drop-down list, and **Collection** (PVS server collection name), as shown in the following screenshot:

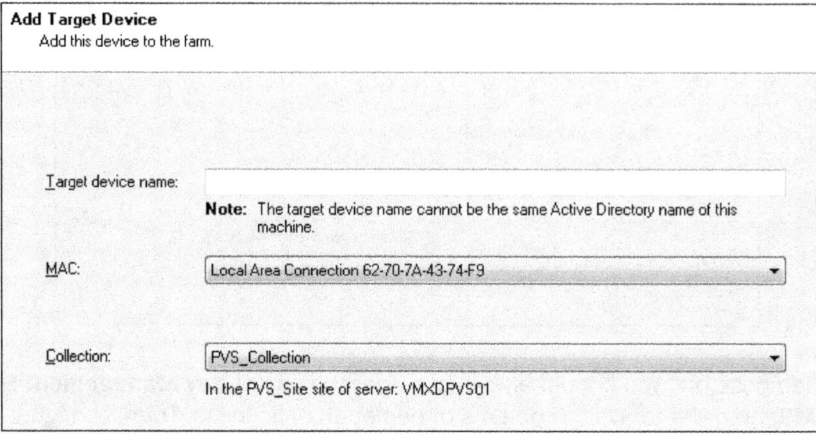


34. Now we're ready to complete the target device installation. After that configuration has completed, in order to set up a network boot for a TD image, we need to reboot the Windows client, and configure the boot order from BIOS.

    Be sure to have enabled the PXE boot on the network card of your client machine.

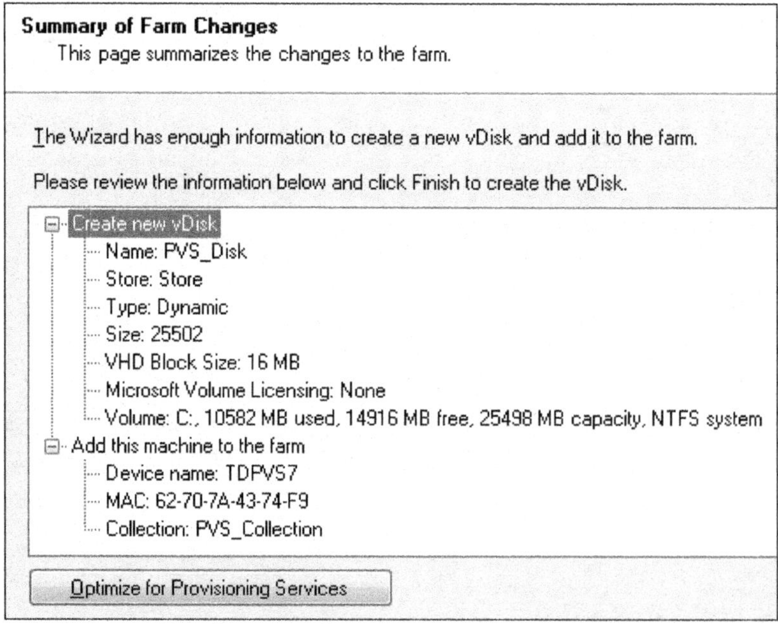

35. After connecting to the PVS server, we can ensure that vDisk has been correctly created under the management console, as shown in the following screenshot:

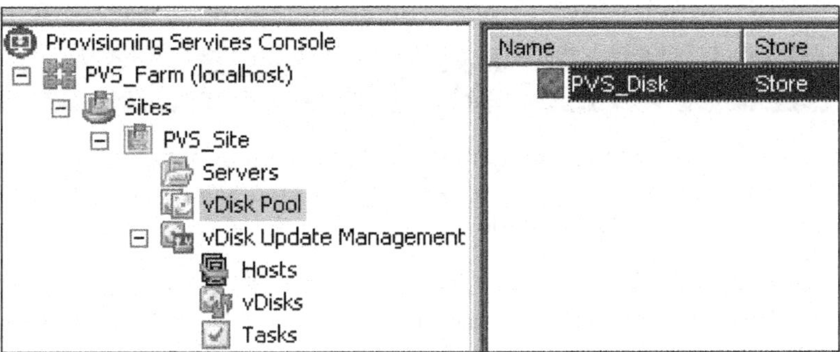


## How it works...

As seen with implementation procedures, after infrastructural components' installation, we have to create a vDisk, which is an operating system's image that is copied by creating a snapshot from an installed operating system (known as Master Target Device). This vDisk will be streamed on demand to clients configured to boot from the network (target devices), pointing to the Provisioning Services server; the desktops are streamed from the memory of the PVS server every time they're needed by users. This process permits having high elevated network performance, dramatically reducing the impact on storage activities.

## There's more...

As discussed earlier in this recipe, when creating a vDisk we have the ability to choose between two kinds of disk formats, fixed disks and dynamic disks. The first type pre-allocates all assigned disk space, while dynamic allocation populates disk files during data writing activities (if you're familiar with virtualization concepts, it's the same as thick and thin disk allocation). The following is a set of information and best practices to understand how to choose between the fixed and dynamic disks:

- Because of the nature of a fixed disk (full space pre-allocation), it could be a waste of storage space.
- PVS uses memory caching mechanisms that reduce disk I/O activities. For this reason, dynamic allocation should be the right choice, because of the huge reduction of storage reading activities. The only interfacing with a disk component is given by writing operations. Also in this case, after configuring a PVS vDisk image in the read-only mode, we'll have almost no more storage activities. To have a responsive system, on the other hand, this infrastructure needs to be supported by 64-bit systems, the right memory sizing (for a PVS server you should have a quantity of RAM between 8 GB and 32 GB), and a block-level storage device (SAN or iSCSI, and not a network share repository on NAS).

Using a fixed disk is a standard way to operate, which at the moment won't offer the advantages that memory cache along with dynamic disk mode could give to IT departments (in terms of performance and cost saving).

# Chapter 1 XenDesktop lab

The main purpose of this lab is preparing infrastructural components, shown in this chapter, to have the base components on which we want to perform advanced configurations and implementations in the next labs throughout the book.

Using a hypervisor supported by Citrix XenDesktop (VMware ESX, Microsoft Hyper-V, Citrix XenServer), install five virtual machines, as indicated:

1. Configure a Windows 2008 R2 virtual machine as a domain controller, with the following parameters:
    - Recommended virtual hardware resources are one vCPU, 4 GB of RAM, 30 GB of hard disk
    - `vmctxdc01` as the hostname
    - `192.168.1.50` as the IP address
    - Domain controller, DNS, and DHCP installed roles
    - `ctxlab.local` as the domain name
    - DHCP IP range from `192.168.1.100` to `192.168.1.150`
2. Configure a Windows 2008 R2 virtual machine as the Citrix XenDesktop platform (follow the installation procedure explained in this chapter), with the following parameters:
    - Recommended virtual hardware resources are two vCPUs, 4 GB of RAM, 50 GB of hard disk
    - `vmctxddc01` as the hostname
    - `192.168.1.60` as the IP address
    - Join it to the `ctxlab.local` domain, before configuring any software role
    - From XenDesktop setup install the components, XenDesktop Controller, Desktop Studio, Desktop Director
    - Select Express edition of SQL Server 2008 R2 for the installation
3. Configure a Windows 2008 R2 virtual machine as the Citrix license server (follow the installation procedure explained in this chapter), with the following parameters:
    - Recommended virtual hardware resources are one vCPU, 2 GB of RAM, 30 GB of hard disk
    - `vmctxlc01` as the hostname

- `192.168.1.70` as the IP address
- Join it to the `ctxlab.local` domain, before configuring any software role

4. Configure a Windows 2008 R2 virtual machine as the Citrix Web Interface (follow the installation procedure explained in this chapter), with the following parameters:
    - Recommended virtual hardware resources are one vCPU, 2 GB of RAM, 30 GB of hard disk
    - `vmctxlc01` as the hostname
    - `192.168.1.80` as the IP address
    - Join it to the `ctxlab.local` domain, before configuring any software role
5. Configure a Windows 7 64-bit virtual machine as master target device for PVS, with the following parameters:
    - Recommended virtual hardware resources are one vCPU, 4 GB of RAM, 30 GB of hard disk
    - `vmctxtd01` as the hostname
    - DHCP assigned IP address
    - Join it to the `ctxlab.local` domain, before configuring any software role

# 2
# Deploying Virtual Machines for XenDesktop

In this chapter we will cover:

- Configuring the XenDesktop site
- Configuring XenDesktop to interact with Citrix XenServer
- Configuring XenDesktop to interact with VMware vSphere
- Configuring XenDesktop to interact with Microsoft Hyper-V

## Introduction

Configuration of the XenDesktop components is the first step to implementing a fully functioning infrastructure. After this, the second and maybe the most important step is deploying virtual desktop instances.

To accomplish this task, you need to interface Citrix servers with a hypervisor, a bare-metal operating system that is able to create, configure, and manage virtual machines. XenDesktop is able to communicate with three important hypervisor systems on the market; Citrix XenServer, VMware vSphere, and Microsoft Hyper-V. The mechanism implemented is that, after you've created a template with a virtual machine with a Microsoft desktop operating system (Windows XP, Windows Vista, or Windows 7) on board, XenDesktop is able to deploy desktop instances to end users, starting with the virtual desktop through the use of different deployment techniques.

In this chapter we're going to implement the communication between hypervisors and Citrix servers.

# Configuring the XenDesktop site

Before any interfacing activities, after you've installed XenDesktop Director, you need to configure a site, which will be the place where you'll configure the hypervisor host.

## Getting ready

In order to complete all the required steps for this recipe, to perform a standard site deployment (non-quick deployment format), you need to be assigned the administrator role for all the machines involved in the site configuration (XenDesktop Controller and the database server).

## How to do it...

In the following steps, we will describe how to create a site for a XenDesktop infrastructure:

1. Connect to Desktop Studio by clicking on the **Start** | **All Programs** | **Citrix** | **Desktop Studio**.
2. Click on **Desktop deployment**, as shown in the following screenshot:

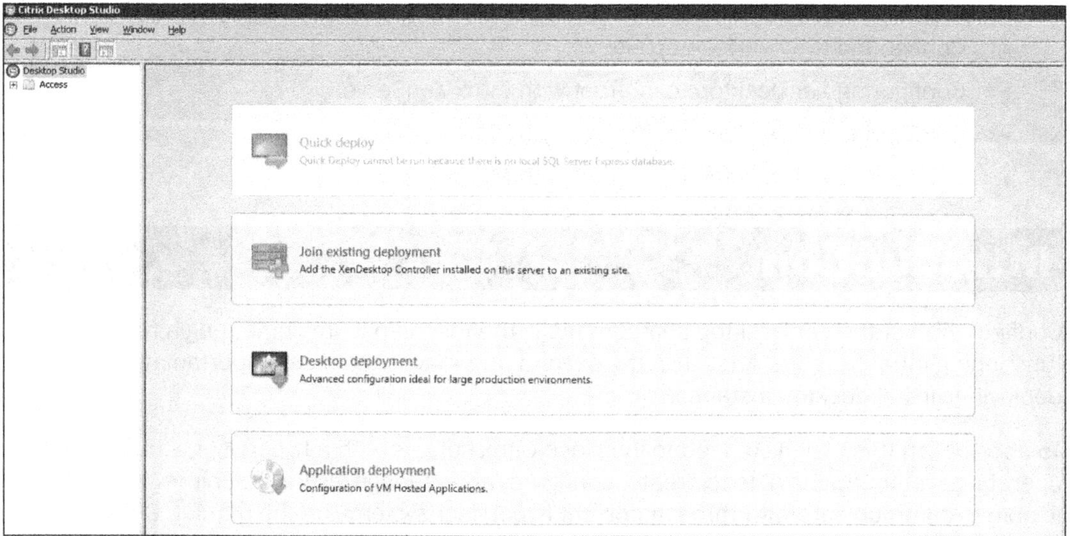

The **Quick Deploy** option is grayed out because of the version of SQL Server that is installed (nonexpress version).

3. Insert a name for the site in the **Site** field, and then populate the **Server location** scope with the DB hostname plus the instance name (in the form `hostname\instance name`) and the **Database name** field with the XenDesktop database name; Then, click on the **Test connection...** button to verify that you're able to contact the DB machine, as shown in the following screenshot:

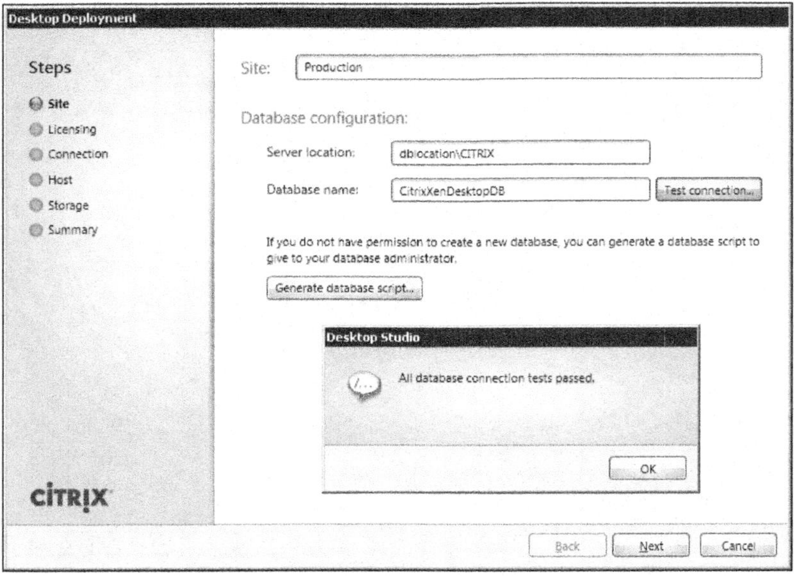


4. If you want to create a database manually, click on the **Generate database script...** button; you'll get back a set of instructions in the form of two scripts, to generate the database for standard and mirrored mode, as follows:

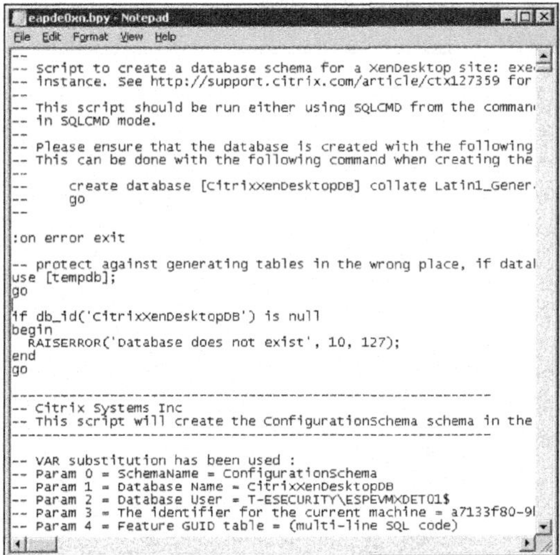

5. After database interfacing, in the licensing section, type your license server's name plus the port number (in the format `hostname:port`), and click on the **Connect** button. If you already have a configured license file, select the **Select from existing licenses** radio button; otherwise, you have to select the **Use XenDesktop 30-day free trial** radio button and insert a correct license file later.

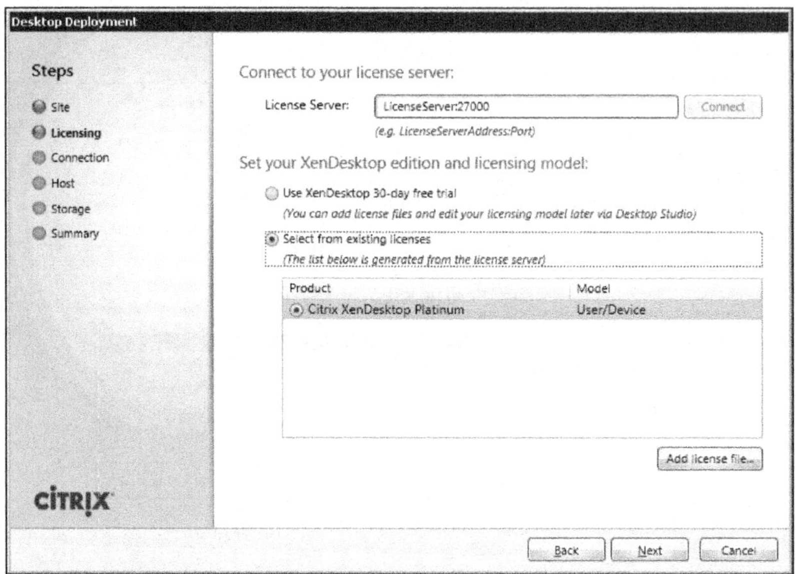


6. For the **Connection** section of the wizard, select the **None** option for the moment; later in this chapter, we'll configure the host connection for every kind of hypervisor host.
7. After reviewing the summary information, in the **Summary** section, click on the **Finish** button to complete site configuration.
8. You'll find confirmation about site preparation on the **Initial Configuration** tab of Desktop Studio's home page:

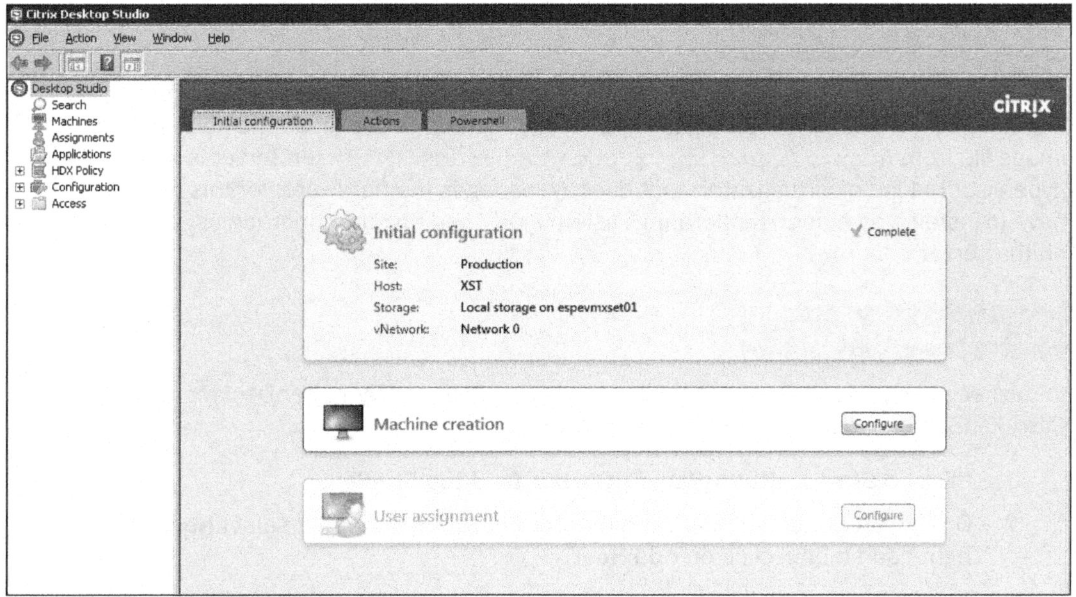


## How it works...

Configuring a site lets you assemble together all the components that you had configured previously; by this creation, Desktop Director is able to connect to the SQL Server machine, and there create the database (or simply populate it with the necessary tables) in which machine information will be archived. Moreover, XenDesktop can connect to the license server, being able to verify the number of configured licenses (important for the number of desktop deployments you'll be able to perform).

## See also

- The *Managing the Citrix Desktop Controller – broker cmdlets* recipe in *Chapter 9, Working with XenDesktop PowerShell*

# Configuring XenDesktop to interact with Citrix XenServer

The first and most common configuration for a XenDesktop site is interfacing it with the Citrix hypervisor, XenServer. Related to XenDesktop 5.6 is the XenServer 6.0.201 release.

## Getting ready

The preliminary work required to perform all the operations in this recipe is to install one or more XenServer hosts. To accomplish this task, you need to download the XenServer ISO image file from `http://www.citrix.com/downloads.html`. XenServer is a bare-metal hypervisor (a kind of virtualizator) that directly manages the hardware; for this reason, you have to install it as a normal operating system (you need no other operating system installed on the server).

## How to do it...

In this recipe, we will perform the operations required to configure XenDesktop to use the Citrix XenServer hypervisor. Perform the following steps:

1. Click on **Start** | **All Programs** | **Citrix** | **Desktop Studio**.
2. On the left-hand menu, expand the **Configuration** node and select **Hosts**, then on the right-hand menu, click on **Add Host**.

3. In the **Connection** section, select **Citrix XenServer** from the **Host type** drop-down menu. In the **Address** field, enter the **Full Qualified Domain Name** (**FQDN**) of the XenServer host (in the form of `http://address`), then type in the username and password in the respective fields, and give a name to the connection (in the **Connection name** input field).

> You should always add the FQDN and the IP address in the host file of your Desktop Controller machine to avoid unexpected resolution name problems.

4. For the **Virtual machines** section, you've got the ability to let XenDesktop automatically create all the required virtual desktop instances within the chosen hypervisor (**Use XenDesktop to create virtual machines**) or to create them manually (**Manually create virtual machines**).

For an automated and better performing desktop deployment, it's better to select the first option, **Use XenDesktop to create virtual machines**.

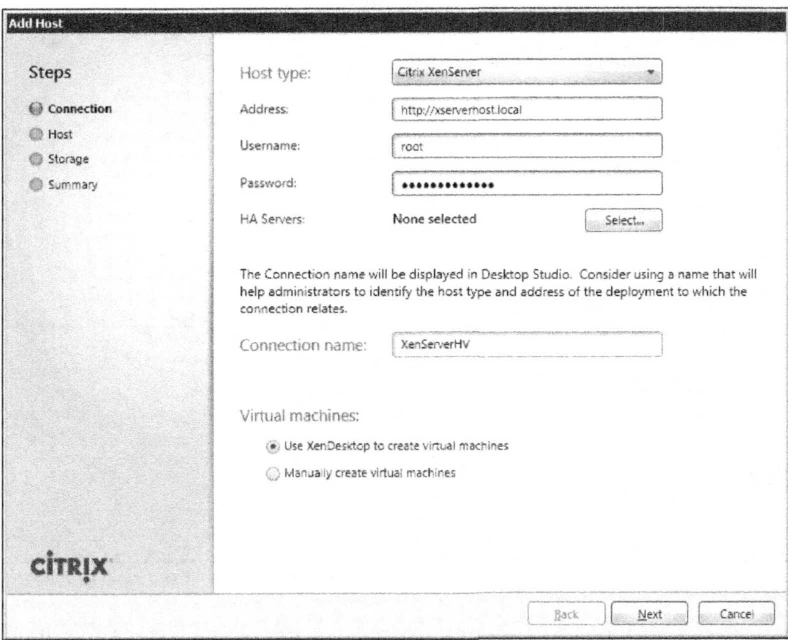


5. If you want to configure more than one XenServer host in high availability, click on the **Select** button from the **HA Servers** section, and choose an additional machine to configure in the HA cluster.

6. On the next screen, which is the **Host** section, choose a configured network (depending on your XenServer host configuration, you could have one or more available networks) on which you want to assign the generated virtual desktop instances, then click on the **Next** button.

7. Next, for the **Storage** section, select an available storage on which you want to create virtual machines and select the desired radio button for personal vDisk location (**Use same storage for virtual machines and personal vDisk** or **Use different storage for personal vDisk**), as shown in the following screenshot:

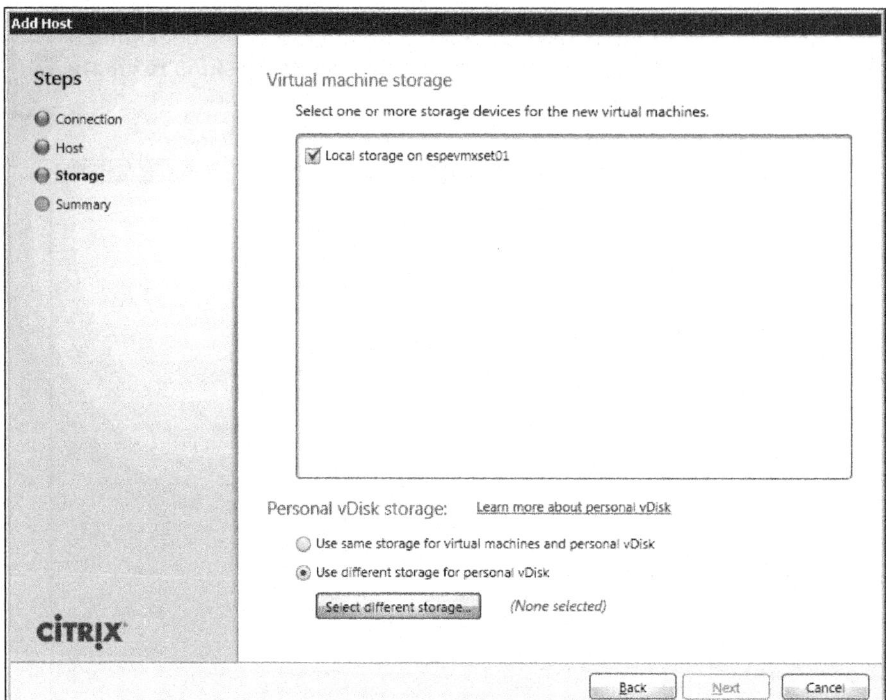

In the presence of available storage, you should consider separating the operating system disk area from personal vDisk storage. Separating these areas could make it easier to locate user disk zones, especially for backup operations or troubleshooting activities.

8. As the last step, on the **Summary** screen, assign a name to the configured host in the **Host name** section, and then click on the **Finish** button.

9. Going back to the first screen, now we can see a XenServer host with a configured connection, as shown in the following screenshot:

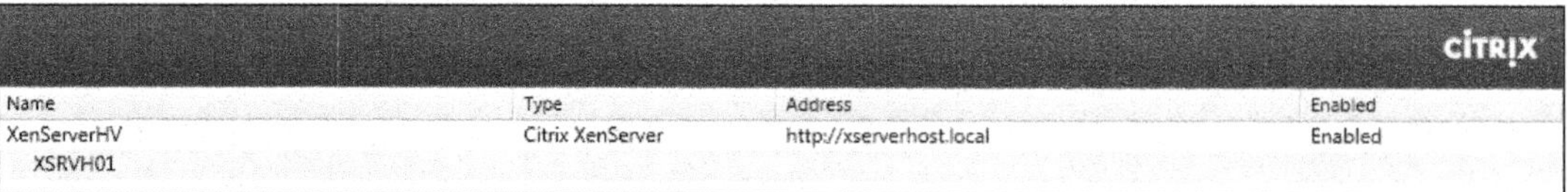


| Name | Type | Address | Enabled |
|---|---|---|---|
| XenServerHV | Citrix XenServer | http://xserverhost.local | Enabled |
| XSRVH01 | | | |

10. If necessary, we could change the connection parameters. Select the connection name that you want to modify, and click on the **Change details** link in the right-hand menu. At this point, it's possible to reconfigure the main information such as **Address**, **User**, and **Password**, and you can also include **HA Servers** where configured, as shown in the following screenshot:

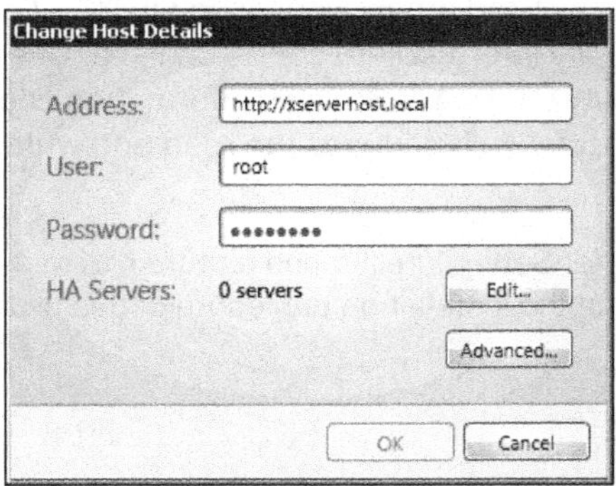


11. Clicking on the **Advanced...** button, the administrator has the capability to configure **Max active actions**, **Max new actions per minute**, **Max power actions as percentage of desktops**, and **Max personal vDisk power actions as percentage**. You can leave the default values; in fact, these parameters are applicable to the most standard infrastructure types.

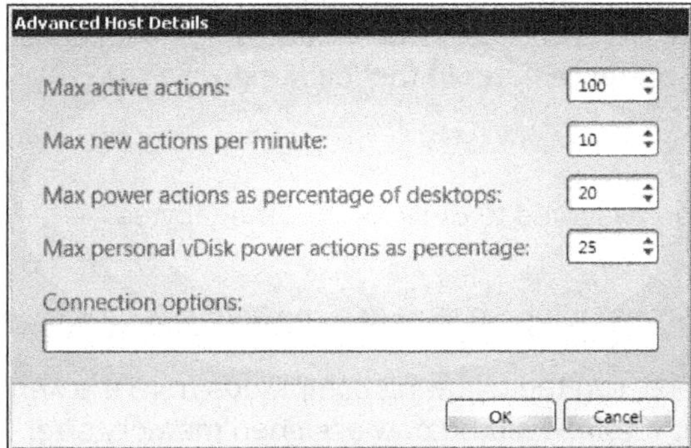

To perform any modification activity on host and connection, you must put them into maintenance mode.

## How it works...

XenServer is the hypervisor included in the Citrix virtualization platform. At this moment, it's the best integrated hypervisor with the Citrix VDI platform, also thanks to the cooperation between the XenDesktop and XenServer teams. The way in which XenDesktop interfaces with XenServer is simpler despite the other hypervisors; in fact, Desktop Controller directly contacts the server, without any intermediate server console. One of the advantages of using this hypervisor is the capability to use XenServer's information caching feature, also known as IntelliCache. This technique drastically reduces the read and write activities for your storage.

The XenServer IntelliCache feature has to be enabled during the installation procedure of this hypervisor.

## There's more...

In the presence of many tens or hundreds of virtual machines, the XenServer hypervisor could have performance issues in terms of lack of physical resources for `Dom0`, the most privileged domain in a XenServer installation and the only domain able to directly interface with the hardware or starting nonprivileged domains, for instance. To solve this problem it is necessary to assign more physical resources to `Dom0`; this operation can be performed by connecting to the desired XenServer machine using the XenCenter console or through the SSH connection, then editing the `/boot/extlinux.conf` file and modifying every occurrence of the `dom0_mem` parameter, assigning it the desired value in MB. You should consider using the advised value from Citrix, setting the parameter in the following way:

```
dom0_mem=2940M
```

The default memory value assigned to `dom0` is 752 megabytes.

To apply the memory changes, you have to restart the XenServer node.

After the reboot operations, run the following commands from the XenServer CLI in order to let XenServer understand how to use all the new assigned memory size:

```
./etc/xensource-inventory
staticmax=`xe vm-param-get uuid=$CONTROL_DOMAIN_UUID param-name=memory-static-max`
echo staticmax=$staticmax
xe vm-param-set uuid=$CONTROL_DOMAIN_UUID memory-dynamic-max=$staticmax
xe vm-memory-target-set uuid=$CONTROL_DOMAIN_UUID target=$staticmax
```

## See also

- The *Configuring the Branch Repeater virtual appliance* recipe in *Chapter 5, Configuring Additional Architectural Components*

# Configuring XenDesktop to interact with VMware vSphere

Citrix XenDesktop not only offers compatibility for Citrix proprietary platforms, but also supports the most important virtualization architectures on the market. VMware is currently the virtualization solution which better permits you to manage the resource over commitment for your virtual environments.

## Getting ready

To ensure that all the activities in this chapter are fully executed, it's required that you have an already functioning VMware vSphere environment, made up of at least two ESX or ESXi servers and Windows Server (on which we want to install the VMware Virtual vCenter software).

After this, the step you've got to perform is to import the VMware vCenter certificate on the XenDesktop server, to allow Desktop Studio to connect with the SSL connection to vCenter SDK.

## How to do it...

The following are the steps that you have to execute in order to activate the communication between the XenDesktop Controller machine and the VMware vSphere infrastructure:

1. Launch your chosen web browser and then type, in the address bar, the hostname of the vCenter server, using the HTTPS connection. When prompted regarding security risks, accept to continue with site navigation.

2. On the certificate status bar, click on the **Status** error and click on the **View certificates** link (the vCenter certificate is currently invalid for XenDesktop), as shown in the following screenshot:

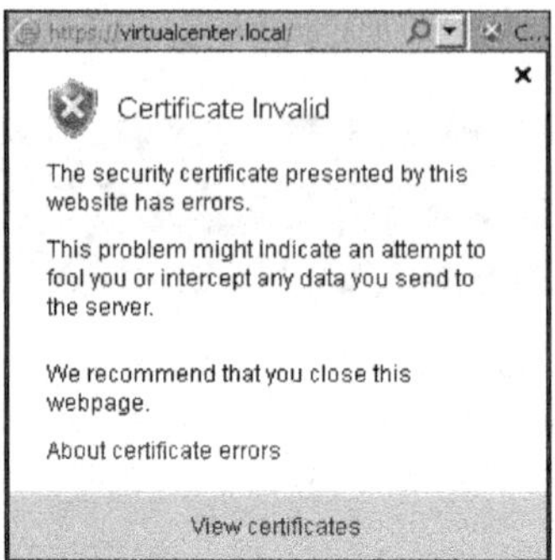


3. After certificate presentation, click on the **Install Certificate...** button, as shown in the following screenshot:

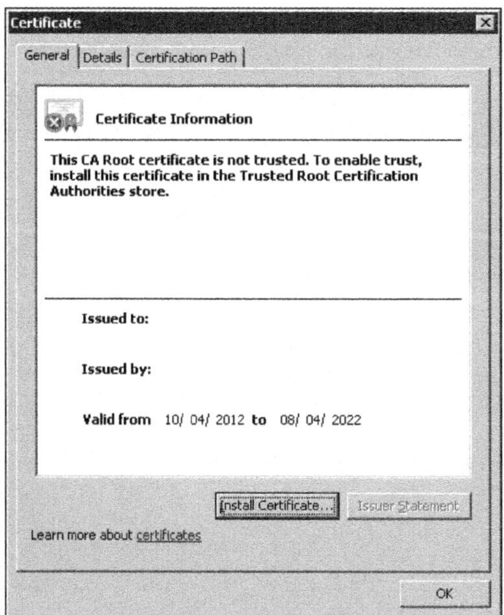

Make sure that the hostname associated with the certificate matches the name assigned to the vCenter server. In case of mismatching, in fact, XenDesktop won't be able to connect with VMware. To avoid this, you could consider adding a record to the local file hosts of XenDesktop server to match the IP address and hostname in the certificate.

4. After clicking on **Next** on the **Welcome** screen, select the **Place all certificates in the following store** radio button option, and then click on **Browse...**.
5. Check the **Show physical stores** checkbox, and select the **Local Computer** subfolder under the **Trusted People** folder. After this, click on **OK**, as shown in the following screenshot:

6. To complete the certificate import activities, click on **Finish**, as shown in the following screenshot:

7. To verify that the certificate import was successful, you must reconnect to the SSL VirtualCenter address (`https://hostname`). If you receive no more prompts about unsecure connections (as previously seen), the import has successfully been completed.

This procedure must be performed for the Desktop Controller server and Provisioning Services server, depending on what architecture you've implemented.

8. Connect to Citrix Desktop Studio and go to **Configuration** | **Hosts**, as seen in the *Configuring XenDesktop to interact with Citrix XenServer* recipe. Then click on **Add Host**, as done for XenServer.
9. Specify the **Connection name**, and then select **VMware virtualization** from the **Host type** drop-down menu.
10. In the **Address** field, specify the VirtualCenter address previously configured for SSL authentication, pointing to the SDK API platform (a URL of the form `https://FQDN/SDK`).
11. For the **Virtual machines** section, specify the right choice for your infrastructure, as described earlier.

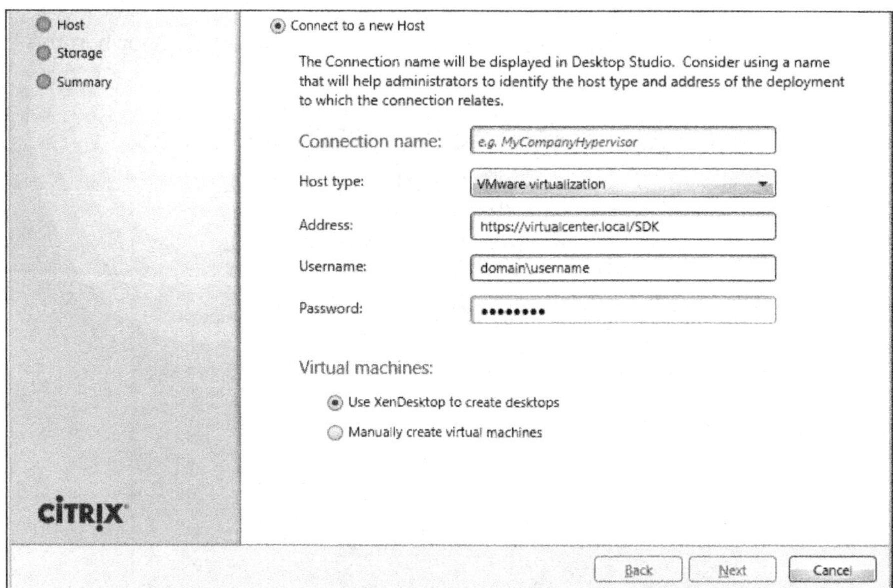

The specified username and password for the connection must be valid domain credentials, with privileges within VirtualCenter.

12. On the **Add Host** screen, click on the **Browse...** button to select a vSphere cluster on which to deploy virtual machines. After this operation, select a network for VDI from the presented list.

13. Also, in this case, select the storage for your virtual machine's system disks (local or shared) and decide whether to select a separate datastore for personal vDisks (recommended).

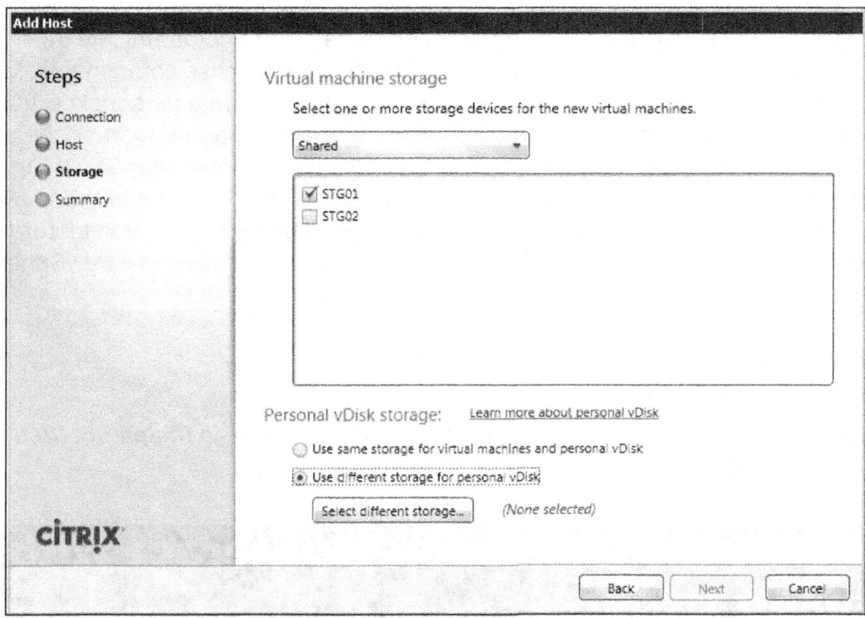


14. As a last step, assign a name to this connection, in the **Host Name** field, and then click on the **Finish** button, as shown in the following screenshot:

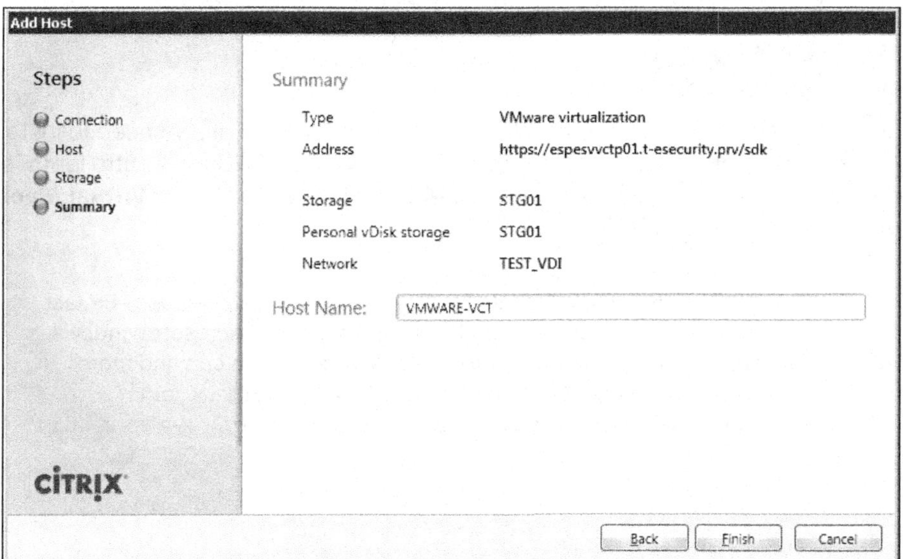

## How it works...

The communication between XenDesktop and VMware VirtualCenter can be realized through two kinds of channels, HTTP and HTTPS. The second is obviously more secure, and this communication is also what is advised by Citrix, so to be able to communicate in HTTP over SSL, you need to import your VirtualCenter certificate. For these components, VMware best practices say that you should create your own certificate from a personal certification authority. Anyway, communication could be established by using and importing the default self-signed VMware certificate. Once this import has been completed, the only thing remaining is to connect to the VMware API by its published SDK. The use of the VMware VirtualCenter is not only necessary, but it is also a way to implement an architecture that is centrally managed and tuned by a controlling platform such as the VMware vSphere VirtualCenter platform, as explained.

## See also

- The *Creating and configuring the machine catalog* recipe in *Chapter 6, Creating and Configuring a Desktop Environment*

# Configuring XenDesktop to interact with Microsoft Hyper-V

In the last few years, collaboration between Citrix and Microsoft has grown so much that they now share the application virtualization and deployment market. Owing to this partnership, it's possible to deploy virtual desktops for Citrix with Hyper-V, the Microsoft hypervisor.

## Getting ready

To be able to use virtual machines with Windows 2008 R2, first of all, we need to install and configure the hypervisor server role. After this, in order to allow Desktop Controller to interact with the Hyper-V server, it's necessary to install **Microsoft System Center Virtual Machine Manager** (also known as **SCVMM**).

> In the November, 2012 tech preview of the Excalibur release—Project Avalon—Citrix has announced the support for the Microsoft Windows 2012 operating system and its Hyper-V version. You can find more details about Project Avalon at `http://www.citrix.com/products/xendesktop/whats-new/project-avalon.html`.

## How to do it...

In this recipe, we will configure the Microsoft Hyper-V system and the XenDesktop installation such that they are able to communicate with each other. Perform the following steps:

1. On a clean Windows 2008 R2 installation, click on the **Server Manager** icon on the Windows taskbar, and then click on **Add Roles**, as shown in the following screenshot:

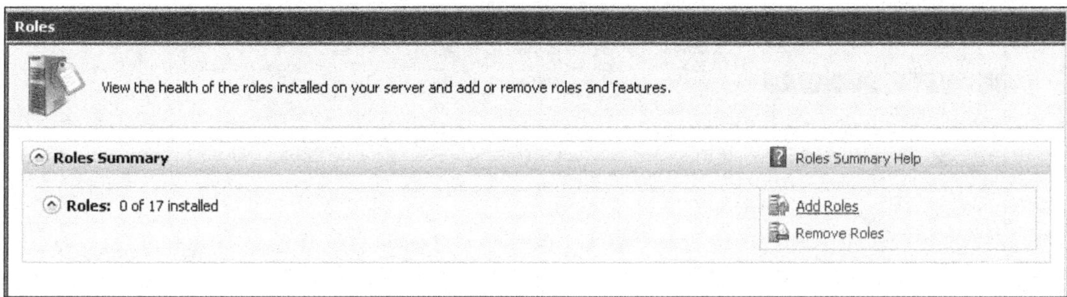


2. After clicking on **Next** on the welcome screen, check the **Hyper-V** checkbox from the **Roles** list, and then click on **Next** twice.

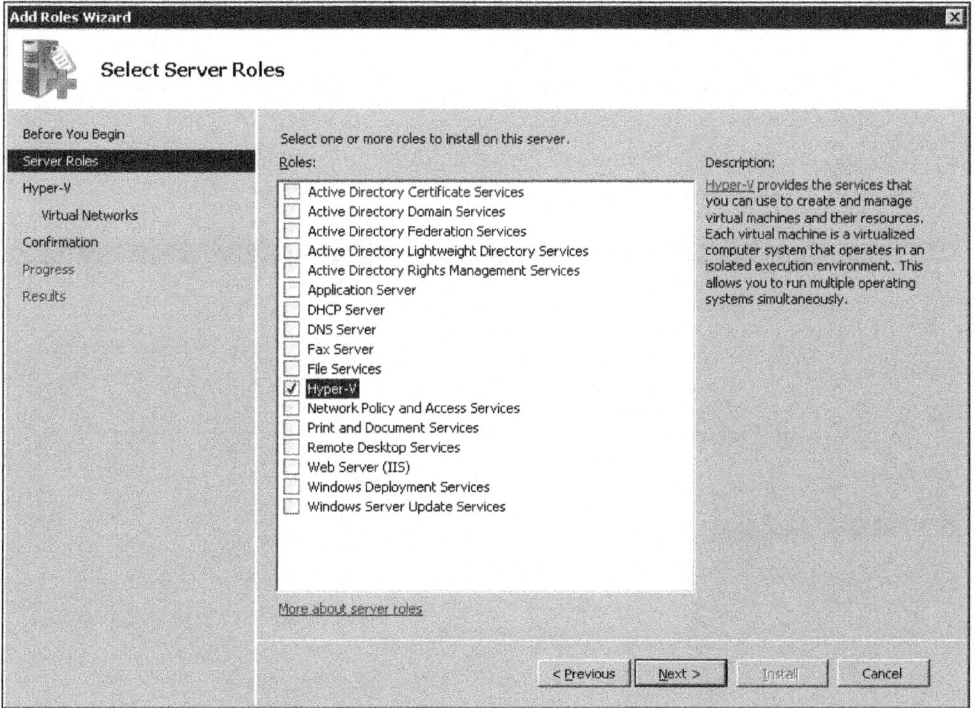

3. After flagging the desired network card from the **Network Adapters** section (by which we erogate network services for the virtual machines that we will attach to the virtual network), click on **Next**.

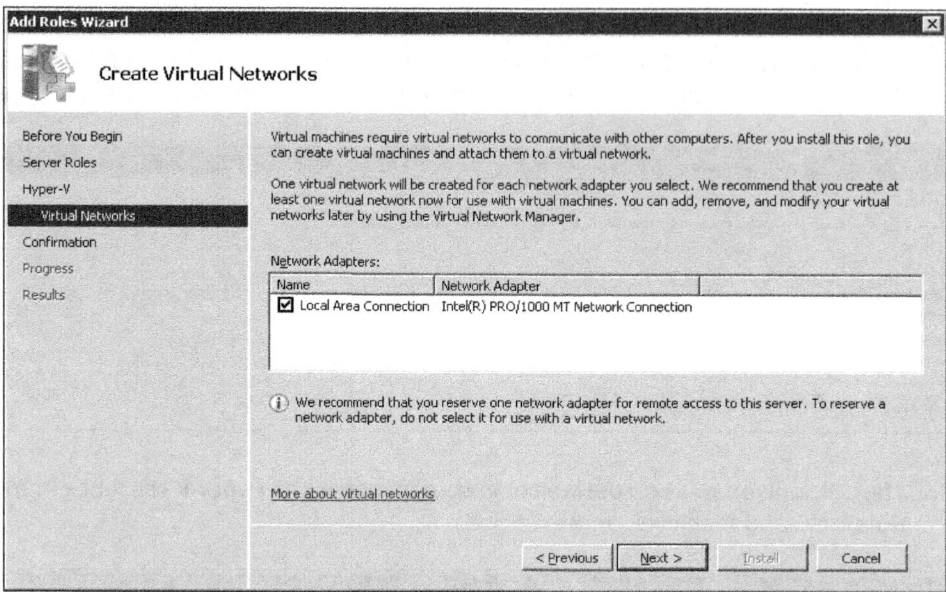


4. If the information in the **Confirmation** section is correct, click on **Install** to complete role installation.
5. Now you have to restart Windows Server in order to complete the installation procedure. Click on **Close**, and then restart the machine.

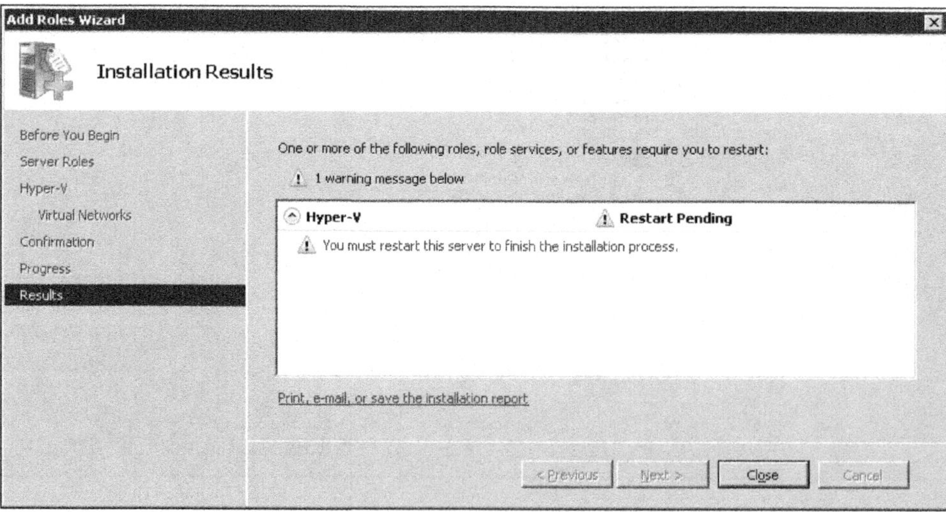

[ The Xendesktop 5.6 release is fully able to use the 2012 version of Microsoft SCVMM. ]

6. After completing role configuration for Windows Server Hyper-V, download the SCVMM software from the Microsoft portal, at `http://www.microsoft.com/en-us/server-cloud/evaluate/trial-software.aspx`.

[ For performance reasons, you have to install SCVMM Server on a machine other than XenDesktop Controller; instead, SCVMM console must be installed where Citrix XenDesktop Controller has been configured. ]

7. On a server different from XenDesktop DDC, run the download archive (`SC2012_VMM`) to extract the software; then, launch `Setup.exe` from destination folder.
8. On the presented screen, click on the **Install** link in the **Virtual Machine Manager** section, and leave the **Get the latest updates to Virtual Machine Manager from Microsoft Update** checkbox checked.

[ Before SCVMM installation, be sure you've installed and configured IIS Web Server and **Windows Automated Installation Kit** (**AIK**) for Windows 7 (available at `http://www.microsoft.com/en-us/download/details.aspx?id=5753`). ]

9. In the **Select features to install** list, select **VMM management server** and **VMM Self-Service Portal**, and then click on **Next**. The **VMM Console** component will automatically be selected, as you can see in the following screenshot:

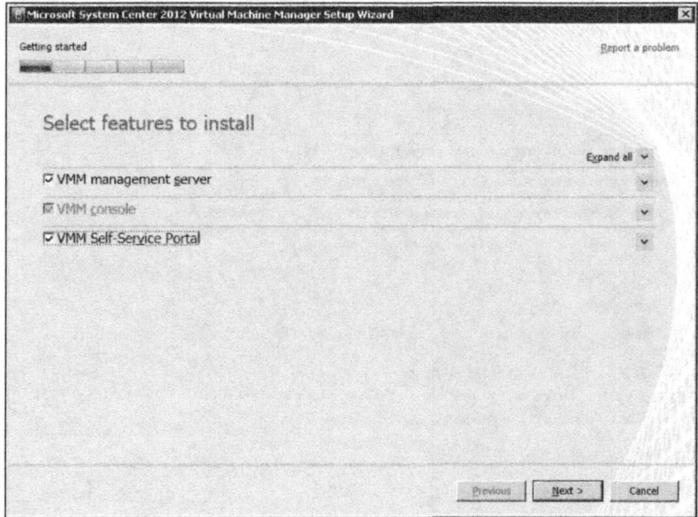

10. Populate the **Name**, **Organization**, and **Product key** fields, and then click on **Next**, as shown in the following screenshot:

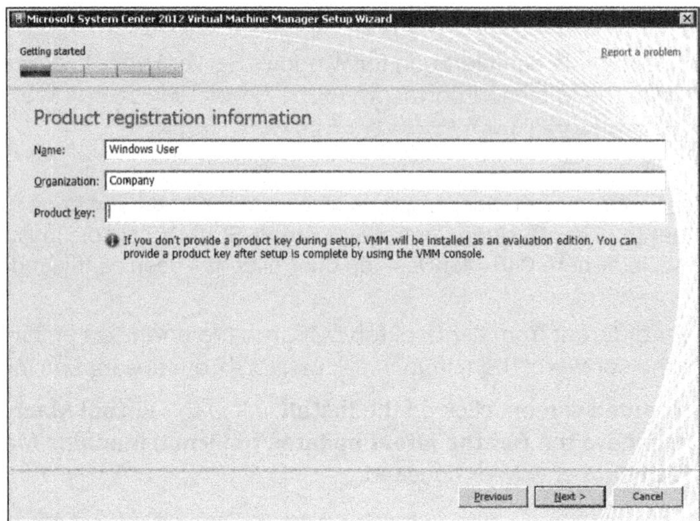


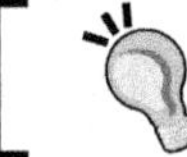

You can also insert your license number after the installation procedure.

11. Accept the license agreement (check **I have read, understood, and agree with the terms of the license agreement**) and click on **Next**, as shown in the following screenshot:

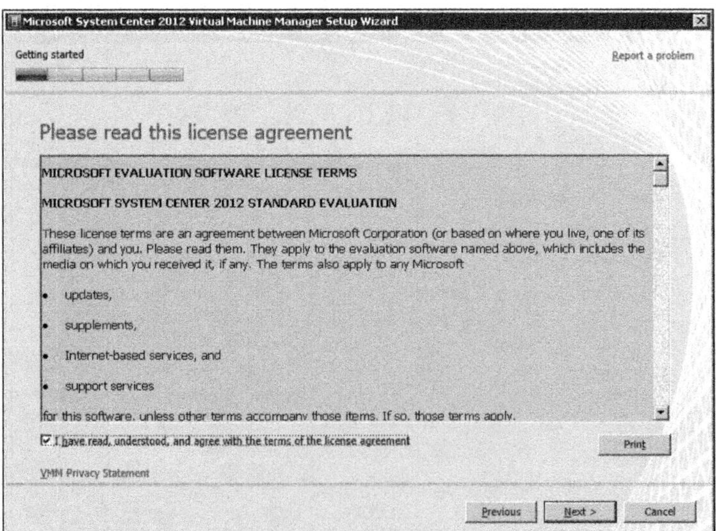

12. Check the appropriate radio button, depending on whether you want to participate in the Microsoft collaboration program or not.
13. Select the installation location by typing it in the **Location** field and proceed by clicking on **Next**, as shown in the following screenshot:

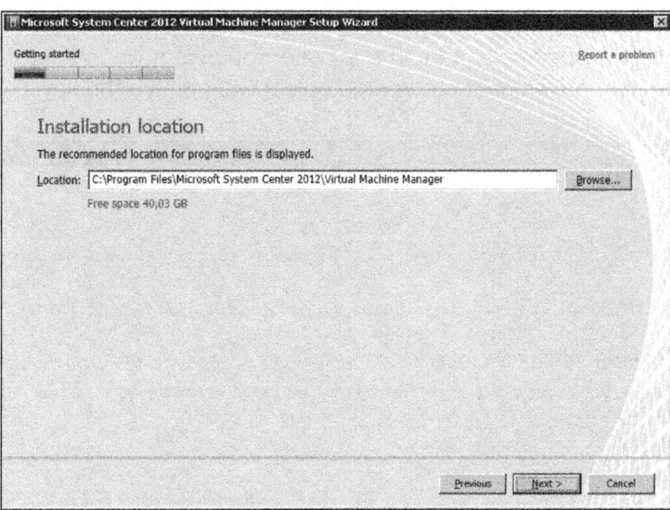


14. After passing the prerequisites check, you must specify the database location (**Server name** and **Port**), Windows administrative credentials (check the **Use the following credentials** checkbox), and **Instance name**. You also need to specify a database name after choosing between the **New database** and **Existing database** radio buttons, as shown in the following screenshot:

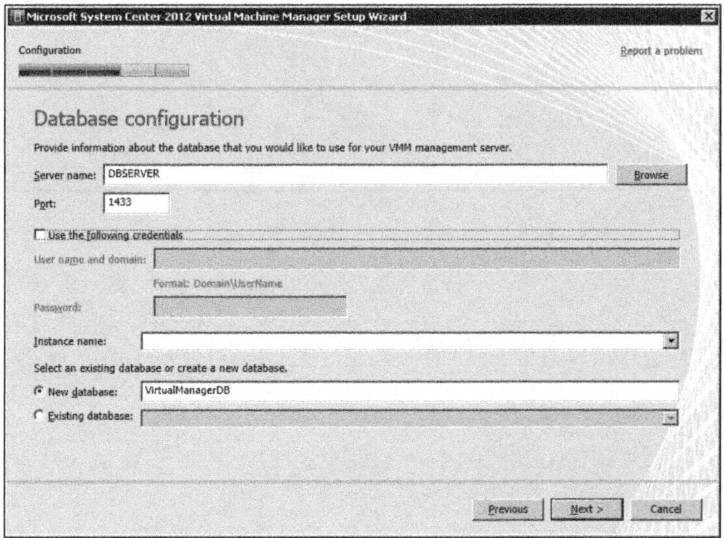

SCVMM 2012 does not support SQL Server Express edition!

15. Select whether you are using local system account or domain account (service type), and decide whether you want to save the encryption keys in Active Directory by checking the specific option; in this case, you also have to specify the location in Active Directory on which the machine object will archive the keys.

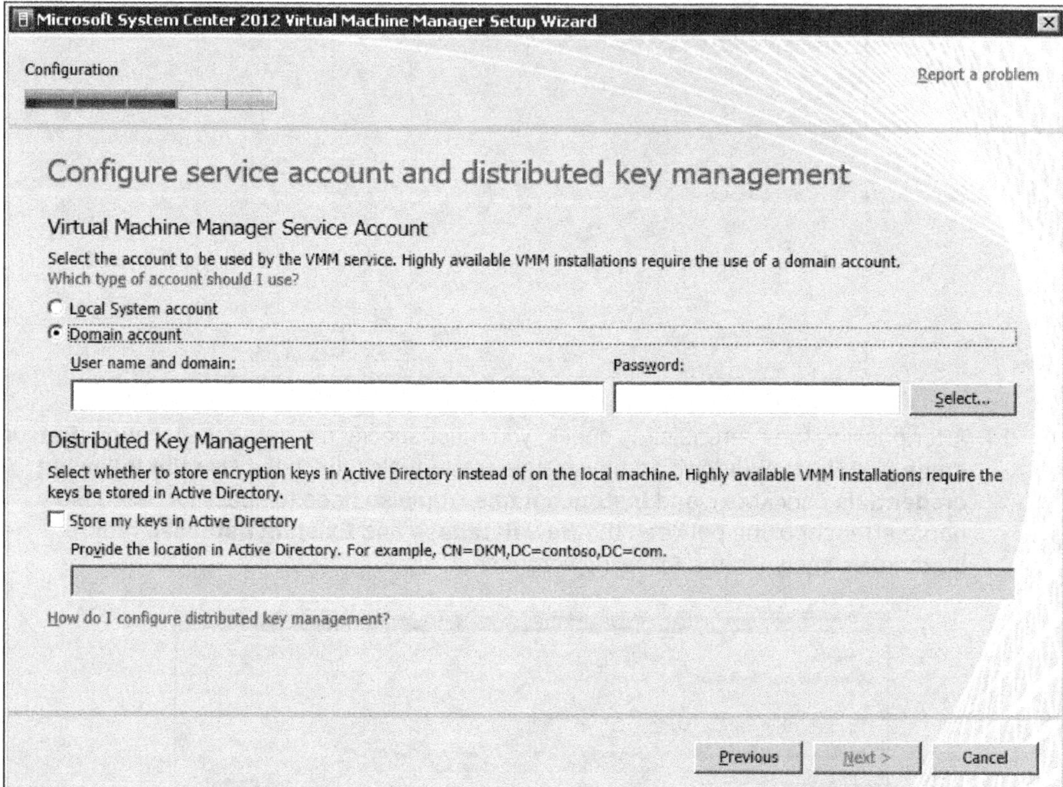

16. Configure the ports for server communication, as shown in the following screenshot:

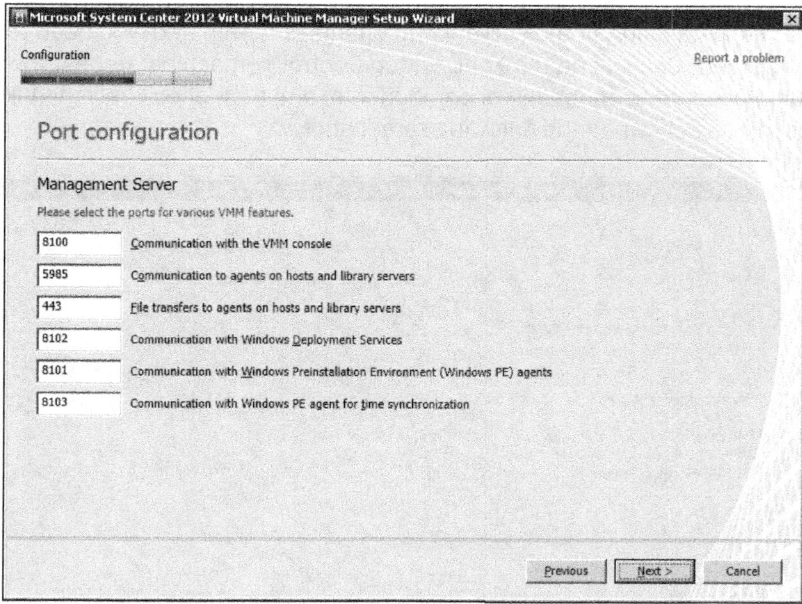


17. On the next screen, you can choose to create a new VMM library (select **Create a new library share**, including a description for the share) or use an existing one (**Use an existing library share**), as shown in the following screenshot:

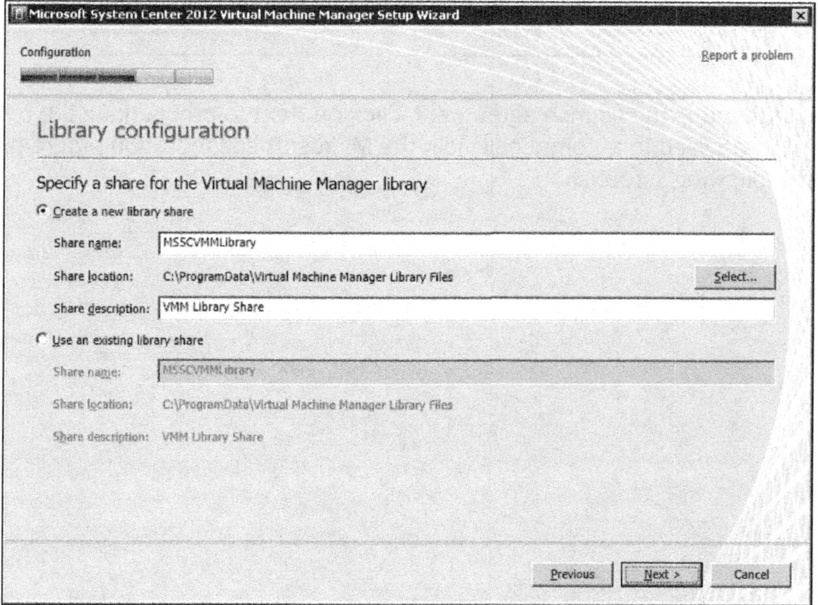

18. If the summary information is right, click on the **Install** button to complete the procedure.
19. Once the installation of the server components is terminated, you need to install Management Console on the XenDesktop Controller machine. Repeat the launching setup procedure seen for server components, and then check only the **VMM console** checkbox, as shown in the following screenshot:

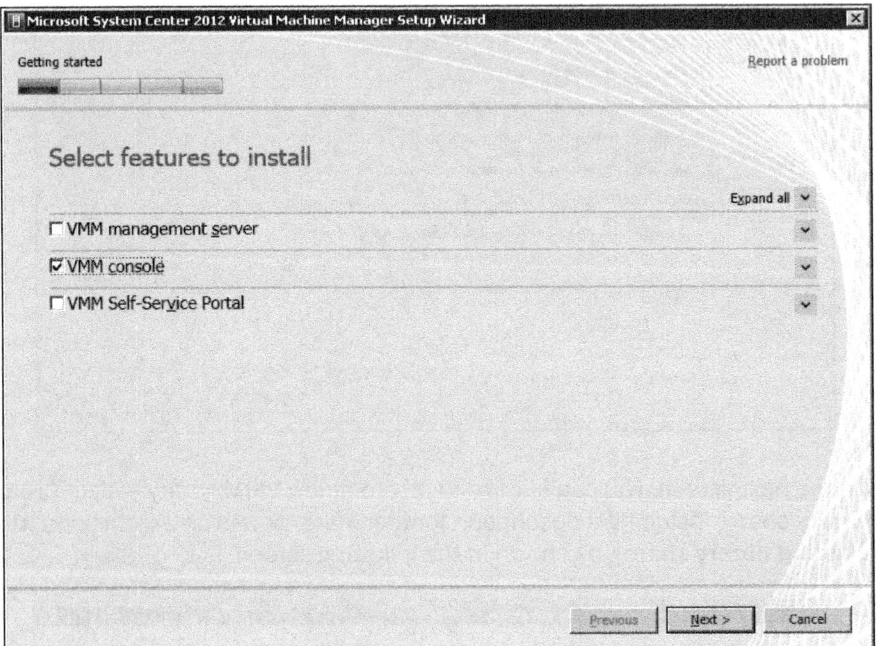


20. After accepting the license agreement, click on **Next** to proceed; on the next screen, you'll be advised to automatically join the Microsoft collaboration program, as shown in the following screenshot:

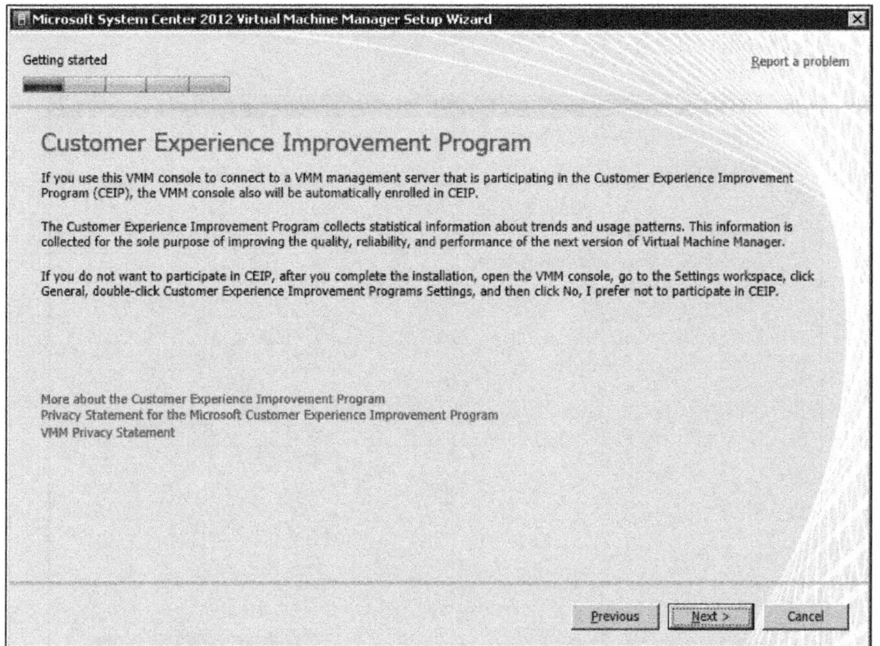


21. Click on the **On (recommended)** radio button to activate updates, and then click on **Next**, as shown in the following screenshot:

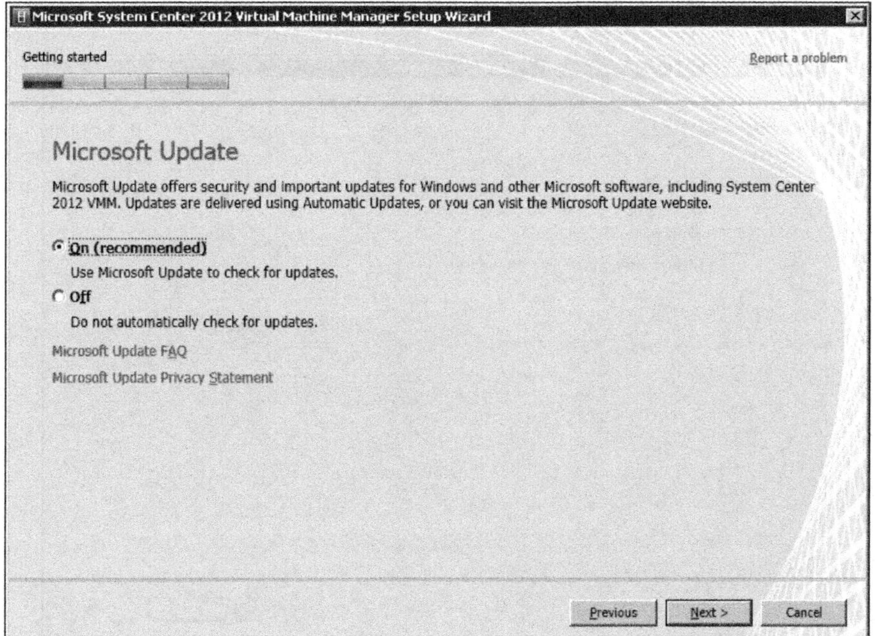

22. Select the installation location by populating the **Location** field, as seen earlier, and click on **Next**.

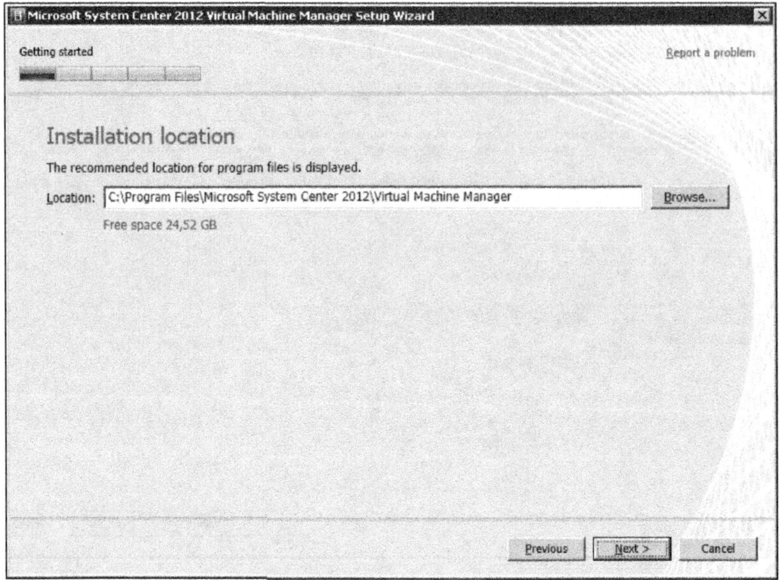


23. Select a port on which you want to configure the console (**Communication with the VMM management server**; default port is **8100**) and click on **Next** to proceed, as shown in the following screenshot:

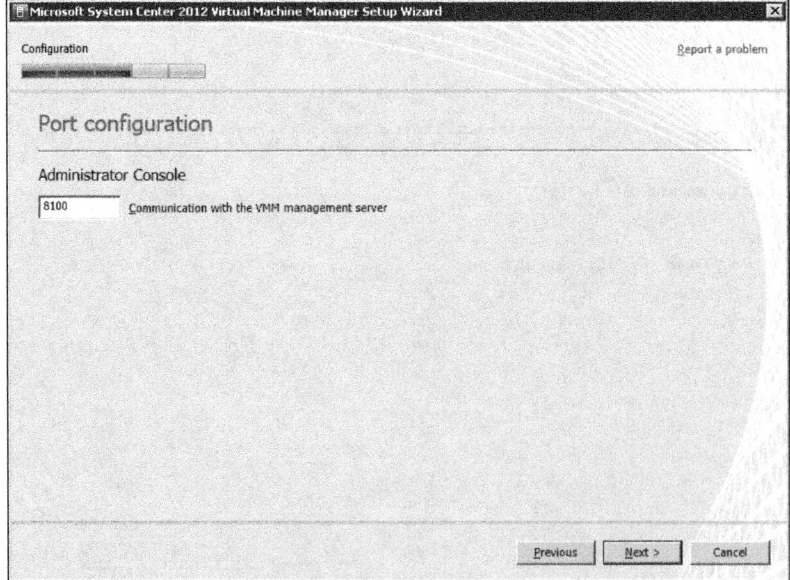

24. If the information on the **Installation summary** screen is correct, click on **Install** to complete this procedure.
25. After setup has been completed, click on **Close** and leave the **Open the VMM console when this wizard closes** checkbox checked.
26. On the logon screen, enter server name and port (in the form `hostname:port`) for SCVMM Server and specify credential access; you can choose **Use current Microsoft Windows session identity** or **Specify credentials**:

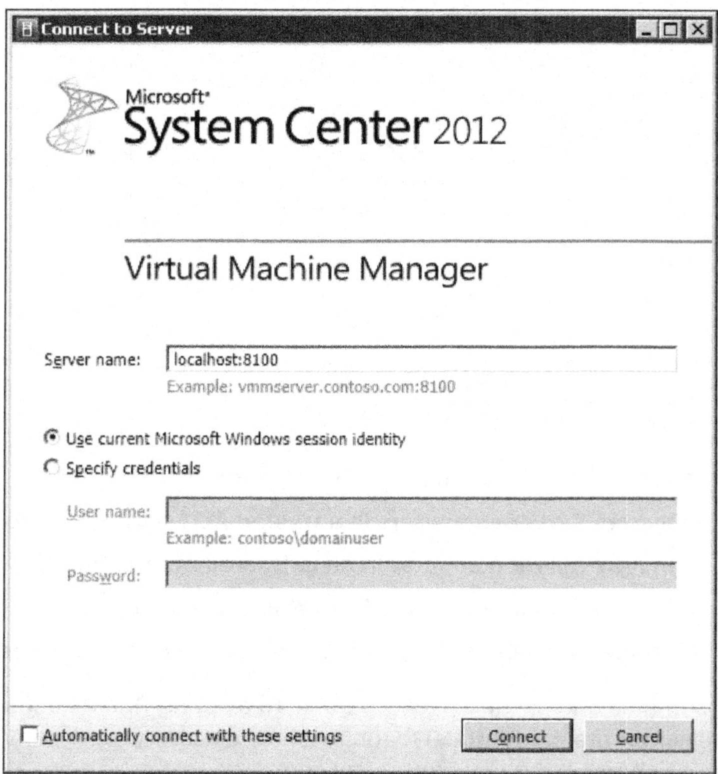

27. Once logged in, right-click on **All Hosts** in the left-hand menu and select **Add Hyper-V Hosts and Clusters**, as shown in the following screenshot:

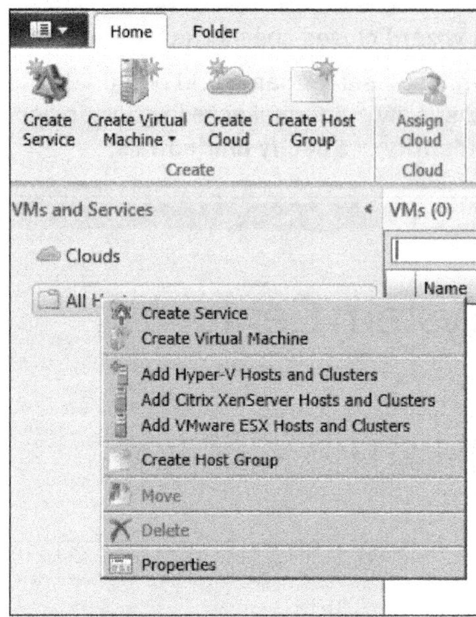


28. Select the Hyper-V host location from one of the following and click on **Next**:
    - **Windows Server computers in a trusted Active Directory domain**
    - **Windows Server computer in an untrusted Active Directory domain**
    - **Windows Server computers in a perimeter network**
    - **Physical computer to be provisioned as virtual machine hosts**

29. Insert username and password (choose **Use an existing Run As account** or **Manually enter the credentials**) to run resource discovery for Hyper-V, and then click on **Next**, as shown in the following screenshot:

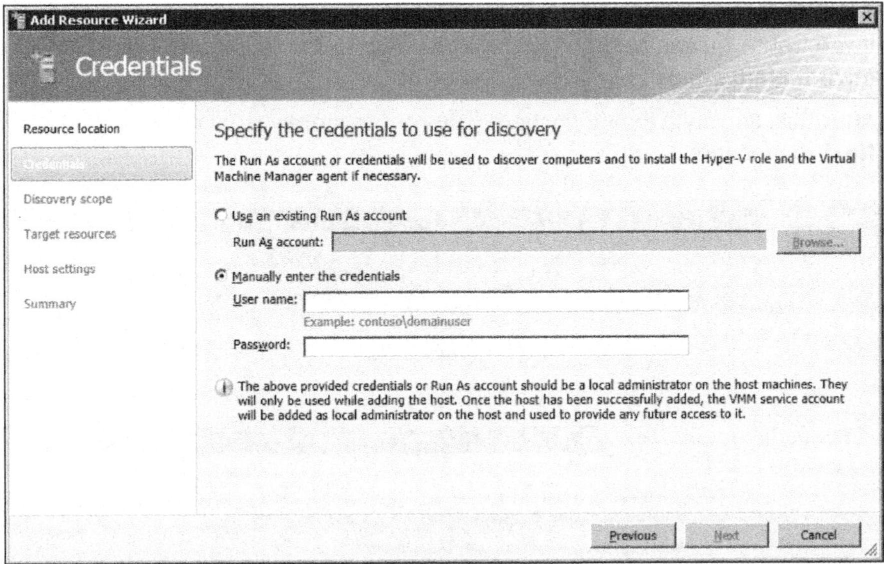


30. Specify a discovery scope (choose **Specify Windows Server computers by names** or **Specify an Active Directory query to search for Windows Server computers**) to reduce the range on which it performs host searches.
31. After you've received query results, flag desired host(s) and proceed by clicking on **Next**:

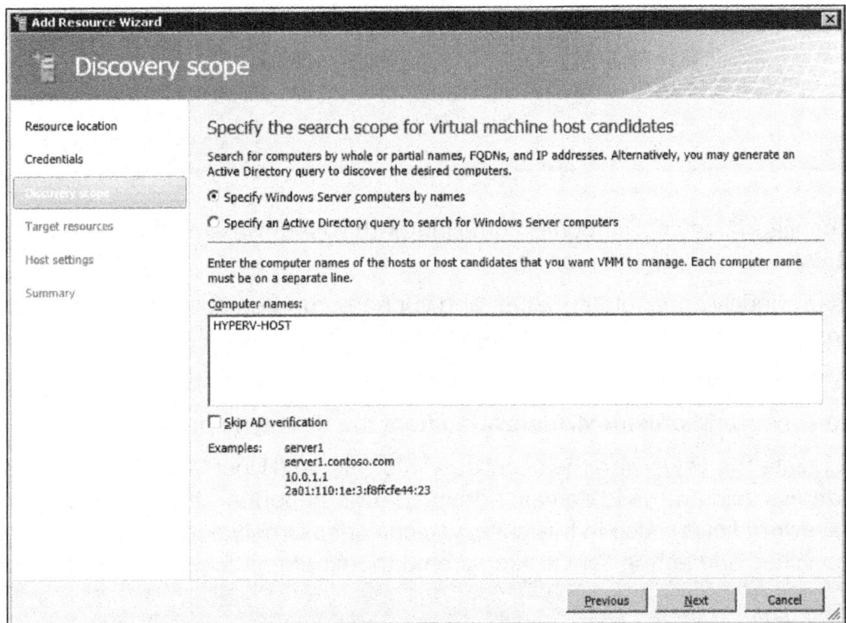

32. Select a host group to which you want to attach the selected Hyper-V server; if you want, you can also check the **Reassociate this host with this VMM environment** checkbox.
33. After this, specify a location where you want to store virtual machines, and click on **Next** to proceed:

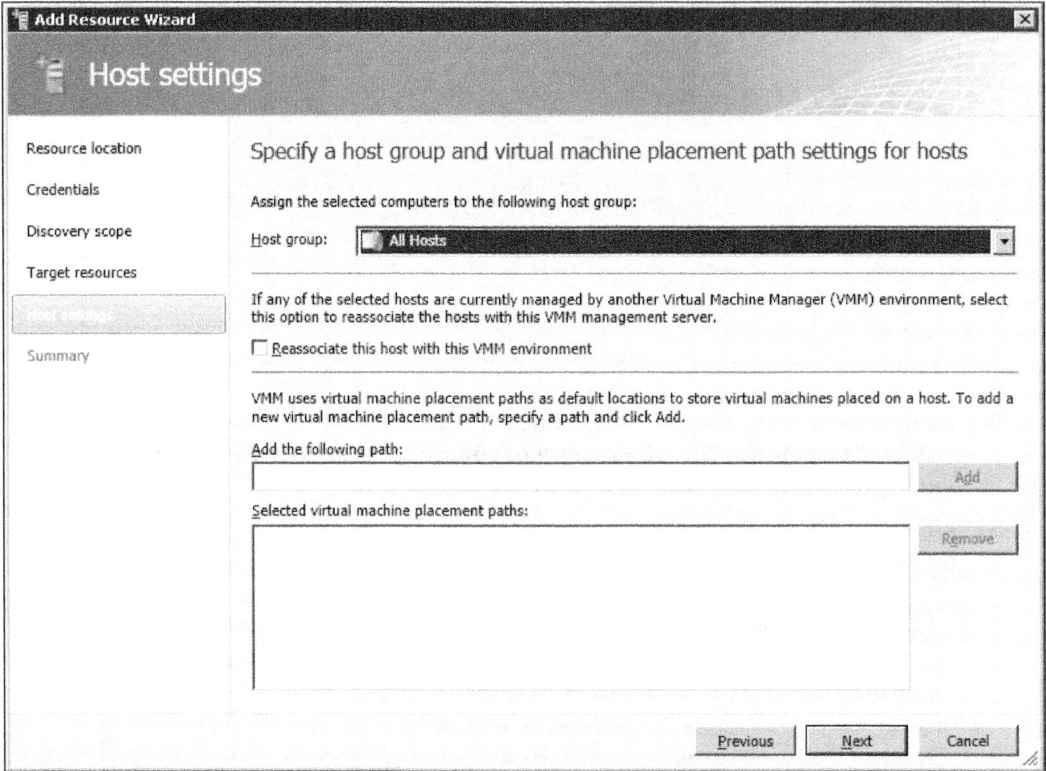


34. If configuration information is compliant with your environment parameters, click on **Finish** to complete the procedure.
35. As previously done for XenServer and vSphere, run Desktop Studio, and select the **Hosts** link from the **Configuration** section.
36. In the right-hand menu, click on **Add Host**.
37. Now choose **Microsoft virtualization** from the **Host type** drop-down menu.
38. Populate the fields with the necessary information (Hyper-V server's address in the **Address** field and valid domain administrative credentials in the **Username** and **Password** fields). Also in this case, you can choose between manually creating virtual machines and letting XenDesktop create them automatically (the better choice).

39. Populate the **Connection name** field and click on **Next**, as shown in the following screenshot:

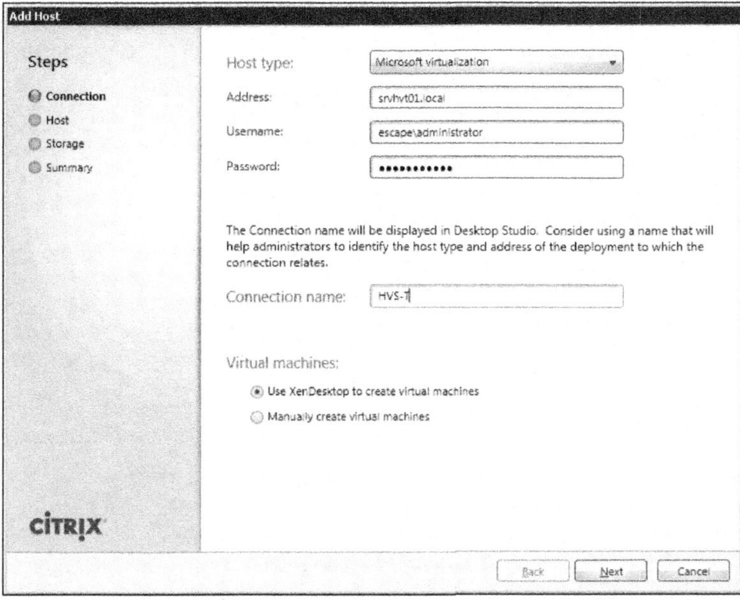


40. Select your Hyper-V cluster from the list, click on the radio button for the desired network , and click on **Next**:

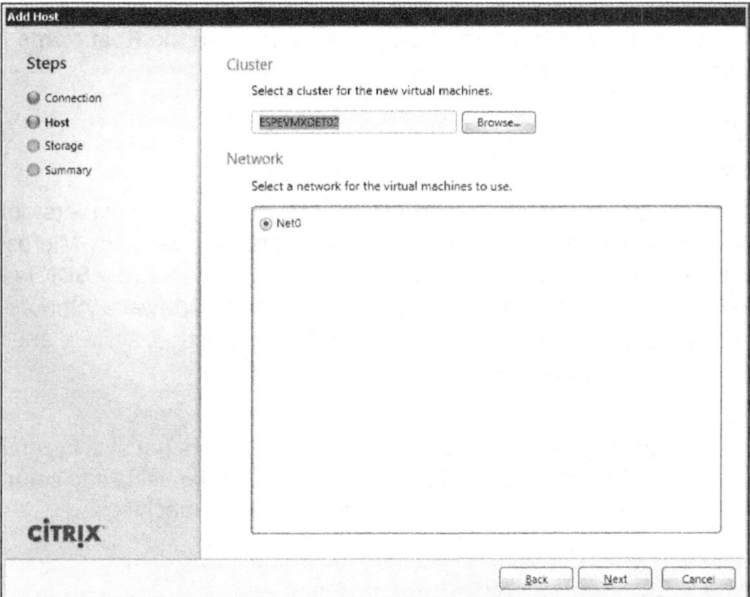

41. Select the storage where you want to archive the virtual machine; it's also possible to separate the VM's operating system storage from personal vDisk storage:

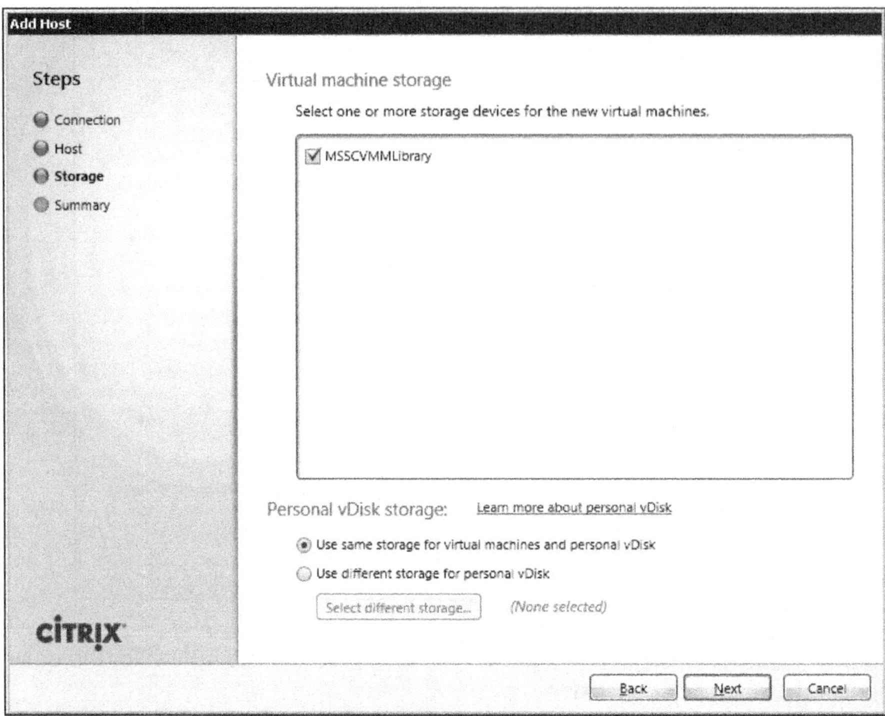


42. After reviewing the setup information, insert a name in the **Host name** field and click on **Finish** to complete the procedure.

## How it works...

Citrix XenDesktop 5.6 is able to communicate with Microsoft Hyper-V servers only by the use of Microsoft SCVMM; more precisely, it uses the SDK platform offered by Microsoft System Center. For this reason, we've previously installed the VMM console (the SDK is included in it) on Xen Controller. This is an interaction similar to that used for VMware vSphere. So, you can consider System Center as similar to VMware VirtualCenter; by this, system engineers can centrally manage all configured Hyper-V hosts in a server farm.

SCVMM is able to manage not only Hyper-V hosts but also hypervisors from different vendors. So, you can also consider using it to centrally manage Citrix XenServer and VMware vSphere machines.

# Chapter 2 XenDesktop lab

The main task to perform in this lab is to install **Microsoft System Center Virtual Machine Manager** (**SCVMM**), to which to attach the hypervisor host(s) you've decided to use to perform the lab in *Chapter 1, XenDesktop Installation and Configuration* (Citrix XenServer, Microsoft Hyper-V, or VMware vSphere). Perform the following steps:

1. First of all, you need to create a virtual machine that will assume the role of SCVMM Server. You need Windows 2008 R2 virtual machine, with these parameters:
    - Recommended virtual hardware resources, that is, two vCPUs, 4 GB of RAM, and 50 GB of hard disk
    - `vmctxscv01` as the hostname
    - `192.168.1.90` as the IP address
    - Join it to the `ctxlab.local` domain before configuring any software role
    - You need to create a SQL Server database, or reuse an existing one, on a SQL Server database machine; as explained earlier, you cannot use SQL Server Express because it's not supported by SCVMM 2012
    - During SCVMM setup, install the VMM Server and VMM Console roles
2. On the XenDesktop Controller machine, with `vmctxddc01` as hostname and `192.168.1.60` as IP address, install the VMM Console role.
3. After you've installed the second console, you can attach your hypervisor under SCVMM. Depending on your platform, add the following:
    - Server address in case of XenServer host
    - Server address in case of Hyper-V standalone host
    - Virtual address in case of Hyper-V failover cluster implementation
    - VirtualCenter address in case of VMware vSphere hypervisor

At the time of this writing, SCVMM 2012 does not support version 5 of VMware vSphere.

4. On XenDesktop Contoller, run Desktop Studio MMC and configure interfacing between XenDesktop DDC and your hypervisor host, as explained in this chapter.

# 3

# Master Image Configuration and Tuning

In this chapter we will cover:

- Installing Citrix Profile Management
- Configuring virtual desktop policies
- Configuring Active Directory policies
- Optimizing the desktop experience

## Introduction

In the previous two chapters, we installed and configured important VDI infrastructural components such as database servers, XenDesktop components, and hypervisor servers for virtual machine creation and provisioning. Now it's time to put aside this class of elements for a while, and concentrate our activities on desktop client components.

End users will interact only with Windows Desktop machines, and not with architectural components shown earlier, so you have to apply particular care to the configuration process of the virtual desktops, in terms of optimization and tuning.

In order to obtain a high-level user experience, without losing agility, performance, and security, most of your activities on clients will be on policy application and optimization.

To do so, in this chapter we'll configure policies at three different levels, Citrix Profile Manager policies, Active Directory policies, and VM base image policies.

# Installing Citrix Profile Management

Citrix Profile Management, also known as Citrix User Profile Manager, is a software suite that a system administrator can use as an alternative to other profile management techniques. With this software, you're able to centrally manage user profiles, applying particular policies configured under your Active Directory domain to them.

## Getting ready

To permit Profile Manager to work correctly, you need to have a centralized and shared store, usually implemented on a file server, with SMB or CIFS protocols. The first part of the recipe explains a procedure to install a file server role on a Windows 2008 R2 operating system.

## How to do it...

In the following steps, the process of implementing the Citrix Profile Management software will be explained:

1. Click on the **Server Manager** icon on the Windows taskbar (or as an alternative, click on **Start** | **Run** and type in `ServerManager.msc`); on the opened windows, click on the **Add Roles** link.
2. After clicking on **Next** on the welcome screen, check the **File Services** checkbox from the **Roles** list, and then click on **Next** twice.

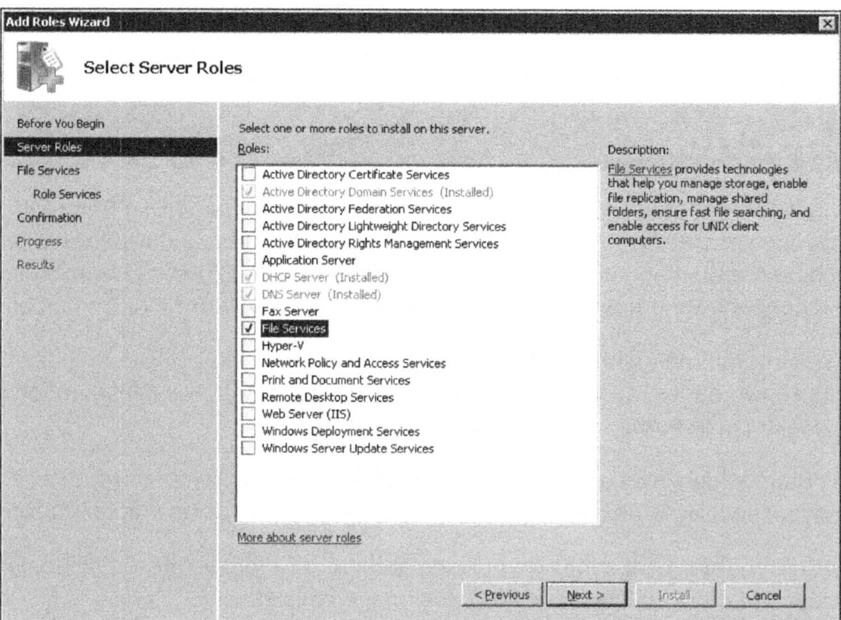

3. Check the **File Server** and **File Server Resource Manager** checkboxes; if you have multiple servers, you can also include the **Distributed File System** (**DFS**) replication topology. Then click on **Next**:

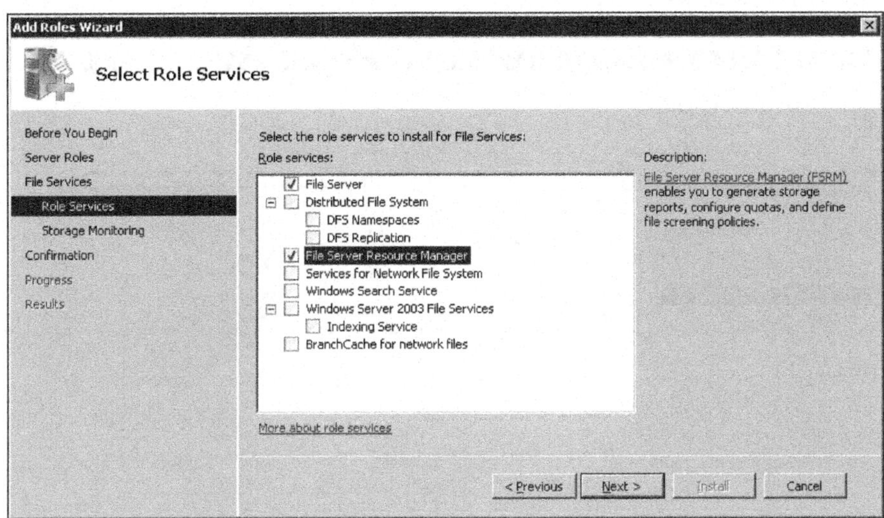


4. Select which volume you want to monitor and include it in reporting activities and click on **Next**, as follows:

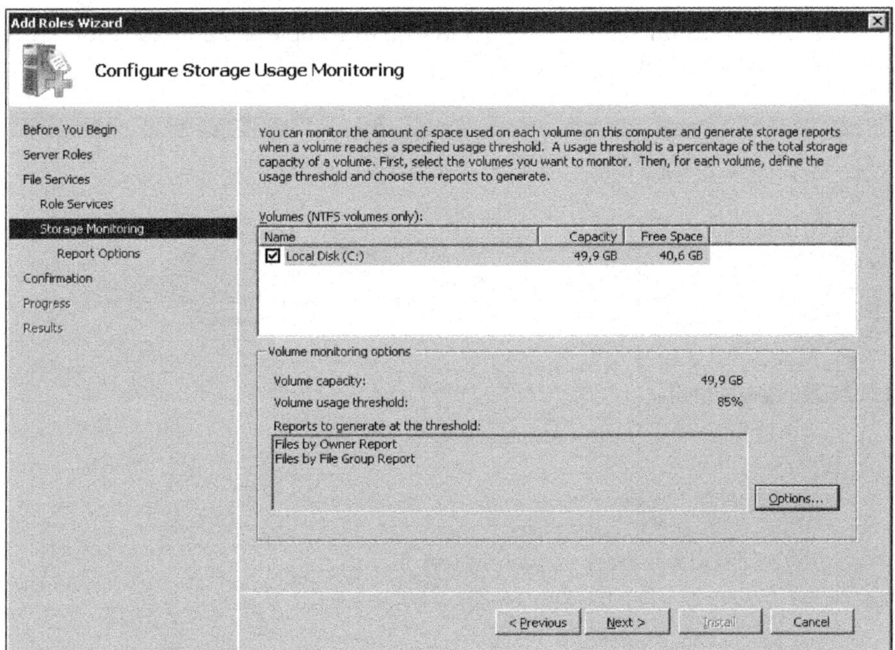

5. Select a location for the **Save reports at this location** section when saving generated reports, then check **Receive reports by email**, and insert a valid e-mail ID to receive reports as well. This option is not mandatory. After this, you can click on **Next** to proceed:

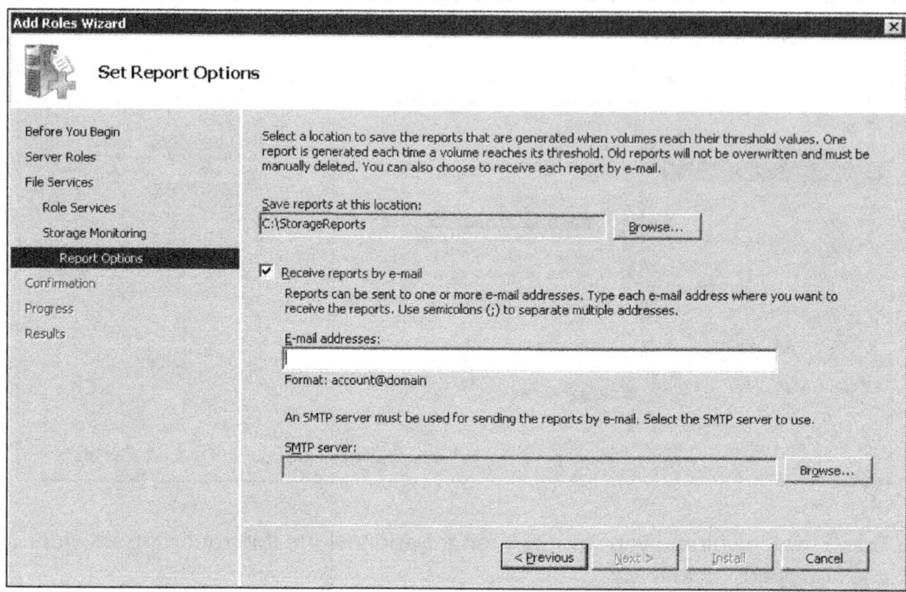


6. On the **Confirmation** screen, click on **Install** to complete the installation procedure, as shown in the following screenshot:

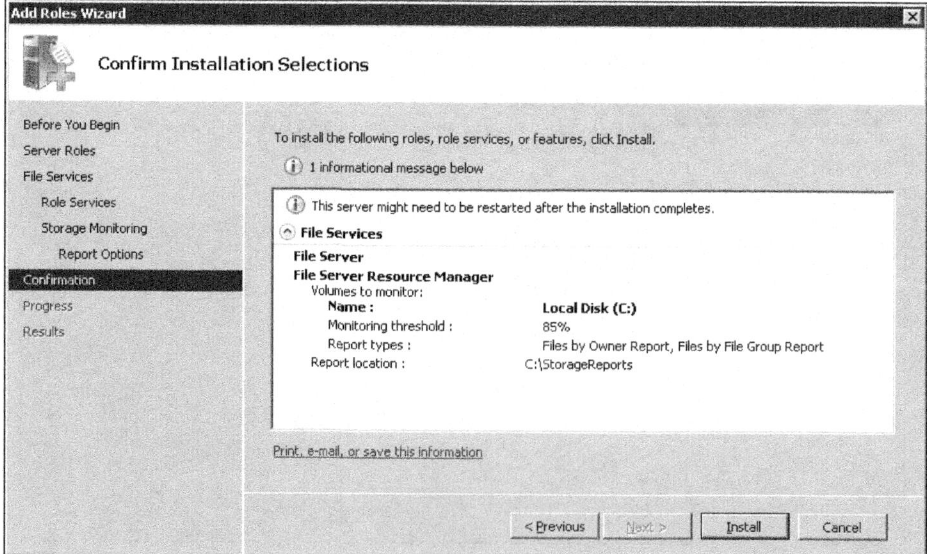

7. Click on **Start** | **Administrative Tools** | **File Server Resource Manager** to open the File Server role console, and further proceed with any advanced configuration, if necessary.

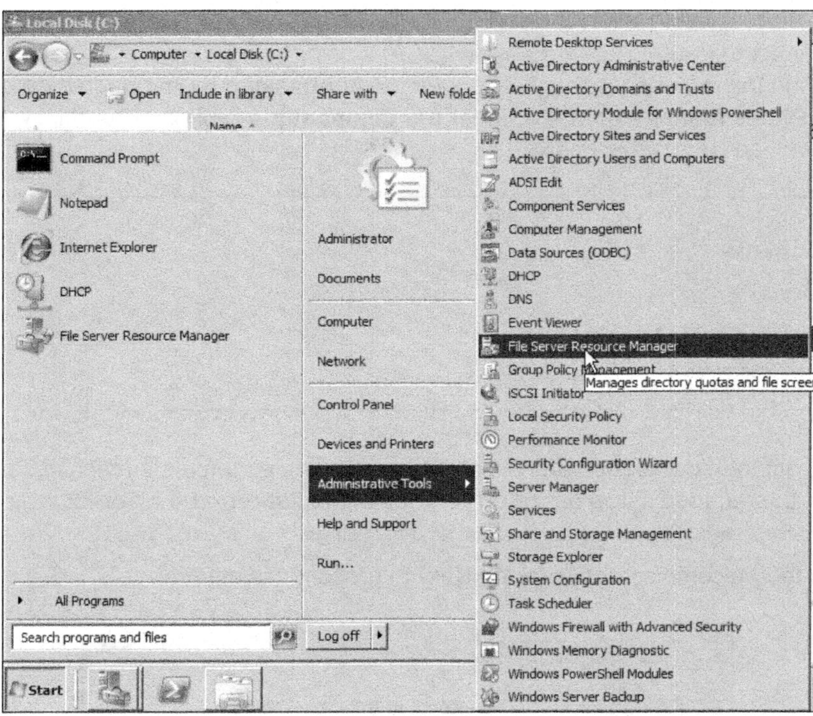

8. The console will allow you to perform operations such as quota assignment or reporting activities management:

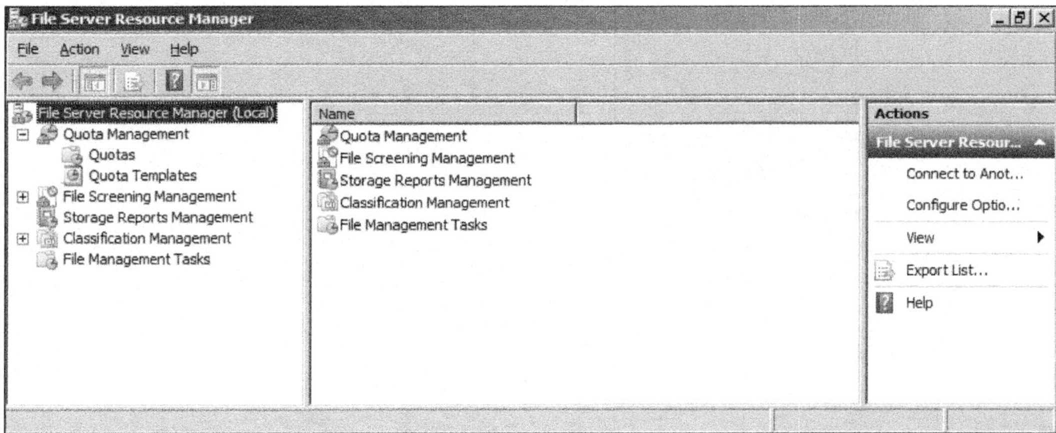

You can find more information on the Windows 2008 R2 File Server role at `http://technet.microsoft.com/library/dd463985%28WS.10%29.aspx`.

9. Connect to `www.citrix.com/MyCitrix` using your personal Citrix account, click on the **Downloads** tab, apply filters for the XenDesktop 5.6 product, then click on **Profile Management 4.1** under the **Components** section. After this, you can download your `.zip` archive.

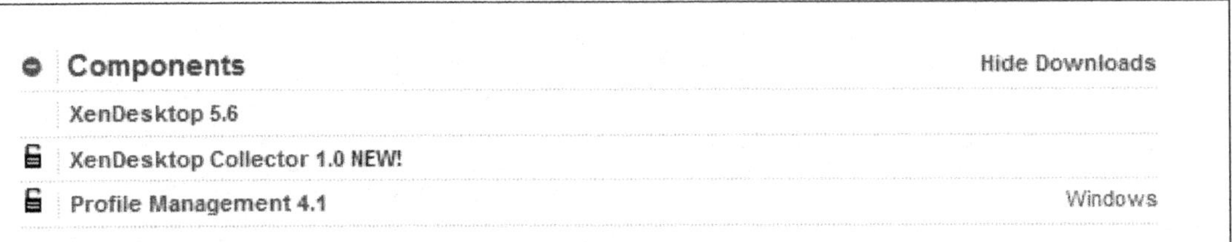


10. Extract the downloaded archive on the master image template machine, and run the required setup based on your machine platform (64 bit or 32 bit), `profilemgt4.1.0_x64.msi` or `profilemgt4.1.0_x86.msi`.
11. On the welcome screen, click on **Next** to proceed, as follows:

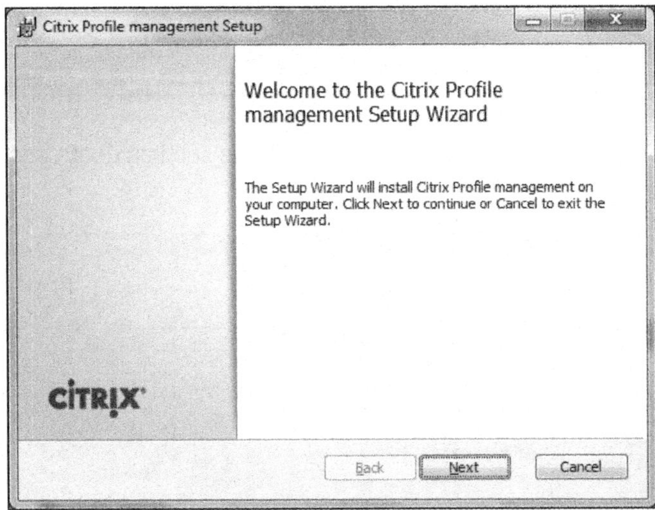

12. Accept the end user license agreement, and click on **Next**, as shown in the following screenshot:

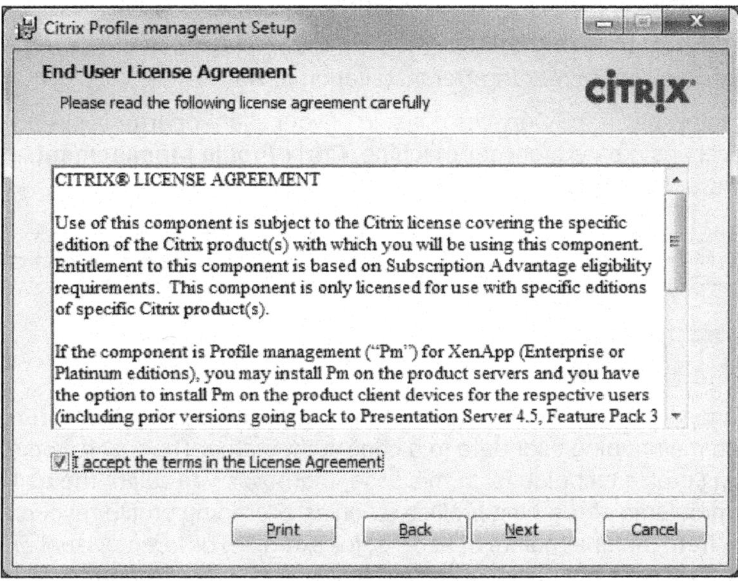


13. Select a path where you want to install the software. You can use the default path, as shown in the following screenshot:

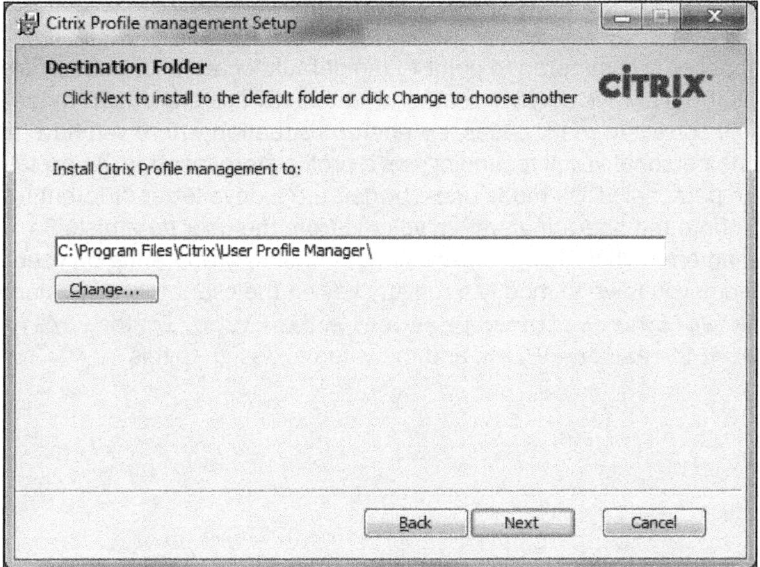

14. Click on **Install** (administrative privileges needed) to complete the installation procedure.
15. Click on **Finish** to close the setup wizard.
16. Restart the machine after the installation is complete. Select **Yes** or **No** depending on whether you want to restart after installation or not.
17. After restarting, in the Services console of your client operating system, you can find a new service created for your machine, **Citrix Profile Management**, as shown in the following screenshot:

## How it works...

Citrix Profile Manager has the responsibility of managing the logon and logoff phase of user profiles and maintaining user data in a consistent status. The way it works is similar to Windows roaming profile techniques. In this case, moreover, you've got the ability to avoid some common problems of roaming profiles (such as overriding profile resources when accessing them from multiple points of access; for example, different virtual or physical desktops). The way it works is quite simple; profiles are saved to a centralized user store; then, for every logon phase, data is copied locally on the machine, and for the logoff phase, every change made to user data or registry keys is synchronized and copied to the central store.

## There's more...

Citrix Profile Manager is configured to point to the default location for user profiles folders. This means that it will always perform read and write activities starting from the `C:` disk path. This can be correct in many cases, except for a situation where you have decided to implement the personal vDisk technology as a profile store location. As explained later in this book, the personal vDisk mode uses, by default, a drive letter different from `C:`, in order to differentiate the operating system volume from the user data disk. So, in this case, you could have an error while trying to retrieve data or simply operating on your profile. To avoid this problem, you have to modify a registry key on the client template machine; it's located at `HKLM\Software\Citrix\personal vDisk\Config`, the key's name is `EnableUserProfileRedirection`, and the value to assign to it is `0`.

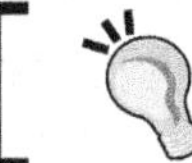

Please refer to this registry modification when you install personal vDisk later in this book.

## See also

- The *Implementing profile architecture* recipe in *Chapter 4, User Experience – Planning and Configuring*

# Configuring virtual desktop policies

After you've completed the installation procedures for the profile management client, it's time to configure the policies for your Active Directory domain that will be applied to the virtual desktop clients.

## Getting ready

To configure the specific domain policies for the VDI environment, you need to have elevated permissions, and you also have to be able to propagate them to the client that will be used as the master image template. You have to apply this custom configuration only to the **Organizational Unit** (**OU**) containing the machines belonging to the VDI architecture.

## How to do it...

The following are the required steps to configure the Citrix Profile Manager policies, which will be applied to the virtual desktop machines:

1. Log in to your domain controller server(s), then copy and extract the Profile Management ZIP archive.

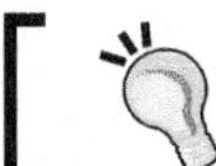

As an alternative, you can install Group Policy Management Console on any Windows 2008 R2 server to manage the domain policies.

2. Click on **Start**, then type in the following command to access the Group Policy Management Console:

```
gpmc.msc
```

3. Expand the **Forest: escape.local** tree, the **Domains** tree, and then right-click on the domain name of your organization and select **New Organizational Unit** to create a container for including all Windows desktop clients; assign it a name.

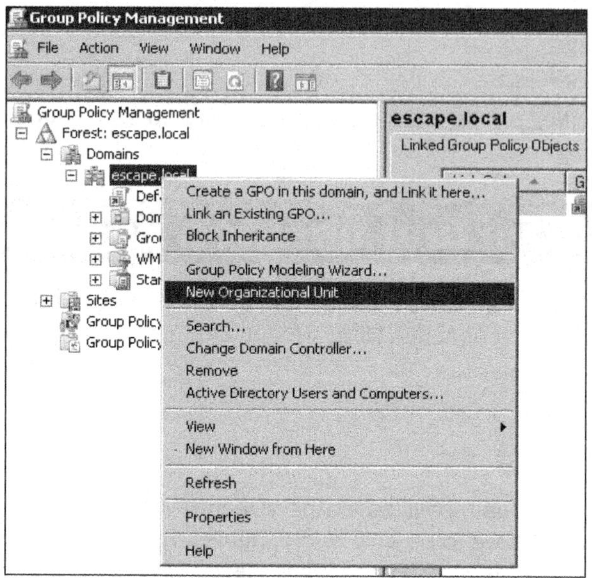


4. Right-click on the created organizational unit, and select **Create a GPO in this domain, and Link it here...**; in this way, we're starting to link Citrix policies to Active Directory.

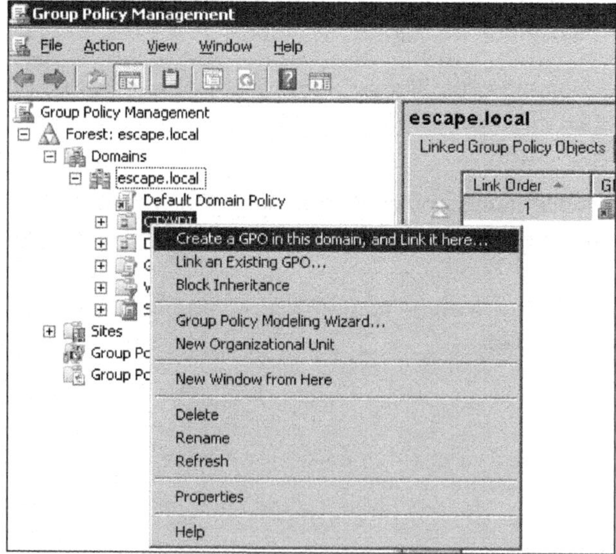

5. Give this policy a name (for example `CTXPMPolicies`), select **(none)** from the **Source Starter GPO** drop-down menu, and then click on **OK**, as shown in the following screenshot:

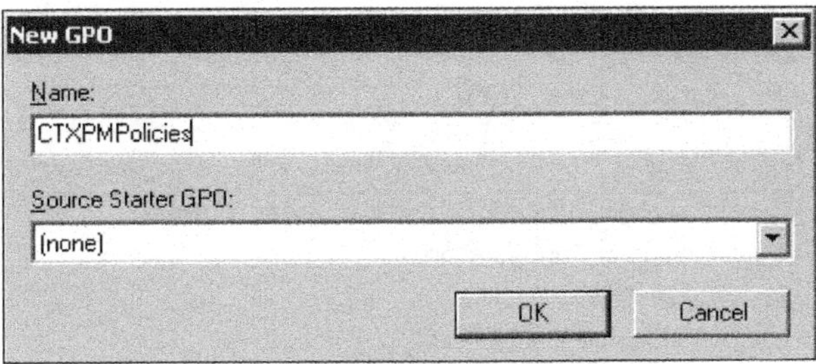


6. Right-click on the policy and select **Edit...** from the menu, as shown in the following screenshot:

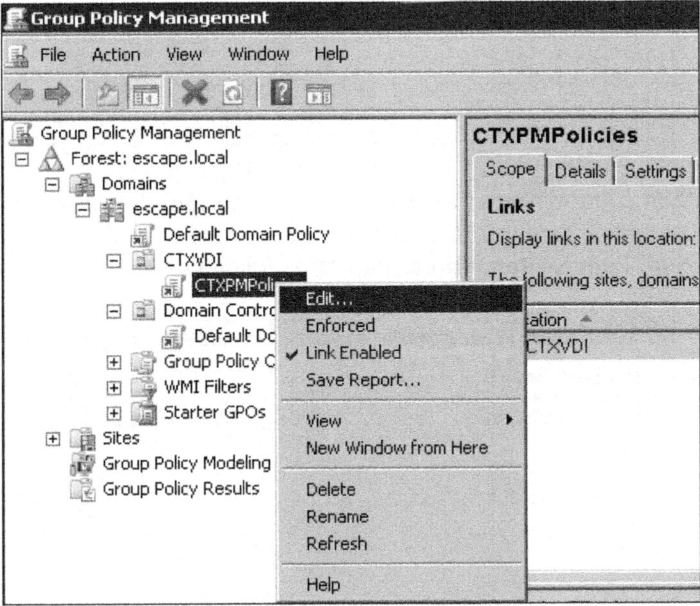

7. On the presented console, expand the **Computer Configuration** tree, then expand the **Policies** tree, and right-click on **Administrative Templates** and select **Add/Remove Templates...** from the menu, as shown in the following screenshot:

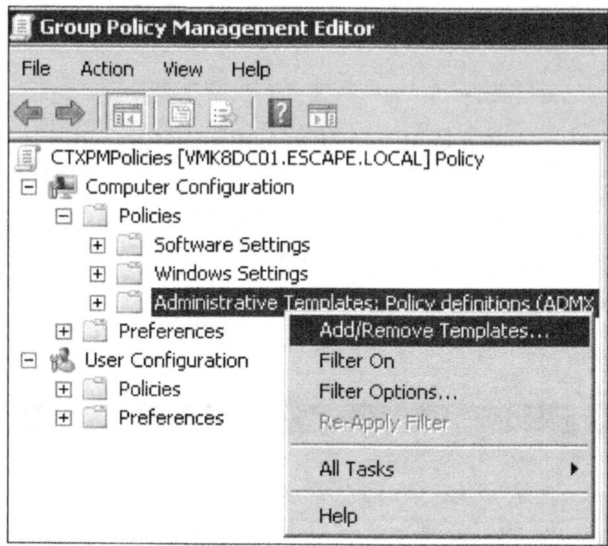


8. Click on **Add...**, then locate the `Profile Management` folder on your DC machine (earlier copied). Before this step, you will not see any kind of information in the opened **Add/Remove Templates** snap-in, as follows:

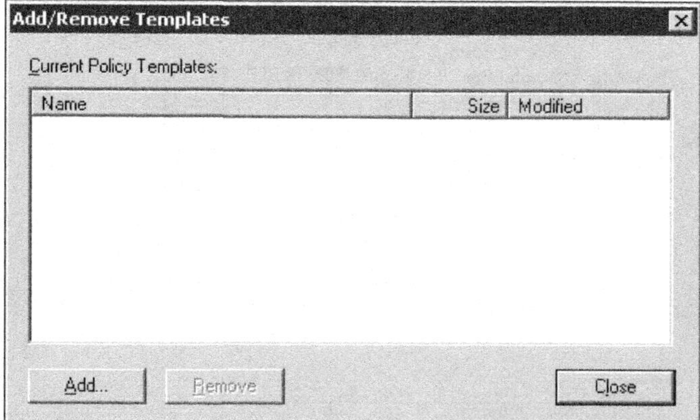

9. Browse the machine disk where you have previously extracted the Citrix Profile Manager ZIP archive, navigate to the `GPO_Templates` directory, select your configured policy language (in our case, the `en` folder, English language), and finally select the **ctxprofile4.1.0.adm** file, as shown in the following screenshot:

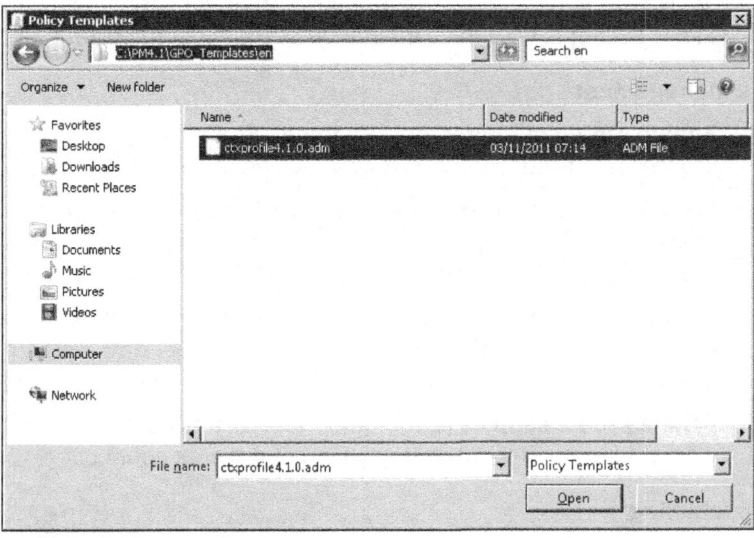


10. Click on **Close** to complete this step.

11. Expand the trees **Computer Configuration** | **Policies** | **Administrative Templates** | **Classic Administrative Templates (ADM)** | **Citrix**. Within this level, you can find all the configurable options about the imported Citrix policies, as follows:

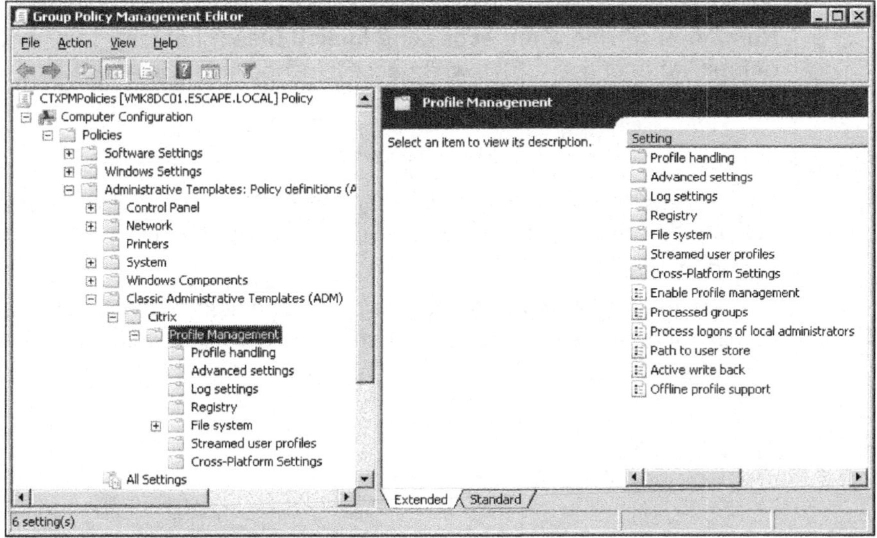

## How it works...

Policies loaded in the previous recipe work in the same way as normal Active Directory policies. For this reason, you have to configure them, modifying their default configuration (the default state is "Not Configured") to the **Enabled** or **Disabled** state. The following is a list of all of the policies sections, with the explanation of the most important among them:

- **Profile Management**
  - **Enable profile management (Enabled)**: Enabling this policy will activate the processing of the logon and logoff phases by the Citrix Profile Manager.
  - **Path to user store (Enabled)**: You must enable this policy to be able to specify the centralized folder on the file server where you want to store the profiles. By enabling this policy you have to specify the right network path.
  - **Active write back (Enabled)**: By enabling this policy, synchronization between a desktop and a user store (only for user data and not for registry keys) will be performed during an active session, before the logoff action.
  - **Offline profile support (Enabled)**: Enabling this policy will permit users to work offline as well, without any kind of network connection.
- **Profile handling**
  - **Local profile conflict handling (Enabled)**: In order to respect the default Profile Management concepts (the only profiles used are domain profiles), you should configure this policy to delete local profiles, in order to substitute any nondomain resources with information stored on central profile manager.
- **Advanced settings**
  - **Number of retries when accessing locked files (Enabled)**: This policy has a default value of five retries when accessing locked files. After being enabled, you can re-use this parameter.
- **Log settings**
  - **Enable logging (Disabled)**: With this, only errors will be logged; if you want to activate the debug mode to log activities in a verbose mode, you can decide to enable the policy.
  - **Log Settings (Enabled)**: Enable this policy and select what you want to log in a more detailed way. You can select the options shown in the following screenshot:

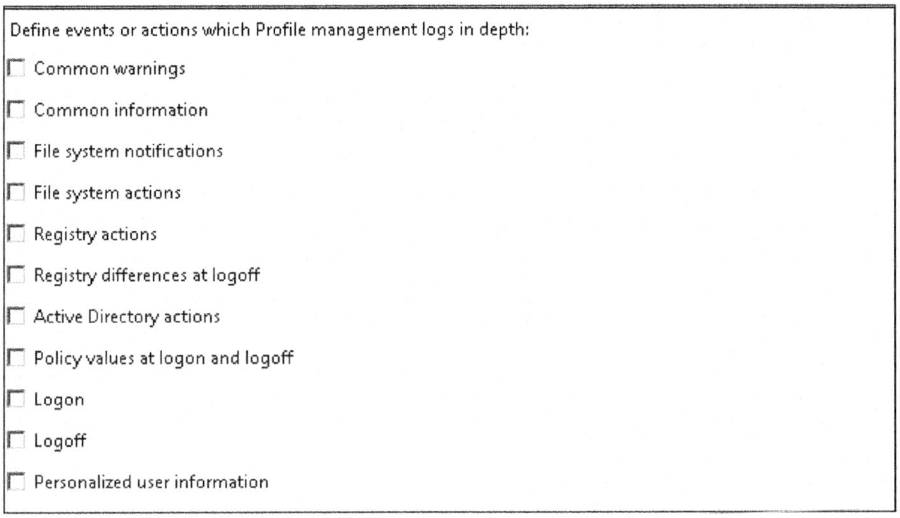

Define events or actions which Profile management logs in depth:

- [ ] Common warnings
- [ ] Common information
- [ ] File system notifications
- [ ] File system actions
- [ ] Registry actions
- [ ] Registry differences at logoff
- [ ] Active Directory actions
- [ ] Policy values at logon and logoff
- [ ] Logon
- [ ] Logoff
- [ ] Personalized user information

    - **Maximum size of the log file (Enabled)**: The default value for the log file size is 1 MB. Define a preferred value in bytes after which the current log will be rotated in a BAK file, and a new active log file will be generated.
    - **Path to log file (Enabled)**: Specify this location, if possible, using a centralized location, as we did for the user profile store.

- **Registry**
    - **Exclusion list**: Depending on your requirements, you can specify a set of registry keys to exclude during synchronization activities. So, any changes made to these values will be discarded and not sent to the user profile store.
    - **Inclusion list**: If you specify keys in this policy, they will be synchronized during the logoff phase.

- **File system**
    - **Exclusion list - files (Enabled)**: Specify the files that you don't want, and they will be saved in the profile store after logoff.
    - **Exclusion list - directories (Enabled)**: Specify the folders that you don't want, and they will be saved in the profile store after logoff.

- **Streamed user profiles**
    - **Profile streaming (Enabled)**: With this policy enabled, profile synchronization activates caching on the local computer only when files and folders are accessed; for registry keys, synchronization is in real time.

## There's more...

The logging activities are, in many cases, the only way to understand what has happened on a computer. We've seen how to enable them from the **Group Policy** snap-in; as an alternative it's possible to enable the log creation from the Citrix Profile Manager configuration file. After you've installed it on the client's machine, you have to go to its installation path, and double-click on the **UPMPolicyDefaults_V2Profile_all.ini** file. Now you can enable the logs for the desired area by assigning it the value of `1`, as shown in the following screenshot:

```
; ----------------------------------------------------------------------
;
; Log settings
;
LoggingEnabled=1
LogLevelWarnings=1
LogLevelInformation=1
LogLevelFileSystemNotification=1
LogLevelFileSystemActions=1
LogLevelRegistryActions=1
LogLevelRegistryDifference=0
LogLevelActiveDirectoryActions=0
LogLevelPolicyUserLogon=1
LogLevelLogon=1
LogLevelLogoff=1
LogLevelUserName=1
MaxLogSize=1000000000
PathToLogFile=C:\UPM_Logs

; ----------------------------------------------------------------------
```

The logs also need to be examined; Citrix helps us in giving the possibility to download a free tool to locate and analyze the UPM logs; this tool is called UPM Log Parser, and it can be downloaded from `http://support.citrix.com/article/CTX123005`. Once you've extracted the ZIP archive, you only have to run the executable file and import the logs that you want to analyze.

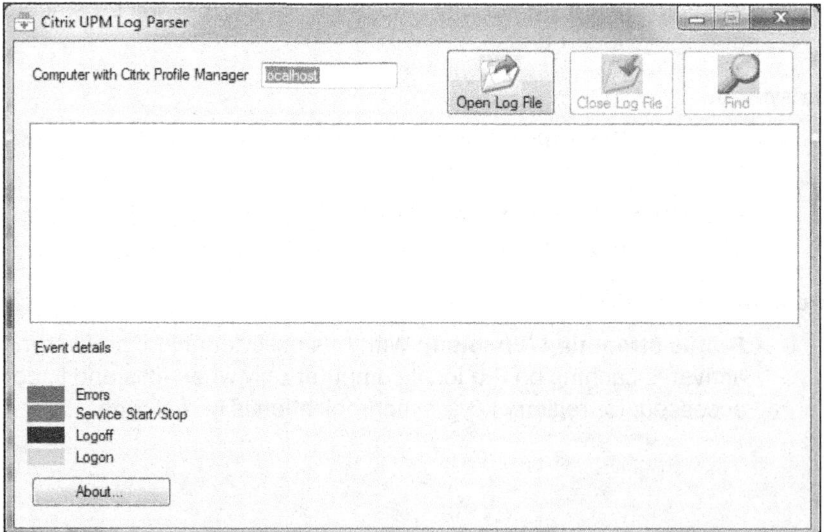

## Configuring Active Directory policies

Now that we have configured the entire Citrix User Profile Management component (both installation and policies confirmation activities), it's time to configure general Active Directory policies for the virtual desktop images, in order to tune and standardize Windows-deployed operating systems.

### Getting ready

The modification activities of the desktop optimization policies only involve the Windows client machine and the domain which it has joined. So you will need domain administrative credentials, in order to be able to modify the necessary policies, and to force their application on the involved clients.

### How to do it...

In this recipe we will explain the procedure to configure the Active Directory domain policies, which will be used by the virtual desktop together with the previously configured Profile Manager policies:

1. Log in to one of your domain controller servers, then click on **Start**, and then type in the following command:

   ```
   gpmc.msc
   ```

2. On the same OU created for user profile policies, right-click on its name and select **Create a GPO on this domain, and Link it here...**.
3. Assign this policy a name, as seen in the first recipe of this chapter, then click on **OK**.
4. After you've created the new policy, right-click on it and select **Edit...**.
5. Configure the policies as follows:
   - Go to **Computer Configuration** | **Policies** | **Administrative Templates** | **Windows Components** | **Windows Update**, and set the **Configure Automatic Updates** policy to the **Disabled** state, then click on **OK**.
   - Go to **Computer Configuration** | **Policies** | **Administrative Templates** | **System** | **System Restore**, and configure **Turn off System Restore** as **Enabled**. After this, click on **OK**.
   - Go to **User Configuration** | **Policies** | **Administrative Templates** | **Control Panel** | **Personalization**, and enable the screensaver by configuring the **Enable Screen Saver** policy as **Enabled** by default. After this, click on **OK** to continue.

- In the same section, configure **Prevent Changing Screen Saver** as **Enabled**, configure **Password Protect Screen Saver** as **Enabled**, and assign a numeric value, in seconds, to the **Screen Saver Timeout** policy after setting it to **Enabled**.

6. After completing the main Active Directory policy configuration, log on to your Windows 7 machine base image, click on **Start**, and run the `cmd` command to open a prompt shell.
7. In the shell, run the following command to force the application of those policies configured earlier for the client:

```
gpupdate /force
```

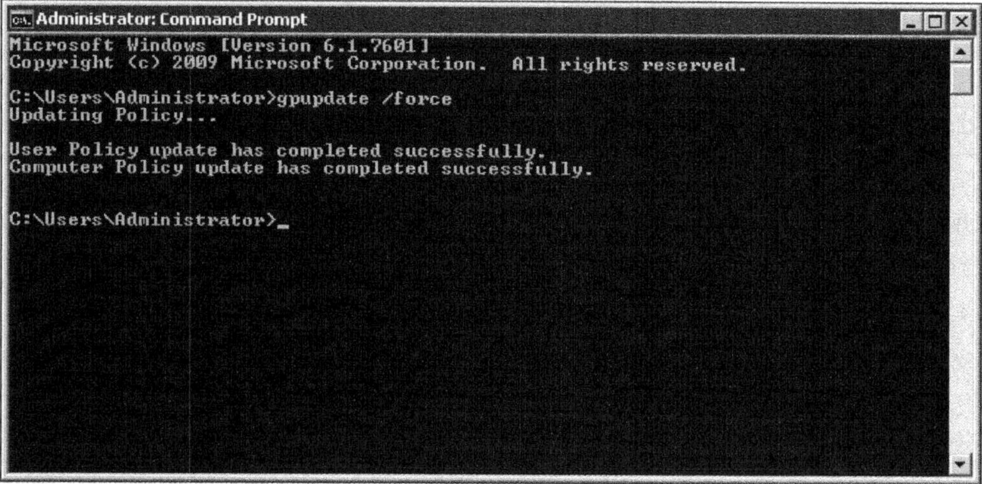


## How it works...

The use of Windows Active Directory policies is due to the necessity to standardize, as much as possible, the Windows image template to deploy to the end users. For this reason, we've disabled Windows Update on the first applied policy; the required updates will be propagated only once to the base image, and the entire set of assigned desktops will be updated every time they will be generated from the source machine. A security plus to this policy is given by using a **Windows Server Update Services** (**WSUS**) server, a centralized Windows Update server manager. This is the only point of contact to the public network, which covers the updates' propagation task in your **local area network** (**LAN**).

Moreover, we've also blocked screensaver customization and system restore points; so the user will be subject to a predefined configuration, in most cases optimized for the company's requirements.

## See also

- The *Managing Active Directory accounts – AD identity cmdlets* recipe in *Chapter 9, Working with XenDesktop PowerShell*

# Optimizing the desktop experience

Windows operating systems, starting from the Vista version in particular, offer the users a lot of graphical enhancements to better appreciate their potential and usability. In a complex VDI architecture, we need to be careful about both of these aspects, as shown in the previous recipe. Consider that the customization process can vary depending on the configured environment; anyway, the steps implemented in this recipe can be generally applied without specific issues.

> You can also refer to the following official Microsoft link to optimize a Microsoft Windows 7 installation:
>
> `http://windows.microsoft.com/en-US/windows7/Optimize-Windows-7-for-better-performance`

## Getting ready

This recipe involves the only Windows client machine; in order to be able to operate all the modifications to the services, the graphical appearance, and the system configuration, you need to use domain or local administrative credentials.

## How to do it...

In this recipe, we will execute a set of operations useful for optimizing the Windows 7 virtual desktops, in order to have a better user experience:

1. Log in to your Windows 7 base image template with administrative credentials.

2. Click on **Start** and type in the `services.msc` command; the Windows **Services** snap-in will be opened, as follows:

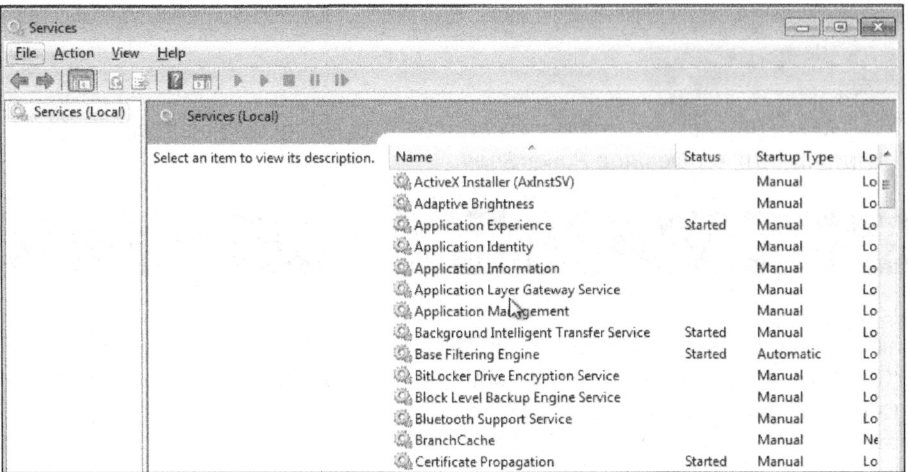

3. From the **Services (Local)** list, search for **Background Intelligent Transfer Service**:

4. Right-click on the name service, and select **Properties** from the menu.
5. From the **Startup type** drop-down list, select **Disabled** as the default state, then click on **Stop** if the service is running. After completing, click on **OK** to exit from this screen.

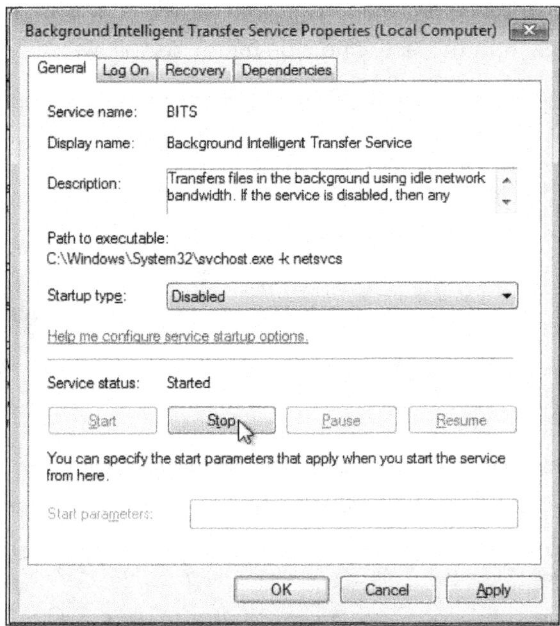


6. Repeat steps 4 and 5 to disable the following services:
   - **Desktop Windows Manager Session Manager**
   - **HomeGroup Listener**
   - **HomeGroup Provider**
   - **Windows Search**
   - **Security Center**
   - **SuperFetch**
   - **Windows Defender**
   - **Windows Media Player Network Sharing Service**
7. Click on **Start** and run the `cmd` command to open a prompt shell, then run the following command required to disable Windows' animation at boot time, in order to perform a faster machine startup:

```
bcdedit /set bootux disabled
```

8. Click on **Start** | **Control Panel**, and click on the **System** icon; then click on **Advanced system settings** from the left-hand side menu, as follows:

9. Select the **Advanced** tab and click on the **Settings...** button in the **Performance** section, as shown in the following screenshot:

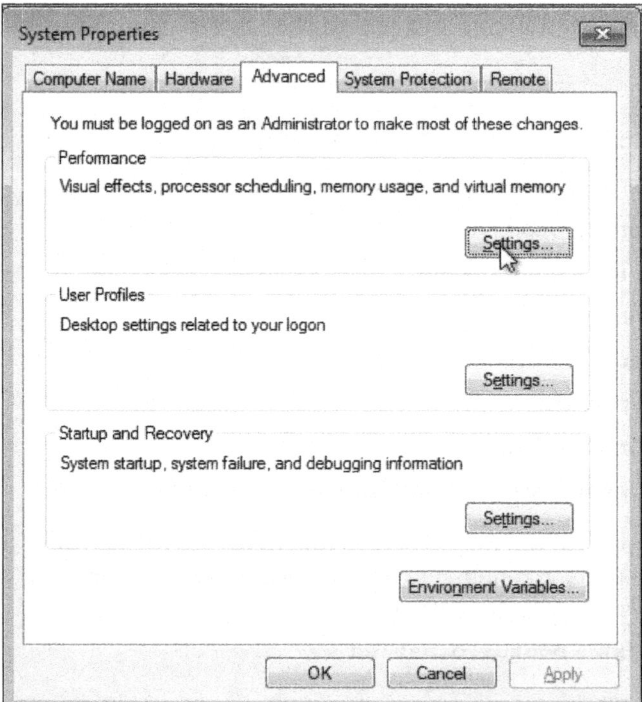

10. Select the **Advanced** tab and click on the **Change...** button in the **Virtual memory** section, as shown in the following screenshot:

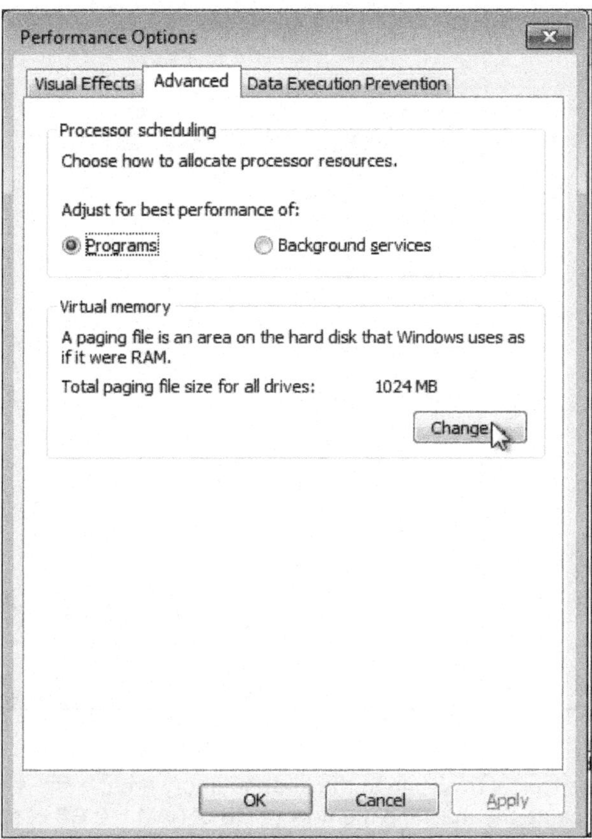


11. Remove the check from **Automatically manage paging file size for all drives**, then select the **Custom size** radio button, and enter the same value for both textboxes.

12. After this, click on **Set**, and then click on **OK**, as follows:

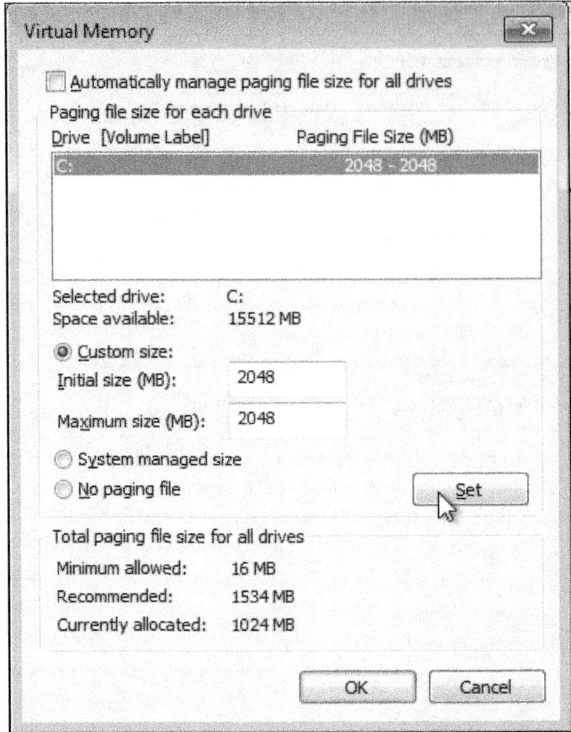

It's typical to assign to the swap memory area, a size equal to double the machine memory (1 GB of RAM = 2 GB of swap size).

13. After the amount of swap has been modified, you need to restart your machine, in order to make the changes available.

## How it works...

To reduce the usual time needed by Windows 7 machines to boot and start up all services, we've turned off a part of them, which are considered not necessary for the normal functionality of this operating system in a VDI environment; so, after disabling the animation presented at boot time (with a time reduction of approximately 20 percent), we have reduced the impact on the network by disabling services such as **Background Intelligent Transfer Services** (**BITS**, used to automatically download programs or information with software such as Windows Update or Windows Live), and impact on the virtual machine's CPU and memory usage (we've disabled Desktop Window Manager Session Manager, the **Desktop Windows Manager** (**DWM**) service, which manages, for example, the Windows Aero graphical user interface). In this second case (CPU/RAM resources), we have also reduced the service's impact on the system by disabling indexing (Windows Search, not required in a nonpersistent VDI environment), operating system's long term performance optimizer (Superfetch service), system protection (Security Center and Windows Defender, substituted by system protection software better integrated with VDI that we're going to explain throughout this book), and unnecessary multimedia components (Windows Media Player Network Sharing Center). The last performed operation is the assignment of a single value (for both minimum and maximum size parameters) for the swap area memory size.

Disable the Windows Search (indexing) service only in the presence of nonpersistent virtual desktops; in any other case, you should maintain it as active to avoid general content search issues.

# Chapter 3 XenDesktop lab

In this laboratory, we will create a Windows 2008 R2 machine to configure and use as a file server where you want to store the centralized profiles under Citrix UPM. Then we'll configure Citrix and Windows native policies, in order to use the centralized profile management and to optimize the performance for the deployed Windows clients, both for PVS and MCS architectures. Perform the following steps:

1. Create a Windows 2008 R2 virtual machine on a supported hypervisor, with the following parameters:
    - Recommended virtual hardware resources, that is, two vCPUs, 4 GB RAM, 40 GB hard disk for system disk (`C:`), and at least 50 GB hard disk for file server volume (assigned driver letter, `F:`)
    - `vmctxdfs01` as the hostname
    - `192.168.1.55` as the IP address
    - Join it to the `ctxlab.local` domain, before configuring any software role

- For File Services installed role, select `F:` as the file server volume.
- Create a directory called `Profiles` under the default shared volume (`F:`)

2. On the domain controller server (`vmctxdc01 - 192.168.1.50`), copy and install Citrix Profile Manager policies, then configure them, as follows:
   i. Enable Profile Management and configure path to the user store as `\\192.168.1.55\Profiles`.
   ii. Enable **Active Write Back** and **Offline Profile Support** policies.
   iii. In case of profile conflict, configure the UPM policy to delete local profiles.
3. On the domain controller server (`vmctxdc01 - 192.168.1.50`), configure Active Directory policies, as follows:
   i. Disable the **Automatic Windows Update** policy.
   ii. Turn off system restore by enabling this policy.
   iii. Disable the user capability of changing the default screensaver enabling the appropriate policy.
4. Install Windows 7 with a 64-bit version virtual machine, on a supported hypervisor, with the following parameters:
   - Recommended virtual hardware resources, that is, one vCPU, 4 GB RAM, and 30 GB hard disk
   - `vmctxtd02` as the hostname
   - IP address as assigned by DHCP
   - Join it to the `ctxlab.local` domain before configuring any software role

This Windows 7 client will be used in future laboratories as the base template for MCS architecture.

5. On Windows 7 PVS desktop base image (`vmctxtd01` – address assigned by DHCP server), perform the following operations:
   i. Copy Citrix Profile Manager software and install it.
   ii. Disable and stop BITS service.
   iii. Disable and stop all the known Windows 7 security services.
   iv. Assign a locked value of `8 GB` as minimum and maximum swap memory size.
   v. Disable Windows 7 animation at startup by using the `bcdedit` command.
   vi. Force policy application using the appropriate command.

6. On the second Windows 7 client (`vmctxtd02` – address assigned by the DHCP server), perform the following operations:
   i. Copy Citrix Profile Manager software and install it.
   ii. Disable and stop BITS service.
   iii. Disable and stop all the known Windows 7 security services.
   iv. Assign a locked value of 8 GB as minimum and maximum swap memory size.
   v. Disable Windows 7 animation at startup by using the `bcdedit` command.
   vi. Force policy application using the appropriate command.

# 4
# User Experience – Planning and Configuring

In this chapter we will cover:

- Implementing profile architecture
- Installing Virtual Desktop Agent
- Configuring advanced user experience – HDX 3D Pro
- Configuring Citrix Receiver

## Introduction

In *Chapter 3, Master Image Configuration and Tuning*, we discussed how to optimize the virtual desktop component in order to optimize and standardize the operating system's base image, which we're going to deploy in future activities.

Now it's time to configure those components that are nearest to the user perspective, such as advanced profile techniques, plugin installations, and appearance configuration settings. These configurations will be more oriented to the tuning and optimization of the user experience, instead of the operations oriented to the installation and configuration of the desktop template, as explained in the previous chapter.

This was formerly known as the user experience, that is, the way in which an end user notices no difference between the use of a standard physical desktop and a virtual desktop deployed by a VDI architecture.

# Implementing profile architecture

When you've decided to implement a VDI architecture for your company, you've got to take care about the location where you will be storing all the user's data, such as documents, projects, and mailbox file data, for example.

So, an important step is deciding what kind of profile architecture you will be implementing for your organization. With XenDesktop 5.6, you have the capability to choose among three kinds of profiles - standard local profiles, Microsoft roaming profiles, and the Citrix solution known as personal vDisk, a new feature implemented in this latest release.

An alternative to Microsoft roaming profiles is using Citrix User Profile Management, discussed in the *Installing Citrix Profile Management* recipe from *Chapter 3, Master Image Configuration and Tuning*.

## Getting ready

To rightly implement any kind of profile architecture, you need to have domain administrative credentials to be able to operate on the AD user objects. Moreover, it's also necessary to have an assigned centralized storage (network share and/or SAN) to implement the roaming profile technique or Citrix personal vDisk technology.

## How to do it...

In this recipe, we will configure the users' profiles based on the technologies supported by Citrix XenDesktop. Perform the following steps:

1. Log in to one of your domain controller servers with domain administrative credentials.
2. Click on **Start** and run the following command to open the **Active Directory Users and Computers** snap-in:

   ```
   dsa.msc
   ```

3. Right-click on the desired **Organizational Unit** (**OU**), and select **New** | **User**, as shown in the following screenshot:

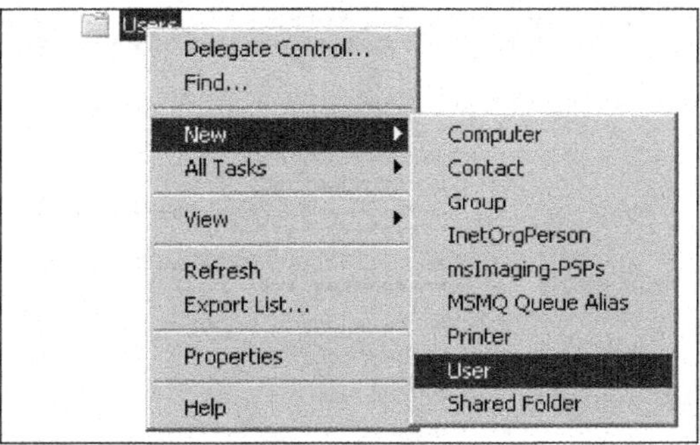


4. Populate the fields with the required information (**First name**, **Last name**, and **User logon name**), then click on **Next** to proceed, as follows:

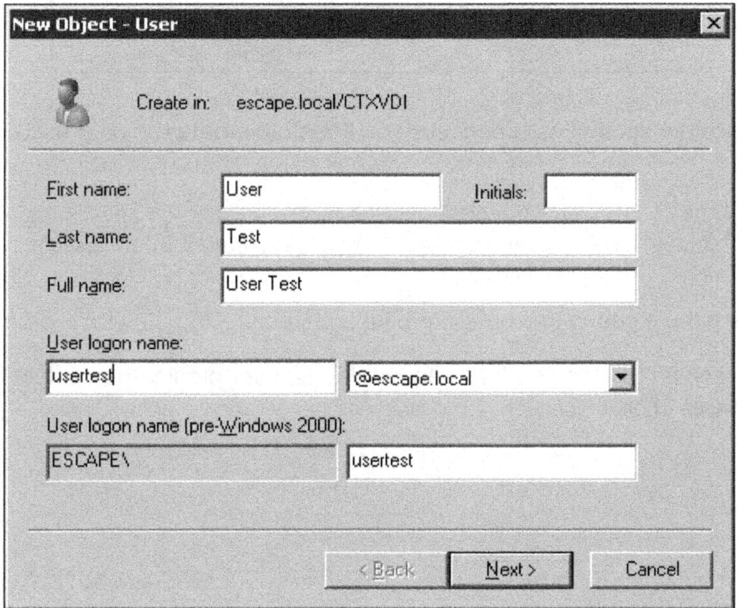

5. Assign a password to the user, then uncheck all the options shown in the following screenshot. Click on the **Next** button after finishing with that.

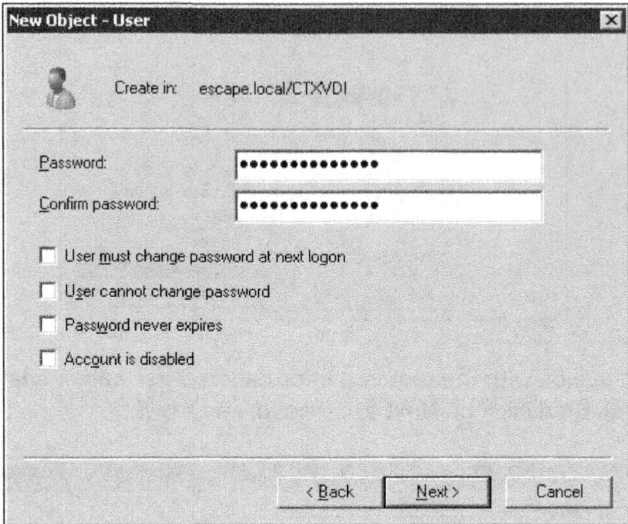


6. On the latest summary screen, click on **Finish** to create the user account.

> You can also configure the profile location on an existing user account; you don't have to recreate it from scratch.

The following are the steps to implement profile architecture by using local profiles:

1. Right-click on the created (or already existing) user profile, then select the **Properties** choice.

2. Select the **Profile** tab, and verify that no network path has been selected. In this way, you're going to implement the user profile on the local machine storage. A copy of the user profile will be created on any machine from which the user will perform the login operations.

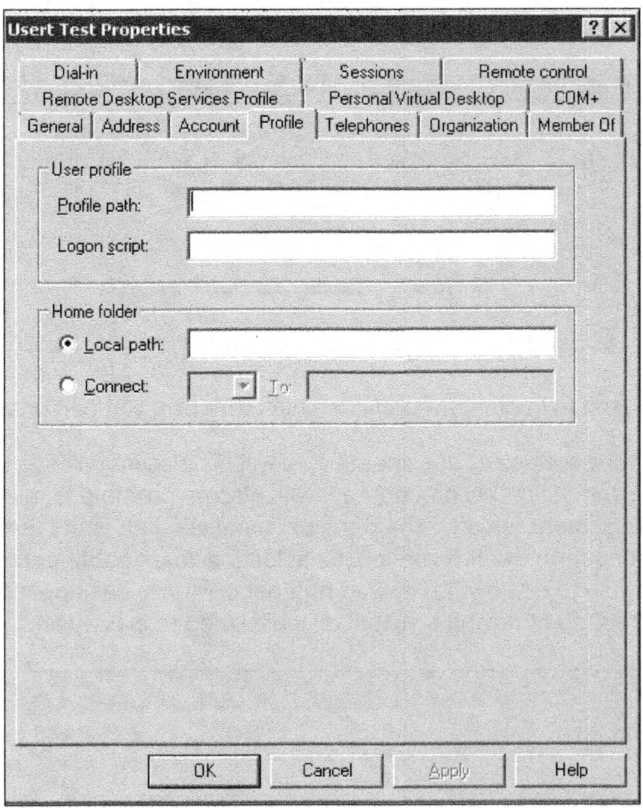

When using the standard local profiles, make sure you've implemented a persistent machine instance, otherwise you'll lose any user data. Virtual machine types will be discussed later in this book.

The following are the steps to implement profile architecture by using roaming profiles:

1. Right-click on the created (or already existing) user profile, then select the **Properties** choice.
2. Select the **Profile** tab, and insert a valid network path (for example, a network share governed by a file server) where you want to store the user data.

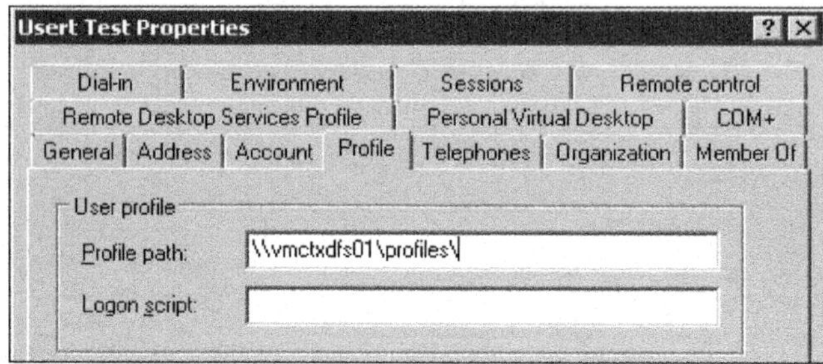


The following is the step to implement profile architecture by using personal vDisk:

1. In the following recipes of this chapter, we will discuss installing a Citrix agent on the client machine; in this procedure, it will also be possible to install another user profile management option – the Citrix personal vDisk. It is the feature included in XenDesktop from the 5.6 version. By selecting **Yes, enable personal vDisk**, it will be possible to deploy the desired number of virtual desktop instances with the additional feature of having a virtual disk assigned to every user.

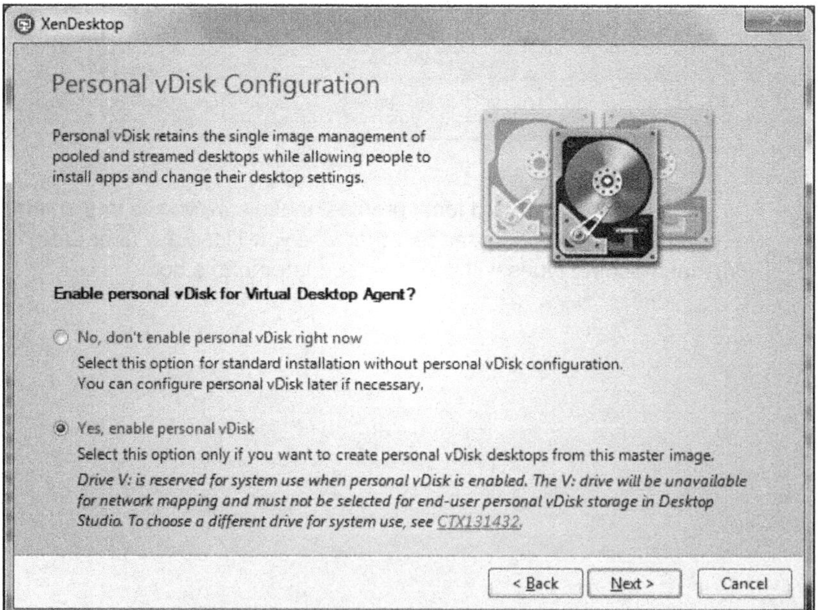

In the next recipe, *Installing Virtual Desktop Agent*, we'll discuss the full agent installation procedure, including the personal vDisk technology.

## How it works...

The user profile is the location where all the user data is usually stored. The first and most common profile is the local profile. With this option, you will have a copy of your user profile for every device from which you will start a user session. This technique is usable only when you have deployed static and persistent virtual desktops (this will be explained better later in this book). In this case, you will not lose your profile data when executing a logoff (persistent deployment), and with the static machine assignment, you can also avoid the profile's duplication on different devices, because you will have a one-to-one association between the user and the assigned machine.

As a second option, we have the Windows roaming profile. This solution is similar to the Citrix User Profile Manager that we saw earlier in *Chapter 3, Master Image Configuration and Tuning*, but with fewer features; also, because of the fact that the Microsoft solution has been developed in the past, we can consider the Citrix product as an evolution of this technique. It's based on a centralized store on a network share, where you want to archive all the user data. This is a way to solve the problem of duplicate information caused by a local profile. In the end, we have the newly implemented feature for XenDesktop 5.6 – Citrix personal vDisk. This is a secondary virtual disk created by the hypervisor chosen for your infrastructure, and assigned to every deployed desktop machine instance associated to only one user; so, in this case also, we'll have a one-to-one association between the user and its personal vDisk. Citrix PvD is made up of two components, a hidden volume identified with the `V` drive letter, which is a sort of catalog of the applications installed by the user, and a visible volume identified with the default `P` drive letter, on which the users can archive their personal data. This last solution permits you to have a huge reduction of storage occupation, giving more flexibility to the users about the applications' installations and data modifications without impacting the operating system's volume.

The following is a table showing the comparison of the pros and cons of every profile method, with a set of real-world application cases:

| **Profile Technology** | **Pros** | **Cons** | **Use cases** |
|---|---|---|---|
| Local profile | Faster than centralized profiles | Data duplication with multiple desktops | Persistent virtual desktops, physical desktops |
| Roaming profile | Centralized profile location, no duplicated data | Slower than local profiles | Nonpersistent (pooled) virtual desktops |

| Profile Technology | Pros | Cons | Use cases |
|---|---|---|---|
| Personal vDisk | Virtualization of the user profile space, no reason to use centralized profiles to maintain the user customization | Backup and restore is a little bit more difficult than other technologies, performed at the hypervisor level | Non-persistent (Pooled) Virtual Desktops |

## There's more...

The personal vDisk drive letters can be modified, but they follow two different procedures. For the user data visible drive (default `P`), you can modify the assigned letter in the phase of creation by using Desktop Studio. For the `V` hidden drive, you have to modify a registry key on the template virtual machine. The key is located at `HKLM\Software\Citrix\personal vDisk\Config` in your Windows machine registry, and its name is `VHDMountPoint`. The only operation to perform is to edit the value of the registry item, specifying the drive letter that you want to assign.

Please remember that you must perform the `V` hidden drive letter modification before creating the personal vDisk inventory and before generating any machine catalog from Desktop Controller!

## See also

- The *Using Citrix Desktop Director* recipe in *Chapter 6, Creating and Configuring a Desktop Environment*

# Installing Virtual Desktop Agent

After you've chosen the way to implement the profile technology, it's time to allow your Windows base image to communicate with your XenDesktop infrastructure; you can accomplish this task by installing Virtual Desktop Agent.

## Getting ready

In order to permit the communication between the virtual machine's base image and Citrix Desktop Controller, you have to turn off the Windows firewall or permit opening the following ports and services:

- **TCP**: `80, 1494, 2598, 3389`
- **UDP**: From `16500` to `16509`
- **Services**: Remote Assistance and Windows Remote Management

## How to do it...

In this recipe, the installation process of Virtual Desktop Agent will be explained. Perform the following steps:

1. Log in to your Windows client template machine, and from the Citrix installation media run the **Autoselect.exe** executable file, to launch the XenDesktop setup.
2. Click on the **Install Virtual Desktop Agent** section, as shown in the following screenshot:

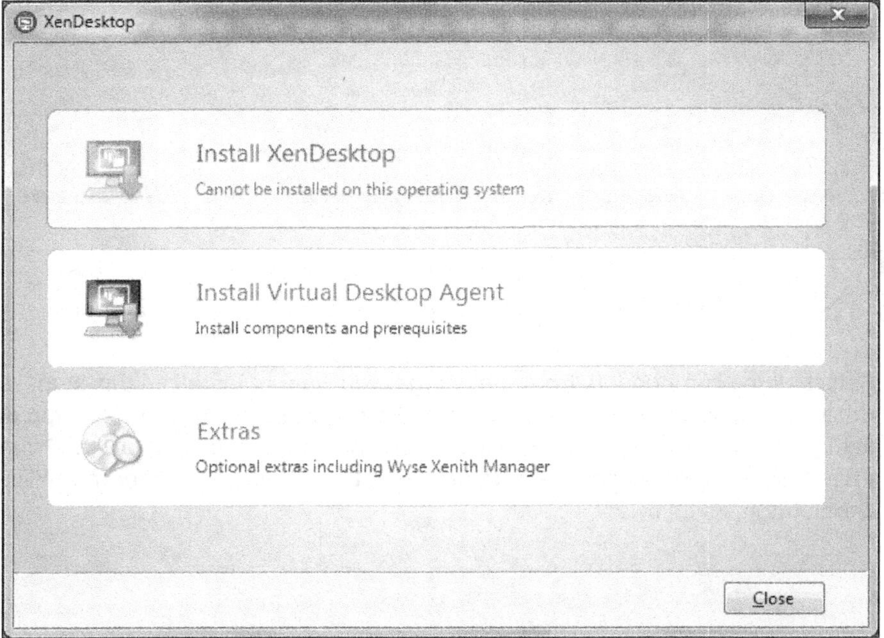

3. Accept the licensing agreement and click on **Next**.
4. Select the **Virtual Desktop Agent** radio button, and click on **Next**, as shown in the following screenshot:

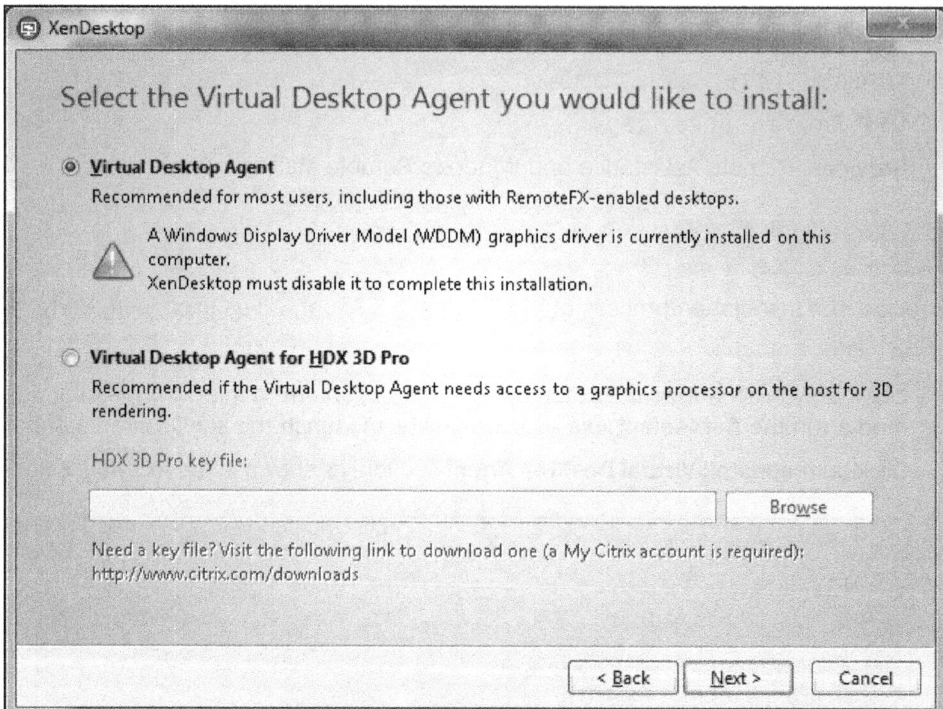

In the next recipe, *Configuring advanced user experience – HDX 3D Pro*, we'll see how to use and configure the HDX 3D Pro suite.

5. Select all the components from the list that you want to install; in this step, please don't enter any Web Interface URL in the **Please enter the URL for XenApp delivery** textbox. If you want, you can also change the default install location (**C:\Program Files\Citrix**) by clicking on the **Change install location...** link. After this, click on the **Next** button, as follows:

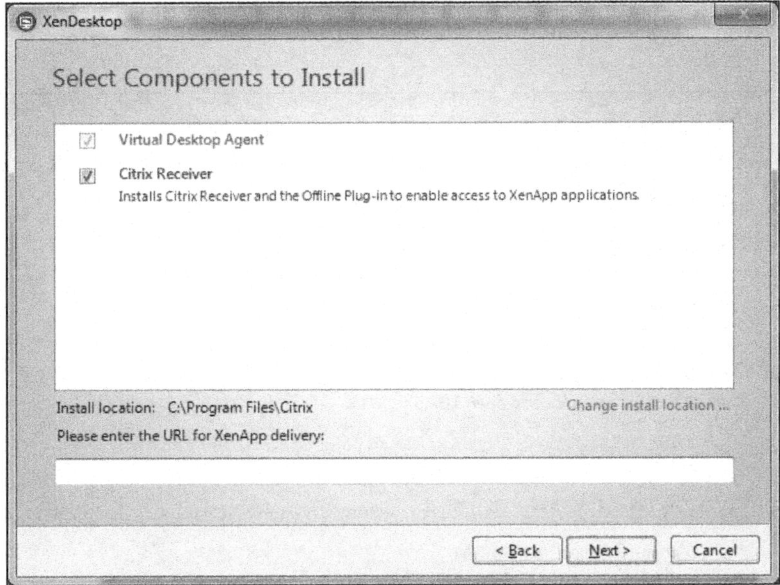


6. Based on your profile policies, you can choose whether you want to use the personal vDisk technology, as shown in the previous recipe. Then click on the **Next** button.
7. Manually enter the FQDN of your controller server, and click on the **Check** button to verify that your client can correctly contact **XenDesktop Desktop Delivery Controller** (**DDC**). If all is ok, click on **Next** to proceed:

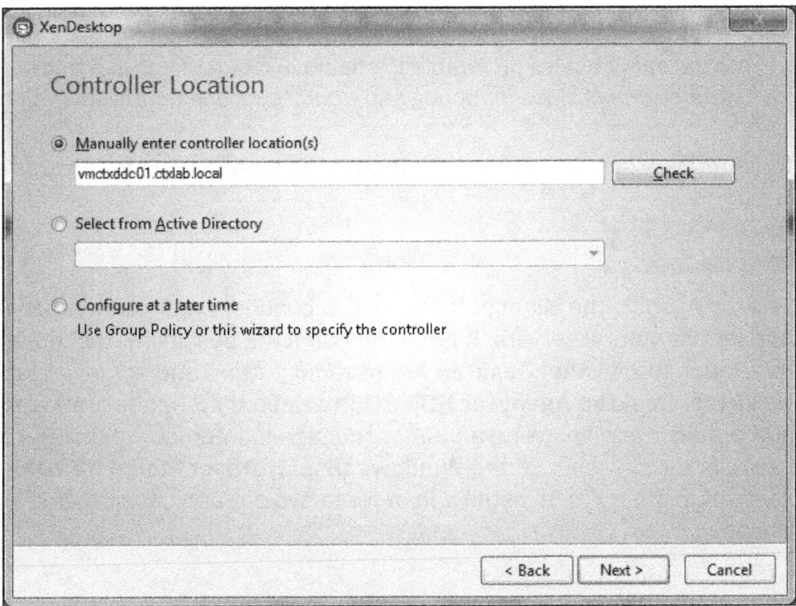

8. Check all the components presented to you, and click on **Next**, as shown in the following screenshot:

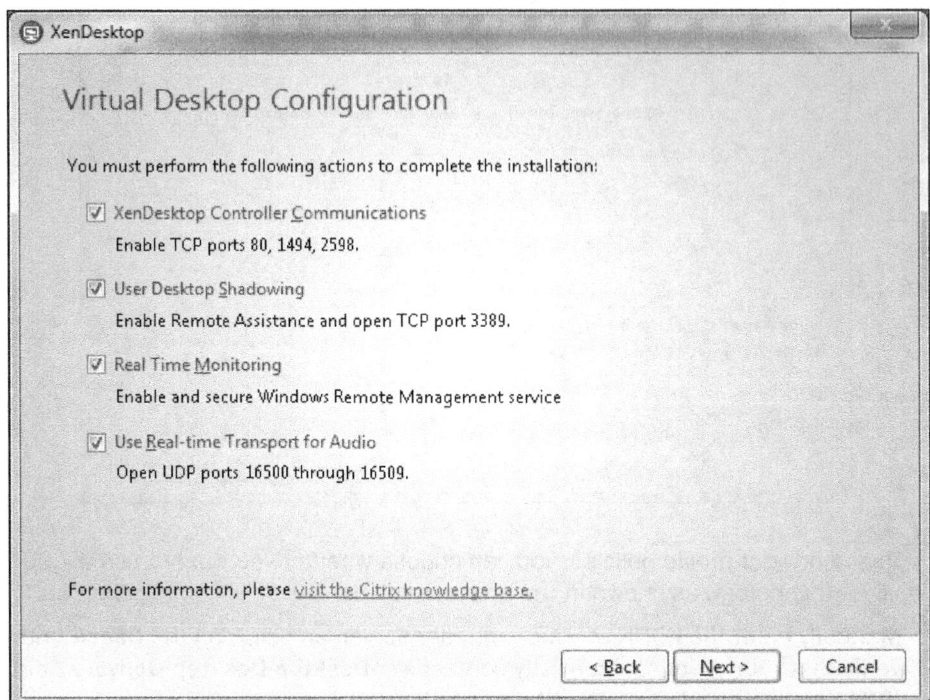

**Real Time Monitoring** is not a fundamental component for your agent installation, but it's preferable to enable it in order to have a trace of your client activities for debug and troubleshooting analysis.

9. On the **Summary** screen, click on the **Install** button to complete the entire procedure.

## How it works...

The Virtual Desktop Agent is the client software which connects your client machine with the XenDesktop infrastructural servers. It gives the users the possibility to choose between a standard installation (the **Virtual Desktop Agent** radio button) and an advanced use of the agent (The **Virtual Desktop Agent for HDX 3D Pro** radio button); the first option will use the normal HDX protocol version, using an ICA connection to interact with the centralized controller servers. In the presence of the **Windows Display Driver Model** (**WDDM**) system driver, the agent setup will try to uninstall it in order to avoid graphical problems with your desktop instances.

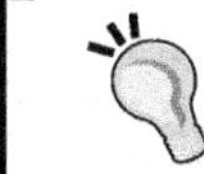

When possible, you should uninstall the WDDM driver before the Virtual Desktop Agent installation, especially when interfacing XenDesktop with a VMware ESX hypervisor host.

The second option (HDX 3D Pro) is particularly useful in the presence of a deployed desktop used for 3D graphical activities. To use this advanced feature, you have to download your assigned license file from your MyCitrix account (`HDX3D_KeyFile.ctx`) and insert it during the installation phase, as shown in the following screenshot:

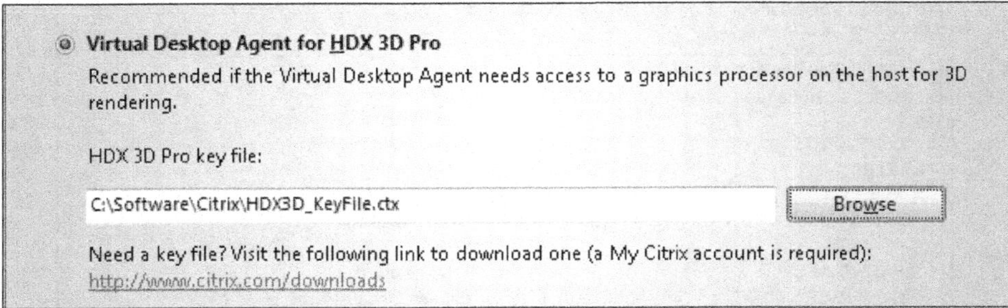


After this section, the installation procedure continues with the selection of the most important components for the VDA client, the Virtual Desktop Agent, and the Citrix Receiver. If you already have a XenApp farm, in this recipe you can also interface your client with the XenApp server.

An alternative way to install the Citrix Receiver is using Merchandising Server, which will be discussed in the next chapter.

Then, the next step requires inserting Desktop Controller's server FQDN and checking its availability. This is not mandatory in this section (you can also configure it later), but in order to complete all the required steps, you should insert this information at this time.

## There's more...

For those users who prefer to run setup from the command line and not from the graphical interface, Citrix offers an executable file that can substitute the previously seen installation procedure.

This file is named `XenDesktopVdaSetup.exe`, and you can find it in your XenDesktop installation media at the location, `x86\XenDesktop Setup` for 32-bit installations or at the location, `x64\XenDesktop Setup` for 64-bit installations. Run it from the command line to perform the required installation. To see the complete options list for this executable file, run the following command:

```
XenDesktopVdaSetup.exe  /?
```

You will receive a pop-up screen with the full list, as follows:

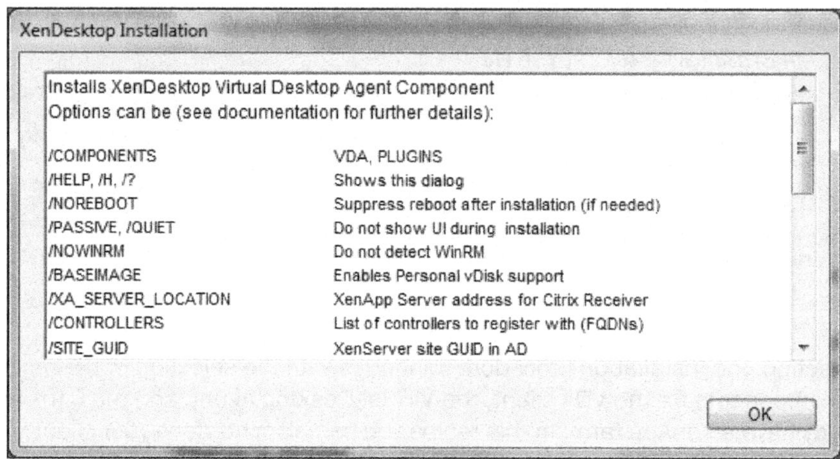


So, for example, to install the Virtual Desktop Agent with the personal vDisk enabled, with both the VDA and Receiver components, without the WDDM driver and with the specified Citrix Controller address, you have to run from the Windows command line the following instructions:

```
XenDesktopVdaSetup.exe  /BASEIMAGE /COMPONENTS VDA,PLUGINS /NOCITRIXWDDM
/CONTROLLERS vmctxddc01.ctxlab.local
```

## See also

- The *Configuring the XenDesktop policies* recipe in *Chapter 8, XenDesktop Tuning and Security*

# Configuring advanced user experience – HDX 3D Pro

The Citrix HDX is a collection of capabilities offered by XenDesktop, which is based on the well-known and stable ICA protocol. HDX has to be considered as a set of features oriented to high performance without losing the resolution quality for both audio and video reproductions. An evolution of this suite is the HDX 3D Pro, which is more oriented to the 3D graphical and rendering activities. In this chapter, we're going to discuss further this powerful feature.

## Getting ready

Citrix HDX 3D Pro is a component of the Virtual Desktop Agent software, so we only need to operate on an already implemented setup, only modifying the necessary parameters. For the HDX Monitor discussed in one of the chapters' section, you have to download it from `http://hdx.citrix.com/hdx-monitor/tech-preview`. Obviously, to perform these configurations, you must choose the HDX 3D Pro agent version during the Virtual Desktop Agent installation procedure.

The HDX Monitor 2.0 tool can only work with XenDesktop 5.5 and 5.6. It's not compatible with any previous versions.

## How to do it...

The following steps will explain how to activate and use the HDX 3D Pro technology:

1. Log in to your desktop client machine with administrative credentials.
2. Click on **Start** and type in the `cmd` command, in order to launch a command prompt shell.
3. Go to the Virtual Desktop Agent folder (the default path is `C:\Program Files\Citrix\ICAService`).
4. Run the following command to check the HDX 3D Pro configuration:

   ```
   HDX3DConfigCmdLineX64.exe DISPLAY CURRENT_OPTIONS
   ```

```
C:\Program Files\Citrix\ICAService>HDX3DConfigCmdLineX64.exe DISPLAY CURRENT_OPTIONS
                DEBUG LOGGING --> DISABLED

C:\Program Files\Citrix\ICAService>
```

Depending on your client architecture, you have to use `HDX3DConfigCmdLineX64.exe` for 64-bit systems or `HDX3DConfigCmdLineX86.exe` for 32-bit architectures. In this recipe we will use the version for the 64-bit systems.

5. Enable the advanced logging for HDX 3D Pro:

   ```
   HDX3DConfigCmdLineX64.exe DEBUG_LOGGING 1
   ```

6. Disable the automatic image adjustment by enabling the `ENABLE_FIXEDQUALITY` parameter, as follows:

   ```
   HDX3DConfigCmdLineX64.exe ENABLE_FIXEDQUALITY 1
   ```

7. Force the Windows Aero graphical feature to be disabled; this option is in a disabled state by default:

   ```
   HDX3DConfigCmdLineX64.exe MIRROR_DRIVER 1
   ```

## How it works...

The HDX 3D configuration utility permits you to configure advanced graphical parameters from the Windows command line. The first operation to perform is checking what configuration parameters are active on your client machine; this is performed by the command launched in step 4 in the *How to do it...* section of this recipe. The use of the `DEBUG_LOGGING` parameter in the second task, that is, step 5, allows the system administrators to have two different types of logging. The first is made up of the standard records registered in the Windows Event Viewer application log; the other is the advanced registration of the system activities in the Citrix log files, thanks to the use of the specified configuration parameter. The advanced logging is disabled by default (value equal to `0`) to improve performance.

To make the log comprehension easier, you can download the DebugView Microsoft tool from `http://technet.microsoft.com/en-us/sysinternals/bb896647.aspx`.

In step 6, we've disabled the automatic image quality adjustment performed by HDX 3D Pro. In this way, the user is free to decide whether to privilege the quality image rather than the desktop reactivity time, based on the available network. The level of the desktop appearance is tunable by the use of a sliding bar in a desktop control panel, which is discussed later in this book. The last performed configuration, that is, setting the `MIRROR_DRIVER` parameter to `1`, has disabled the Windows Aero component in order to privilege the desktop streaming fluency. This parameter is disabled by default, but we've performed it anyway to better root this concept. The opposite value, "enabled", is equal to `0`.

## There's more...

To check the configuration's quality for our desktop images, Citrix offers a free tool called HDX Monitor, which is an information collector for performance levels configurations such as normal and 3D graphics, Adobe Flash reproduction, and USB devices mapping. After the installation procedure (you can decide between online and offline modalities), you only have to double-click on the generated icon to launch it. On the first screen, you have to specify the machine for which you want to execute the data collection. You can manually insert its data or browse your Active Directory domain for the required desktop client.

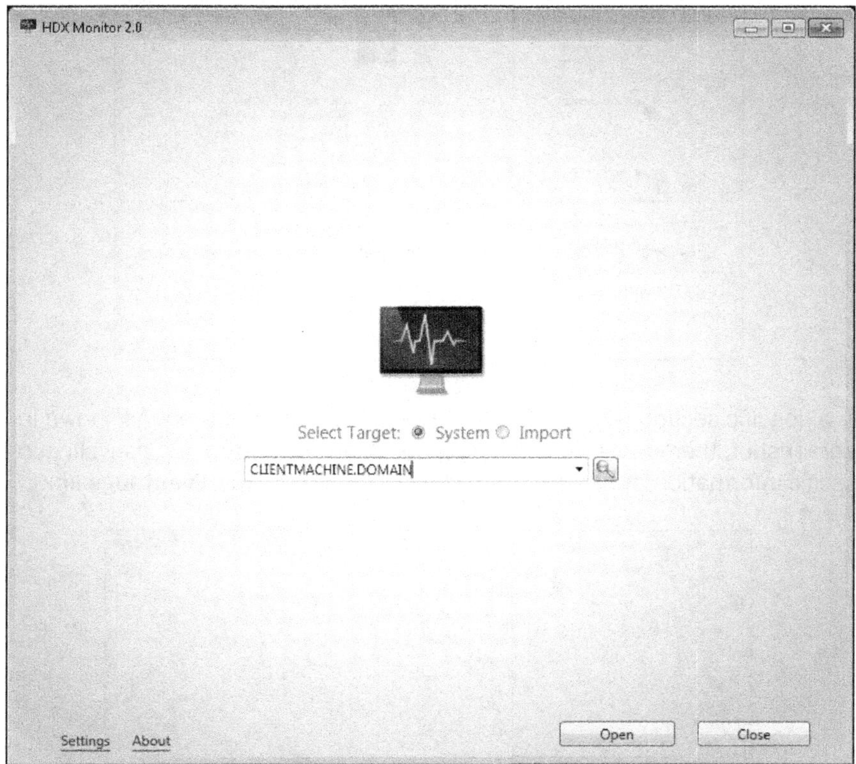

After HDX Monitor has established the connection with the specified system, you will receive back the status of that configuration; this monitor will assign a score to your client, as shown in the following screenshot:

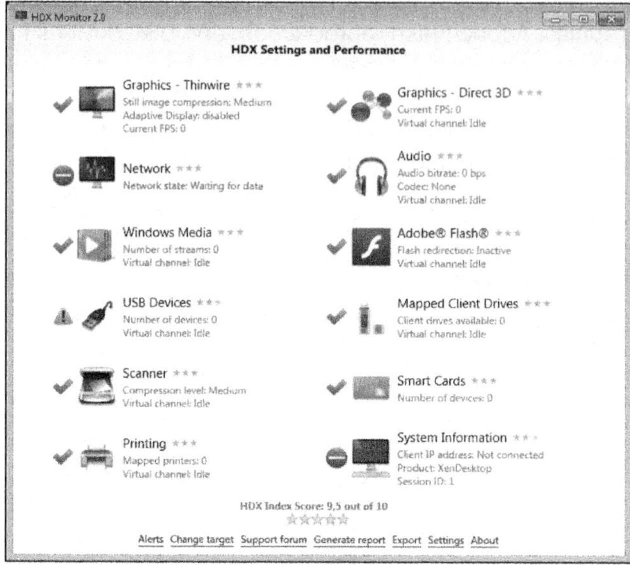


Clicking on a specific section will give you more details about that area. As shown in the following screenshot, there is a link for filtering the Windows system log as well, in order to receive specific information about the section we're analyzing (the **Event logs** link):

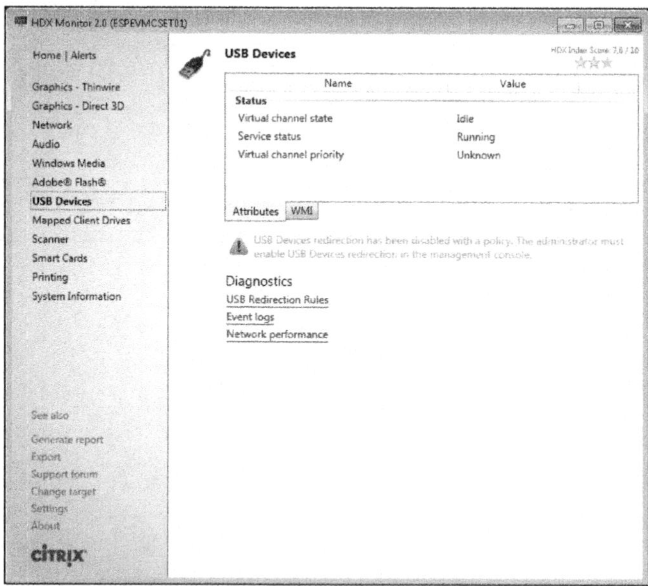

This is an extremely useful tool to analyze the quality of your client's configuration at different levels (media redirection, USB mappings, network usage).

In order to trace the evolution of your infrastructure, you should periodically use the **Generate report** feature, which generates files in the HTML format.

## See also

- *Chapter 7, Deploying Applications*

# Configuring Citrix Receiver

Citrix Receiver is the last component to configure for the Virtual Desktop Agent. This plugin, which will be installed and used within the virtual desktops and/or the user's endpoints, is the connector used by any device (laptops, smart phones, tablets) to connect with the server's farms, both XenDesktop and XenApp types, in order to receive the assigned desktops or the published applications.

## Getting ready

No preliminary operations are required to perform the configuration for Citrix Receiver. In fact, you have already installed all the necessary components to use the Citrix plugin. On the other side, a XenDesktop-configured server or a XenApp working farm is required to use the plugin for its main purpose, the interaction with the hosted or streamed applications.

## How to do it...

In this recipe, we will explain in detail the operations to perform for configuring the Citrix Receiver agent:

1. Log in with administrative credentials to the Windows client image template.
2. Right-click on the **Receiver** icon on the Windows taskbar, and select the **Preferences** voice, as shown in the following screenshot:

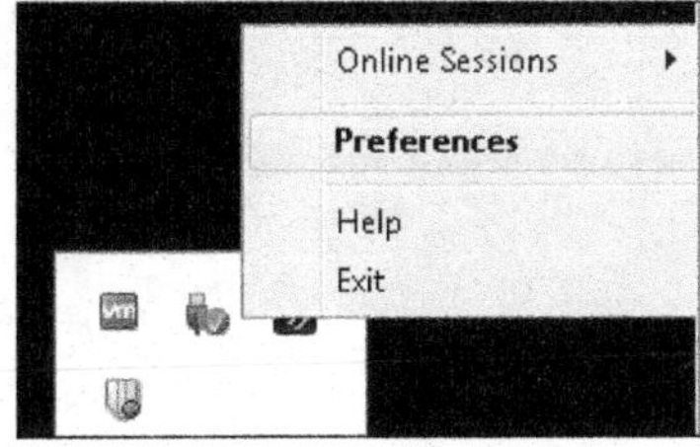

3. In the **User settings** section, you can flag both the presented options; these are the recommended parameters that you should activate for your client:

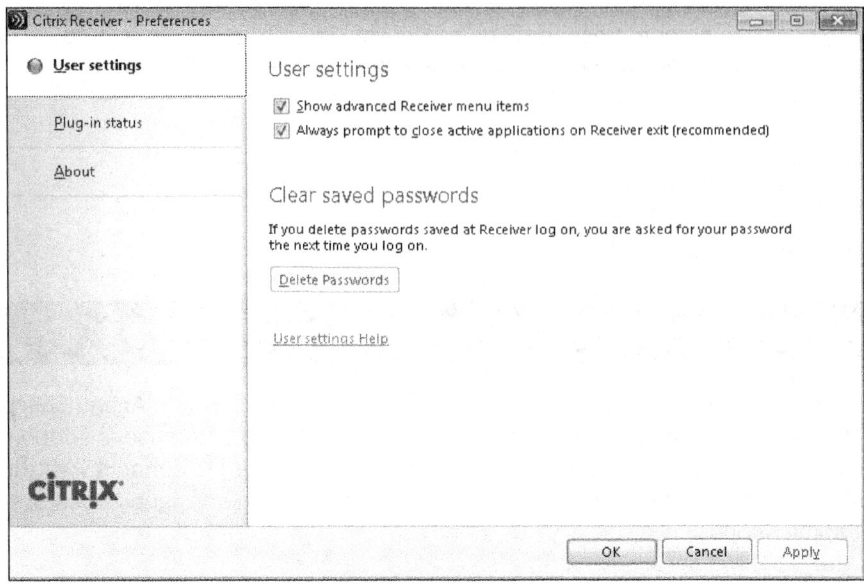


4. Select the **Plug-in status** section and right-click on the **Online Plug-in (13.1.0.89)** option, and then select **Logon to Refresh Applications** for logging in to the application farm and receiving all the published applications, as shown in the following screenshot:

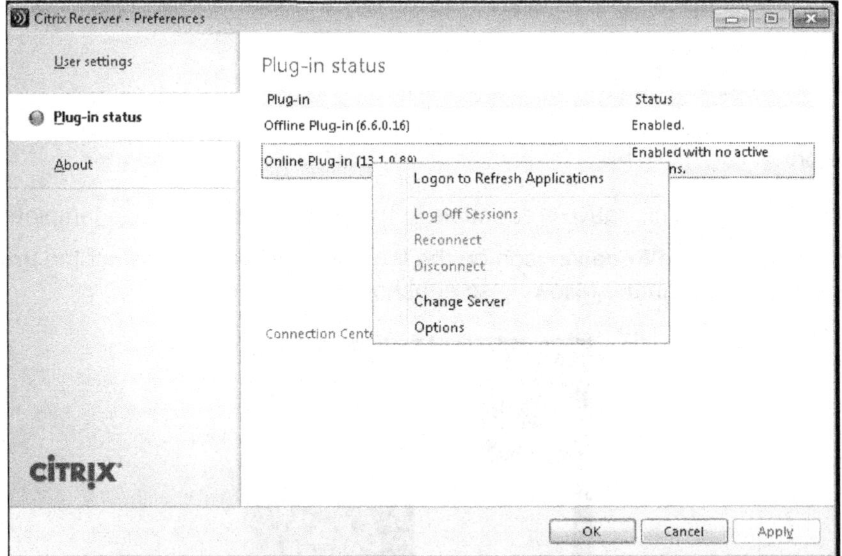

5. Select the **Change Server** option if you want to modify the application server from which you want to receive the applications. This can be a XenDesktop or a XenApp server. After entering a valid URL, click on **Update**, as shown in the following screenshot:

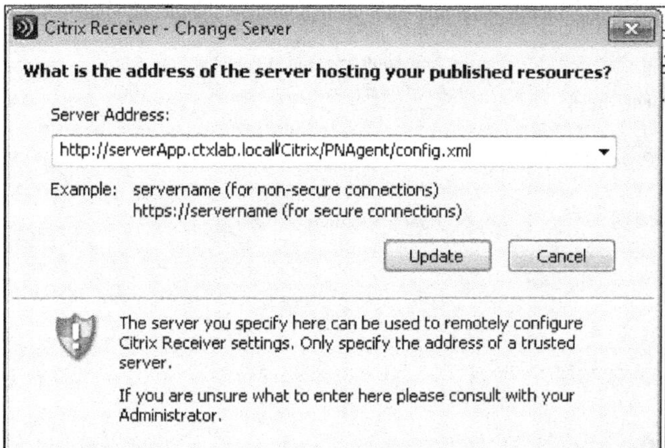


6. In the **Server Options** subsection in the **Citrix Receiver – Options** window, you can configure **Logon Mode** to ask for the credentials (**Prompt user**) or to use the Windows machine credentials currently in use (**Pass-through authentication**), as follows:

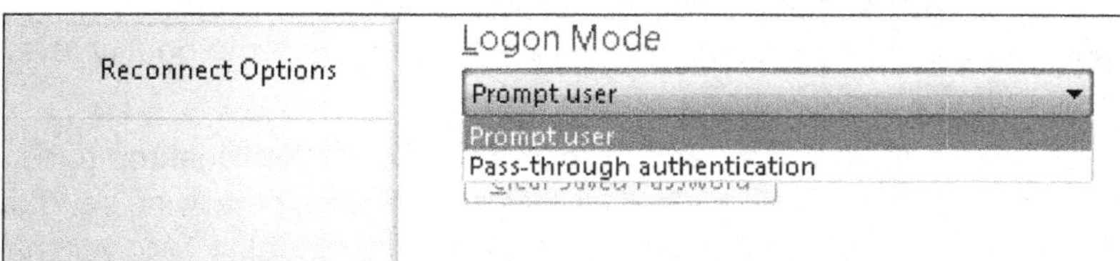

The advantage of **Pass-through authentication** is given by the fact that you do not need to retype the credentials after the login to the endpoint machine; on the other hand, you have to properly configure your entire desktop environment to avoid security issues.

7. In the **Application Display** subsection in the **Citrix Receiver - Options** window, you can decide to show the published applications in your **Start** menu and/or on your desktop, as shown in the following screenshot:

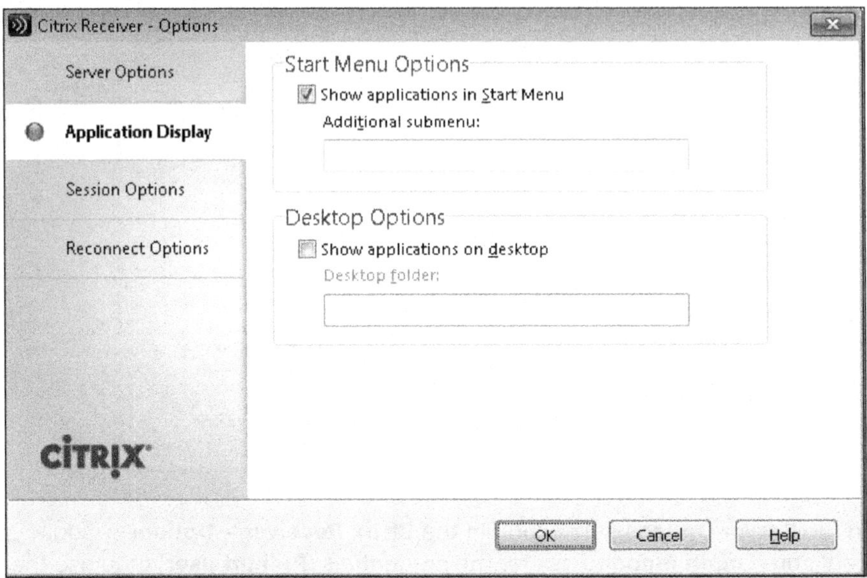


8. In the **Session Options** subsection in the **Citrix Receiver - Options** window, you can configure the Windows display size together with the quality level for the color and the audio.

   Configuring the Windows size as full screen will permit XenDesktop to adjust the resolution equal to the physical client's screen size; otherwise you have to configure the virtual desktop's resolution with a size equal to or lower than the physical endpoint.

9. Now that all the configuration steps have been completed, Citrix Receiver is ready to work with the server farm's components.

In the next chapter, *Configuring Additional Architectural Components*, we will discuss about the pre-packaging of Citrix Receiver and the way to deploying it through a centralized Citrix platform.

## How it works...

Citrix Receiver is a set of features used to receive the applications installed and presented to the end users, or streamed and published for them. It's made up of two main components, the offline plugin used with the XenApp server farms to be able to receive the streamed applications, and the online plugin (a Receiver component also used to receive the hosted applications and the assigned desktops published under the XenDesktop server farms). After you've logged in with your domain credentials, you will see your applications published on your desktop or on your **Start** menu, if configured as we saw earlier. All the changes made to your applications, such as new software assigned to your user or a previously existing application removed from your area, are immediately replied to your running desktop. You can also customize the appearance and the quality of your applications, in order to privilege the speed in some situations, or decide to have a higher-quality image with a probable impact on the general performance. All these features permit having an extremely flexible approach; you could have a Windows client machine without any installed application, and populate it with software from other clients and servers, based on the permissions assigned to a user on that specific application. This could permit you to reduce the operating system's attack surface, separating the applications from the operating system area, using application packaging platforms such as Citrix XenApp or Microsoft App-V.

## There's more...

When using a remote application published on a XenApp or a XenDesktop server, you should have a content redirection problem while double-clicking on a file associated to a specific software; for instance, you could have Microsoft Word published to your virtual desktop and there may arise a necessity to open a `.doc` file located on your desktop instance. Without any further operation on the client, you could probably receive an error about the file path location. To avoid this problem, you have to perform the following tasks:

1. Modify the registry key, **NativeDriveMapping** located at `HKEY_LOCAL_MACHINE\SOFTWARE\Citrix\ICA Client\Engine\Configuration\Advanced\Modules\ClientDrive` (32-bit machines) or located at `HKEY_LOCAL_MACHINE\SOFTWARE\Wow6432Node\ Citrix\ICA Client\Engine\Configuration\Advanced\Modules\ClientDrive` (64-bit machines), assigning the value of **TRUE** to it, as shown in the following screenshot:

| | | |
|---|---|---|
| MaxWindowSize | REG_SZ | 8650 |
| MaxWindowSize2 | REG_SZ | 62500 |
| NativeDriveMapping | REG_SZ | TRUE |
| SFRAllowed | REG_SZ | FALSE |

2. Modify the `module.ini` file located at your Citrix Online plugin installation path (usually `C:\Program Files (x86)\Citrix\Online Plugin\Configuration`). Search for the `[ClientDrive]` section, and assign the value of `TRUE` to the `NativeDriveMapping` key, as shown in the following screenshot:

```
**
** Client Drive Virtual Driver
**
** This virtual driver is responsible for providing client disk drive
** access to supplement the ICA 3.0 driver.
**
*****************************************************************************

[ClientDrive]
 DriverName                  = VDCDM30.DDL
 DriverNameWin16             = VDCDM30W.DLL
 DriverNameWin32             = VDCDM30N.DLL
 MaxWindowSize               = 8650
 MaxWindowSize2              = 62500
 MaxRequestSize              = 1440
 MaxRequestSize2             = 4116
 CacheTimeout                = 600
 CacheTimeoutHigh            = 0
 CacheTransferSize           = 0
 CacheDisable                = FALSE
 CacheWriteAllocateDisable   = FALSE
 DisableDrives               =
 CDMReadOnly                 = FALSE
 NativeDriveMapping          = TRUE
 SFRAllowed                  = FALSE
```

After that is complete, you will receive no more errors while trying to access a file type redirected to its native application.

## See also

- The *Configuring the Merchandising Server* recipe in *Chapter 5, Configuring Additional Architectural Components*

# Chapter 4 XenDesktop lab

In this laboratory, we're going to configure the previously created Windows 7 machine with Virtual Desktop Agent, by following the instructions given in this chapter:

1. Connect to the domain controller server (`vmctxdc01 - 192.168.1.50`) and create two new users, as follows:
   i. Create a user named `userRoaming01`, setting it as a roaming profile with location as `\\192.168.1.55\Profiles`.
   ii. Create a user named `userPVD01`, without any remote profile location configured.

2. Connect to the Windows 7 machine template dedicated to the PVS infrastructure (the `vmctxtd01` - address assigned by the DHCP server) and perform the following operations:
    i. Disable Windows Firewall.
    ii. Install the Virtual Desktop Agent with the HDX standard version and enable the personal vDisk.
    iii. Do not select the Citrix Receiver component during the installation phase.
3. Connect to the Windows 7 machine template dedicated to the MCS infrastructure (the `vmctxtd02` - address assigned by the DHCP server) and perform the following operations:
    i. Disable Windows Firewall.
    ii. Install the Virtual Desktop Agent with the HDX 3D Pro version and do not enable the personal vDisk feature.

> If there is no possibility of obtaining the HDX 3D Pro license file, please skip this step.

    iii. Select the installation of all the components (Virtual Desktop Agent and Citrix Receiver).
    iv. Configure the Citrix Receiver to show the published applications only on the desktop and not in the **Start** menu; configure **Logon Mode** as **nonPass-through authentication**.
    v. Configure the HDX 3D Pro to have a fluent desktop deployment, referring to the parameters, `ENABLE_FIXEDQUALITY` and `MIRROR_DRIVER`. Use only the Windows application log to register the client activities.
    vi. Modify the right registry key and the receiver configuration file in order to avoid the client-to-server content redirection error, while clicking on a file associated to an application.

# 5

# Configuring Additional Architectural Components

In this chapter we will cover:

- Configuring the Merchandising Server
- Configuring the Branch Repeater virtual appliance
- Installing and configuring XenDesktop Collector

## Introduction

XenDesktop 5.6 has to be considered as a suite made up of a lot of different features, some of them as an addition to the core architectural software. In this chapter, we're going to discuss the important features that have the purpose of improving the quality, the performance, and the manageability of your VDI architecture, such as the Merchandising Server, the Branch Repeater virtual appliance, and the XenDesktop Collector.

# Configuring the Merchandising Server

In the previous chapter, we've seen why and how to configure the Citrix Receiver plugin; this is a fundamental component to view and use the applications and the desktops assigned to a user. It requires an installation on any device that needs access to the online or offline resources; this could need an ulterior effort in the maintenance tasks such as upgrading activities. How could you avoid this problem? By the use of the Merchandising Server, a centralized store for any receiver version (for example, Linux or Windows OS, iOS, and/or Android devices), you can download the latest version of the client, to be able to have a single and centralized point of maintenance.

## Getting ready

The Citrix Merchandising Server is a virtual appliance developed for the hypervisors such as Citrix XenServer (a `.bz2` template type) and VMware vSphere (an OVF template type). So you need to download it from your MyCitrix account, and import it to your hypervisor. The Merchandising Server also needs to interface with a Windows Active Directory domain; so, it will also require you to have administrative credentials for your company domain.

## How to do it...

In this recipe we will deploy and configure the Citrix Merchandising Server virtual appliance. Perform the following steps to do so:

1. After you've imported the virtual appliance to your hypervisor, connect to the console of the created virtual machine. You will find a text menu with seven options, as shown in the following screenshot:

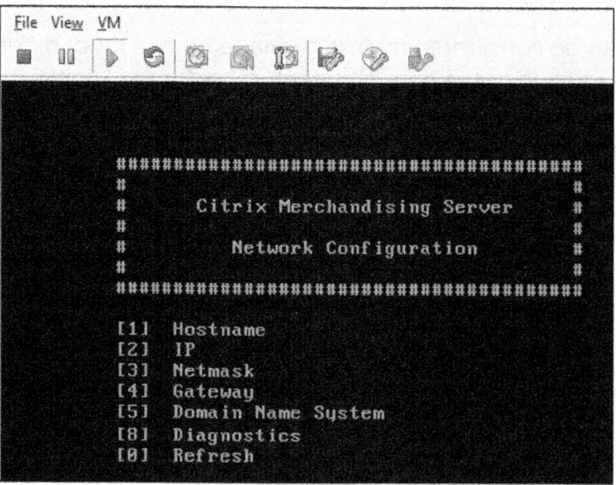

2. Select the option, `[1] Hostname`, to assign a hostname to the virtual appliance. After completing this, press *Enter* to confirm.
3. Select the option, `[2] IP`, to assign an IP address to the Merchandising Server. Press *Enter* to complete the procedure.
4. Assign a net mask by selecting the option, `[3] Netmask`, and press the *Enter* key to proceed.
5. Configure the default gateway by selecting the option, `[4] Gateway`. After you've typed the required IP address, press the *Enter* button.
6. Insert all the required DNS servers information in order to configure a complete name resolution for the option, `[5] Domain Name System`. After this, press *Enter* to complete this task:

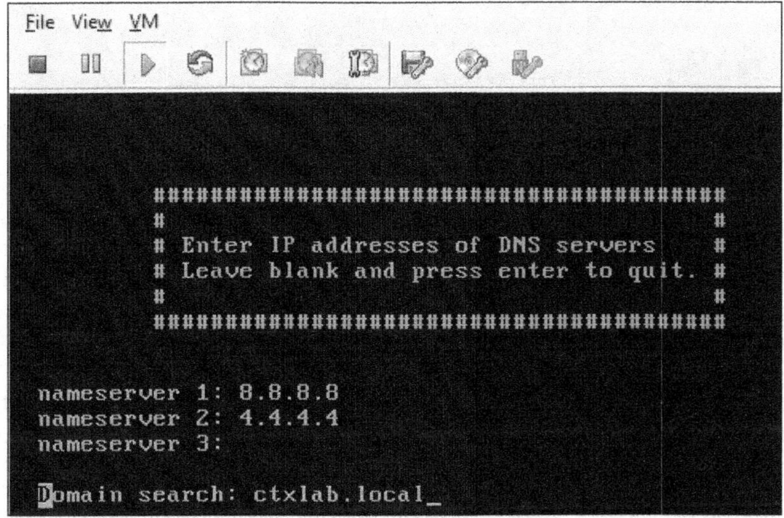


7. Select the option, `[8] Diagnostics`, if you want to verify the availability of a network address by using the `ping` and `tracert` commands. This option also permits you to connect to the appliance terminal, by inserting the required username and password, as shown in the following screenshot:

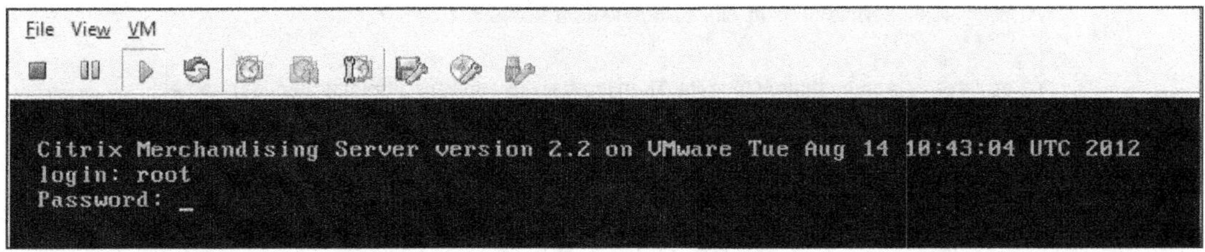

8. After completing all the console configuration, you can open a compatible web browser and type the Merchandising Server administrative address in the form of `protocol://hostname/appliance`. So you need to type in a URL, such as `https://merchandising.ctxlab.local/appliance`. The default credentials to log in are `root` as **User Name** and `C1trix321` as **Password**, shown as follows:

9. On the **Setup Guide** welcome screen, click on the first link, **Configure Active Directory**, in order to interface your Merchandising Server with your company domain, as follows:

**Welcome to the Citrix Merchandising Server Administrator Console**
The root login to the Citrix Merchandising Server Administrator Console gives you access
Once you complete these tasks you can log back in with your user account name to have

1. Configure Active Directory
You must enter your Active Directory server information and perform a sync to load your co

2. Set Permissions
Grant Auditor permissions to your corporate user account.

3. Log off
Log off of the Administrator Console. Then log back in with your administrator user name

10. Configure two valid **Primary** and **Back up** DC servers, by specifying the domain name (the **Source Name** field), checking or unchecking the **Secure connection** checkbox (for security reasons you should activate this), and specifying **Server Address** and **Server Port** for both the machines. You also need to specify the username and password of a domain service user (the **Bind DN** and **Bind Password** fields), **Base DN**, and the time interval on which you want to synchronize the server with your Active Directory domain (you can select any of **Day**, **Week**, **Month**, or **3 Months** from the drop-down menu). For this last option, you should consider to activate the syncs every day. After filling up the fields from every section, click on the **Save and sync** button, as follows:

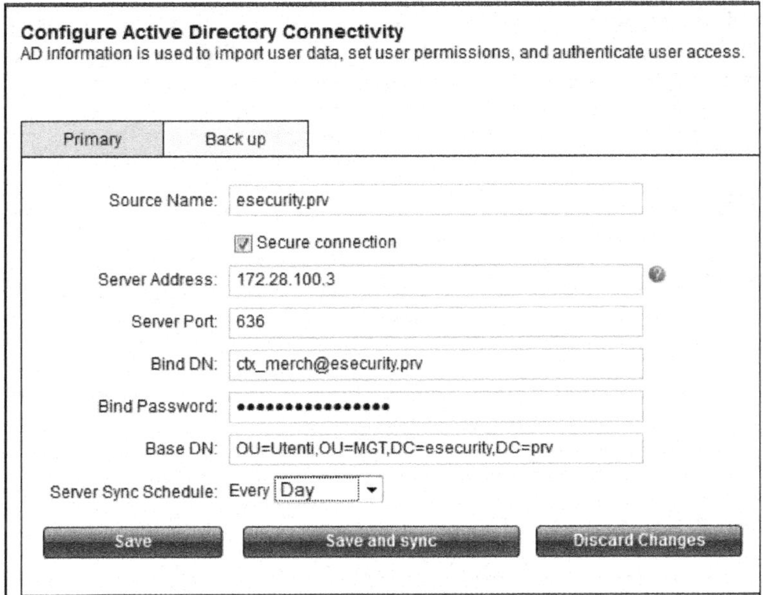

To find the correct BASE DN, people can use the ADSI Edit Microsoft tool. You can visit `http://technet.microsoft.com/en-us/library/cc773354(v=ws.10).aspx` for more information.

11. On the left-hand side panel, click on the **Set Up Guide** link to come back to the previous page, and then select link number two on the welcome screen, **Set Permissions**, in order to configure a domain user other than root, to administer the Merchandising Server.

12. In the **Search Users** textbox insert a valid name of a user belonging to your domain, then click on **Search** to proceed, as shown in the following screenshot:

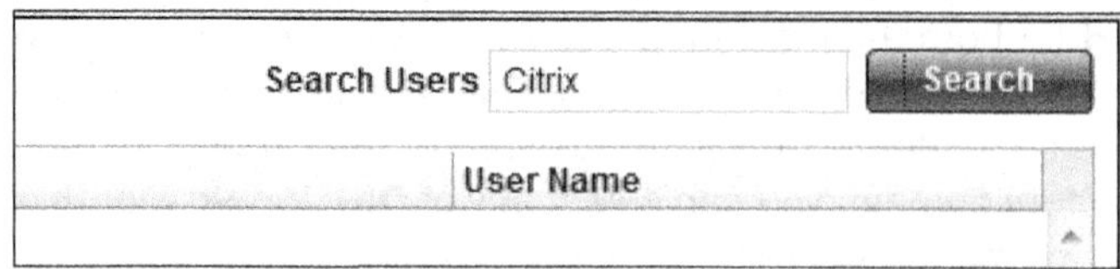


13. A pop-up box will be presented to you with the found domain user. Select the corresponding radio button and click on the **Edit** button to assign a role to this user (**Administrator**, **Auditor**, and **None**; **None** is to set no roles for the user). In this case, you have to assign the **Administrator** role. Click on the **Save** button to complete the procedure, as shown in the following screenshot:

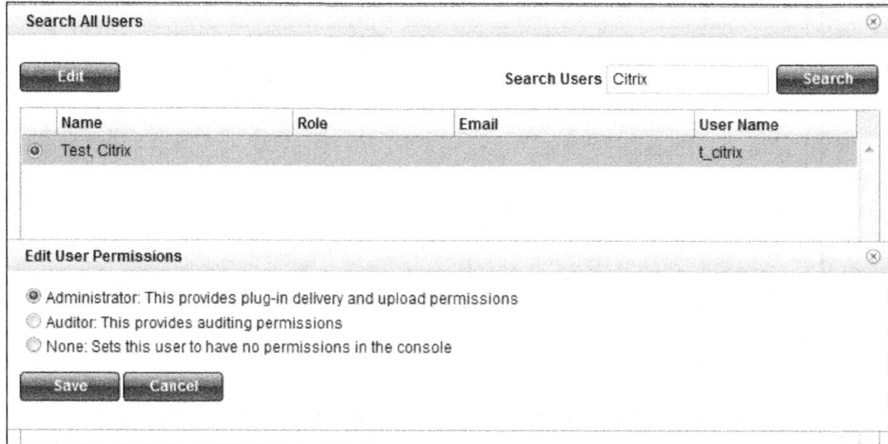


14. In the left-hand side menu, click on the **Change Root Password** link, and assign a new password for the root user in order to change the default installation parameter.
15. Log off from the application and log on again using the last configured administrative user, in the form of `domain/username`.
16. You will find a new version in the left-hand side menu, and on the welcome page, you will have some useful links such as **Documentation**, **Video Links**, and a counter for the new available plugins for your infrastructure (the **New Plug-ins available** section). Click on the **View New Plug-ins** link to proceed with the required operations.
17. Select the desired plugin by checking its radio button and click on **Download Plug-in** to copy it to your local machine. If you want to download all the available plugins to the Merchandising Server, you have to click on **Download All to Server**.

18. After downloading all the required plugins, click on the **Uploaded Plug-ins** link in the left-hand side menu, in order to view the terms and conditions agreement (the **View Readme** and **View EULA** buttons) and/or delete the imported components (the **Delete** button).

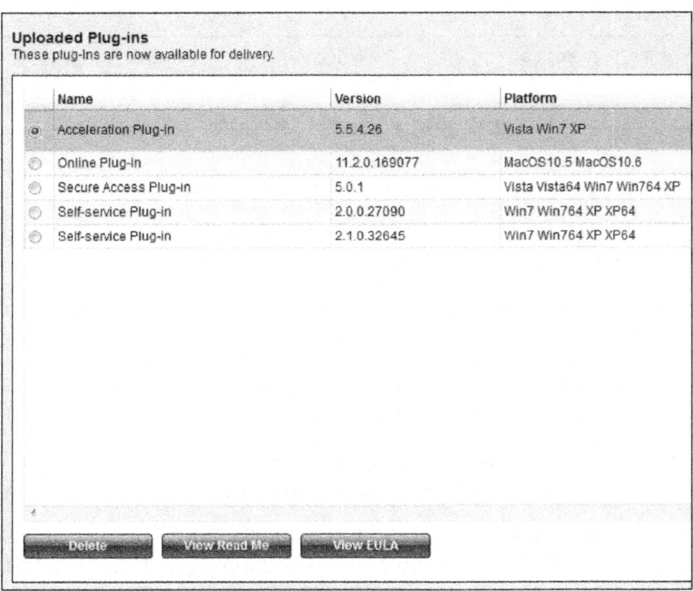


19. In the left-hand side menu, in the **Deliveries** section, click on the **Rules** link. In this area, you can create the delivery rules specific to your company, based on destination targets such as user or computer domain membership, operating system type, machine name, or IP address range. Populate all the required fields (**Name**, **Description**, **Field**, **Operator**, and **Value**) and click on **Save** to create the rule, as shown in the following screenshot:

Rule Create/Edit
Use this screen to create and edit delivery rules.
Name: OS_W7_x64
Description: Windows 7 x64 operating system delivery rule.
Field: Operating System
Operator: Is
Value: Windows 7 64 bit
Save
Cancel

20. In the left-hand side menu, in the **Deliveries** section, click on **Create/Edit** to generate a delivery action or edit an existing one:

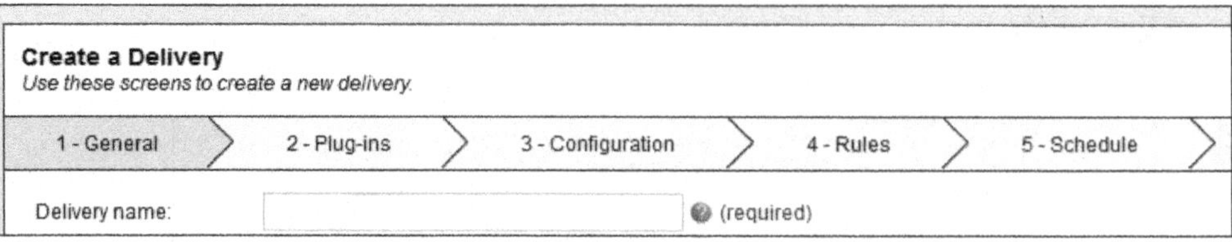


21. Click on the **1 – General** tab, and populate the following fields:
    - **Delivery name**: This decides the name to be assigned to your delivery. This field is mandatory.
    - **Evaluation order**: This decides the priority assigned to a delivery when distributing it among the users.
    - **Default delivery**: This is a checkbox, which when checked, is considered as the default plugin release technique.
    - **Silent install**: You can decide whether to allow users to see and stop the component installation by selecting the **Yes** or **No** radio button.
    - **Check for Updates**: In this field, you can specify how many days should pass before clients contact the Merchandising Server for updates check.
    - **Completion text**: You can insert here the message that you want to send to the users at the end of the component's installation.
    - **Support email address**: If you want, you can insert an e-mail address that refers to a support area. This e-mail will be displayed in the Citrix Receiver support panel.
    - **Support website**: This field is for the possible website support that will appear in the Citrix Receiver support panel.
    - **Support phone number**: This field is for the contact number for the support shown in the Citrix Receiver support panel.

Only one delivery group can be the default delivery!

22. Click on the **2 – Plug-ins** tab, and then click on the **Add** button to select the quantity of plugins that you want to assign to this delivery. Please specify the action to be performed on these components in the destination client as well (**Install/Uninstall**), as shown in the following screenshot:

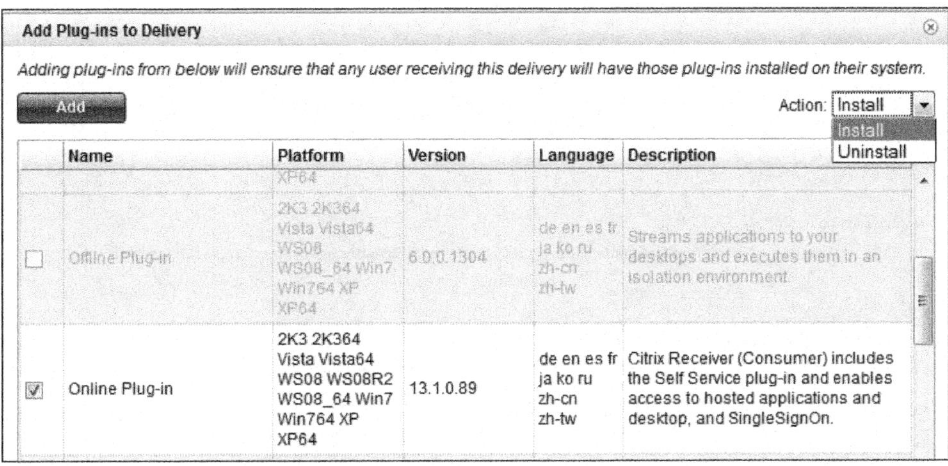


23. The **3 – Configuration** tab covers the configuration parameters for Citrix collateral components, such as Dazzle and StoreFront. You have to enter the information for the following fields, as they are mandatory:
    - The **Store configuration** field under the **Online Plug-in** section
    - The **Hostname(s) or IP Address(s)** field under the **Acceleration Plug-in** section for the Branch Repeater server

**Online Plug-in**

Enter configuration information to accompany the Dazzle delivery. Users' store configurations are updated w one or more application stores.

Open Dazzle for new users when Receiver starts

Store configuration (required)

(Example: Store name;https://xenapp.citrix.com/Citrix/PNAgent/config.xml)

Create a new item

**Acceleration Plug-in**

Enter the Signaling IP addresses of the Branch Repeaters separated by commas and without spaces. If the

Hostname(s) or IP Address(s) (required)

(Example: 10.20.30.40,some.domain.com:4433)

- The **Store configuration** field under the **Online Plug-in** security section
- The **Allow users to add stores** and **Allow users to save passwords for PNA based stores** under the **Online Plug-in** security section

Security: Enable ICA file signature verification

Security: Prompt user for questionable certificates

Security: Enter Trusted Certificate Thumbprints

(Example: e5 d0 ea 68 3f 21 90 77 4e 33 05 3c f6 12 20 f5 a1 ba 6f b7)

Create a new item

Store configuration (required)

(Example: Store name;https://storefront.citrix.com/Citrix/Store/discovery/;on;Store description)

Create a new item

Allow users to add stores (required)

(Example: Never (N), Always (A), Secure connections only (S))

Allow users to save passwords for PNA based stores N (required)

(Example: Never (N), Always (A), Secure connections only (S))

Install SSON

Start menu folder

Use legacy FTA icons

Reconnect apps on Windows logon

Reconnect apps when users start or refresh apps

Allow users to change reconnect options

Add Advanced User Menu Items Disabled Enabled(shown by default) Enabled(hidden by default)

24. In the **4 – Rules** tab, click on the **Add** button and select one of the previously created rules. After you've performed the selection, click on **Add** again to complete the task.

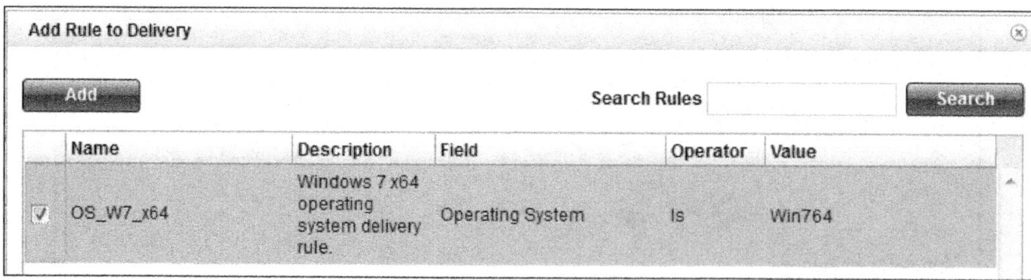

25. In the last tab for this section, **5 – Schedule**, please select **Deliver Now** or **Deliver Later**. If you select **Deliver Later**, please specify the date and time for the action, and then click on the **Schedule** button:

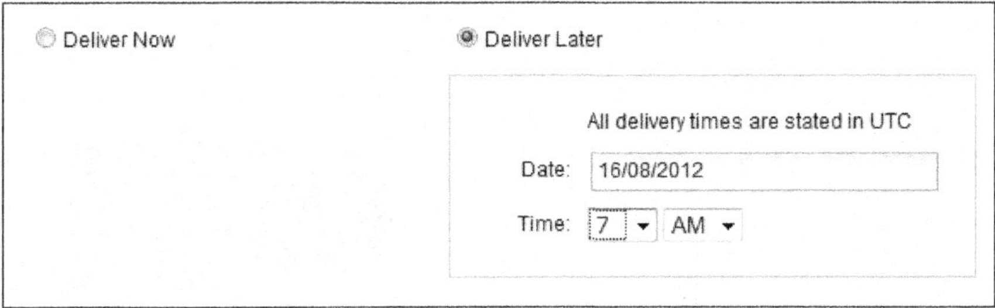


26. After you finish with the delivery configuration, you can choose one among the following options from the **Reporting and Logging** section in the left-hand side menu:

    - **Delivery Reporting**: With this option, you can export the reports for the Citrix packages delivery activities.
    - **Enable/Disable Logging**: For every configured user in the Merchandising Server, you can decide to enable or disable the logging activities by flagging the record referring to it. Moreover, you are also able to activate the system logging.

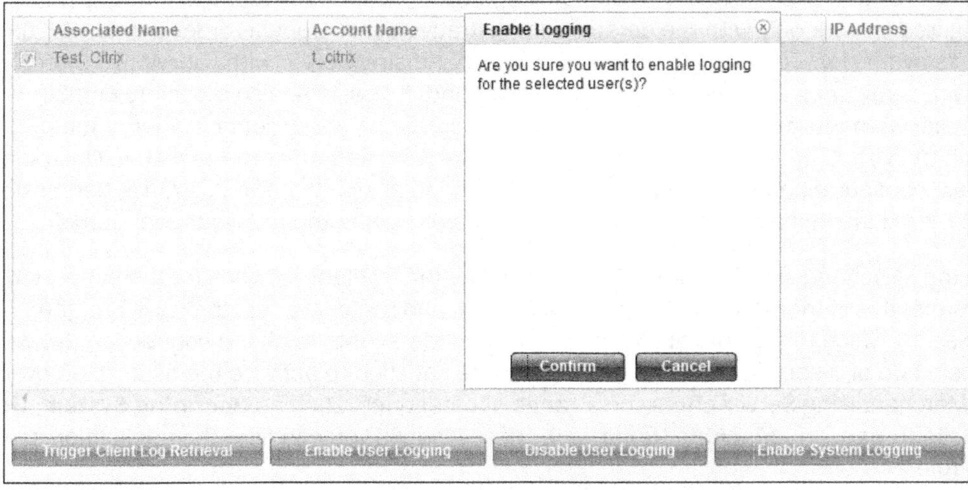


    - **View Log Files**: By using this option you will be able to view and download the client and server log files for troubleshooting and analysis activities.

27. Once you complete all the configuration tasks, you can test the availability of your Citrix Receiver by typing its FQDN in your browser's address bar, in the form of `http://hostname.domainname` or `https://hostname.domainname`. A website will appear, giving you the possibility to manually download the latest release in your infrastructure of the Citrix Receiver, as follows:

## How it works...

The Citrix Merchandising Server allows you to make the plugins delivery easier, more centralized and secure, for both the internal and remote user categories, giving the user the ability to work with both online and offline plugin types. The virtual appliance is initially configured to work only with the default administrative user - root. In order to make all the options available, you have to interface the Merchandising Server with your Active Directory domain, configuring a primary domain controller and, if possible, also a backup domain controller. To perform this operation, you need to create a user account in your domain, to permit the virtual appliance to read your Active Directory and synchronize with it. Once the domain configuration has been completed, it's time to assign the administrative permission to one of the domain users; a good solution could be assigning them to your user domain.

With the Merchandising Server, you can archive all the available plugins for the supported platforms; this is the base for structuring the rules and the deliveries, the ways and the policies, by which this virtual appliance distributes the agents to all the connection devices. A rule is made of a set of conditions, which must be satisfied to activate the associated event. The Merchandising Server offers you a range of categories, such as **Operating System**, **IP Address Range**, and **Machine Name**; with these choices you can filter the application scope for a rule.

After a rule has been created, it can be associated with a delivery, which is the container of the distribution policies applied to the devices. In this area, you have to configure the priority assigned to the delivery (which will reflect the distribution priority), the plugins to send to the PCs or the smart phones, for instance, the configuration information for the components in the distribution process, such as the Branch Repeater WAN accelerator, the application store platform known as Dazzle, or the XenApp application repository. In this way, you're linking the central repository with all the involved infrastructural components, required and optional.

After linking a previously created rule to the delivery, the last step is to configure a valid schedule time to execute the components' distribution, deletion, and/or upgrade; if you've correctly planned the deliveries and the rules contained in it, you could have a huge reduction in the manual and repetitive activities.

## There's more...

The Citrix Merchandising Server optionally offers you the possibility to connect with the Citrix Receiver through an SSL secure channel; to use this kind of connection, you need a certificate in order to validate the communication established with the server. In the left-hand side panel of the management area, you have the **SSL Certificate Management** link; in this section, you will find a drop-down menu with all the possible activities for certification authority management, as follows:

- **Manage SSL certificates**: In this option the server will display the current certificate configuration. No further operational activities are permitted.
- **Generate self-signed certificate**: A self-signed certificate is generated by default from the Merchandising Server, with a validity of 30 days. Selecting this option requires the certificate regeneration every month. To regenerate after the expiration time period, you have to populate all the required fields (**Common Name**, **Organization Name**, **Organization Unit**, **Locality Name**, **State Name**, and **Country Code**).
- **Export certificate signing request**: With this option, you will generate a request to obtain an SSL certificate. As previously seen, you have to populate all the required fields to generate a valid request (**Common Name**, **Organization Name**, **Organization Unit**, **Locality Name**, **State Name**, and **Country Code**) plus the certificate's **Key Size** (**2048**, **4096**, or **8192**).

Remember that you have to populate the **Common Name** textbox with the Merchandising Server FQDN for both the generate and export tasks.

- **Import certificate from a certificate authority**: In the presence of an already existing CA architecture, the Merchandising Server gives you the way to import an SSL certificate located on an external CA server (for instance, a certification authority based on Microsoft Windows technology). As a mandatory object, you have to load the public certificate file; optionally, you can insert the intermediate certificates and the private key files, and populate the last textbox with the private key password.
- **Import root certificate**: This is an optional operation to perform in case of a certificate generated by an external certification authority. In this case, you need to import the root certificate file and insert the alias certificate in order to make the certificate identification process easier. Both options are mandatory.

## See also

- The *Publishing the streamed apps with XenApp 6.5* recipe in *Chapter 7, Deploying Applications*

# Configuring the Branch Repeater virtual appliance

When we refer to a Citrix architecture, we usually intend a complex infrastructure located on the same area or building. In some cases, especially in presence of huge organizations, you could have a central infrastructure used by many remote locations or branch offices. In this case, the native optimization of the ICA protocol could not be sufficient to have the performance needed by the remote users to work without having performance issues, because of the WAN connection. In this scenario, Citrix presents Branch Repeater, which is a WAN optimizer developed for these kinds of situations. It is in the form of some physical network devices and a virtual appliance; in this chapter, we're going to discuss about this second solution.

## Getting ready

The Branch Repeater virtual appliance is downloadable from your MyCitrix account as a single component, or as a part of XenDesktop 5.6 suite's Platinum version. Also in this case, this element is in the form of a template for XenServer and vSphere hypervisors. After downloading Branch Repeater, you need to import it into your infrastructure, and assign a network to both the configured network cards, one connected to the LAN area and the other pointing to the WAN network. You also need to generate a license file for this platform from the license portal in your MyCitrix account; you have to assign the required number of licenses to allow all the users to work from the remote locations. Then you have to import the generated file in your license server, as shown in the *Installing and configuring license server* recipe from *Chapter 1, XenDesktop Installation and Configuration*.

To generate a valid license file for the Branch Repeater appliance, you have to insert the host ID of your license server. You can find this information in the **System Information** section of the **Administration** panel.

## How to do it...

In the following steps, we will perform the installation and configuration of the Citrix Branch Repeater virtual appliance:

1. Mount or extract the Repeater ISO file, select the template version for your hypervisor (VMware vSphere or Citrix XenServer), and import the template in your virtual infrastructure.
2. Connect to your hypervisor host and open the console of the imported virtual appliance.
3. Insert the default administrative credentials (`admin/password`) in the **command-line interface** (**CLI**) login screen and then press the *Enter* button.
4. Following the instructions on the screen, type the `help` command followed by pressing the *Enter* key if you want to have the complete CLI command list.

```
Login: admin
Password:

Citrix Branch Repeater V45 Command Line Interpreter
Copyright 2011 Citrix Systems, Inc. All Rights Reserved.

Hit <TAB> once for command completion or context-sensitive help.
Hit <TAB> twice to see a list of all available commands.

Use the "help" command to display help for a specific command.
Example: help show config-script

admin> _
```

5. Configure the adapter network parameters to make the Web Interface available, by typing the next command. Press *Enter* after you've completed the following task:

```
set adapter apA -ip x.x.x.x -netmask x.x.x.x -gateway x.x.x.x
-vlan [enabled|disabled] -vlan-group [VLAN_ID]
```

You have to populate the indicated fields with a valid IP address, a netmask, and a default gateway. Optionally, you can enable the `vlan` parameter and specify the VLAN ID.

6. After you have configured the network interface, run the following command and press the *Enter* key, in order to restart the virtual appliance and apply all the configuration modifications:

```
restart
```

7. After the restart has been successfully completed, verify it by pinging the IP address assigned to the Branch Repeater network adapter, open a web browser, and type the URL `https://Branch_Repeater_IP_address` in the address bar. You will receive back the web login interface for this virtual appliance.

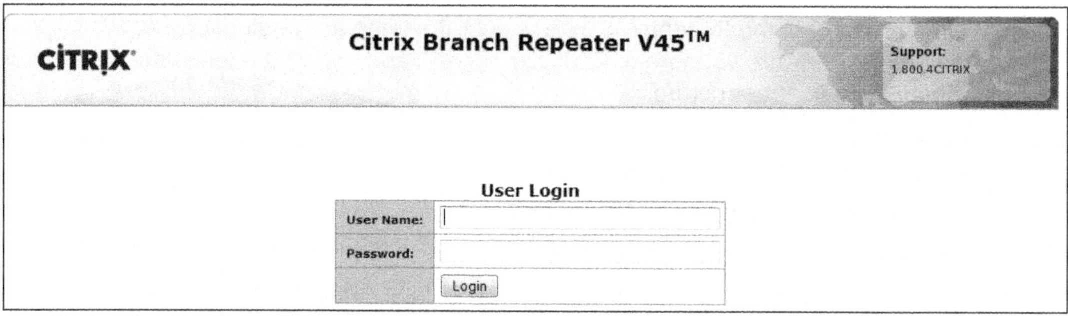


8. Insert the default credentials used for the CLI environment and click on the **Login** button.
9. In the left-hand side menu, expand the **Configuration** section and click on the **Licensing** link. On the **License Server Location** tab, click on the **Remote** radio button and populate all the required fields with the details of your license server. Then click on the **Apply** button, and wait for the time needed to restart the repeater.

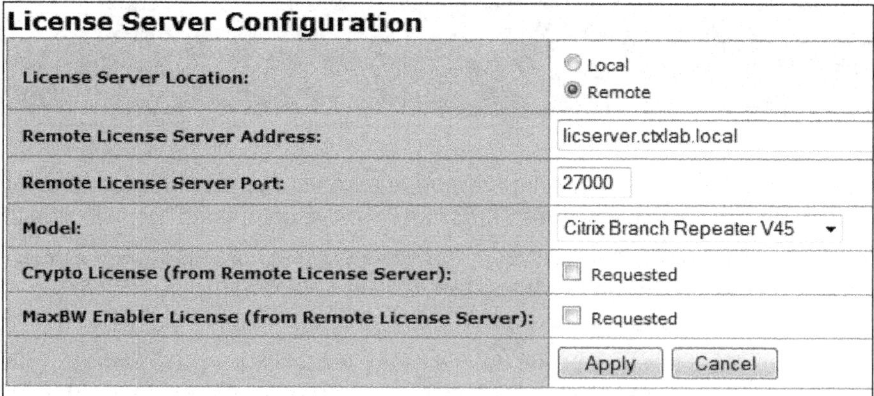

Remember that you need to pre-allocate the licenses to your license server by generating the required file containing the Branch Repeater licenses.

10. In the **Configuration** section in the left-hand side menu, click on the **Administrator Interface** link, then select the **User Accounts** tab and modify the default password for the admin user. If you want, you can also add additional users.

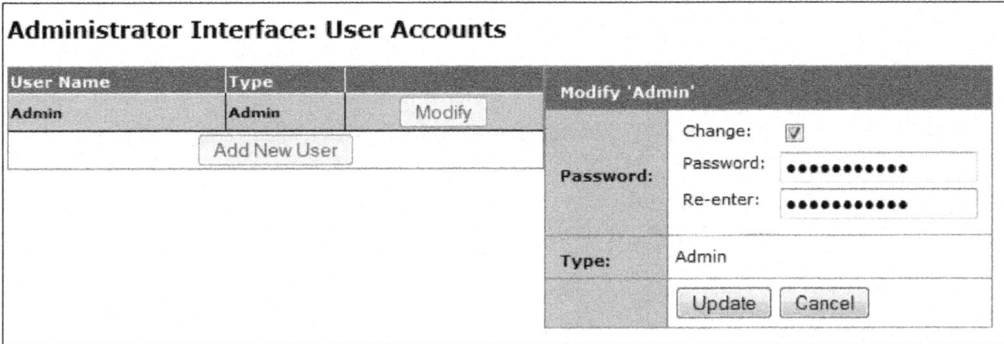


11. In the left-hand side menu, click on the **Windows Domain** option from the **Configuration** section; this will open a domain configuration page. Click on the **Join Domain** button, and populate the information fields to complete the task. After this, please click on the **Join** button, as shown in the following screenshot:

12. In the **Configuration** section located in the left-hand side menu, select the **Application Classifiers** link; in this section, you are able to view and edit the application group(s) configured by Citrix, and you can also create new applications to permit the Branch Repeater to identify them during acceleration activities. Select an application category from the drop-down list, then click on the **Edit** button in the **Action** column. In the following screenshot, we've selected **Citrix Protocols** as **Application Group**, exploding the ICA application:

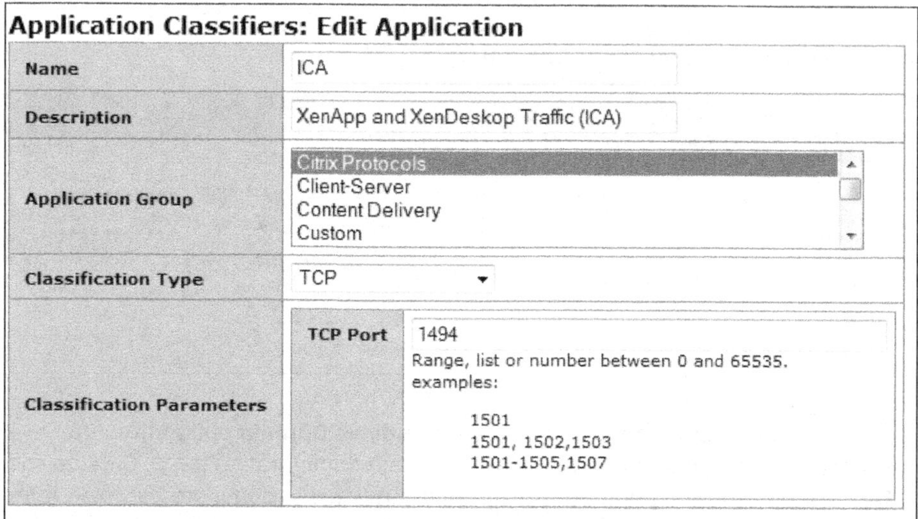


13. In the **Configuration** section from the left-hand side menu, click on the **Logging/ Monitoring** link. In the first tab, **Log Options**, select a suitable **Log Max Size** in MB (default is 1024), the number of displayed lines (default is 30), **Max Export Count Default**, and the log category that you want to collect (**Log System Records**, **Log Adapter Records**, **Log Flow Records**, **Log Connection Records**, **Log Open/Close Records**, **Log Text Records**, and **Log Alert Records**).
14. In the **Alert Options** tab of the **Logging/Monitoring** category, you can configure the monitoring sensor to assign to the configured system groups (**Alerted**, **Logged**, and **Disabled**), and the percentage threshold levels wherever possible. After configuring the monitor sensor, click on the **Update Alert Message Settings** button.
15. Select the **Syslog Server** tab in the **Logging/Monitoring** category if you have got a syslog server to which you are sending the collected logs; in this case, you have to check the **Send To Syslog Server** checkbox, specifying **Syslog Server IP** and **Syslog Server Port**. After completing this, click on **Update**.

16. In the **Configuration** section, click on the **Links** menu and edit the traffic link shown in the **Link Definition** tab. For all of these links, you can configure **Name**, **Link Type** (**LAN** or **WAN**), **Bandwidth In**, and **Bandwidth Out**, and if necessary you can implement filter rules by specifying network parameters such as source and destination IP addresses, or network adapters MAC addresses. After it's completed, click on the **Save** button.

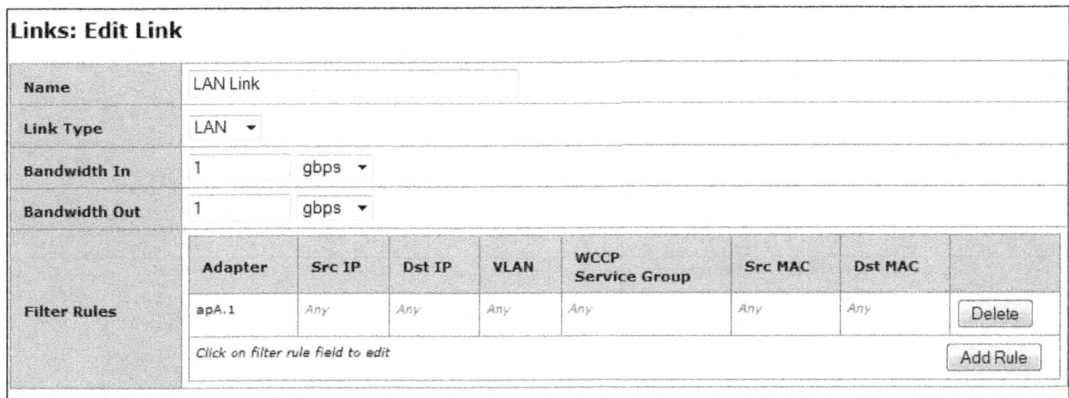


17. In the **Monitoring** section from the left-hand side menu, click on the **Citrix (ICA/CGP)** link. In the **ICA Statistics** tab you can find the statistics about the use and the optimization of the ICA protocol. In the same section, by clicking on **Acceleration Graphs Last Minute**, you will obtain a real-time graphical representation of the optimized ICA traffic.

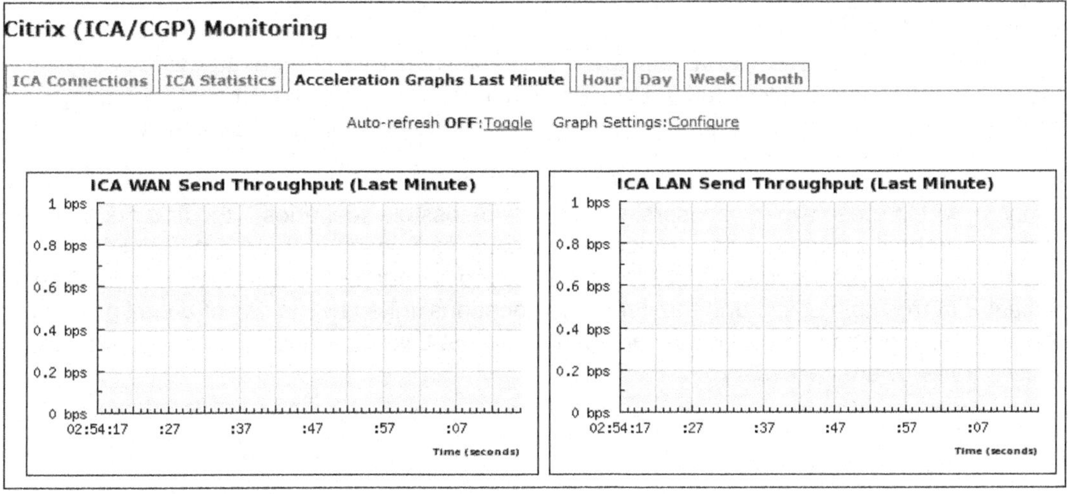

18. You can obtain similar information about the network filesystems or the Outlook MAPI protocol use by clicking on the left side menu links called **Filesystem (CIFS/SMB)** and **Outlook (MAPI)**.
19. Click on the **Usage Graph** link in the **Usage Graph Monitoring** section from the left-hand side menu, to have general traffic information about the WAN and LAN network usage, with the **View Last Minute**, **Hour**, **Day**, **Week**, and **Month** views, as shown in the following screenshot:

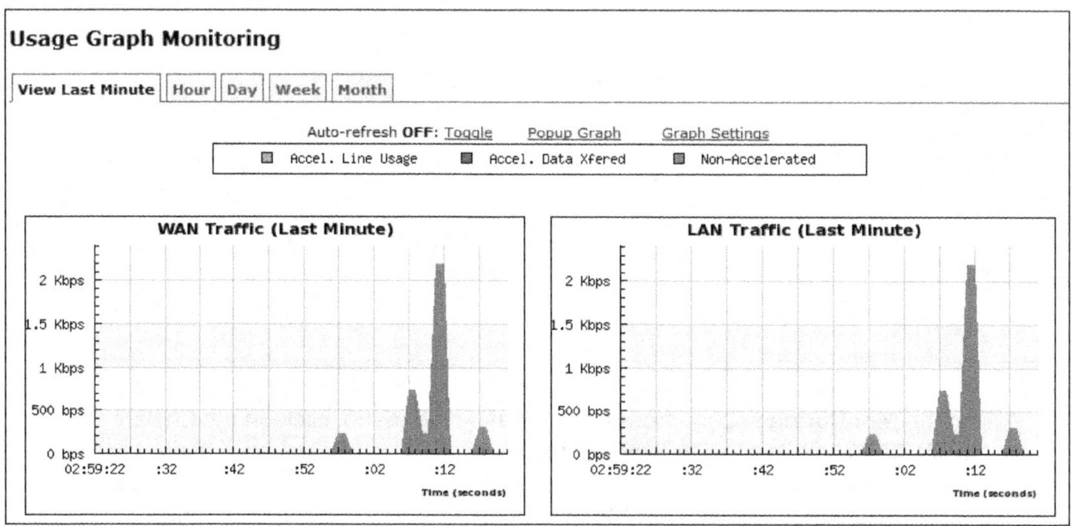


## How it works...

The Citrix Branch Repeater virtual appliance, also known as Branch Repeater VPX, is a less expensive and more flexible solution to optimize and improve the WAN connection among remote locations; the opposite product is the set of physical appliance products by Citrix.

It has been developed to run as a virtual machine under Citrix XenServer and VMware vSphere; within these two hypervisors, you have two possible scenarios - the first made up of a set of repeaters equal to the number of remote offices, each of them in communication with the main Branch Repeater office, and the second scenario constituted by a single Branch Repeater in the main office, and the peripheral locations linked by the use of a plugin called Repeater Acceleration. With this second scenario, an SSL VPN connection and the Citrix Access Gateway are necessary.

If using two or more virtual appliances, in the common configuration's best practices, you can choose between two different network topologies, as follows:

- **Inline mode**: With this modality, you need two network interfaces, which can be attached to two physical interfaces, or to one physical interface and one virtual interface, or to two virtual interfaces. This last case is used only for test and simulation purposes.
- **One arm mode (WCCP)**: In this case as well, you need two network adapters, but one of them must be directly attached to a router through a physical network card, and the other must point through a virtual interface to the Branch Repeater VPX.

You can find further details about the network configurations at `http://support.citrix.com/article/CTX131015`.

With the VPX version, the only way to implement an HA configuration is given by the high availability of the hypervisor system. You can't configure two virtual appliances in an active/passive clustered configuration.

Once you've installed the virtual appliance, the first operation to perform is its configuration by the use of the CLI. In this way, you will configure the virtual network adapters (identified with the name apA.x, where x is a number of configured interfaces) by assigning the network parameters, such as the IP address or the VLAN ID. After every critical configuration, a restart is needed in order to make the changes active. Now the web management console is available, and you can log in with the same username and password used to connect to the CLI (default `admin/password`). Once logged in, the first action to perform is interfacing the Branch Repeater with the license server of your company. Remember that with the nonexpress version of this product, you must use the standard license server; to use the internal repeater license platform you need the express version. You have to license the right version; be careful about the final part of the product name (Vx). The associated number refers to the speed of the network link in Mbps for which you've bought the licenses (V1, V2, V10, and V45 are the licenses for a network speed of 1 Mbps, 2 Mbps, 10 Mbps, and 45 Mbps, respectively). After completing this step, it is really important to modify the default administrative password. Moreover, by joining the Branch Repeater to the company domain, you'll be able to add users other than the default account.

The latest version of the VPX is loaded with pre-configured applications divided by a category. Each application has its communication ports already configured, thanks to this implementation, as the Repeater is able to optimize by default the network use of critical applications such as Citrix Protocols, Microsoft Exchange, LDAP, or database platforms. You can also create and insert any missing application. This section is strongly linked to the traffic shaping policies and the service classes section; for every configured application, you have the capability of specifying the acceleration policy (disk, memory, or flow control) and the traffic priority for the specified application. In this way, you have the full control and regulation over the use of the network by the application's users.

An important configuration parameter is the available bandwidth assigned to the WAN and LAN areas. Don't forget to rightly configure these two values in the links section!

As usual, Citrix offers the logging feature in this case as well. This feature is configurable to perform troubleshooting activities. In addition to the log size and the areas you are logging on, you can decide to generate a message alert or an event log for every configured alert option, such as **WAN or LAN loss rate**, **Out of CPU or Memory resources**, and **Compression Error detected**.

The point of strength for the Branch Repeater is its great ability in the compression and deduplication of the network traffic. You can monitor these activities in real time, thanks to the integrated monitoring platform offered by the Branch Repeater VPX.

## There's more...

The Branch Repeater plugin, which is an alternative way of allowing the remote users to communicate with the Branch Repeater located in the main office, is configurable using two different approaches, as follows:

- **Redirector modality**: With this configuration, the plugin transfer traffic is directed to a server machine by passing it from the user client to the repeater VPX. The accelerator then transfers the request to the destination server. To enable this mode, you have to select the **Repeater Plug-ins** link in the left-hand side menu of the VPX appliance and select the **Redirector** radio button. This configuration should be used only when it's necessary for your infrastructure to use the target appliance as a proxy that redirects the traffic from the plugin to the destination server and back.
- **Transparent modality**: With this configuration, you have a situation similar to the connection between two appliances. So after the plugin has successfully contacted the VPX, it downloads the acceleration rules, which will be seen to verify whether the established connection is regulated with the acceleration policies. To enable this mode, you have to select **the Repeater Plug-ins** link in the left-hand side menu of the VPX appliance and select the **Transparent** radio button. This option should be used in the presence of a set of pre-configured Branch Repeater appliances, using a pass-through connection between the client plugin and the destination virtual appliances. Citrix recommends using this second plugin mode.

For both the options, you have to specify a private IP address (which will be available only after you've established the secure VPN connection) and a port in the **Signaling IP** and **Signaling Port** textboxes, as shown in the following screenshot:

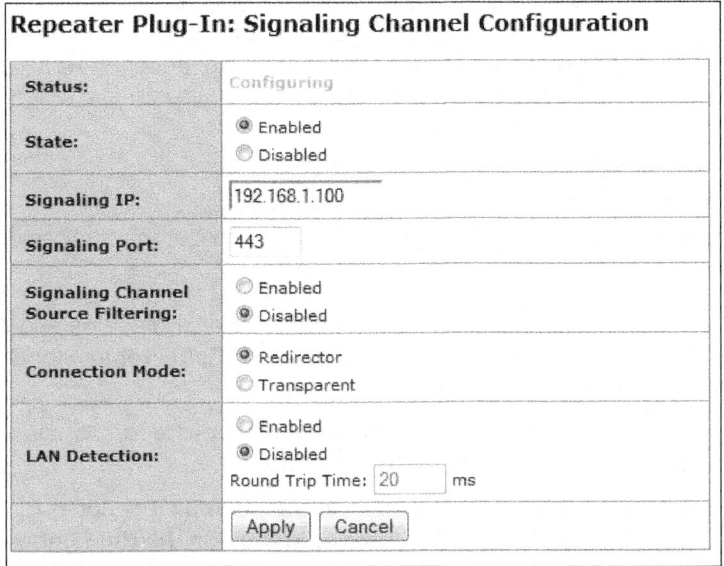

For the virtual appliance area, only VPX v45 supports the use of the Repeater plugin for the branch offices. VPX v45 is included in XenDesktop Platinum Edition.

## See also

- The *Configuring the Citrix Access Gateway virtual appliance* recipe in *Chapter 8, XenDesktop Tuning and Security*

# Installing and configuring XenDesktop Collector

In some situations, even an expert IT system administrator could not be capable of understanding a problem during the log collection and analysis activities. In this case, the vendor support could be the only way to solve the problem. Citrix offers the IT professionals a log collector software, which can directly upload the required information to the support working team. This is the XenDesktop Collector program.

## Getting ready

Citrix XenDesktop Collector is a part of the XenDesktop 5.6 Feature Pack 1; so, you need to download it from your MyCitrix account in this specific section. It's a ZIP archive which contains two setups in the form of an MSI package, for both 32- and 64-bit operating system versions. You need to connect to your Desktop Controller server with administrative credentials in order to be able to install this program.

## How to do it...

In this recipe, we will configure the Citrix software used to collect the XenDesktop system logs. Perform the following steps to do so:

1. Extract the Collector archive on your Desktop Controller machine and double-click on the setup for your operating system version (**XDCollector.msi** for 32 bit and **XDCollectorx64.msi** for 64 bit).
2. On the Welcome screen click on the **Next** button to proceed, then accept the end user license terms and click on **Next** to continue.
3. Select the installation path for the Collector; the default location is `C:\Program Files\Citrix\XenDesktopCollector\`. Click on the **Next** button to proceed.
4. To complete the installation procedure, click on the **Install** button.
5. After completing the installation, leave the **Launch Citrix XenDesktop Collector** checkbox checked and click on the **Finish** button, as shown in the following screenshot:

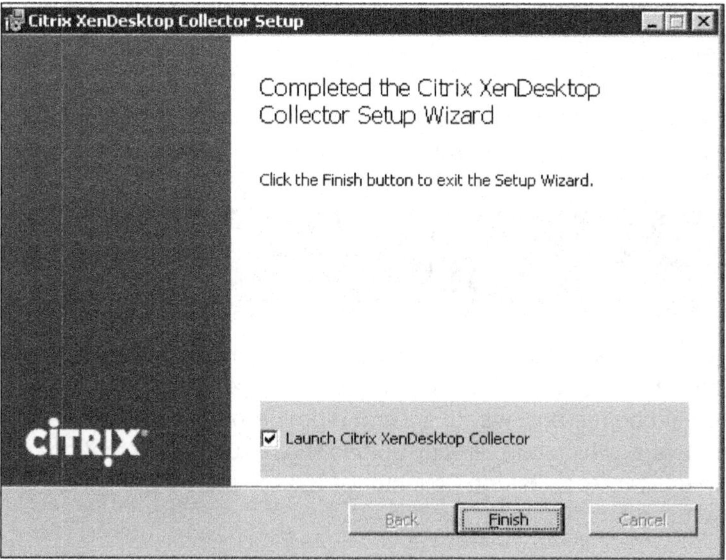

6. On the first Collector screen, you can find information about the configured controllers on which you are operating. If you want to register an error trace during an error reproduction, you have to click on the **Run CDF Trace** button.

The acronym, **CDF Trace** stands for **Citrix Diagnostic Facility Trace**.

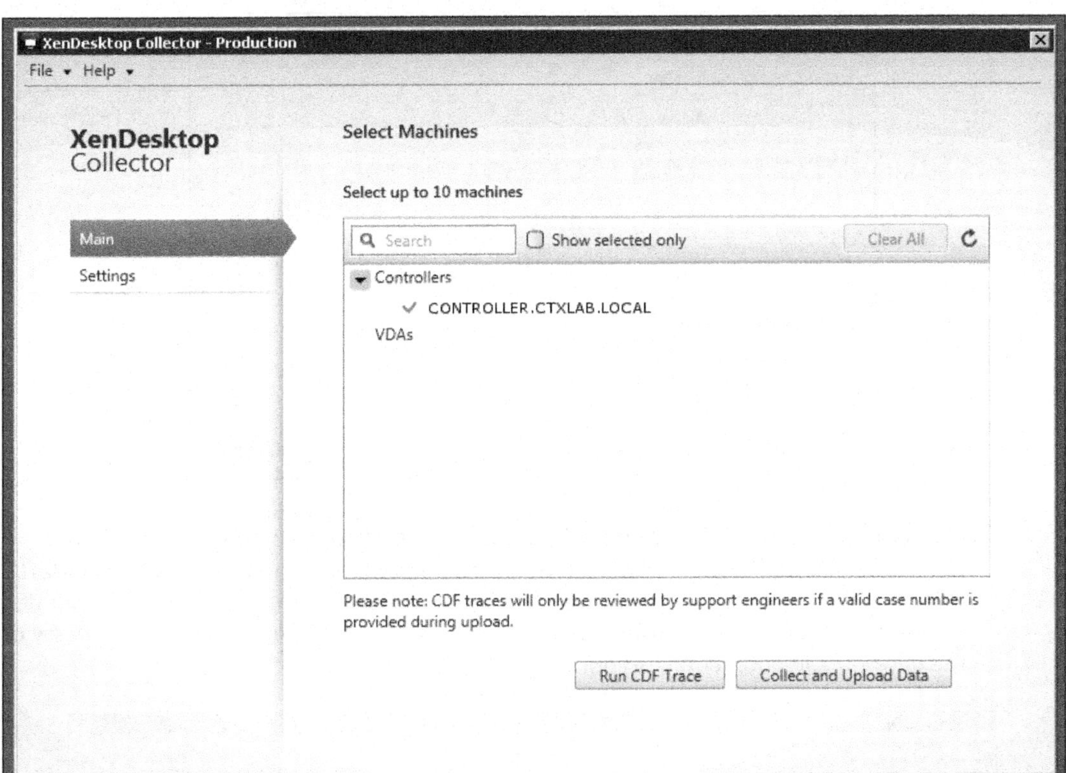

7. To start the error and data collection on the selected Desktop Controller, click on the **Collect and Upload Data** button. After it's completed, the XenDesktop Collector will present you with a login screen on which you have to insert a username and a password for the **Citrix Tools as a Service** platform in order to upload your data to the Citrix Support; to populate an optional field, you can insert a ticket number assigned by the support to analyze the generated CDF traces. If you want, you can view the collected items by clicking on the **View Data** link.

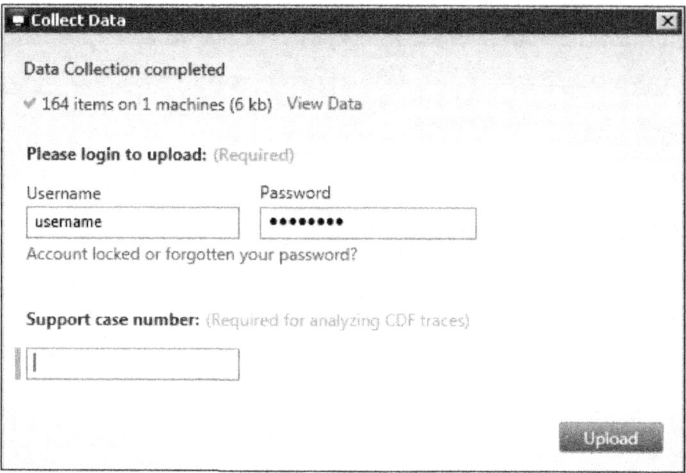


8. After completing the first log collection, you can modify the default configuration by clicking on the **Settings** link in the left-hand side panel. On the **Settings Panel Alert** pop-up screen, click on the **Continue** button to bypass the Citrix advice and continue with the operations. In the **Advanced Settings** main menu you will find an overview of the current collection configuration.

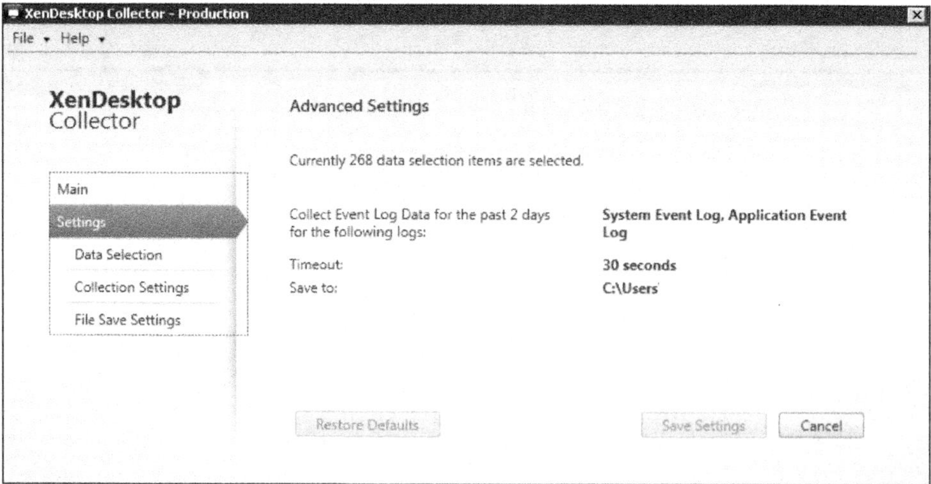

9. Click on the **Data Selection** link and select the collection options for the categories shown ahead; when possible you should leave all the default options as checked:
    - **Site**
    - **Controller**
    - **VDA**
10. Click on the **Collection Settings** link and choose whether to collect all event logs or specify the interval data collection in days. After this, flag the log types to collect (**System Event Log**, **Application Event Log**, or **Security Event Log**) and specify **Collection Timeout** in seconds, and the maximum number of machines on which you are collecting the data. If you've modified at least one of these settings, please click on the **Save Settings** button to register your changes.

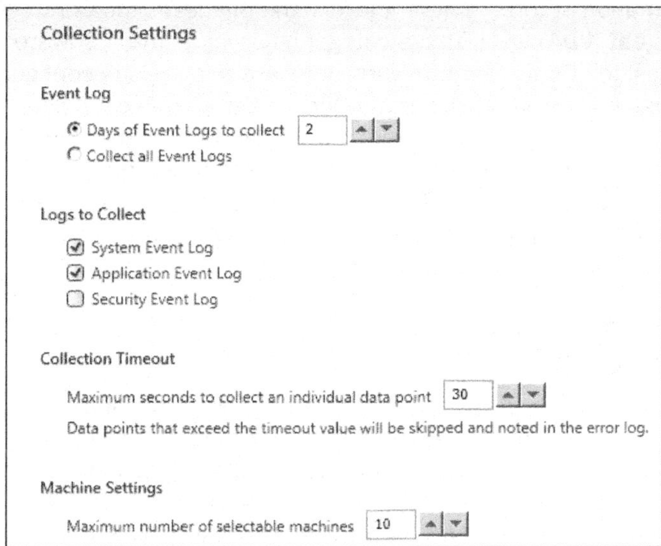


11. By clicking on the **File Save Settings** link in the left-hand side menu, you can specify the location where you want to save the generated reports. If you want to delete them after a successful upload, please check the **Delete reports after they are successfully uploaded** checkbox, as shown in the following screenshot:

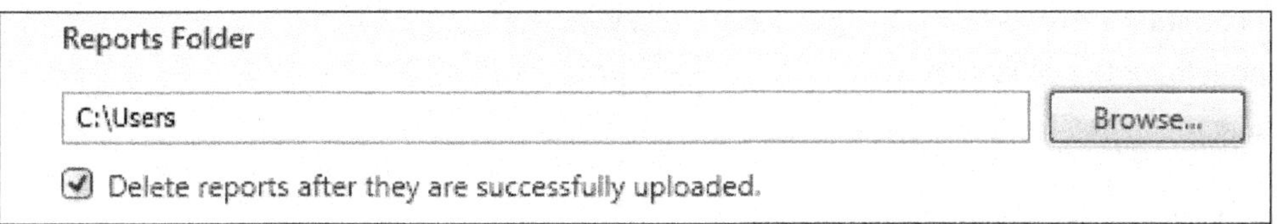

## How it works...

The Citrix XenDesktop Collector tool helps the system administrators in automating the log collection activities. This software cooperates with the **Citrix Tool As A Service** platform, also known as **TAAS**, which is a public cloud portal on which you can transfer the result of the collections in your infrastructure, allowing the Citrix Support to analyze them to work on your architectural issues.

You can log in to the Citrix TAAS platform (`https://taas.citrix.com`) with your MyCitrix account credentials.

The Collector's way to work is quite simple, because it runs a series of queries to collect configuration information at three different levels, the Site level, the Controller level, and the **Virtual Desktop Agent** (**VDA**) level. These categories cover all the hardware and software aspects such as Desktop Controller hardware, software and registry configurations, the XenDesktop catalogs and desktop groups, the Virtual Desktop Agent software parameters, and all about concerning the Citrix policies implementation. You also have the possibility to choose the time period to run these system statistics and how many machines to include in the reporting activity. You can perform the collection in two different ways – the first, called CDF Trace, runs during the reproduction of a specific problem, and the second, called Collect, is a full gathering of all the system information.

## There's more...

If you want, you can work with the XenDesktop Collector in an advanced way, by using its CLI. This is a powerful tool to manage and control the log collection, so GUI is not the only way to manage and control it. At the software installation location (the default location is `C:\Program Files\Citrix\XenDesktopCollector`), there is an executable file to run the CLI command, `XDCollector.exe`. The following table shows the CLI principal commands and their abbreviations:

| Description | Command | Abbreviation |
|---|---|---|
| Run in GUI mode | `--gui-mode` | `-g` or `-gm` |
| List infrastructure machines | `--list-machines` | `-m` or `-lm` |
| Collect data | `--collect` | `-c` |
| Output file for the collection data | `--output-file=filename` | `-o` or `-of` |
| Include machines by their FQDNs (comma separated) | `--include-machines=FQDN1,FQDN2...` | `-q` or `-im` |
| Upload the collected archive | `--upload` | `-U` |
| Username for the upload action | `--upload-user` | `-u` or `-uun` |

| Description | Command | Abbreviation |
|---|---|---|
| Password for the upload action | `--upload-password=your password` | `-p` or `-up` |
| Server for the upload action (default is `https://taas.citrix.com`) | `--upload-server=server address` | `-S` or `-us` |
| Run the trace collection on the machines specified by their FQDNs (comma separated) | `--trace-machines=FQDN1,FQDN2...` | `-Q` or `-tm` |
| Run CDF Trace | `--trace` | `-t` |

So, for instance, if you want to list all the configured controllers for your infrastructure, you have to run the following command:

```
XDCollectore.exe --list-machines
```

To avoid resource lock problems, you have to run the XenDesktop Collector GUI or CLI, but not both.

## See also

- The *Configuring the XenDesktop logging* recipe in *Chapter 8, XenDesktop Tuning and Security*

# Chapter 5 XenDesktop lab

In this laboratory, we will configure the Merchandising Server virtual appliance to deploy two kinds of plugins to all the Windows 7 machines created in our infrastructure. From a network perspective, we will perform the WAN optimization test by installing two Branch Repeater virtual appliances, which will work in the inline mode. After completing these steps, we will collect logs and data about the Controller machine. Perform the following steps to do so:

1. Connect to the Domain Controller server (`vmctxdc01 - 192.168.1.50`) and create two users, as follows:
    i. Create a user named `citrix_bind` and assign to it the administrative permissions to give access to the Active Directory service.
    ii. Create a user named `merch_admin`; this user will be used as the administrator of the Merchandising platform.

2. Download from your MyCitrix account the Merchandising Server virtual appliance, and import it into one of the supported hypervisors. After completing the import, configure it as follows :
    i. Assign `vmctxmrc01` as the hostname.
    ii. Assign `192.168.1.95` as the IP address.
    iii. Download all the available plugins and make them reside on the server.
    iv. Create a rule called `W7_x64`, which performs a filter on the Windows 7 64-bit operating systems.
    v. Create a default delivery action, which will use the created rule, to deploy the online and offline plugins for the Windows 7 operating systems; this delivery task has to be executed after the creation.
    vi. Update the default server certificate by generating a new version of the self-signed certificate. The key size must be 8192.
3. Download from your MyCitrix account the Branch Repeater VPX, and import it into one of the supported hypervisors. After completing the import, configure it as follows :
    i. Assign `vmctxbrv01` as the hostname.
    ii. Assign `192.168.1.98` as the IP address.
    iii. Join the virtual appliance to the `ctxlab.local` domain.
    iv. Configure the repeater to generate a log file of maximum 512 MB.
    v. Configure the network bandwidth to be coherent with your network configuration.
4. Import a second repeater virtual appliance and configure it, as follows:
    i. Assign `vmctxbrv02` as the hostname.
    ii. Assign `192.168.1.99` as the IP address.
    iii. Join the virtual appliance to the `ctxlab.local` domain.
    iv. Configure the repeater to generate a log file of maximum 512 MB.
    v. Configure the network bandwidth to be coherent with your network configuration.

To perform the compression and optimization tests, please consider installing a virtual machine with the role of a WAN emulator. A useful free tool is the Tata WANem, which can be downloaded from `http://wanem.sourceforge.net/`.

5. Configure your repeaters' architecture to be in inline mode, then start a file transfer operation between the two simulated network locations (over a WAN), and analyze the traffic report within both the virtual appliances.
6. On the XenDesktop Controller machine (`vmctxddc01 - 192.168.1.60`), install the XenDesktop Collector in order to run a log collection of the only Desktop Director component. After this, run the collection and upload tasks.
7. Repeat the previous step to run collection and data upload for both the Controller and the Virtual Desktop Agent; everything must be performed from the CLI.

# 6
# Creating and Configuring a Desktop Environment

In this chapter we will cover:

- Creating and configuring the machine catalog
- Modifying an existing machine catalog
- Using Citrix Desktop Director
- Configuring printers
- Configuring USB devices

## Introduction

In the first five chapters of this book, we have installed and configured all the main architectural components used to implement the XenDesktop suite and different useful technologies.

Now it's time to proceed with the creation of the virtual desktop instances; the linked clone of the virtual image template will be released to and used by the end users. In this chapter we'll learn how to perform this task, and how to maintain and modify the desktop collections.

# Creating and configuring the machine catalog

All the virtual resources released to the end users are part of a group collection called a catalog; this contains information about the type and number of virtual desktop instances, the configurations, and the assignment, based on the Active Directory objects (users, groups, computers). In this recipe we're going to perform a full creation and configuration of all these elements.

## Getting ready

To correctly perform the configuration tasks, you need administrative credentials for the XenDesktop Controller server, and to be able to use the created virtual desktop, you first need to install and configure the required VDA plugin on the client device, as explained in the previous chapter.

You also have to generate a snapshot within your hypervisor environment for the master image virtual machine created to deploy the virtual desktop instances; the VM creation has been discussed in *Chapter 3, Master Image Configuration and Tuning*.

## How to do it...

In this recipe we will explain how to create and manage a XenDesktop machine catalog. Perform the following steps to do so:

1. Connect to the Desktop Controller server with an administrative domain user.
2. Select **Start** | **All Programs** | **Citrix**, and click on the **Desktop Studio** link. Now we will see how to create the machine's catalog.
3. Based on the connection to your hypervisor explained in *Chapter 2, Deploying Virtual Machines for XenDesktop*, select the **Machines** link from the left-hand side menu. After selecting it, click on the **Create Catalog** link from the right-hand side panel, as shown in the following screenshot:

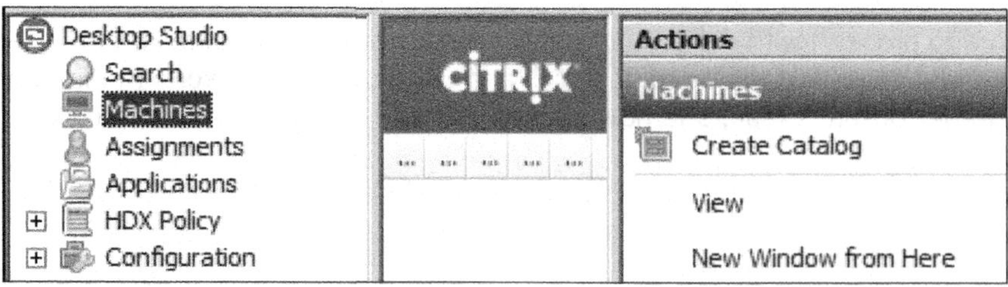

Alternatively you can click on the **Configure** button, in the **Machine creation** section from the main menu of the **Desktop Studio** link.

4. In the **Machine Type** section, from the drop-down list, select the type of deployment to be performed (**Pooled**, **Pooled with personal vDisk**, **Dedicated**, **Existing**, **Physical**, **Streamed**, and **Streamed with personal vDisk**). In the **Machine Assignment** section select the appropriate radio button (**Random** or **Static**). After completing this click on the **Next** button.

Please refer to the *How it works...* section of this recipe to understand the differences between the listed catalogs.

The options available under the **Machine Type** section are shown in the following screenshot:

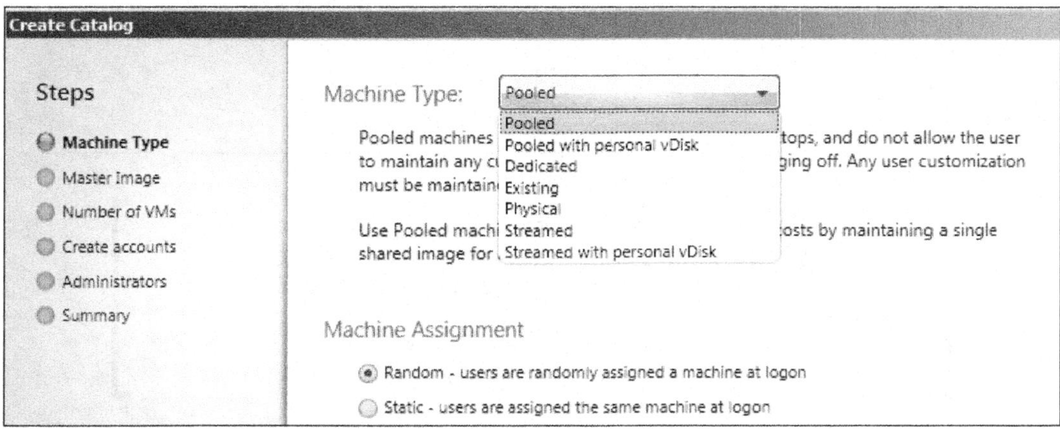


5. Select a master image from the list, from which we will generate the desktop instances. Then click on **Next**.

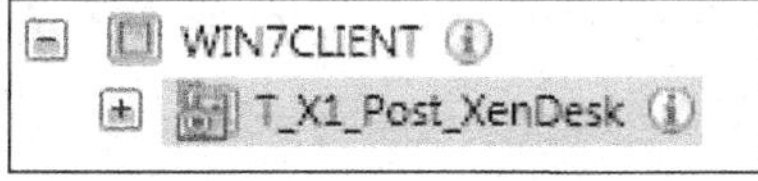

The image selected from the list is a snapshot that refers to the original virtual machine disk.

6. Select how many machines are generated by incrementing the value of the **Number of virtual machines to create** field. After this you need to configure the resources to assign to any virtual desktop instance (**vCPUs** and **Memory**), and select **Create new accounts** or **Use existing accounts** in the **Active Directory computer accounts** section. To better understand all the creation features, in this section we will select the creation of new computer accounts. After finishing with this click on **Next**.

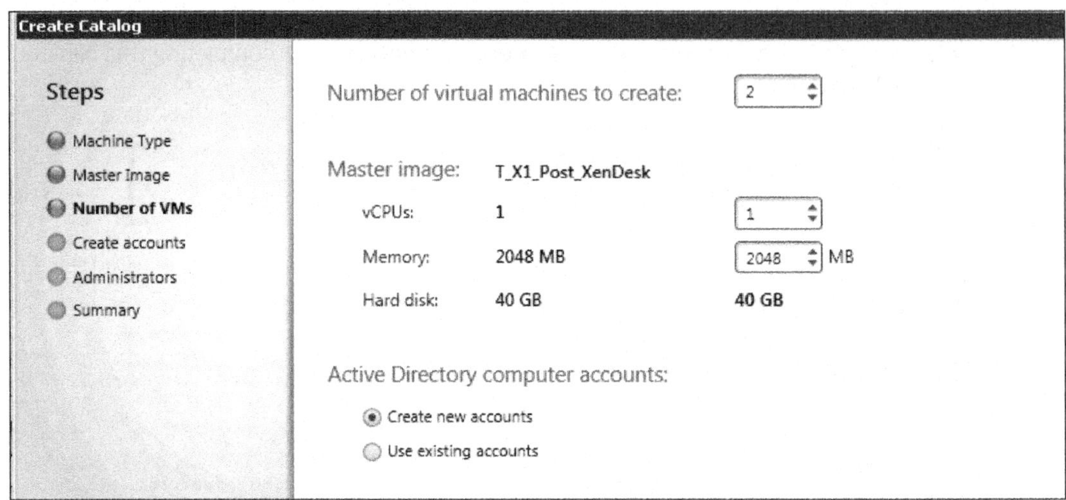

Note that you can't modify the operating system's disk size parameter, because it depends on the master image template configuration. On the template, make sure that you have mapped the virtual disk with the ID `0:0` (the first created disk for the machine), otherwise you will receive an error during this configuration step.

7. In the **Active Directory location for computer accounts** section, select from the drop-down list the domain on which you are working, and choose an organizational unit on which you are creating the computer accounts, then select an account naming scheme, in the form of **MachineName##**, where the two final characters identify a progressive code made up of letters or digits (A - Z or 0 - 9). After completing this click on the **Next** button.

8. If you want, you can insert a catalog description to help administrators in identifying the generated pool. To continue click on **Next**.

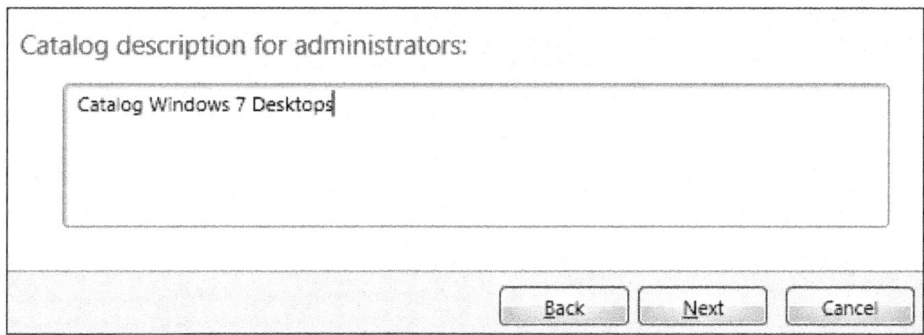


9. On the **Summary** screen, assign a name to the catalog, and click on the **Finish** button to complete the procedure, as shown in the following screenshot:

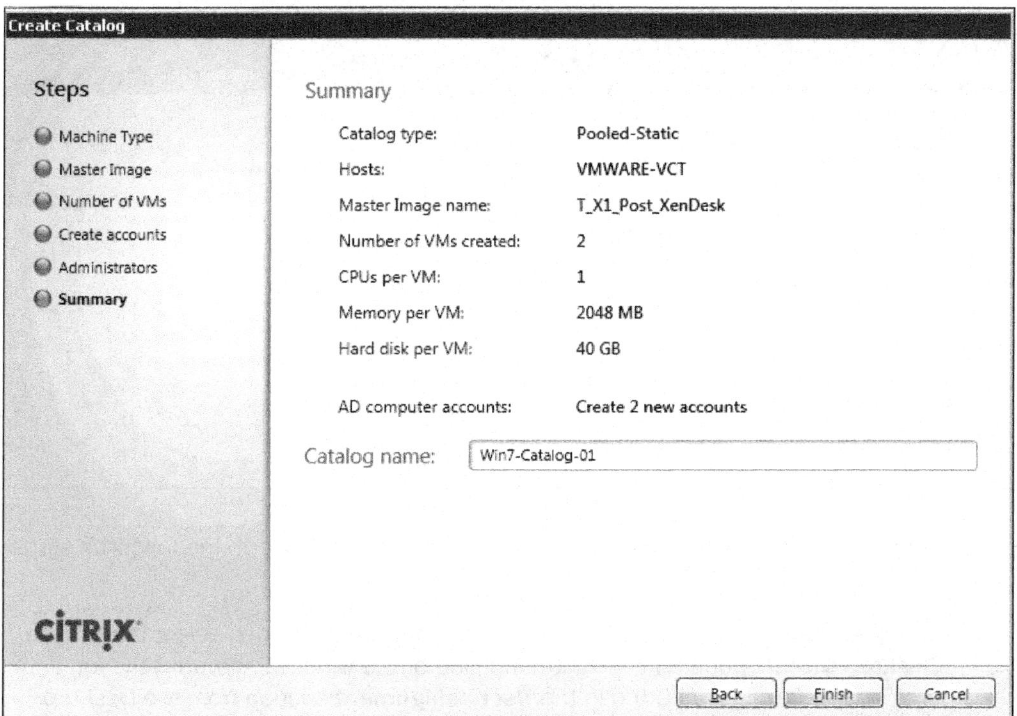

10. To verify that the catalog has been successfully created, click on the **Machines** link in the left-hand side menu.

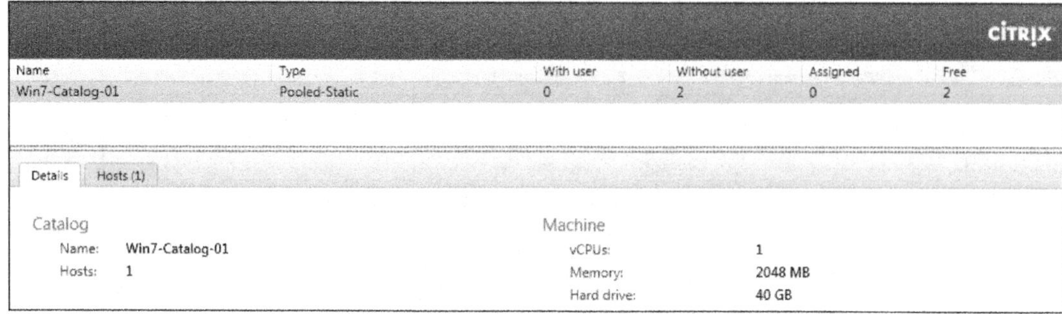


11. To verify that all the required machines have been generated, right-click on the catalog name in the **Machines** section and select the **View machines** option. You will get back the full list of generated desktop instances, as follows:

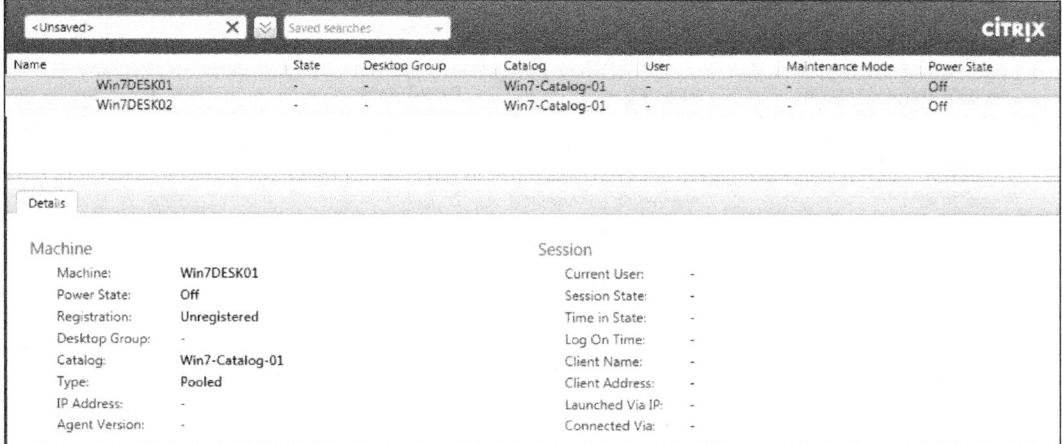


Now we will perform the machine assignment operation phase. Perform the following steps to do so:

1. In the left-hand side menu, click on the **Assignments** link, then select the **Create Desktop Group** option on the right-hand side of the window. Alternatively, you can click on the **Configure** button in the **User assignment** section from the Desktop Studio's main menu, as shown in the following screenshot:

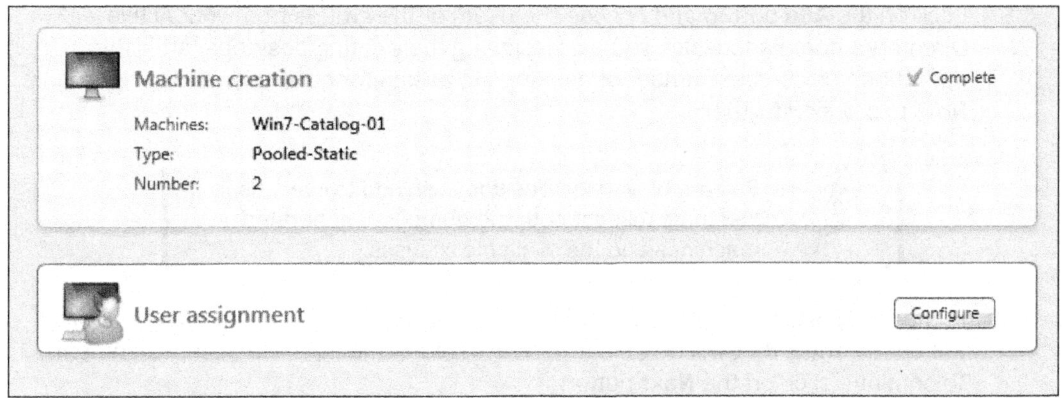


2. Select an existing catalog from the list and then choose the number of machines to assign to the users in the **Add machines** section from the available machine pool(s). After completing this click on **Next**.

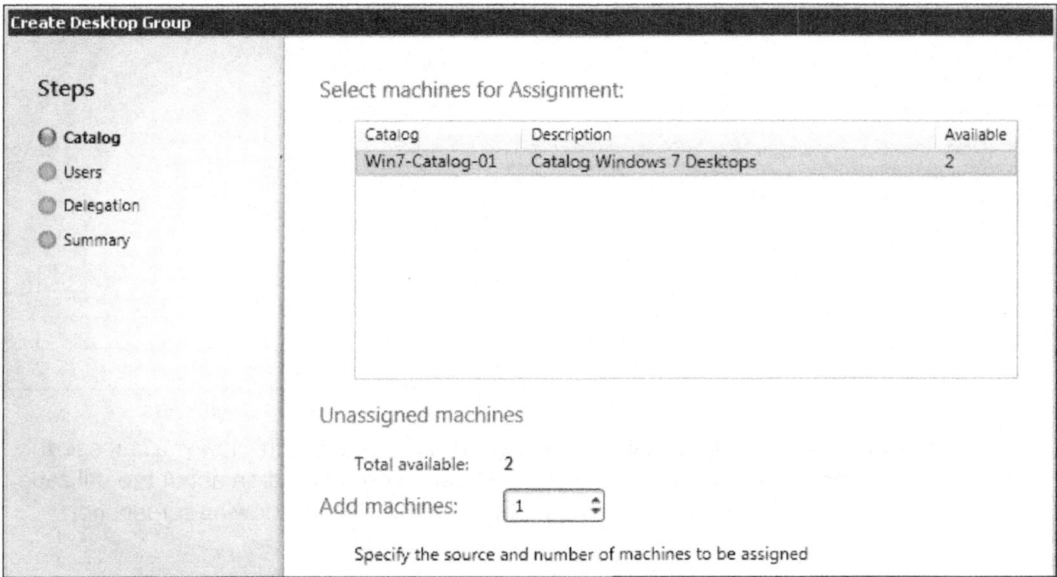

3. Click on the **Add** button and choose the users or the groups from your Active Directory's domain to which you are assigning the existing desktops. After this operation, choose the number of desktops to assign for each user and click on **Next** to proceed further.

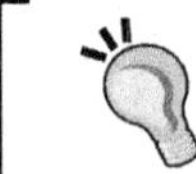

Be careful with the desktop assigned to every user. You must respect both the number of generated machines and the available licenses.

4. In the **Delegation** section, leave checked the configured administration group; this will be the entity that will be able to manage and administer the user assignment. To continue click on the **Next** button.

5. On the **Summary** screen specify **Display name** for the assigned virtual machines, specify **Desktop Group name**, and click on **Finish** to complete the configuration.

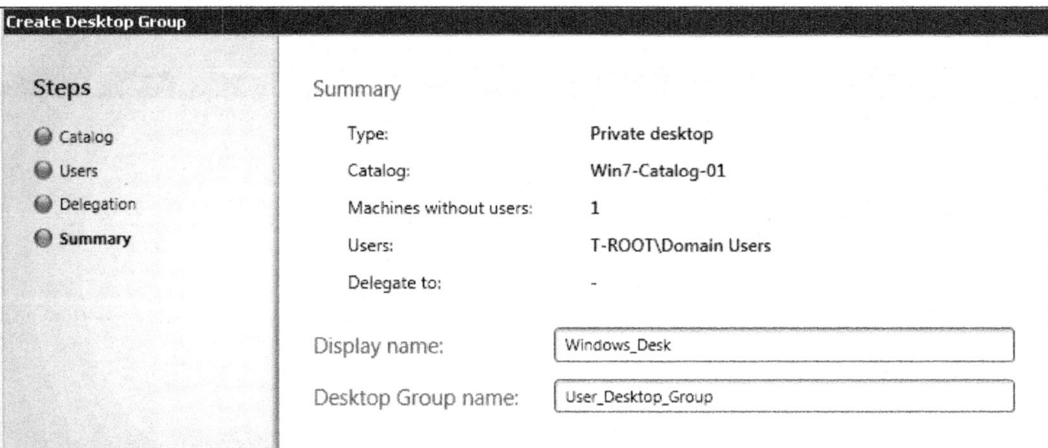


6. Again click on the **Assignments** link in the left-hand side menu. Now you can see the results of the last performed operations, with an information area about the utilization of the assigned desktops (the **Details** tab), as shown in the following screenshot:

| Name | Total desktops | Available | In use | Disconnected | Unregister... | Enabled |
|---|---|---|---|---|---|---|
| User_Desktop_Group | 1 | 1 | 0 | 0 | 0 | Enabled |

Details | Catalogs (1)

Desktop Group

| | |
|---|---|
| Name: | User_Desktop_Group |
| Display Name: | Windows_Desk |
| Description: | |
| Type: | Private desktop |
| Users: | T-ROOT\Domain Users |
| Enabled: | Yes |
| Maintenance mode: | Disabled |

Usage (last 24 hours) Weekdays Weekend

Machines: 1, 0,8, 0,6, 0,4, 0,2, 0

Time: 0.00 3.00 6.00 9.00 12.00 15.00 18.00 21.00 0.00

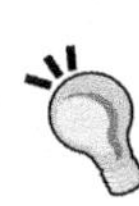

You would have problems with the virtual desktop registration (presence of virtual machines in the unregistered state). Please refer to the following URL, where you can find the Citrix official article to solve this issue:

`http://support.citrix.com/article/CTX126992`

7. Using a configured client device, open a web browser and type in the URL of your Citrix Web Interface in the address bar. Log in with the credentials of one of the users with an assigned desktop. After the login phase, you will receive a screen with the desktop published to that user. Connecting through the PNAgent services site, in the presence of a single resource assigned to the user, this will be directly sent to the Windows logon.

> The virtual desktop icon shown in the preceding screenshot will turn blue in the presence of an available virtual desktop instance, otherwise it will be gray, waiting for an available resource.

8. Click on the published resource or wait for some minutes in order to let Citrix connect to the desktop. Once connected, the desktop instance is available for use.

Now we will manage the power and access management. Perform the following steps to do so:

1. Click on the **Assignments** link located in the left-hand side menu, right-click on the desired desktop group, and select the **Edit Desktop Group** option, as shown in the following screenshot:

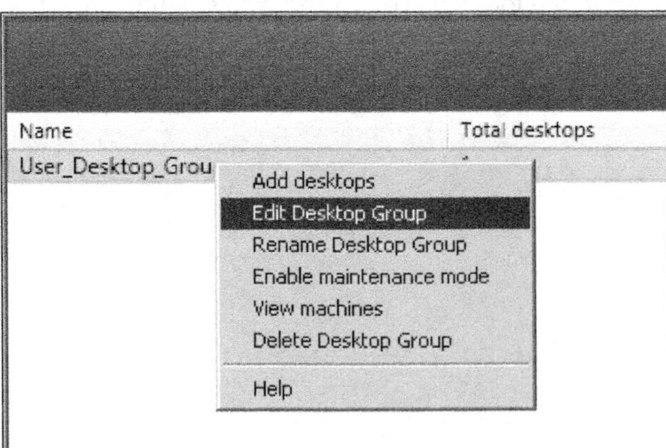

2. Select the **Power management** section, and choose from the **Power on/off machines** area the week period to configure (**Weekdays** or **Weekend**). Click on the **Peak hours** bar to set the time interval to consider as the highest working activities' period (in the screenshot it's configured from 9 a.m. to 6 p.m.):

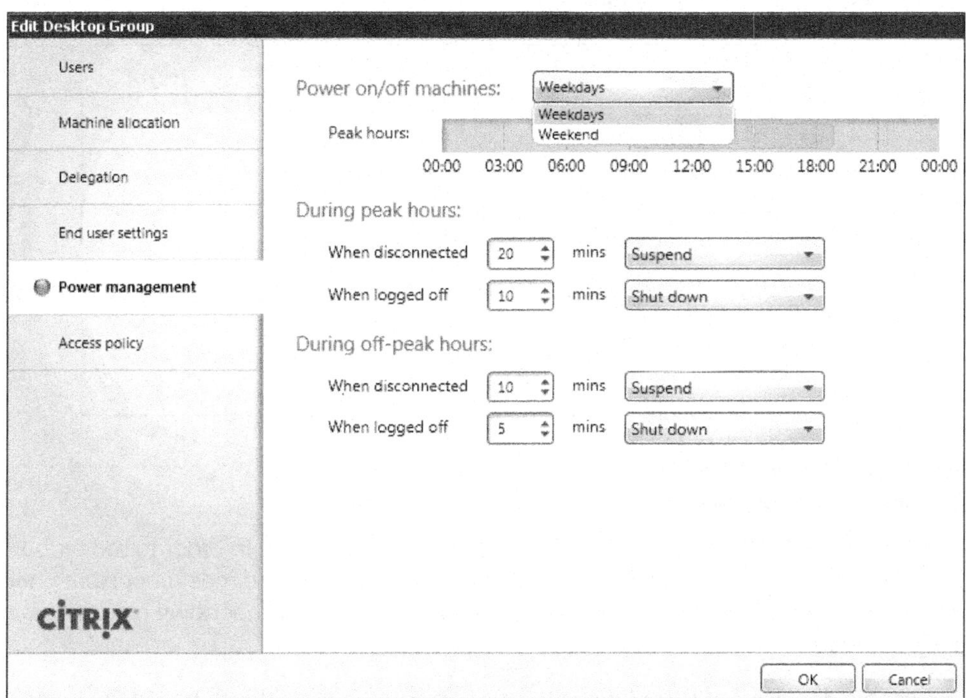

In the presence of more than five virtual machines, if you specify to start up only one virtual desktop, the XenDesktop broker will automatically power up three virtual desktops, in order to prevent a user from having to wait till a virtual desktop is powered up.

3. In the **During peak hours** area, assign a time period in minutes for the two configured conditions (**When disconnected** and **When logged off**), and select the action to execute in case of a condition verification (**Suspend** for the disconnection, and **Suspend** or **Shutdown** for the logoff). Repeat the same steps for the **During off-peak hours** section.

4. Select the **Access policy** section, and choose the desired option(s) in the **Allow the following connection** area (**All connection not through Access Gateway** or **Connections through Access Gateway**). If you want, you can configure personalized filters by flagging the third option, **Connections meeting any of the following filters**, and clicking on the **Add** button to insert the filter rule.

5. Click on the **End user settings** section and configure **Color depth** (**16 colors**, **256 colors**, **High Color**, or **True Color**) and **Time zone** of the clients, then if you want to use an encrypted connection between the client and the XenDesktop farm, check the **Enable Secure ICA** checkbox. After completing this, click on the **OK** button to register all the modifications.

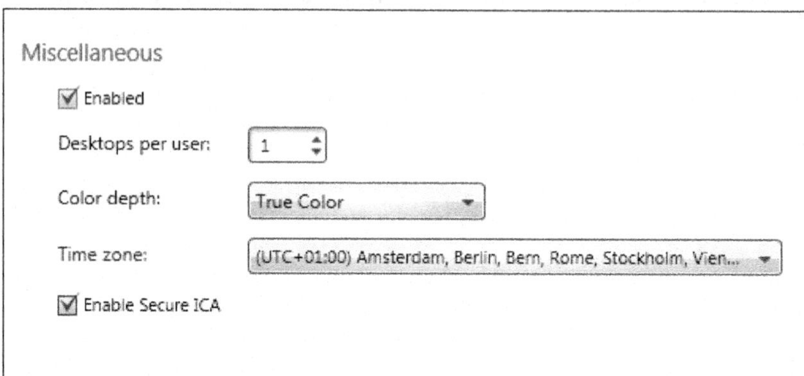


## How it works...

The creation of the XenDesktop catalog is a fundamental operation in order to redistribute the desktop and application resources to the end users devices. The most important choice to make is what kind of machines you want the catalog to create, depending on specific company requirements.

The first usable deployment technique is the pooled catalog type; this is based on a single virtual machine template, which shares the virtual disk for all the generated desktop instances; this way you can reduce the storage utilization, because to every desktop instance only a snapshot of the original disk will be assigned (in order to register all the changes), and not the entire space allocated for the desktop template image disk. The desktop assignment can be performed in two different ways—Random, which means that every user is able to use any machine in the catalog, based only on the logon priority, and Static, which will always assign the same machine instance to the same user, after the first logon is performed.

This catalog type, based on the MCS architecture, has the limitation to use only one NIC for the virtual desktops. To be able to use more network cards, you have to refer to the streamed catalogs (PVS architecture).

You have to take care about where the users save their profile data; no critical information must be saved on the operating system disk, because with this form of catalog, the machines are in a nonpersistent state. This means that after every logoff, reboot, or shutdown activity, all the changes made to the main disk will be lost. To avoid this problem, as previously seen in this book, you can choose to deploy a different kind of catalog, pooled with a personal vDisk. The manner of operating the operating system disk is the same as that of the general pooled catalog, but in this case, additionally you have the persistent disk assigned to the users for their profiles. The personal vDisk is a virtual disk created on the hypervisor's data store; this file will be paired to the quota assigned in the user disk creation procedure according to the size, but it will be generated as a thin virtual disk. In this case, the virtual disk's file size will increase only when the space will actually be used by a user, up to the predefined maximum size.

The third kind of catalog is made up of dedicated machines; in this case, you will move from a nonpersistent machine state to a persistent pool of desktops, which means that any changes made to the operating system disk will be saved and maintained. This solution is necessary when using a noncentralized user profile technique (local profiles), or when it's an alternative in the presence of centralized profiles (Microsoft roaming and/or Citrix Profile Manager).

In the fourth case, we can generate a catalog of an existing virtual machine. By the use of XenDesktop Controller, it will be possible to import already generated virtual machines with a supported hypervisor, and assign them to the domain users. This way to operate is quite different from the general purpose of a VDI infrastructure; you could use this way to manage the existing virtual machines under the central XenDesktop management console, but this is not the standard VDI pooling approach.

Similar to the existing catalog type is the physical pool; in this way, you can attach a physical machine to the XenDesktop management console, permitting access to the virtual resources using the physical devices of the attached machine. For instance, this could be useful when you need to use a CD or DVD recorder in order to create a removable media. By default, XenDesktop does not support the mapping of these kinds of peripherals under a Citrix virtual desktop. By publishing the physical machine to the users, they will be able to perform the previously shown operation.

The last available catalog is the streamed catalog; in this case, the Desktop Controller will create machines starting from an existing desktop, physical or virtual, generated under the Citrix Provisioning Services machine, as explained in *Chapter 1, XenDesktop Installation and Configuration*. For this kind of deployment you have to connect to the PVS server created in *Chapter 1*. Right-click on the configured site, and select the **XenDesktop Setup Wizard...** option from the menu, as shown in the following screenshot:

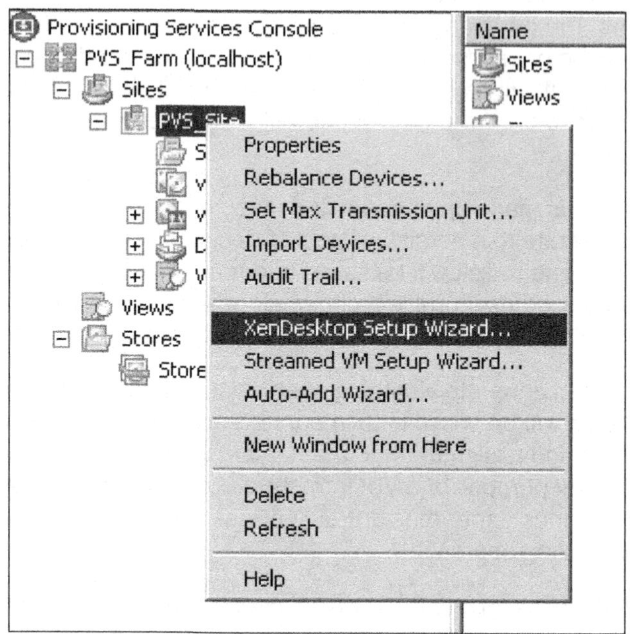


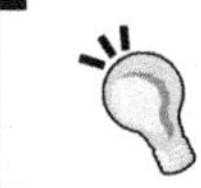

Make sure that you have configured at least one of your PVS configured vDisks in Standard Image access mode, otherwise you will not be able to deploy a XenDesktop Streamed catalog.

You can also create the streamed catalog from the XenDesktop Desktop Studio wizard (typing the PVS server address, specifying the Windows domain to operate, and the type of the existing target device (virtual or physical)). This method should be used only to synchronize Desktop Studio with an already existing streamed catalog created under the PVS server.

For all the supported catalogs, except the existing and physical types, you have to specify the operating system disk size and the way by which you are creating the computer accounts under your Active Directory domain. In this last situation, you can re-use already existing domain accounts or generate them from scratch, choosing the right naming convention for your company.

Be sure to create the computer and the user accounts within an OU included in the Citrix Policies application, as discussed earlier in this book.

An important component contained by the catalog is the desktop group; this object allows you to allocate all or some of the available machines in the catalog to the domain users. You can create more than one desktop group; the only required parameter that you should have available is machine instances to populate the group.

In the next chapter, we'll discuss about another kind of resource group, called application desktop group.

## There's more...

In the previously explained **Machine Creation** section, we've seen how to create desktop instances and how to configure all the related parameters. For some of these desktop pools, however, some more options need to be discussed.

When selecting the **Pooled with personal vDisk** machine type, we need to specify, in the **Number of VMs** section, **Total size of end-user personal vDisk** and **End-user drive letter**, as shown in the following screenshot:

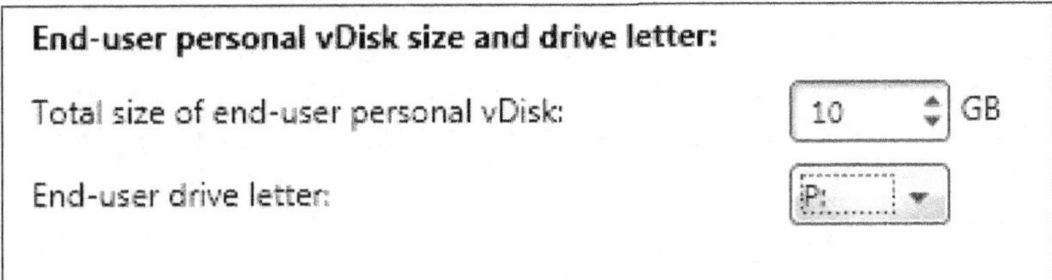

We have explained what the personal vDisk is and how it works in *Chapter 4, User Experience – Planning and Configuring*.

With the **Existing** and **Physical** machine types, you need to select and configure an existing virtual machine and an already installed physical machine, respectively. After importing them you need to configure a computer account for each of them under your Active Directory domain.

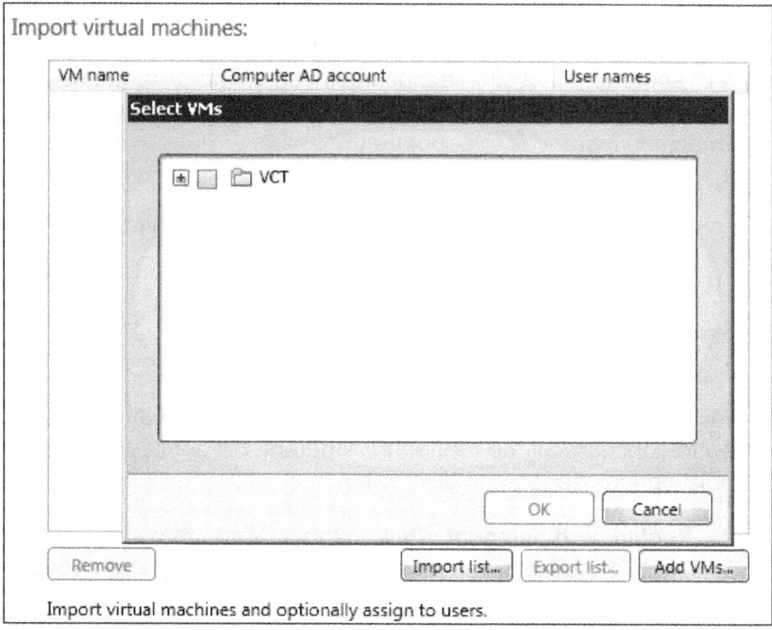


If you have decided to deploy streamed machines in a PVS configuration, you need to configure this from the Provisioning Service console by specifying the **Streamed with personal vDisk** option as **Machine Type**, assigning a name and a description to the catalog, selecting a domain administrative account, and then choosing the vDisk parameters shown in the following screenshot:

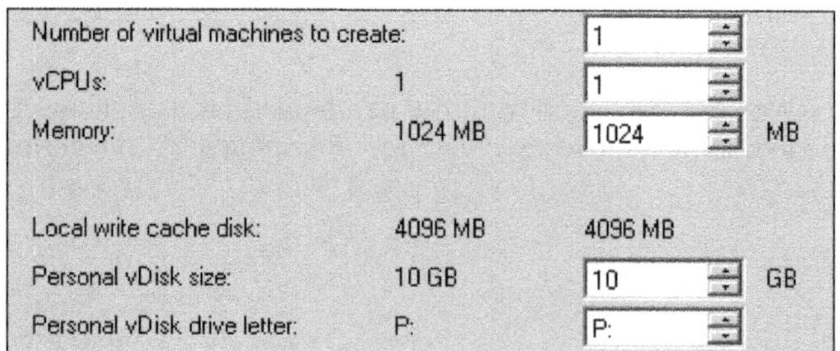


## See also

- The *Configuring the XenDesktop policies* recipe in *Chapter 8, XenDesktop Tuning and Security*

# Modifying an existing machine catalog

Now that we've deployed and configured the machine catalog, we will be able to use and work on the Citrix Desktop Infrastructure. In some cases it could be necessary to modify the configurations, for instance, when it's necessary to add a new desktop to the catalog because of a new colleague in the company. In this recipe we will explain how to modify the machines, their assignments, and the configured catalogs.

## Getting ready

All the operations performed in this recipe are on the already existing objects; so, all you need is to have administrative credentials at two different levels. You have to be the administrator of the involved virtual machine's templates and administrator of your XenDesktop architecture to be able to modify the director configurations.

## How to do it...

Let's start by updating the existing virtual desktop machines. Perform the following steps to do so:

1. Log in to the Windows desktop template, apply all the system and configuration changes you need, and then log off.
2. Connect to your hypervisor machine(s) or management console with administrative credentials on the specific machine, and generate a new snapshot for the virtual machine disk, in order to register the applied modifications.
3. Connect to the Desktop Controller server, click on the **Machines** link in the left-hand side menu, right-click on the desired desktop catalog, and select the **Update machines** option, as shown in the following screenshot:

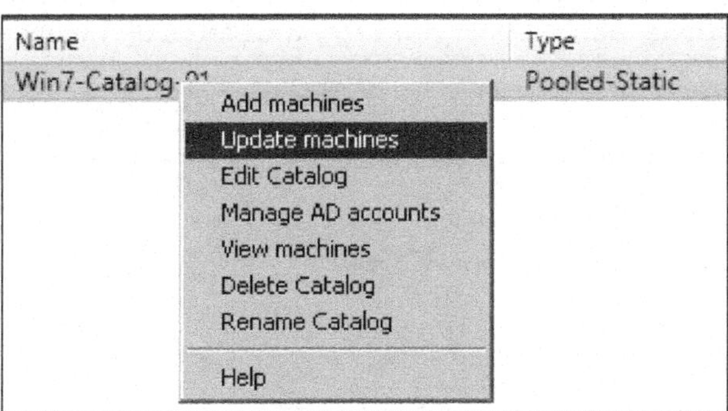


4. Select the desktop group you want to update in the **Overview** section, then click on the **Next** button.

5. Select the most recently created virtual machine's snapshot as your master image, then click on **Next** as shown in the following screenshot:

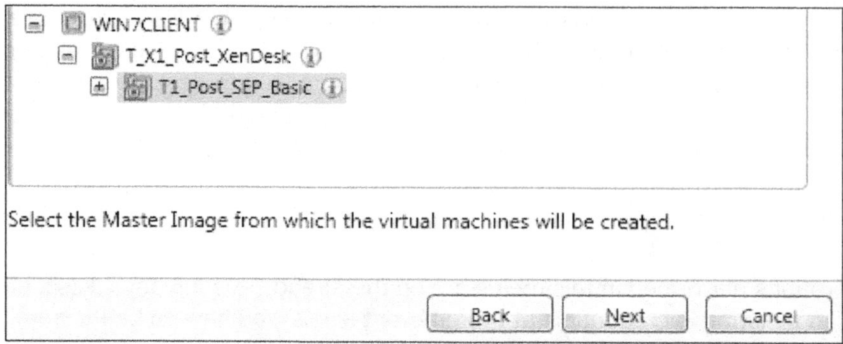


6. In the **Strategy** section select an option from the **Rollout strategy** drop-down menu (**None**, **Send message**, **Restart immediately**, or **Send message then restart after delay**). After selecting it click on the **Next** button.

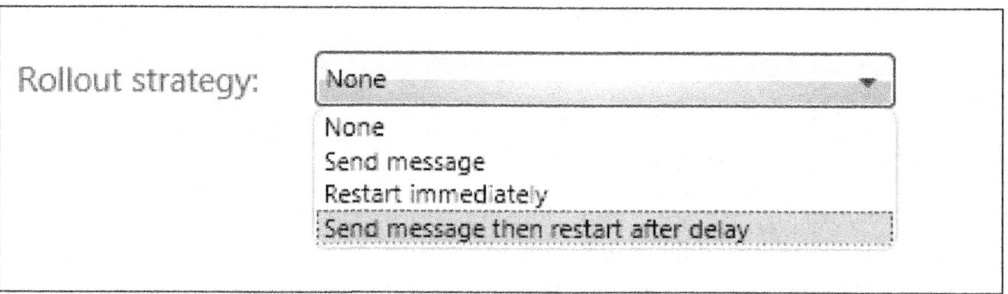


7. After reviewing the information in the **Summary** section, click on **Finish** to complete the machine's update.
8. Click on the **Desktop Studio** link in the left-hand side menu, and in the main panel select the **Actions** tab; here you can verify the status of the updating task.

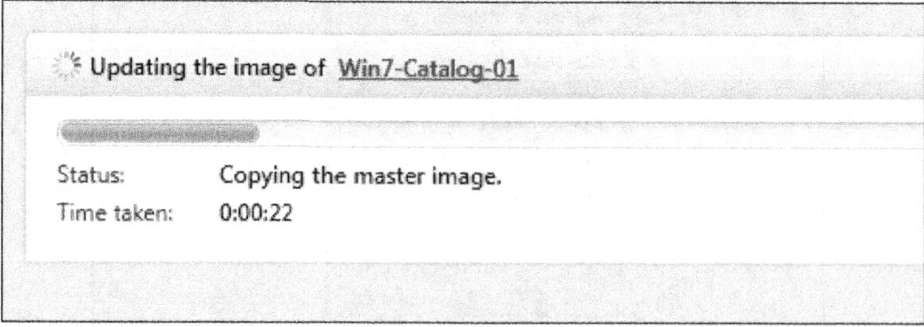


9. After all the operations have been completed, connect to a desktop instance through the Web Interface, and verify if all the updates are available.

Now we will explain how to modify the machine assignment. Perform the following steps:

1. In the left-hand side menu select the **Assignments** link, then right-click on the desktop group that you want to modify, and select the **Edit Desktop Group** option, as shown in the following screenshot:

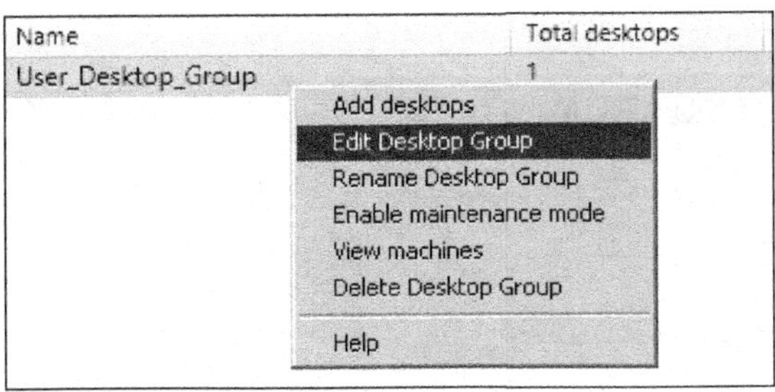


2. Select the **Machine allocation** section, then click on the button in the **Users** field to browse for a configured domain user to which you want to assign the virtual desktop instance.
3. To add more users to the desktop group, in order to let them use any available desktop instance in the pool, click on the **Users** area of the **Edit Desktop Group** window and browse for the desired domain users to add to the group. If you want, you can modify the number of assigned desktops per user. After completing all the configurations, click on the **OK** button.

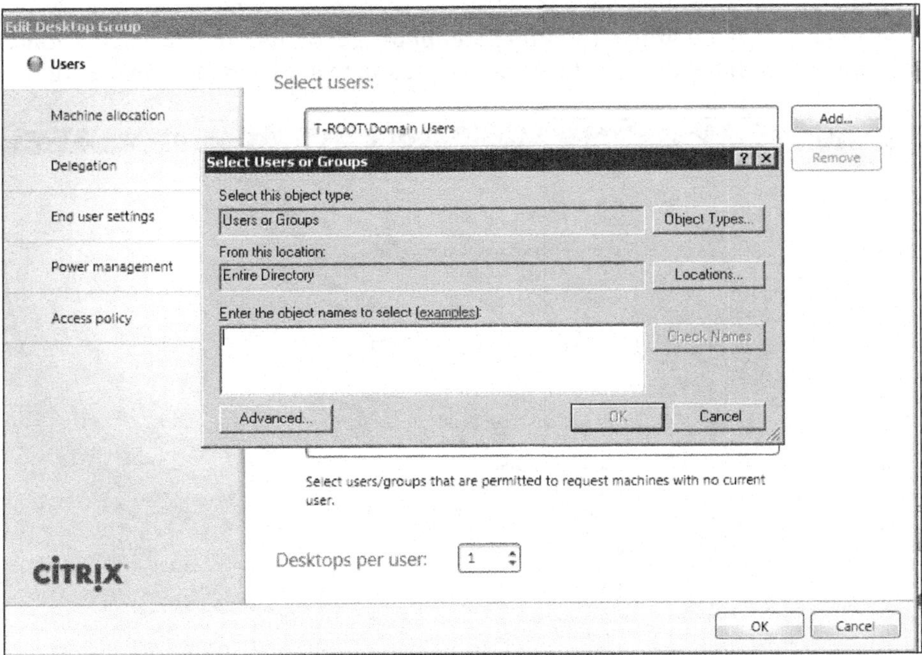

4. You can also configure the machine assignment in another way; in the left-hand side menu, select the **Machines** link, then right-click on the desired machine catalog, and select the **View Machines** option.
5. On the newly opened screen right-click on the virtual machine instance you want to modify, and select the **Change user** option; now you can remove the configured user and add the new virtual machine owner.

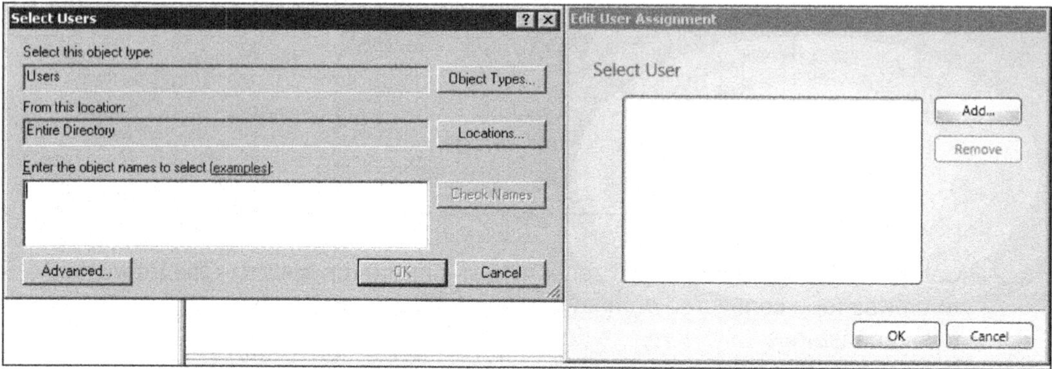


The following are the steps used to add new machines to an existing catalog:

1. In the left-hand side menu select the **Machines** link, right-click on the desired catalog, and click on **Add machines**.
2. In the **Virtual Machines** section select the number of instances you want to add to this catalog. In the **Active Directory computer accounts** section, select **Create new accounts** or **Import accounts**. After completing this, click on the **Next** button.

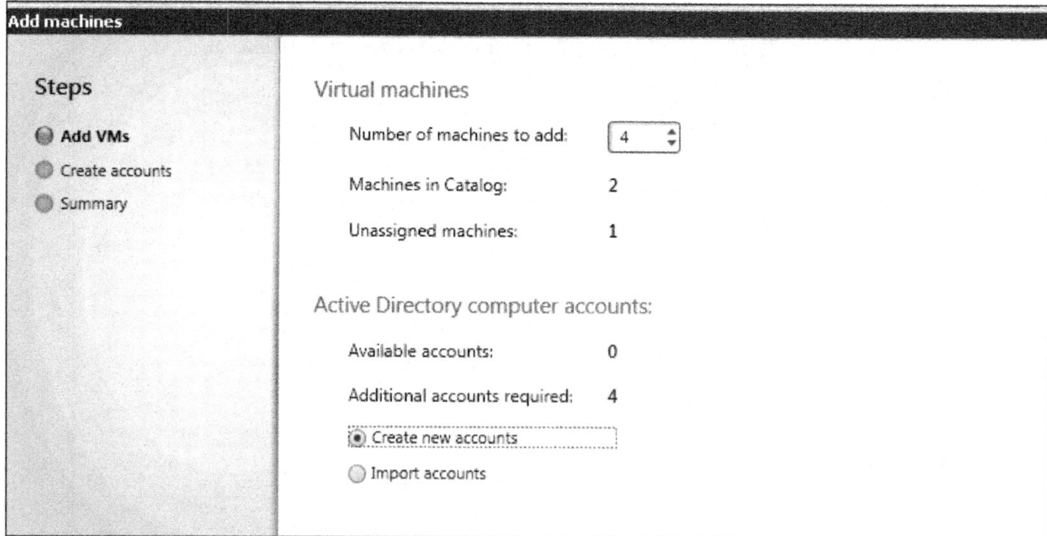

3. If you've chosen to generate new computer accounts, you should consider maintaining the same naming convention used for the other desktop instances in the catalog. If you have decided to import existing accounts, you have to browse for existing Active Directory computer objects, and then select one of the **Reset all account passwords** and **All accounts have the same password** radio buttons. After this click on **Next**, as shown in the following screenshot:

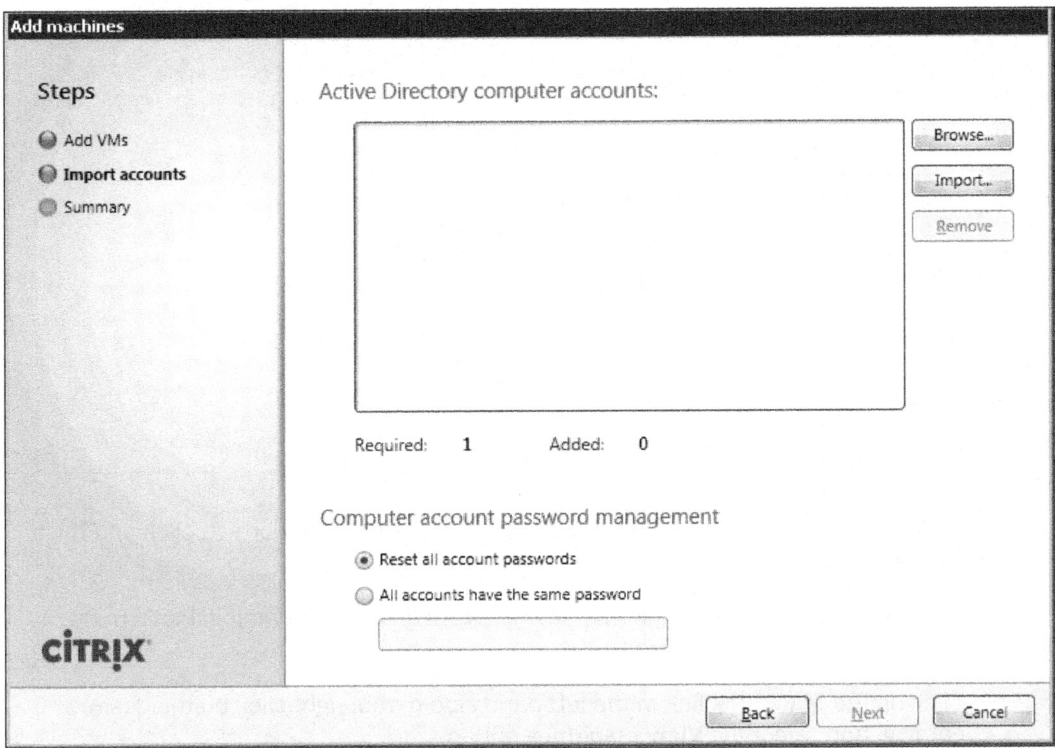


4. On the **Summary** screen, click on the **Finish** button to complete the procedure.
5. After the task has been completed, click on the **Assignments** link from the left-hand side menu, right-click on the desktop group that you want to modify, and select the **Add Desktops** option.

6. Highlight the catalog and insert the number of machines you want to add. This number must be equal to or less than the number of machines listed in the **Available** column. After this click on **Next**.

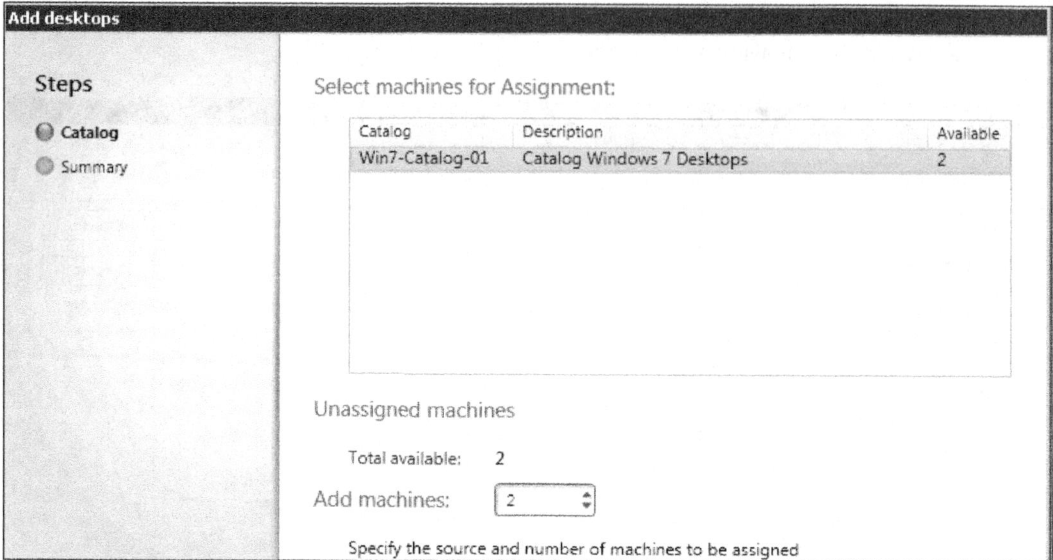


7. If all the information on the **Summary** screen appears to be correct, click on **Finish** to complete.

Now we will see how to remove assigned machines from an existing catalog. Perform the following steps:

1. Click on the **Machines** link in the left-hand side menu, right-click on the desired catalog, and select the **View machines** option.
2. In the machine list, select the machine that you want to remove from the desktop group in the catalog, right-click on it, and select **Enable maintenance mode**. Click on the **Yes** button to confirm the operation.
3. After the operation has been completed (you can verify it by checking the presence of the **Enabled** value in the **Maintenance Mode** column), right-click again on the desktop instance, and select the **Remove from Desktop Group** option. Click on **Yes** to confirm the operation.
4. After completing this, you will find no more information about desktop group assignment for the desktop machine. To completely remove the desktop right-click on it and select the **Delete** option.

5. In the **Machine Deletion Options** section select what kind of operation you want to perform. In case of the **Delete virtual machines** option (which will perform an instance deletion at the hypervisor level), you have to choose whether to reuse the virtual machine instance, or remove the machine from XenDesktop and leave, disable in, or delete from Active Directory. After selecting this, click on the **Next** button.

What do you want to do with the virtual machine?

- ( ) Remove machines from XenDesktop but leave virtual machines intact
- (•) Delete virtual machines

  What do you want to do with the Active Directory computer accounts?

  - ( ) Remember for re-use with other machines
  - ( ) Remove from XenDesktop and leave in Active Directory
  - ( ) Remove from XenDesktop and disable in Active Directory
  - (•) Remove from XenDesktop and delete from Active Directory

6. If all the information on the **Summary** screen is correct, click on **Finish** to complete the task.

To be able to complete this procedure, make sure to force the shutdown of the desired virtual desktop instances before proceeding.

Now we will perform the deletion of a configured XenDesktop catalog. Perform the following steps:

1. Select the **Machines** link in the left-hand side menu, right-click on the right catalog, and select the **View machines** option.
2. Put every desktop instance in the desktop group in the maintenance mode, then repeat the deletion procedures, as seen earlier.
3. After finishing with all the removing activities, return back to the **Machines** section, right-click on the catalog, and select the **Delete Catalog** option.
4. In the **Summary** section of the opened window, click on the **Finish** button to complete the deletion procedure.

## How it works...

The XenDesktop machine catalog is a modifiable entity, which allows you to update or roll back the previously implemented configurations.

In the presence of the MCS architecture, the machines update is, maybe, the most used and important modification task; this procedure is usually executed when modification occurs to the desktop base image template; for instance, software changes that must be applied to all the created desktop instances. This procedure is made up of four main steps; after all the required updates to the machine template have been completed, you have to regenerate a virtual machine snapshot under your hypervisor platform, then update the desktop instances content through the Desktop Studio console starting from this last created snapshot. An important option is the Rollout strategy; with this option, you can choose the correct way to interact with the users in order to complete the regeneration step; so, before restarting the desktop instances that are necessary to effectively apply the changes, you have to decide whether to send a message to the connected users about the required restart, that is, restarting the desktops immediately, or alerting the users and then restarting after a configured delay time.

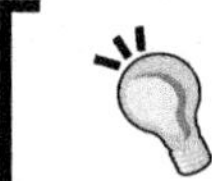

In order to avoid problems when stopping the desktops during the working hours, it should be better to update the machines during the off-peak working hours, and restart the desktops immediately.

You can also add or remove machines from the catalog; these are quite simple operations, which contain all the powerful maintenance tasks of a VDI architecture. In fact, you can add instances simply by selecting the number of desired desktops; the bigger part of this activity has already been performed during the creation and the configuration of the desktop base image template. In the same way, you can remove single desktop instances from the catalog by right-clicking on a particular instance and selecting the appropriate deletion option; in this case, you can choose whether to completely delete a computer account (from both the XenDesktop architecture and Active Directory), or simply to remove its assignment and preserve the desktop instance to be re-used by another user.

## There's more...

In case your users face problems after updating the desktop image, Desktop Studio allows you to roll back to a previous consistent machine state.

In the **Machines** section that we have already used in this chapter, by right-clicking on the desired catalog name, you will have the possibility to use the Rollback machine update command. This will let you choose from previously created restore checkpoints, which are equivalent to every machine's update performed previously.

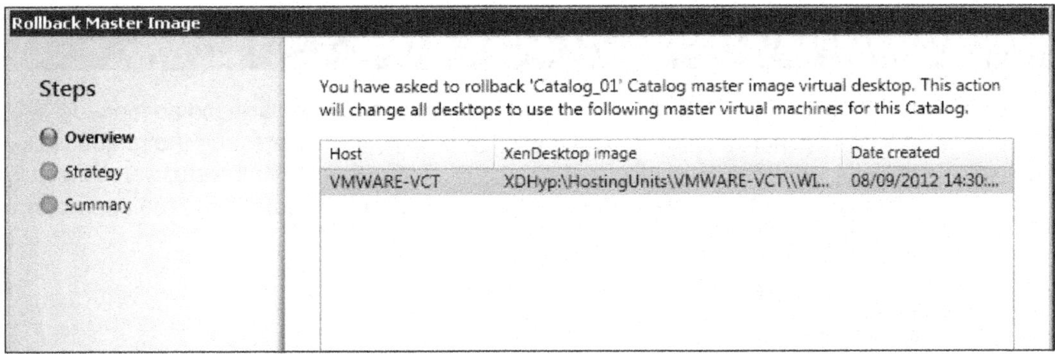


Also, in this case, you need to select a Rollout strategy when stopping the desktop instances to complete the rollback activities; as previously described, you should plan a rollback strategy with a really low impact on the user operations during the working hours.

For the Provisioning Services infrastructures, a rollback activity is managed in a quite different way; the vDisks are based on versions and categories. Every disk has a version number assigned to it and a category (**Access version** of **Maintenance**, **Test**, or **Production**). In case of failure after a disk update, you have the ability to revert a disk from **Production** to **Test** or **Maintenance**; in this way, the previously generated disk version will become the production disk, permitting the virtual machines booting from it after they have been rebooted. This method permits you to easily manage multiple disks versions within your XenDesktop environment.

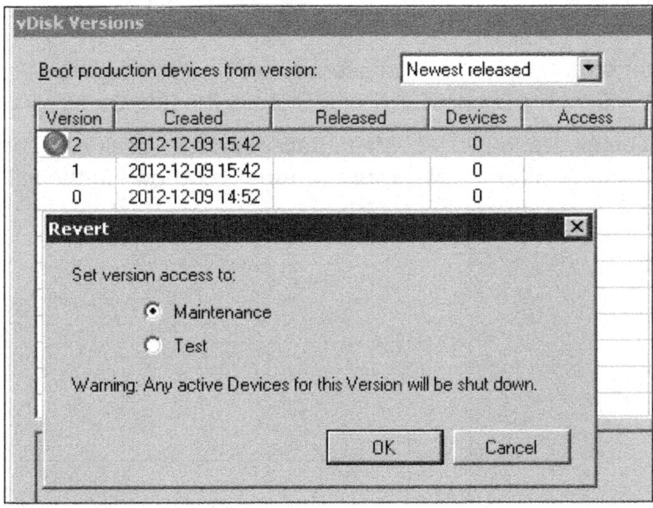


## See also

- The *Managing the Citrix Desktop Controller – broker cmdlets* recipe in *Chapter 9, Working with XenDesktop PowerShell*

# Using Citrix Desktop Director

In the presence of huge VDI architectures, it could be hard to find standard and advanced information about the generated desktop instances, the configured users, and the relations that may occur between these two objects. The Citrix Desktop Director is a useful web console that helps system administrators to easily find information about the status and the operation of the desktop infrastructure.

## Getting ready

To use the Desktop Director, you need an already installed and configured Citrix XenDesktop architecture; because of its necessity to interface with your Active Directory domain, you need to configure and use a username that is able to read your AD structure.

In order to view the generated graphs under the Director console, it's necessary that you have installed Adobe Flash Player 10 or a later version.

## How to do it...

In this recipe we will explain the Citrix Desktop Director platform and how to use it. Perform the following steps:

1. Connect to the XenDesktop Controller machine, then click on **Start** | **All Programs** | **Citrix** | **Desktop Director**.
2. On the login screen type in a valid username and password, specifying the domain on which XenDesktop is operating, and click on the **Log On** button.
3. In the **Machines** section, select **All** as **Category**, then click on one of the available views (**Servers**, **Catalogs**, or **Desktop Groups**), as shown in the following screenshot:

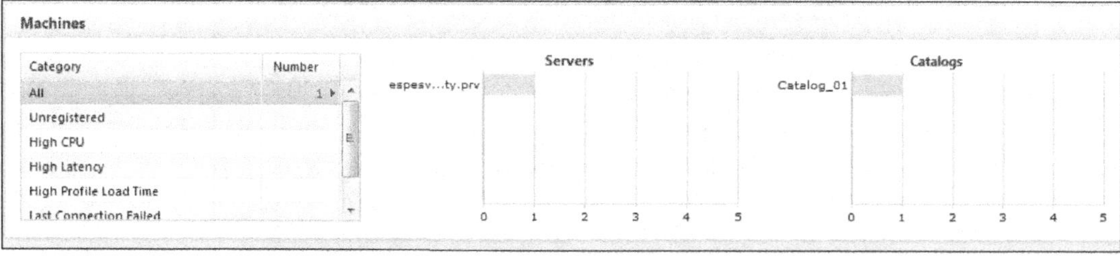


4. In the **Filters** section, apply the required filters to list all the necessary machines by selecting from the list of available filters and conditions. If you want, you can save the generated query by clicking on the **Save** or **Save as...** button.

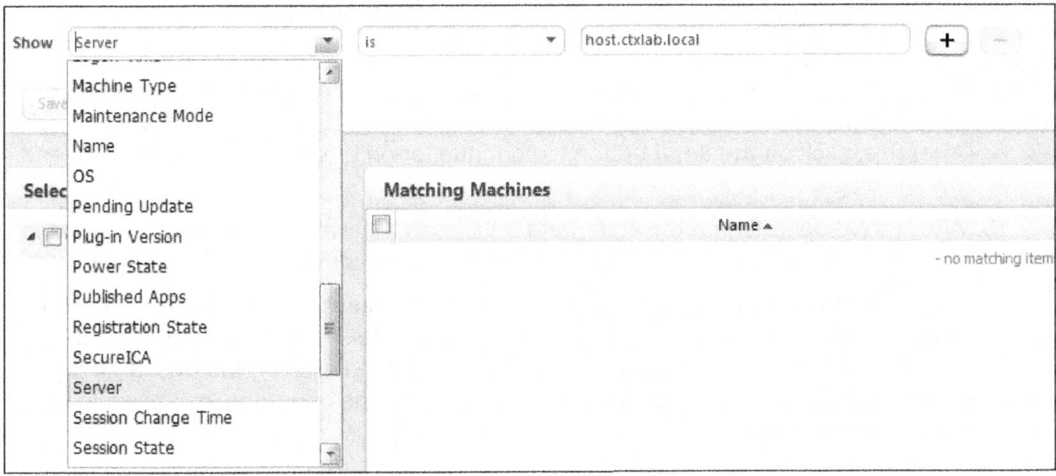


5. In the **Select Columns** area on the left-hand side, you can flag information options to display in the **Matching Machines** area. After you have finished selecting your choice, click on the matching machine name and flag it, as follows:

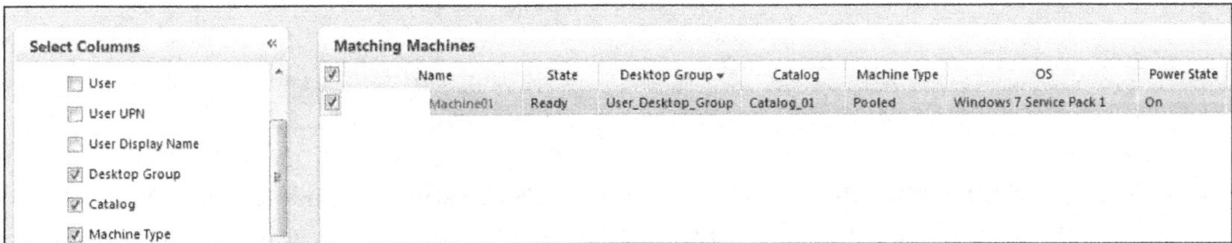


6. To execute one of the available power management operations, click on the **Power Control** button at the end of the page, and select one of the available options (**Restart**, **Force Restart**, **Shut Down**, **Force Shutdown**, **Suspend**, **Resume**, and **Start**).
7. If necessary, you can activate or deactivate the maintenance mode for the selected client directly from the Director web console by clicking on the associated button, as shown in the following screenshot:

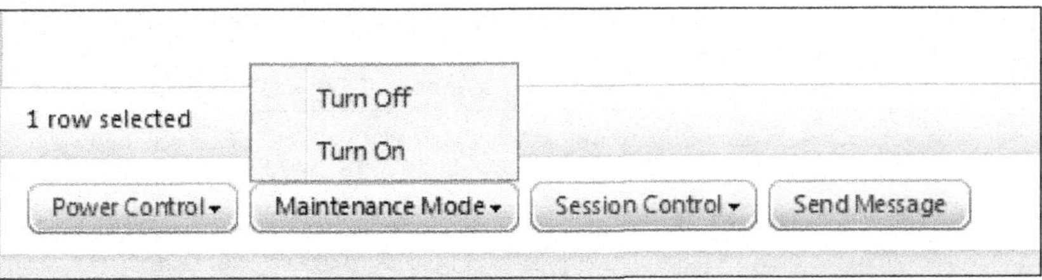

8. To force the logoff of an active session, click on the **Session Control** button and select whether to log off or disconnect the user.
9. Click on the **Send Message** button and populate all the required fields (the **Subject** and **Message** textboxes) to send a communication message to every logged on user. After this, click on the **Send** button to continue, or on the **Cancel** button to not send the message.
10. After you've operated on the command buttons in the web console, flag the desktop that you want to manage, then click on the hyperlink corresponding to its name.
11. In the **Machine Details** section, click on the **Assignment** button and select **Assign User** or **Unassign User** from the drop-down list. In the second case, you have to select the user from the presented list of accounts and click on the **Unassign User** button to proceed, or on the **Cancel** button to abort the operation, as shown in the following screenshot:

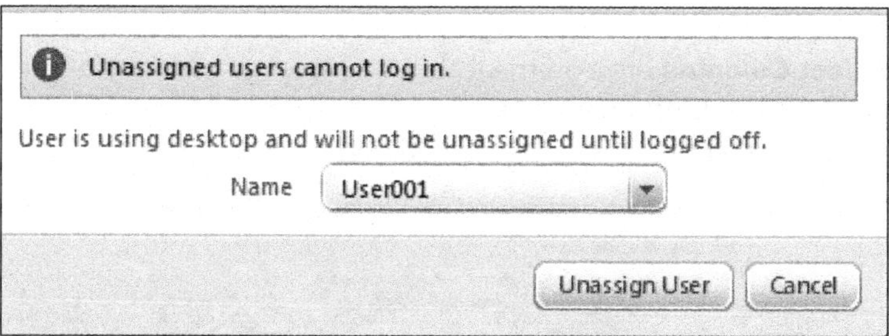


12. In the **Machine Details** section, click on the **Maintenance mode** button to turn on or turn off this modality, as follows:

13. In the **HDX** section click on one of the available categories in order to retrieve statistics and information about the chosen section. You can also retrieve the HDX performance rating assigned to every category.

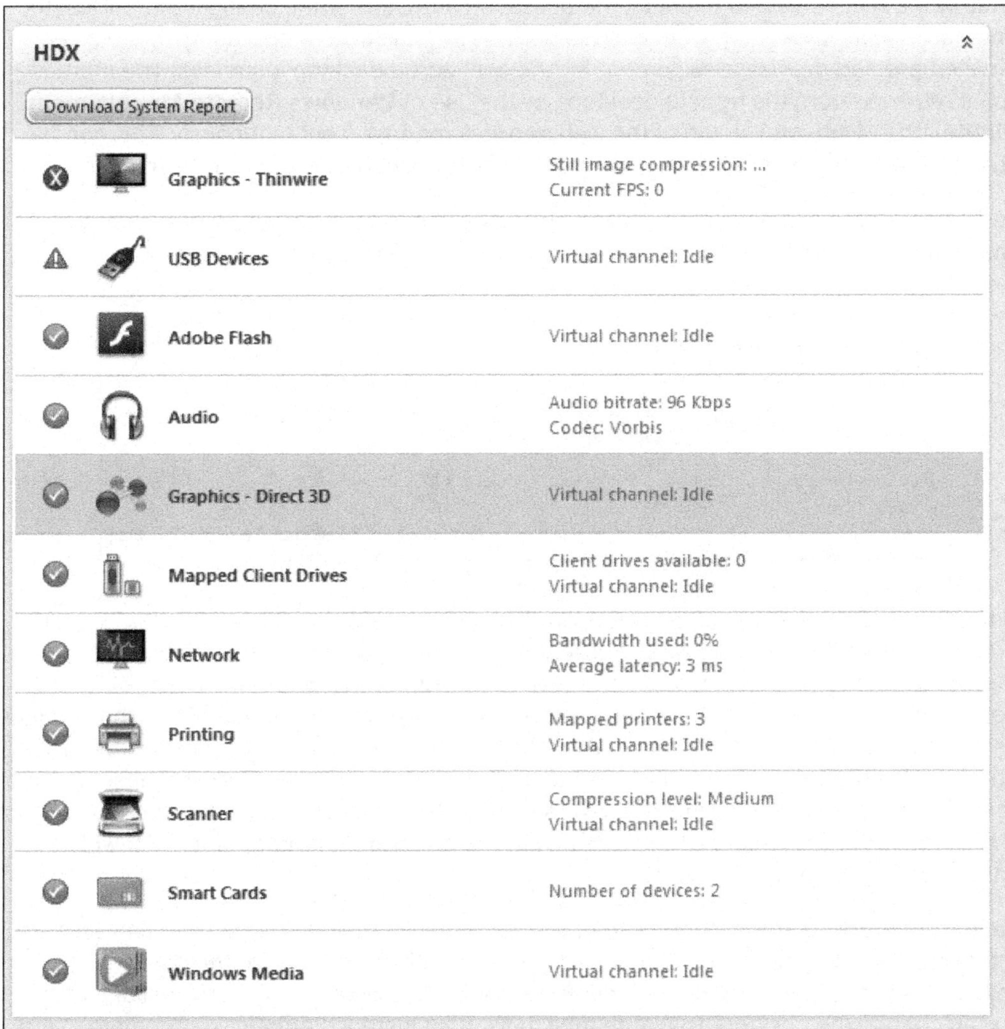


14. Click on **Download System Report** to download the report file about the registered utilization and configuration metrics. This is an XML file type.

## How it works...

The Citrix Desktop Director is a web application that allows system administrators to verify the status of the machines and to check the utilization statistics of the configured XenDesktop infrastructures. The Desktop Director also permits administrators operating on the power management and the user assignment for the configured desktop instances. The metrics can be retrieved from the remote desktops by the use of **Windows Remote Management** (**WinRM**), the Microsoft version of the web services management technology. This can be activated either by the XenDesktop installation process or manually by the administrators.

The Desktop Director portal is composed of a website configured under the IIS Web Server installed on the server that hosts the Desktop Director installation.

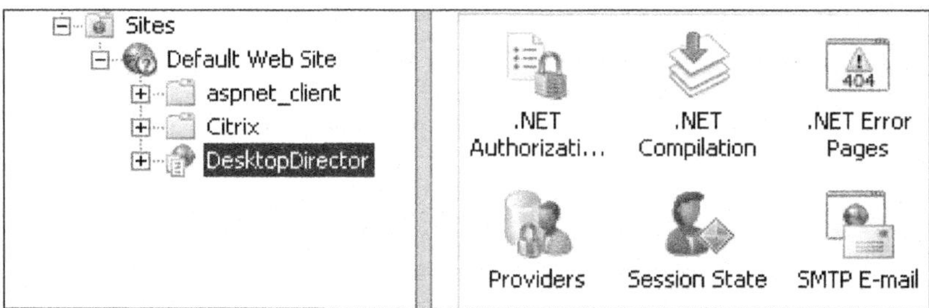


On the first screen after the login phase, the Director presents a summary status of your infrastructure. By this you can verify the real-time resource occupation, or the status of the main parameters of any configured controller server (**Online**, **Service**, **DB Access**). Going deeper in terms of the level of details, you can obtain a lot of information about the configured desktop instances; use the filters to find the specific resources on which you are operating, and apply the information fields you want to get back on the results. Some of these are about the machine identification data (**Name**, **Desktop Group**, **Machine Type**, **OS**), the power state for the machines, or the connection status (**Last connection** and **Endpoint**, from which the connection has been established).

The most interesting part is composed of the set of active operations that you can execute on the desktop machines; for instance, it's possible, in fact, to manage the power state of the machines, thereby being able to restart or power on a desktop when necessary. Moreover, you can change the desktop assignment by moving an instance among your domain users, because of the ability of the Desktop Director to interface with the Active Directory structure in order to manage and retrieve information about the domain users.

To manage the power state of the virtual machines created under a VMware hypervisor, you need to install the VMware tools on the guest machine.

**Reset Personal vDisk** is a powerful task; in case of desktops configured with the personal vDisk technology, the Director will allow you to check the status of the assigned user disks, and if necessary, reset their configuration to the fabric default.

All the collected metrics are exportable from the Desktop Director as a report, in the form of an XML file.

The Citrix Desktop Director is also able to retrieve information about the applications created and published from a XenApp farm.

## There's more...

Another powerful tool offered by the Desktop Director is the ability to remotely control the desktop of a user in order to offer remote assistance to troubleshoot issues. This technique is known as **shadowing**.

You have two ways of enabling the remote control on the desktop machine base image, the first one that has already been seen is selecting the **User Desktop Shadowing** option during the installation phase of the Virtual Desktop Agent. The second one is enabling it in the domain group policies applied to the desktop; the location is **Computer Configuration** | **Policies** | **Administrative Templates** | **System** | **Remote Assistance**, the policy name is **Offer Remote Assistance**, and the value is **Enabled** with the **Allow helpers to remotely control the computer** option selected to give full control over the desktop. Click on the **Show** button in the **Helpers** section and insert a valid username or a group name configured to work as a remote assistant.

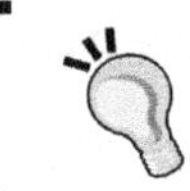

For an easily manageable architecture, you should consider using a group instead of a list of users.

After performing the listed steps, select and click on the desktop instance machine name under the Director console, and in the **Session Details** section, click on the **Shadow** button, as shown in the following screenshot:

On the desktop instance accept the remote control request; from the newly opened windows you will be able to remotely manage the virtual desktop generated from XenDesktop.

> Be sure to have considered all the security aspects of the Remote Management implementation!

## See also

- The *Configuring advanced user experience - HDX 3D Pro* recipe in *Chapter 4, User Experience - Planning and Configuring*

# Configuring printers

To give the users the feeling of working on a virtual system as near as possible to a standard physical workstation, you have to furnish all the peripherals available in a non-VDI architecture. One of these is given by the configuration and use of printers. With the latest release of XenDesktop, Citrix has implemented a set of improvements to manage and choose the quality of the launched prints. In this recipe we're going to discuss about these kind of policies.

## Getting ready

Depending on your company requirements, you could have a lot of different network printers to configure within the virtual desktop environment. In this case, a prerequisite (and also a best practice) is configuring a print server on which you want to install all the devices, and then deploying them through the use of Microsoft domain GPO.

In case of a single printer for the entire organization, you can install the required drivers for the printer using which the users will do their jobs on the desktop base image template; as you've already seen, by this way, you will propagate the printer mapping to all the desktop instances in the pool.

## How to do it...

In this recipe we will perform the configuration of the printers within the XenDesktop environment. Perform the following steps to do so:

1. Connect to the Desktop Controller machine and run the Desktop Studio by clicking on **Start** | **All Programs** | **Citrix** | **Desktop Studio**.

2. In the left-hand side menu expand the **HDX Policy** link and select the **Users** category, as shown in the following screenshot:

3. Click on the **New...** button in the **Users** menu area, enter a name for the new policy, choosing it to match the printer policy configuration, optionally write a description for the policy, and click on the **Next** button.

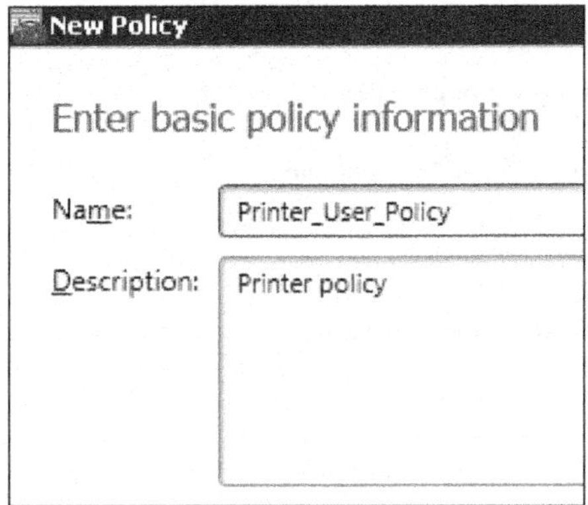


4. In the **Categories** list, select the **Printing** section and choose whether and how you are going to configure the following policies:
    - **Client printer redirection**
    - **Default printer**
    - **Printer auto-creation event log preference**
    - **Session printers**
    - **Wait for printers to be created (desktop)**

5. In the **Printing** section select the **Client Printers** subsection and choose whether and how you are going to configure the following policies:
    - **Auto-create client printers**
    - **Auto-create generic universal printer**
    - **Client printer names**
    - **Direct connections to print servers**
    - **Printer driver mapping and compatibility**
    - **Printer properties retention**
    - **Retained and restored client printers**

    The settings discussed for the **Client Printers** subsection are shown in the following screenshot:

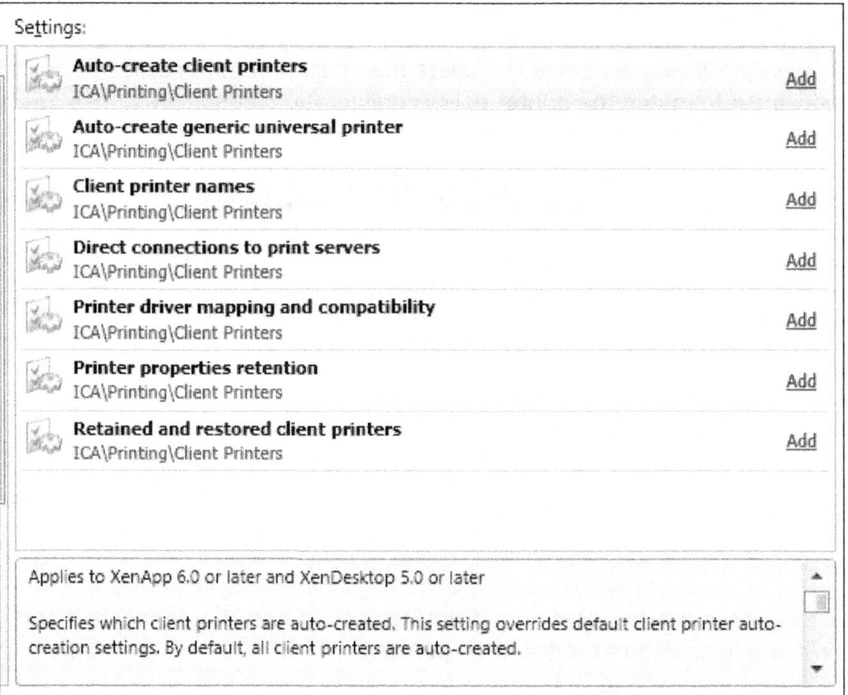


6. In the **Printing** section select the **Drivers** subsection and choose whether and how you are going to configure the following policies:
    - **Automatic installation of in-box printer drivers**
    - **Universal driver preference**
    - **Universal print driver usage**

The settings discussed for the **Drivers** subsection are shown in the following screenshot:

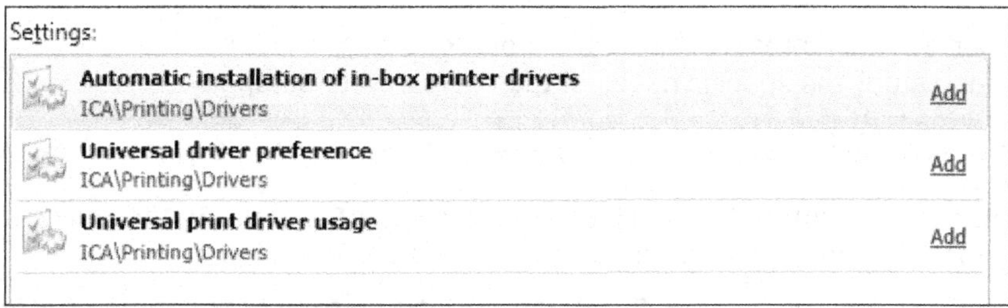


7. In the **Printing** section select the **Universal Printing** subsection and choose whether and how you are going to configure the following policies:
    - **Universal printing EMF processing mode**
    - **Universal printing image compression limit**
    - **Universal printing optimization defaults**
    - **Universal printing preview preference**
    - **Universal printing print quality limit**

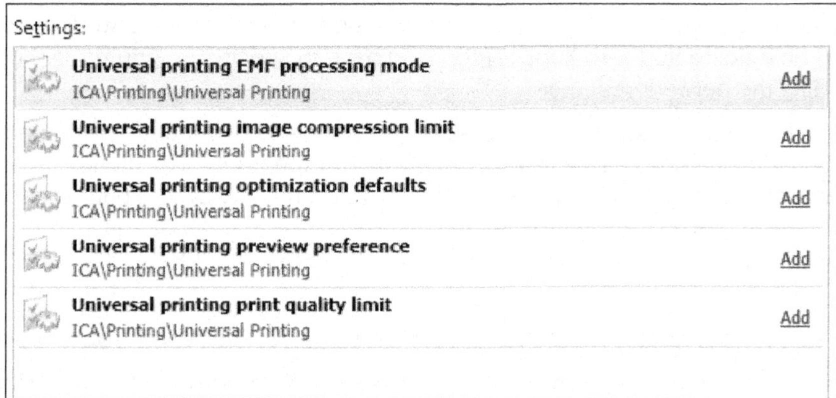


8. After completing the configurations click on the **Next** button.
9. For the moment, do not apply any kind of filter; so on the filters screen, click on the **Next** button to proceed.
10. After completing all the steps click on the **Create** button to generate the printer policy group.

Later in this book, we will discuss, in a deeper way, about the configuration of the most important machine and user XenDesktop policies.

## How it works...

The printer configuration process is a quite complex activity, which requires you to deeply understand and study the specific needs of the users in your company.

The following is an explanation about the main configuration policies in the **Printing** section:

- **Client printer redirection**: (Values are **Allowed** or **Prohibited**) **Allowed** by default, this policy permits you to redirect to a server the client printer mapping.
- **Default printer**: (Values are **Set default printer to the client's main printer** or **Do not adjust the user's default printer**) With this policy you can configure the way by which you have chosen the default user printer. The first option uses the current configured printer as a default device, the second instead loads the printer from the user profile, based on the domain policies and the loaded printer driver. This technique is usually used for the proximity printing approach, the technique of publishing the closer network printer to a user.
- **Printer auto-creation event log preference**: (Values are **Log errors and warnings**, **Log errors only**, or **Do not log errors or warnings**) This policy allows you to configure the level of logging for the printer autocreation activities. You can decide to log no errors and warnings, or errors, or both.
- **Session printers**: This policy permits you to add the list of the network printers, which can be autocreated with XenDesktop. You have to specify the printer UNC path when adding the network resource.
- **Wait for printers to be created (desktop)**: (Values are **Enabled** or **Disabled**) With this parameter you can decide to wait or not wait for the printer creation process when connecting with your user profile. You can't apply this policy to a published resource.

The following is an explanation about the configuration policies in the subsections of the **Printing** section:

- The following are the configuration policies for the **Client Printers** subsection:
    - **Auto-create client printers**: (Values are **Auto-create all client printers**, **Auto-create local (non-network) client printers only**, **Auto-create the client's default printer only**, and **Do not auto-create client printers**) With this policy you can decide whether to autocreate all the listed categories by default, or one of them, including local attached printers. You can also configure to not automatically operate on the creation of the printers.
    - **Auto-create generic universal printer**: (Values are **Enabled** or **Disabled**) With this policy you can decide whether or not to use the Citrix Universal Printer object. As explained earlier, this could be a useful option when trying to avoid printer and drivers fragmentation, because of the use of a single generic printing driver.

- **Client printer names**: (Values are **Standard printer names** or **Legacy printer names**) This policy permits you to choose the naming convention to use in phase of generic printer creation. You should always use the standard naming convention, and only use the other option when a compatibility with old Citrix versions is required.
- **Direct connections to print servers**: (Values are **Enabled** or **Disabled**) With this configuration, you can permit the users to directly access the network printer in order to make printing faster. This is only available in case of LAN connections. In case of WAN printer mappings you have to use a nondirect connection.
- **Printer driver mapping and compatibility**: With this policy you can import a set of printer drivers on which you are operating to define compatibility and substitutions for the client drivers. This means that you can define a rule to override customized settings, in order to standardize the printing architecture.
- **Printer properties retention**: (Values are **Held in profile only if not saved on the client**, **Retained in user profile only**, **Saved on the client device only**, or **Do not retain printer properties**) This policy lets you decide whether and where you are saving the configured printer settings. You should consider saving these settings in the user profile, especially in the presence of a centralized profile manager and a nonpersistent desktop machine.
- **Retained and restored client printers**: (Values are **Allowed** or **Prohibited**) In case of customized printer configurations, you can have the ability of maintaining these settings and restoring them in case of configuration problems.

- The following are the configuration policies for the **Drivers** subsection:
    - **Automatic installation of in-box printer drivers**: (Values—**Enabled** or **Disabled**) This policy permits or blocks the automatic installation of the drivers that are collected in the form of packages and deployed through the use of the Citrix Receiver plugin component called PnPUtil.
    - **Universal driver preference**: By the use of this policy you can choose the order of use of the Universal Printer drivers, such as PCL in its different versions, XPS or PS.
    - **Universal print driver usage**: (Values are **Use only printer model specific drivers**, **Use universal printing only**, **Use universal printing only if requested driver is unavailable**, or **Use printer model specific drivers only if universal printing is unavailable**) This policy manages the situations in which you are using the Universal Printer driver. By default, this driver is used only when a specific driver is not available.

- The following are the configuration policies for the **Universal Printing** subsection:
  - **Universal printing image compression limit**: (Values are **No compression - Best quality (lossless compression)**, **High quality**, **Standard quality**, or **Reduced quality (maximum compression)**) This is an important policy that allows you to configure the quality level of the printed images, deciding to give precedence to the quality level or to the compression level.
  - **Universal printing print quality limit**: (Values are **No limit**, **Draft (150 DPI)**, **Low Resolution (300 DPI)**, **Medium Resolution (600 DPI)**, or **High Resolution (1200 DPI)**) The configuration of this policy permits you to force the users to print documents at the preconfigured resolution.

When possible, you should only use the generic Citrix Universal Printer driver instead of many different printer drivers, and avoid automatically installing the printer drivers on the desktop instances, in order to reduce the troubleshooting activities in case of issues. If you do not have client printers, consider using unified printer drivers and try to consolidate the printer types in your company, if possible.

## There's more...

In the wide range of the Citrix free tools, you can find the Citrix StressPrinters software, which allows you to simulate multiple sessions using a configured printer driver, in order to test the capability of using the driver and its response in terms of physical and virtual resources usage.

You can download the ZIP file archive from `http://support.citrix.com/article/CTX109374`.

Run the correct version for your infrastructure by double-clicking on the 32-bit or 64-bit executable file. The software will let you select the driver on which you want to perform the load tests. You have to specify the printer name and port (for instance, LPT1 for a local printer or the configured IP address for a network device), the number of concurrent events, and the number of times you will repeat the tests. If you want, you can run the test in verbose mode by checking the appropriate checkbox. By clicking on the **Save** button you can archive, in a text file, the configured tests to be loaded and run them again afterwards. To execute the tests you have to click on the **Run** button, as shown in the following screenshot:

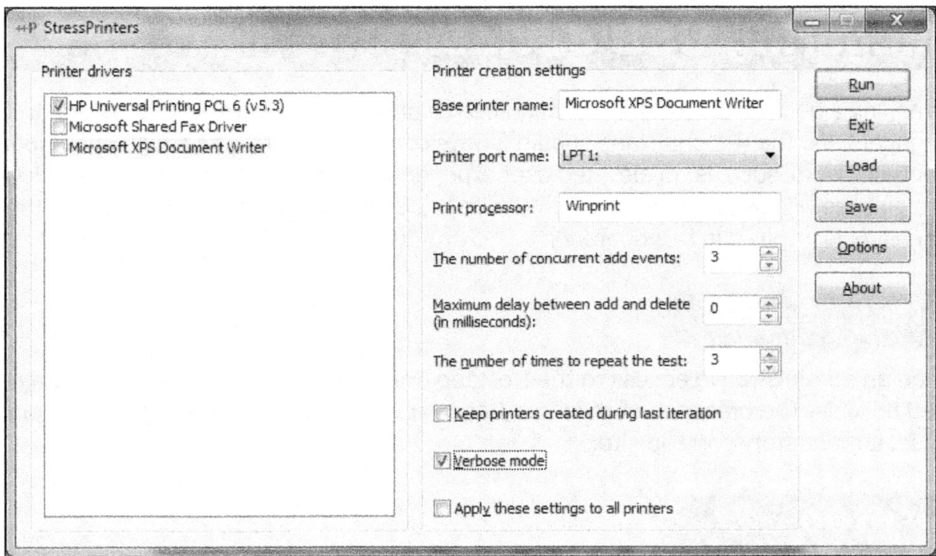


After completing this you'll receive back a summary of the executed tests; if you want, you can save the related log file by clicking on the **Save log** button.

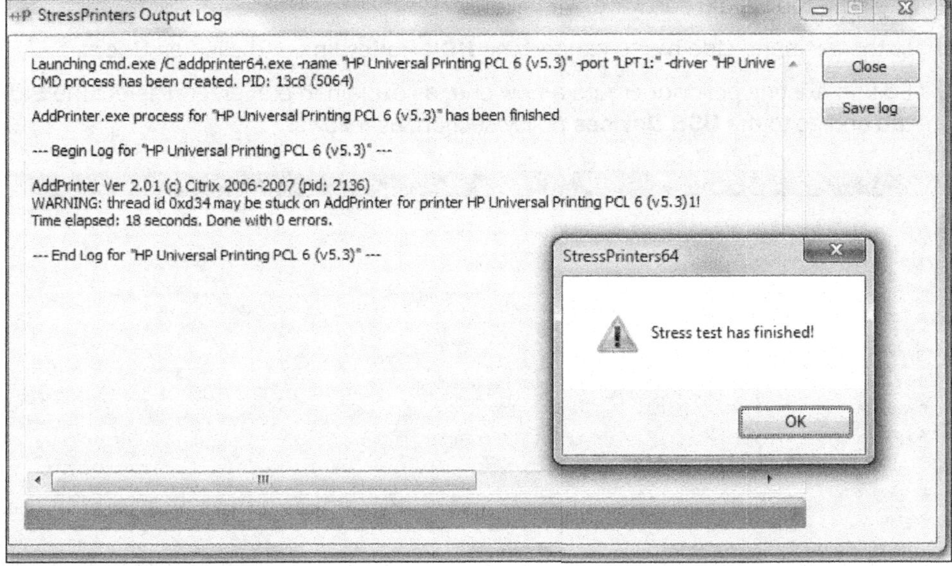


## See also

- The *Configuring the XenDesktop policies* recipe in *Chapter 8, XenDesktop Tuning and Security*

# Configuring USB devices

When making a decision about the migration from a physical to a virtual desktop infrastructure, the managers and the IT technicians should always consider maintaining a high operational level for their users, such as an elevated user experience, or the ability to use external devices. In this recipe we will discuss how to use and map the USB devices, also with an eye on the security aspects involved in this operation.

## Getting ready

You need an administrative access to the Desktop Controller machine in order to configure the required policies. The presence of the Citrix Receiver on the desktop base image template is, of course, a mandatory prerequisite.

## How to do it...

In this recipe we will explain how to configure the use of the physical USB devices within the Citrix XenDesktop virtual environment. Perform the following steps:

1. Connect to the Citrix broker machine, click on **Start** | **All Programs** | **Citrix**, and run the Desktop Studio software.
2. In the left-hand side menu expand the **HDX Policy** link and click on **Users**.
3. Edit an existing policy or create a new one, as explained earlier, and select the **Settings** tab and go to the **USB Devices** policy section, as follows:

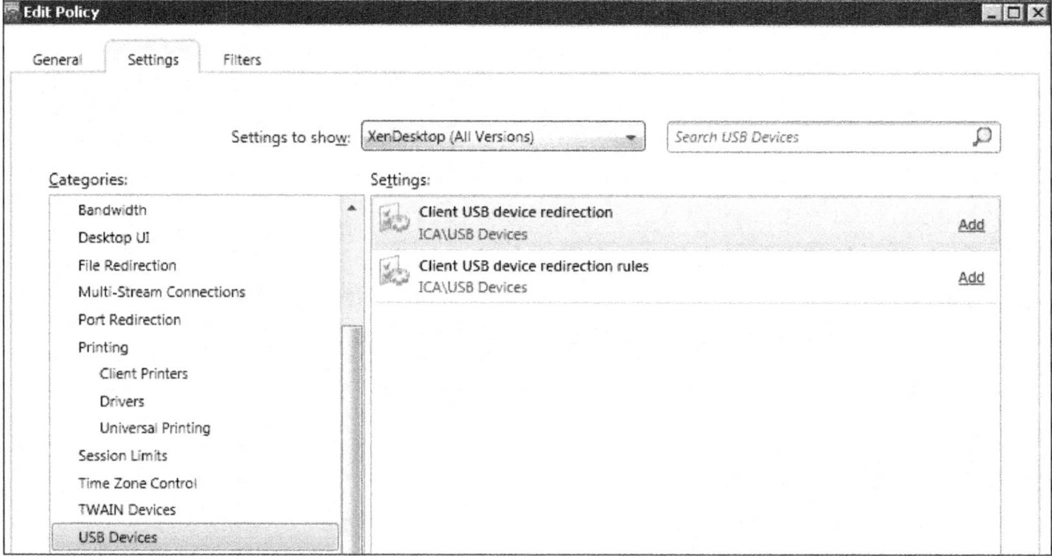

4. Edit the **Client USB device redirection** policy, by choosing to allow or prohibit the mappings of the USB devices. After selecting, click on the **OK** button.
5. Connect to one of the desktop instances, and in the Citrix Receiver menu bar, click on the **Preferences** tab, as shown in the following screenshot:

6. Select the **File Access** section, and decide which type of access to the USB device, you want to give the virtual desktop (**No access**, **Read only**, **Read and write**, or **Ask me each time**). After selecting this, click on the **OK** button, as shown in the following screenshot:

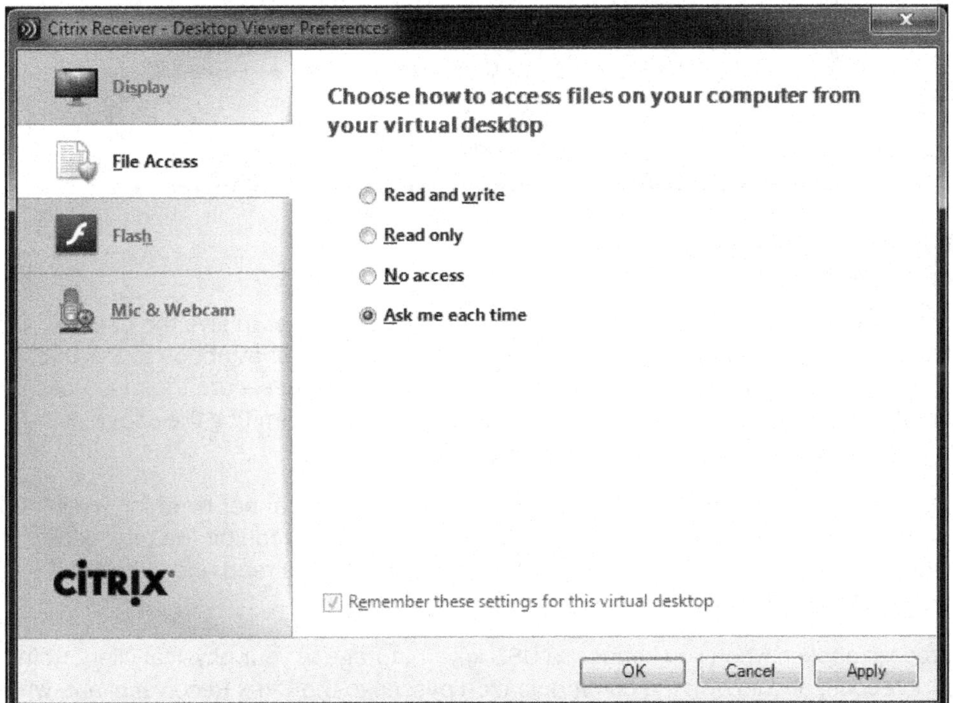

7. Attach a USB disk to your physical client to test the ability of the Citrix Desktop to see and interact with it.

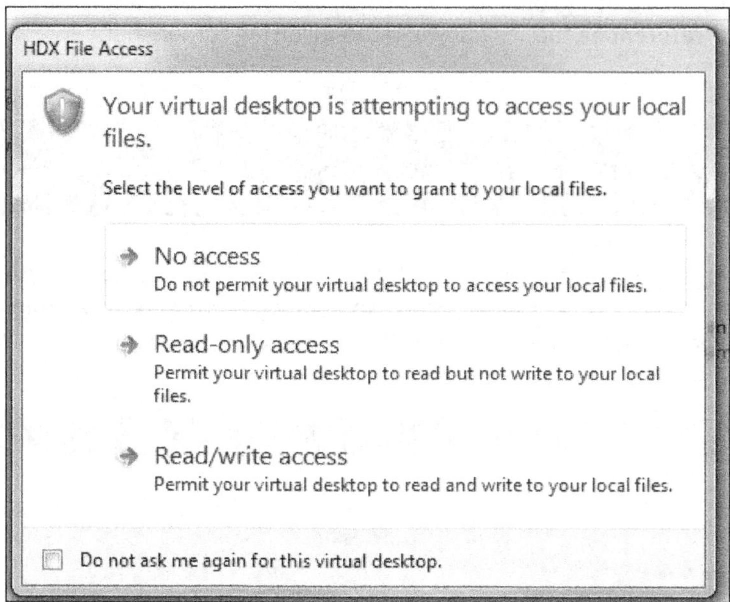


## How it works...

With the USB devices policies, administrators can decide whether to give the user the possibility of mounting and using external devices, with particular attention to the USB mass storage devices. As explained later in this chapter, you can secure the resources in your infrastructure by implementing a kind of device control, limiting the usage and the access only to the configured USB peripherals.

After the configuration of the policies, you have to choose the manner by which a desktop instance can access data on a mounted USB device; you could prohibit the total access to the resource, allowing a basic read-only access, or giving the full read and write privileges to fully operate on the available data.

This process applies when you connect a USB key or storage to your physical client (thin client, notebook, and so on); the communication passes to the Citrix Receiver client, which performs a check on the applied system policies, thereby deciding if it will permit you to view the content of the devices.

## There's more...

The second USB devices policy (**Client USB device redirection rules**) permits you to implement a filter based on the model of the USB product you're going to mount on your virtual desktop; this means that you can allow or deny the use of a specific USB disk, based on hardware parameters such as **Vendor ID** (**VID**), **Product ID** (**PID**), or **Release ID** (**REL**).

To create a rule, edit the discussed policy, and click on the **New** button to create a rule, or click on **Edit** to modify an existing one.

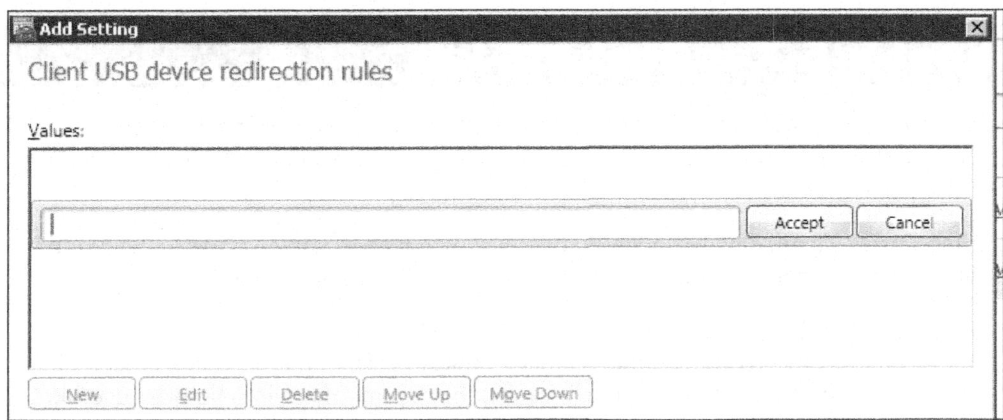


The filtering rule must be generated by using the following parameters:

*[Allow/Deny] : [Category] = [Category Code]*

In the Category section, you have to use one of the following parameters:

- **VID**: The Vendor ID for the USB device
- **PID**: The Product ID for the USB device
- **REL**: The Release ID for the USB device
- **Class**: The category to which the USB device belongs
- **Subclass**: The subcategory part of the Class earlier described
- **Prot**: The communication protocol used by the device

The following is an example of a configured USB device rule:

```
Allow: Class=08 SubClass=03 # Mass storage devices
```

Please refer to the USB corporation (`http://www.usb.org/home`) to find all the required information about the Vendor and Product IDs of the USB devices.

## See also

- The *Configuring the XenDesktop policies* recipe in *Chapter 8, XenDesktop Tuning and Security*

# Chapter 6 XenDesktop lab

In this chapter we've seen how to create and configure the Desktop's catalog containing the resources to distribute among the end users, and how to implement specific configurations such as the ability to use printers and USB devices.

In this laboratory we're going to configure one of the available catalog types, configuring a set of printers and USB devices policies. Perform the following steps to do so:

1. Connect to the domain controller server (`vmctxdc01 - 192.168.1.50`) and generate a group called `MCSDesk-GRP`, assigning to it the membership of four users. If you have no sufficient user accounts, create them in a number useful to cover the required number.
2. Still connected with administrative credentials to your DC server, configure the domain GPO to permit the remote assistance on the machines that are part of the VDI domain OU.
3. Connect to your MCS desktop base image template with administrative credentials, and force the applications of the domain policies.
4. Connect to your hypervisor infrastructure, and after you've completed all the necessary modifications to the MCS desktop base image virtual machine, generate a snapshot disk for it.
5. Connect to the Desktop Controller machine (`vmctxddc01 - 192.168.1.60`) and run the configuration wizard in order to create a desktop catalog with the parameters given next. Perform the following steps to do so:
    i. Create a pooled machine type catalog with a static machine assignment technique.
    ii. Set number of generated instances equal to 4—allocation of the resources that are same as that of the master image.
    iii. Create new machine accounts in the form of `MCSDesk<progressive-number>`.

   iv. Assign the generated machines to previously created `MCSDesk-GRP`.

   v. Configure the peak and the off-peak hours based on your company's working hours with the parameters such as suspending the machine if disconnected for 15 minutes, of turning it off if logged off for 10 minutes.

   vi. Enable the use of the Secure ICA protocol, and set color desktop resolution at the maximum level.

6. Connect to the Citrix Desktop Director web console, and try to change the assignment of a desktop for one of the configured users. After completing this step, check the metrics collection and export them to a report.
7. Using the Desktop Director web console, run a shadow session for one of the existing virtual desktop instances.
8. Connect to the Desktop Controller machine (`vmctxddc01 - 192.168.1.60`) and configure the following policies:
   - Permitting to the client only mappings of the Citrix Universal Printer driver.
   - Allowing users to map external USB devices, and asking them for confirmation of the type of access to the resources.
   - Connecting to the appropriate site, retrieving information about an available USB mass storage device in your company, and creating a filter rule to only use that hardware on your virtual desktops.

# 7

# Deploying Applications

In this chapter we will cover:

- Publishing the VM-hosted apps with XenDesktop
- Publishing the streamed apps with XenApp 6.5
- Publishing applications using Microsoft App-V

## Introduction

When you think about the Citrix XenDesktop suite, you only consider the virtual desktop implementation part. This approach could be correct when creating a machine with the full set of applications already installed, but not when considering to deliver only the specific applications for every domain user.

In this chapter we're going to discuss this second approach, with the use of the three supported technologies to deliver applications to the users' desktops: the creation of the VM-hosted apps with XenDesktop, the streamed applications with Citrix XenApp, and the most recent way to publish applications, the App-V platform developed by Microsoft. The scope of this chapter is not to compare these technologies, but maybe, to explain the main and most important application delivery techniques on the market.

# Publishing the VM-hosted apps with XenDesktop

The VM-hosted apps approach is the simplest and nearest to a standard, preinstalled desktop instance. With this technique, anyway, you will be able to reduce the impact on the infrastructural components because of the absence of the terminal server licenses required in the other application deployment solutions, such as Citrix XenApp. On the other hand, you have to consider the necessity to have more XenDesktop licenses.

## Getting ready

To be able to deploy VM-hosted applications, you need to have the right number of licenses within your infrastructure; remember that for any single application, or a set of applications, you need a XenDesktop license corresponding to a deployed desktop instance.

Moreover, you need to generate a number of desktop instances in your catalog, equal to or greater than the number of users accessing the applications.

## How to do it...

In the following steps we will explain how to publish the VM-hosted apps based on the XenDesktop application catalogs:

1. Connect to the Desktop Controller machine with administrative credentials, then click on **Start** | **All Programs** | **Citrix**, and click on the **Desktop Studio** link.
2. Click on the **Machines** link in the left-hand side menu, and choose if creating a new catalog (the **Create Catalog** link in the right-hand side menu), or editing an existing one (right-click on its name and select the **Add machines** option).

   We've already seen in the previous chapter how to create a catalog, so we will work on an existing catalog in this case.

3. After all the intermediate operations, select the number of machines that you want to add, and select **Create new accounts** or **Import accounts**, then click on the **Next** button.

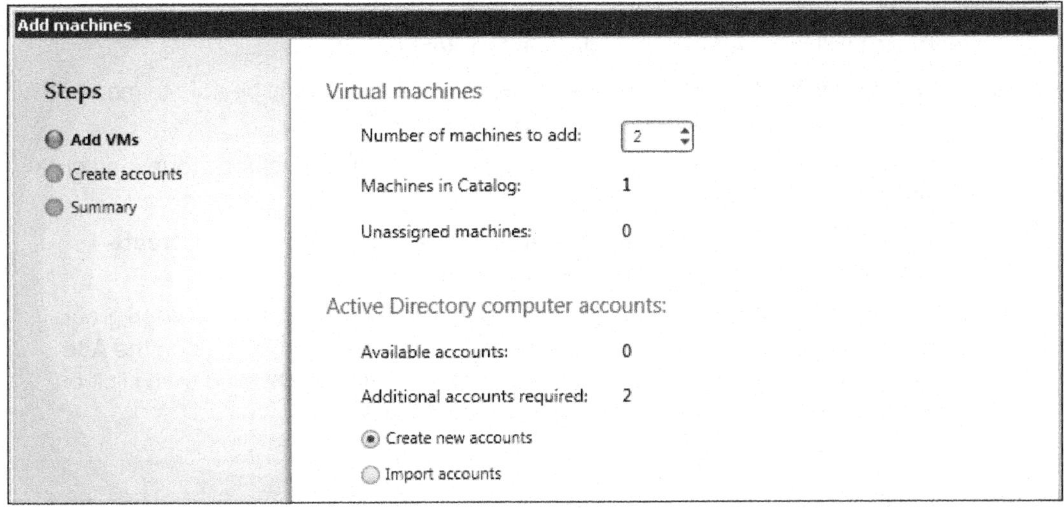

To differentiate the machines in a desktop group from that in an application group, you should always create new machine accounts with a naming convention other than the machines in the desktop group.

4. Select the **Organizational Unit** (**OU**) within creating the computer accounts, and choose a coherent naming convention, in line with the scope of the machines. After completing this click on **Next**, as follows:

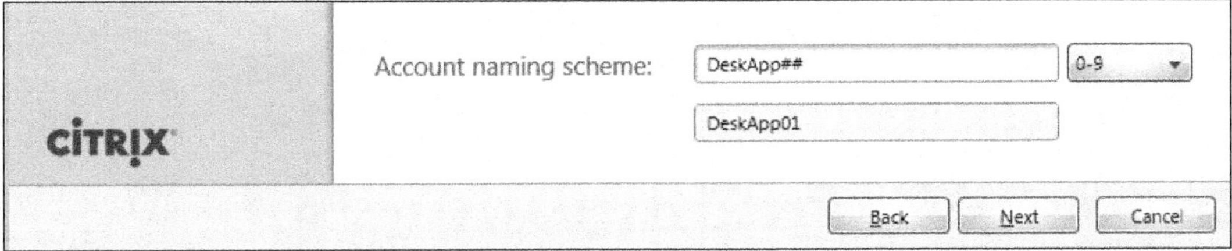


5. On the **Summary** screen, after reviewing all the information, click on the **Finish** button to complete the procedure.
6. Click on the **Assignments** link in the left-hand side menu, then select **Create Application Desktop Group** on the right-hand side of the screen.
7. On the **Catalog** screen select the catalog from which you want to take the desktop instances, and select how many machines you are adding, with a number equal to or less than the number of available machines, then click on **Next**.

8. In the **Users** section select the users or the groups to which the application desktop instances will be assigned, then click on the **Next** button.
9. In the **Delegation** section flag the administrative user who will be able to manage the created desktop instances, and click on the **Next** button.
10. On the **Summary** screen assign a name to the application desktop group, and click on **Finish** to complete the procedure.
11. In the left-hand side menu select the **Applications** link, then click on **Create Application** located in the right-hand side panel.
12. In the **Desktop Groups** section select if you are adding an existing desktop group or creating a new one. Because of the previously created group, click on the **Add existing...** button, select the desktop group to add, click on **OK**, and then click on the **Next** button, as shown in the following screenshot:

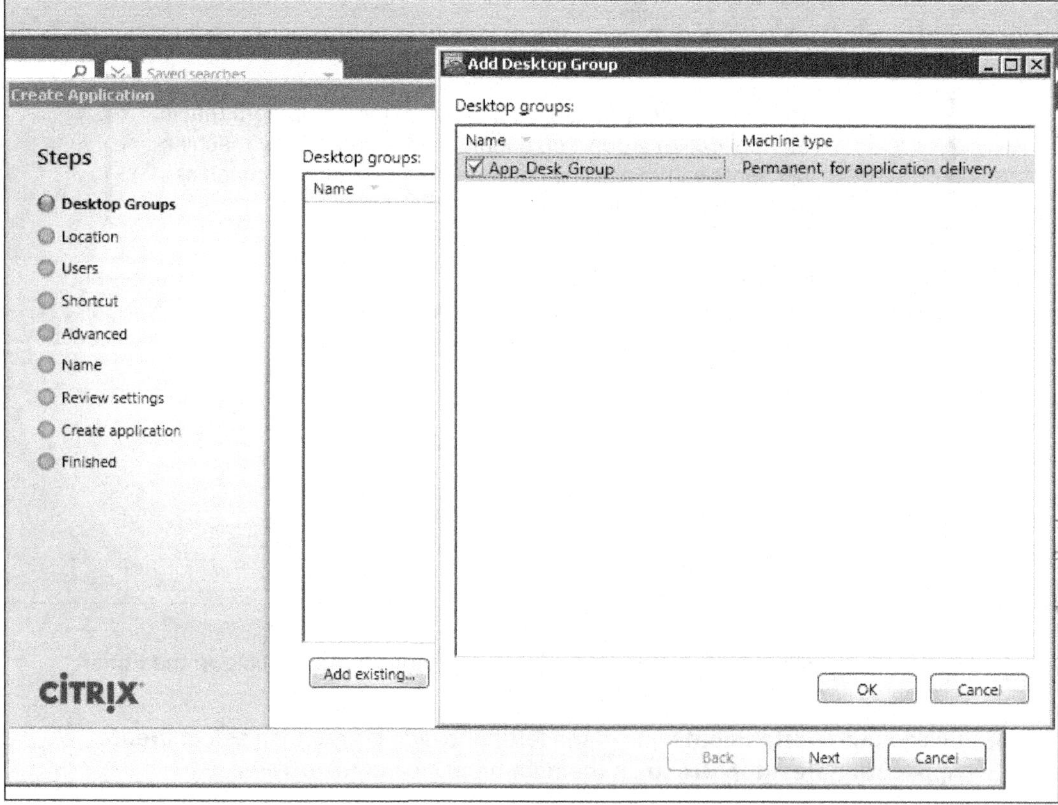


13. In the **Location** section, browse for an application executable file to publish by clicking on the **Browse...** button of the **Program executable** section, as shown in the following screenshot:

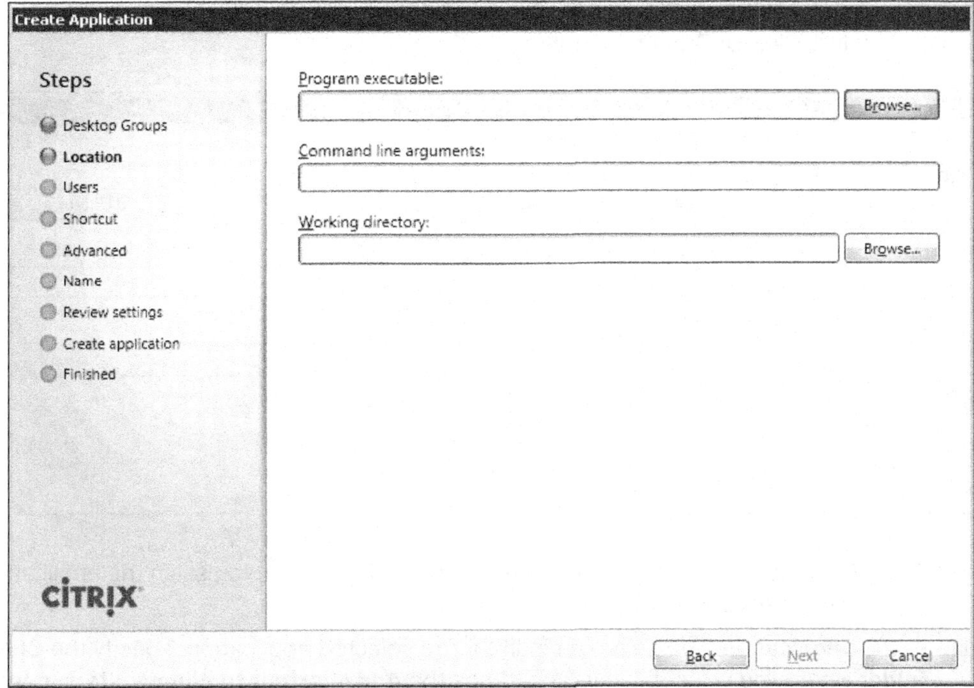


14. On the **Browse for File** screen select the radio button for **Local computer** or **Associated machine**; in this second case, select either **Show only machines in maintenance mode** or **Show only available machines** by checking one or both the checkboxes. After selecting the right available option, select the system share from which you will browse the applications, and click on the **Browse...** button to add the required software.

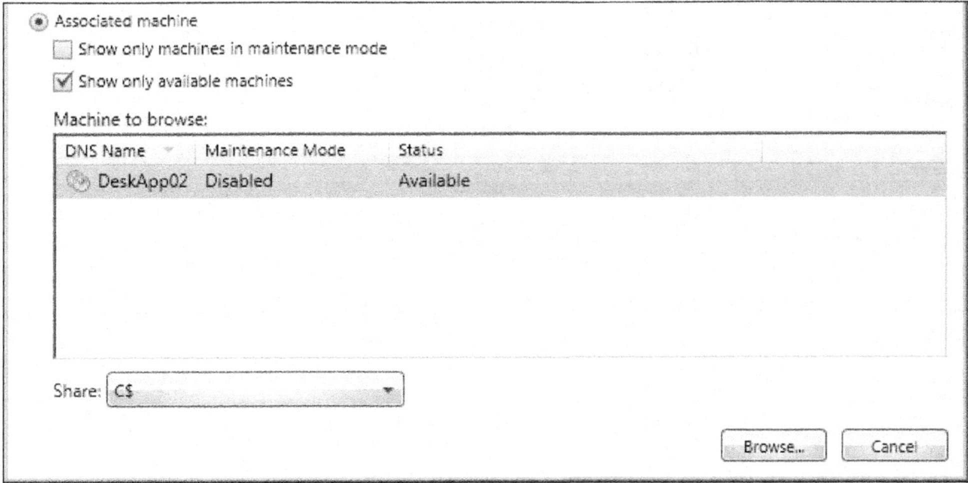

15. After selecting the application the **Working directory** field will be automatically populated. Click on **Next** to continue.

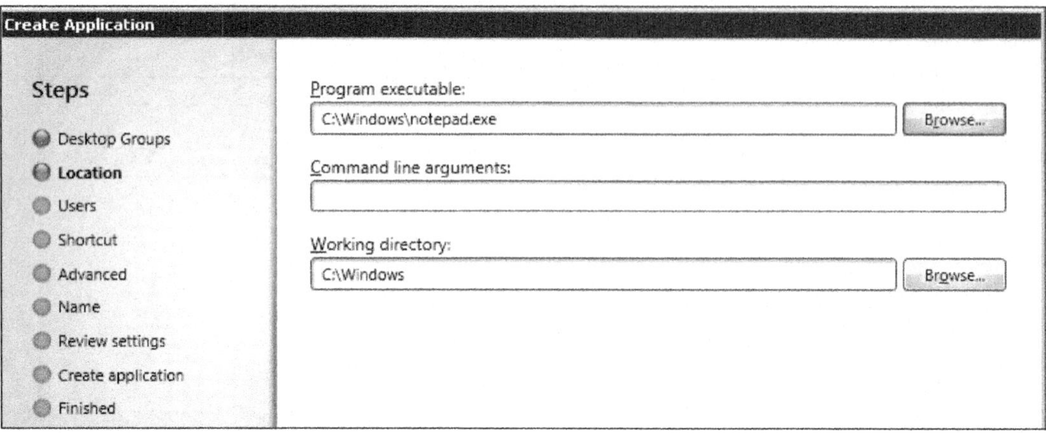


16. In the **Users** section add the domain users to which you want to assign the applications, then click on **Next**.

17. In the **Shortcut** section select an icon for the selected application, specify the **Client folder** where you will publish it, and check the **Add shortcut to client's start menu** and **Add shortcut to client's desktop** checkboxes. These shortcuts will be put on the user profile locations by the Citrix Receiver; in the first selection case, you also have to specify **Start menu location**. After completing this click on the **Next** button.

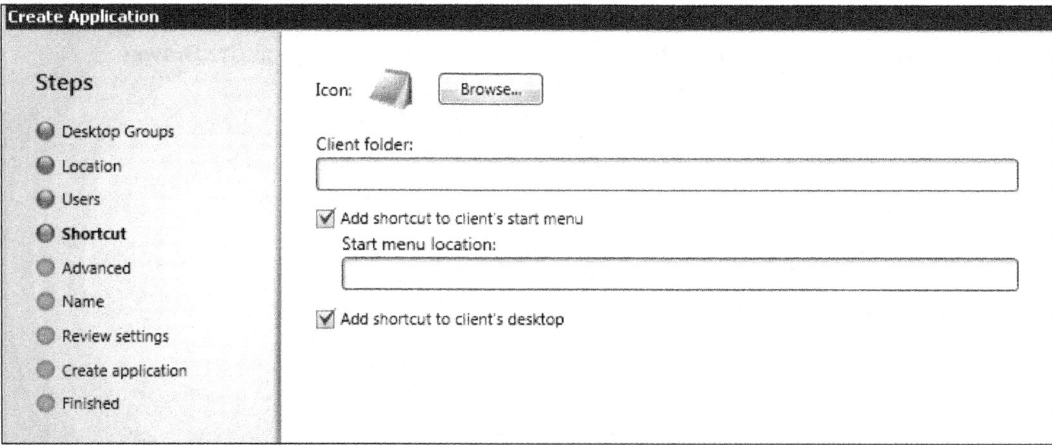

18. In the **Advanced** section configure the following parameters as necessary, and click on **Next** after it's done:
    - **Advanced access control**
        - **Allow connections made through Access Gateway** – **Any connection** or **Any connection that meets any of the following filters**. With this last option, you have to select an existing application farm and a matching rule.
        - **Allow all other connections.**
    - **Appearance**
        - **Windows size** – **Full screen**, **Exact pixel size**, or **Percent of client display**
        - **Color depth** – **16**, **256**, **High color**, or **True color**
    - **Content redirection**
        - **Multimedia**
    - **Enable legacy audio**
    - **Resources**
        - **CPU priority level** – **Low**, **Below normal**, **Normal**, or **Above Normal**. Decide if checking or unchecking the **On startup, wait for printer creation** checkbox.
    - **Security**
        - Decide if checking or unchecking the **Require client to use encryption** option

You'll have more details about the **Content redirection** section later in this recipe.

Steps

Desktop Groups
Location
Users
Shortcut
**Advanced**
Name
Review settings

The settings below are optional. If you do not change them, smart defaults will be used.

▸ Advanced access control
▸ Appearance
▸ Content redirection
▸ Multimedia
▸ Resources
▸ Security

19. In the **Name** section select a name for the published application, specify **Description/Tool tip**, check **Enabled**, **Visible**, or both under the **Availability** section, and then click on the **Next** button.

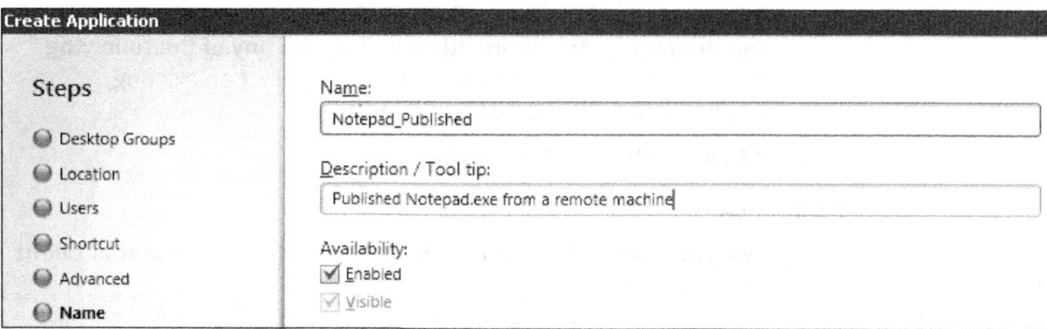


20. On the **Review** settings screen, after you've verified all the configured parameters, click on the **Next** button to complete the publishing procedure, and then click on **Finish** to close the window.
21. In the **Applications** menu, now you can find the published software. Click on the application in order to change the configured properties wherever necessary.
22. Connect to the Web Interface and log in using the credentials of a user holding one or more published applications. In the resources menu you can now find the linked software. You can click on the application link to start using it.

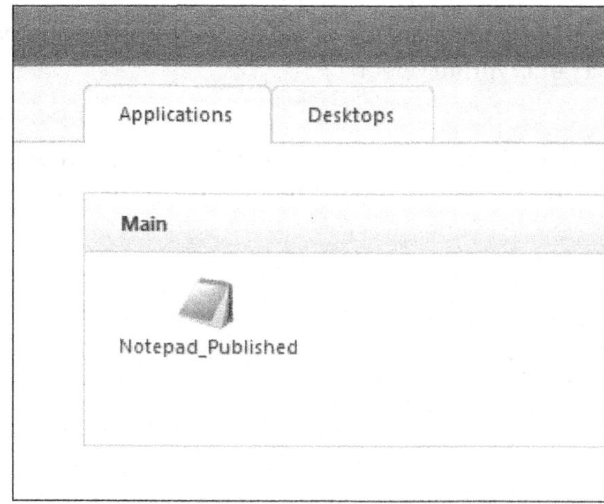

23. Using the same Web Interface session, access a configured desktop instance, right-click on the Citrix Receiver plugin in the sidebar, and select the **Preferences** option.
24. Select the **Plug-in status** section, right-click on the **Online Plug-in (13.1.0.89)** link and select **Change Server**, as shown in the following screenshot:

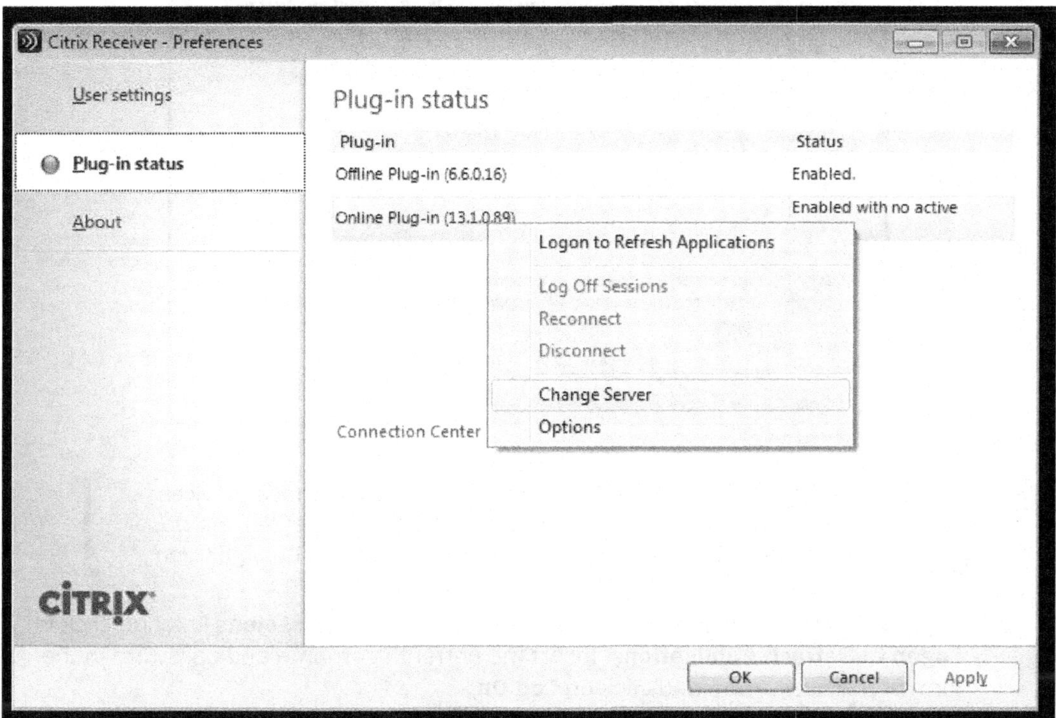

25. Specify the address of the Desktop Controller machine, in the form of, <protocol>://<hostname>/Citrix/PNAgent/config.xml, and click on **Update**, as shown in the following screenshot:

The specified site is the address of the Web Interface Services site explained in the *Installing and configuring the Web Interface* recipe in *Chapter 1, XenDesktop Installation and Configuration*.

26. Right-click again on the Citrix Receiver, select the **Online Sessions** link and click on **Logon to Refresh Applications**. Insert the current username and password in the form of Domain\User and click on **Log On**.

27. Now you can find the published application on your machine's desktop and in your **Start** menu.

## How it works...

The VM-hosted apps is the most recent technique offered by Citrix to deploy applications to the users. Through this approach you can deliver software to the published desktops or simply let the users run the single application without the necessity of the Terminal Server licenses, as required for instance in Citrix XenApp. For this reason, every application associated to a delivered desktop instance allows only one connection, and not multiple accesses to the assigned software. In some way this is the price you have to pay for approaching in a modality other than the XenApp style. This deployment approach could also be useful when you don't want to use the application streaming offered by XenApp or App-V for that software that can only be installed on the desktop machines (XenApp, for instance, can only deploy applications hosted on the server edition of Microsoft Windows).

All the VM-hosted apps are part of a desktop group quite different from the standard group used till now; it's called application desktop group, and it is an applications container in which it is possible to assign permissions and specific software's parameters.

You can decide to publish an application link on the user desktop, and also populate the **Start** menu with a shortcut; this way, the user will tend to run the application locally on his desktop.

This last discussed user experience is less richer than the impression given by XenApp. In fact, when you'll run an application in the VM-hosted modality, you will see it execute an effective machine logon operation; in XenApp, this operation is not visible to the end user.

An important part in the applications configuration is given by the software appearance; you can configure the way in which the application has to run, in terms of color resolution and windows size (the **Appearance** section discussed earlier). Furthermore, you can decide to enable the audio as well for an application, and set its priority level when accessing the CPU resources.

In the presence of the Citrix Access Gateway, it's possible to configure the advanced access control policy; instead of allowing any kind of connection, you can permit the connections to the applications only through the Citrix Gateway, and eventually decide if filtering them through it.

## There's more...

To complete the application publishing process, it's necessary to assign the file type (or types) to the software; to execute this task, you need to perform a process called content redirection.

To be able to operate on the file extension assignment, you need to put the desktop—which is offering the application—in maintenance mode. After this, select the application on which you want to operate, and edit its properties. In the **Content redirection** section click on the **Update file types** button, and select the machine from which you are importing the file type's definition. At this time you will be able to select one or more file extensions to associate to the application (in this example, the `.bat` and `.txt` file types have been associated to the published Microsoft Notepad) as follows:

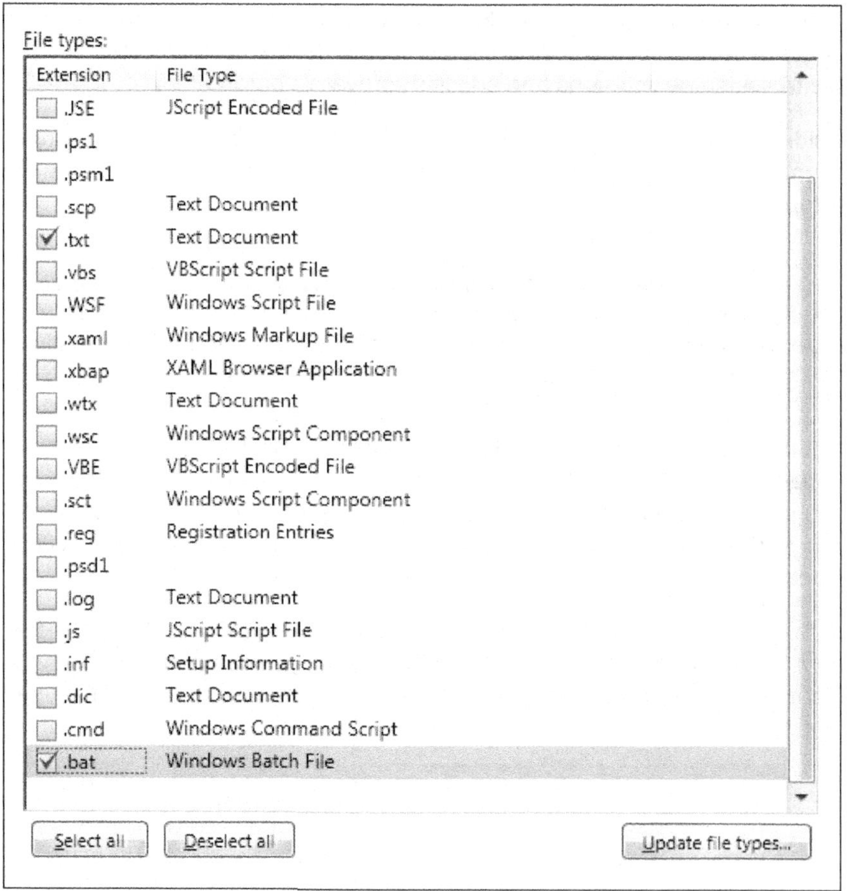

This operation will allow the users to double-click on the associated files and open them using the associated software with the VM-hosted app technique.

Remember to disable the maintenance mode after completing this procedure!

## See also

- The *Configuring Citrix Receiver* recipe in *Chapter 4, User Experience - Planning and Configuring*

# Publishing the streamed apps with XenApp 6.5

Citrix XenApp is the oldest and most famous software of the Citrix family, which is used to publish applications, contents and server's desktops for the end users. These operations can be performed using different approaches. During this chapter we will explain how to assign software to the clients through the streaming technique and redirecting the application execution to the XenApp servers by moving or streaming the application to the client machine.

## Getting ready

To be able to publish streamed applications, you need to install and configure a Citrix XenApp farm, installing and configuring one or more Windows Servers as member servers of this farm. After this you need one or more servers to use as Profiler; on this machine, you have to install the Citrix Streaming Profiler software, create a network share accessible with full privileges for the users who need to access the published applications, and copy all the setups of those applications which will be deployed. All the machines must be attached to the Windows domain on which you have configured the Citrix XenDesktop infrastructure.

Refer to the book *Getting Started with Citrix XenApp 6.5, Guillermo Musumeci, Packt Publishing* to understand and implement a full functioning Citrix XenApp farm.

## How to do it...

In this recipe we are going to explain how to generate and deploy streamed applications within a Citrix XenApp environment. Perform the following steps:

1. Connect to one of the profiling servers with domain administrative credentials, and run the Citrix Streaming Profiler software.
2. In the Profiler menu click on the **New Profile** button to proceed with the application publishing, as follows:

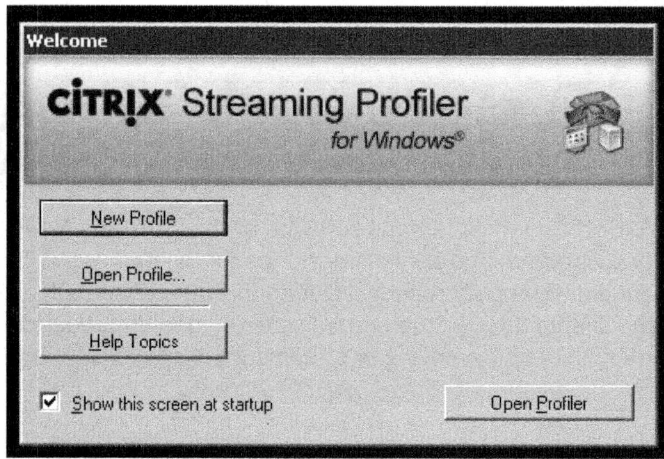


3. On the first wizard screen click on the **Next** button to proceed with the operations. If you want to stop receiving the explanation screen, check the **Skip this screen in the future** checkbox.
4. Select a profile name for the application profile you're going to create and click on the **Next** button.
5. Choose to check or uncheck the **Enable User Updates** option, and flag the **Save these settings and skip this screen in the future to stop the prompt of this screen the next time you will run the wizard** option. After completing this click on **Next**.
6. Check **Enable support for 6.0 Offline Plug-ins** if you want to support older plugins and profiles versions under the Windows XP SP2 operating systems, then click on the **Next** button.
7. In the linked profiles section click on **Next**. We will discuss this later in the recipe.
8. In the **Target operating system** section select the system target for which this application is created (Service Pack selection included). In the **Target language** area select one, multiple, or all the listed operating system languages. After completing this click on the **Next** button.

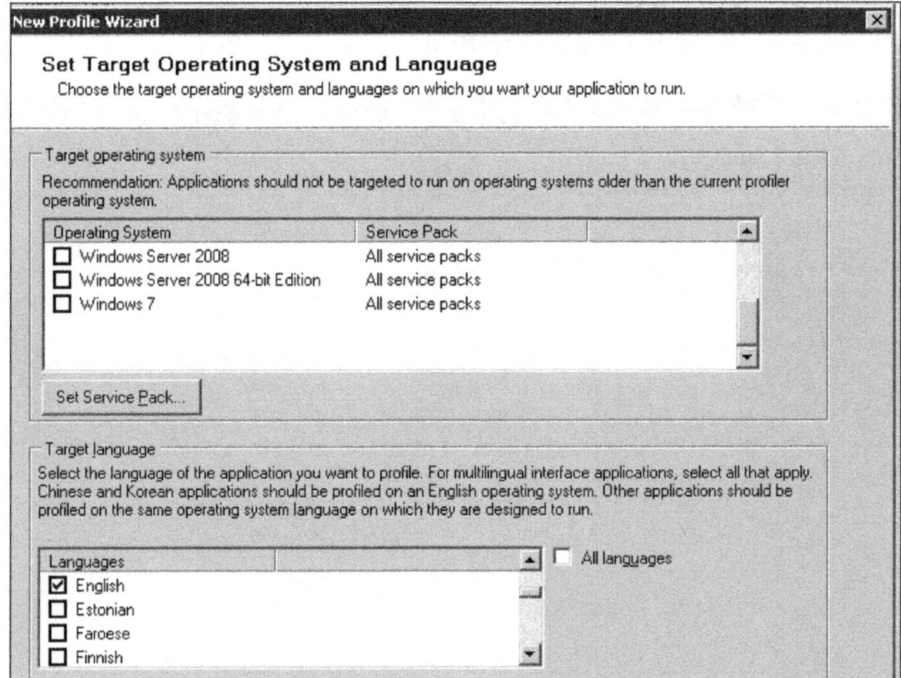

You have to select an operating system version that is coherent with the current profiler machine. So, you should not select a target operating system that is older than the profiler server!

9. Select the **Advanced Install** radio button on the **Select Install Option** screen, and click on **Next**.

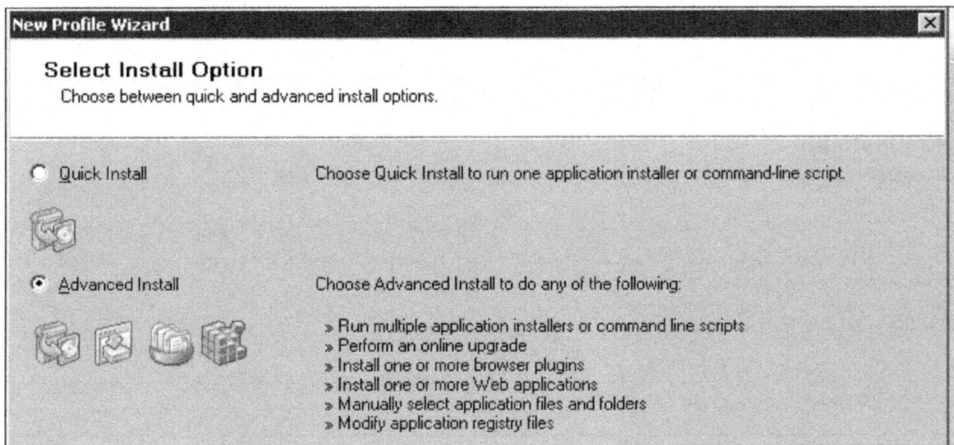

10. On the **Select Install Method** screen select the **Run install program or command line script** radio button and click on **Next**.

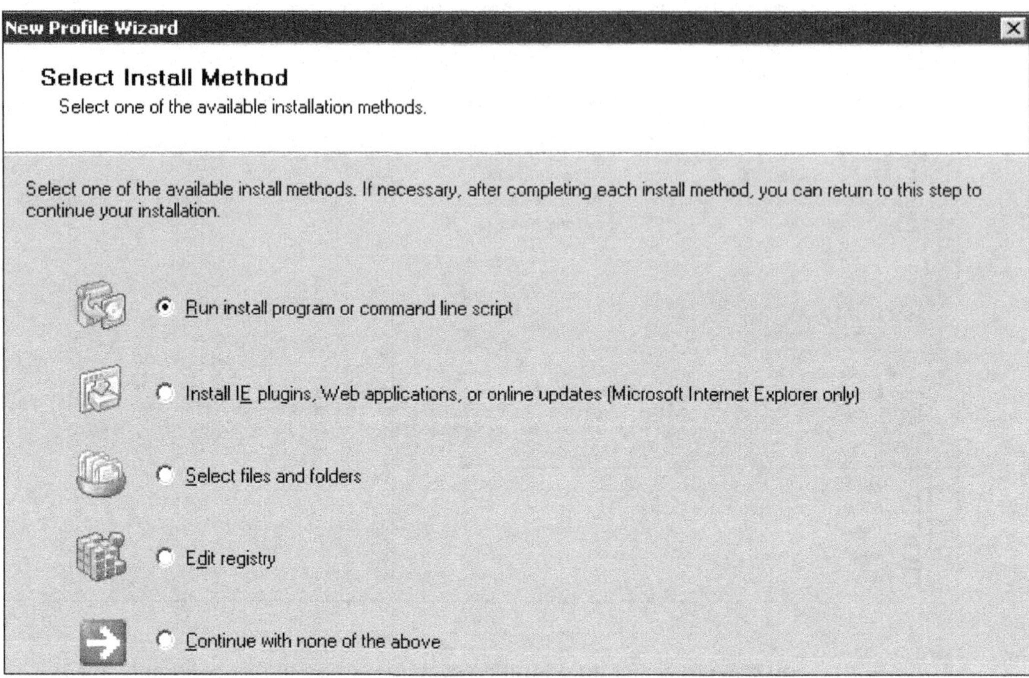


11. On the **Choose Installer** screen browse for one of the copied software setups (in this case Mozilla Firefox 15.0.1), enter an optional command-line parameter, and click on **Next**.
12. On the **Run Installer** screen click on the **Launch Installer** button. At this point the software setup will run under the profiler environment, but nothing will be installed on the profiler machine. After the setup has been completed, click on the **Next** button.

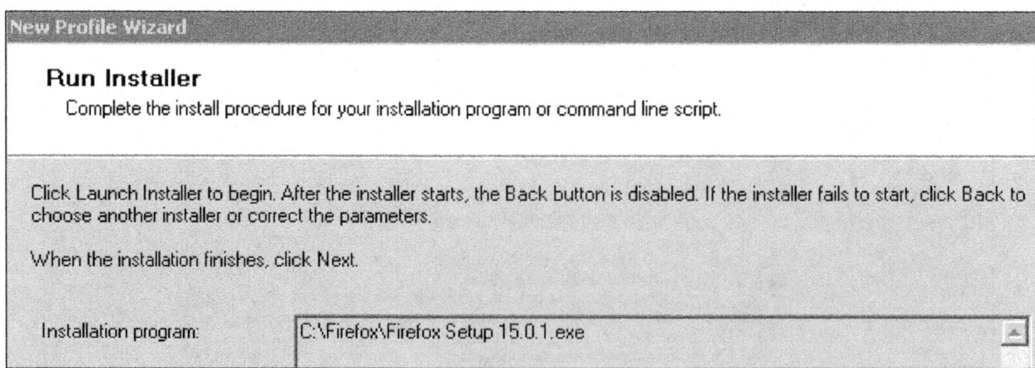

13. Select either **Finish installations** or **Perform additional installations** (for example patches, updates, and so on). In our case we have to choose the first option, and then click on **Next**.
14. Select the application and click on the **Run** button to execute its first launch. This task is necessary to complete the configuration of the installed software. It's also possible to configure command-line parameters for the application execution. After completing this click on the **Next** button.

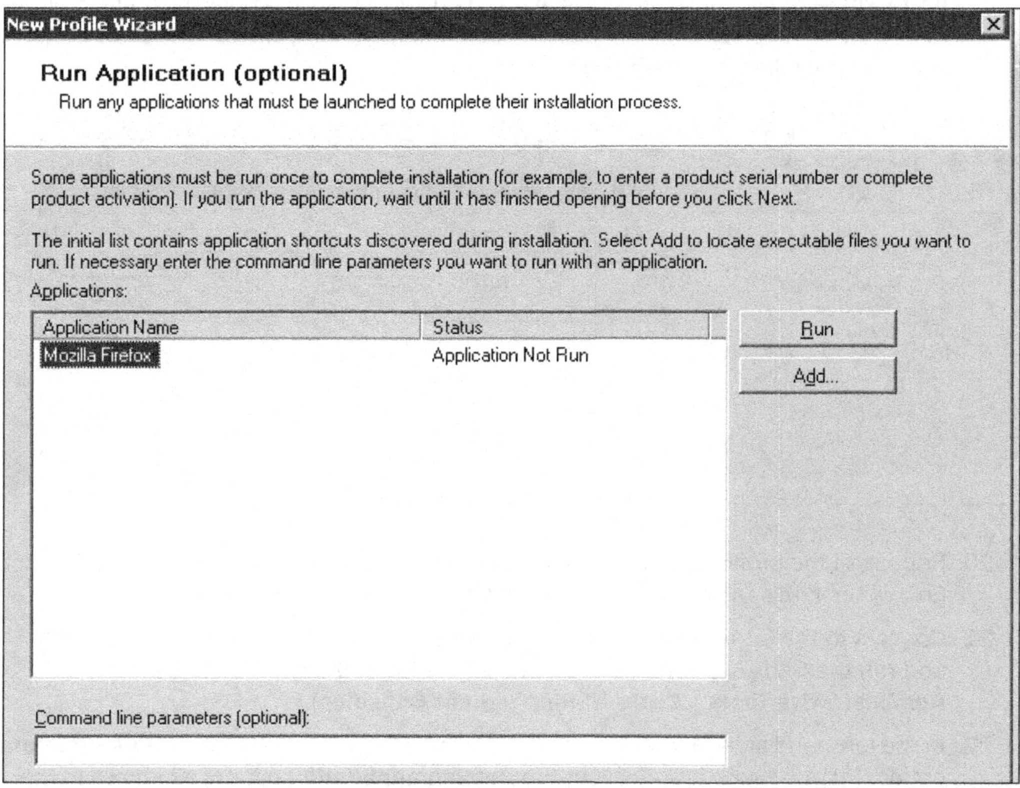


15. On the **Select Applications** screen you can delete, modify, or recover the existing applications, or add a new one. Click on **Next** to continue.

> If you accidentally delete the application during the creation phase, the **Recover** button will permit you to roll back the operation and restore the deleted profile.

16. If you want you can create a **virtual hard disk** (**VHD**) to associate to the application by checking the **Create virtual hard disk (VHD) for this target** checkbox. After completing this click on **Next**.

17. If you are signing your profile with a certificate, select the appropriate radio button (**Sign using key from selectable file**, **Sign using locally installed certificate**, or **Do not sign profile**), and then click on **Next** to proceed.
18. On the **Build Profile** screen review the listed information, and click on **Finish** to complete the profile creation procedure.
19. In the **Streaming Profiler** menu you can now find the generated application profile. Click on **File** | **Save** to save it, and specify **Profile name** and **Profile directory (UNC path)** where you will save the application. The UNC path is the network share generated during the required preliminary tasks. After completing this, click on the **Save** button, as shown in the following screenshot:

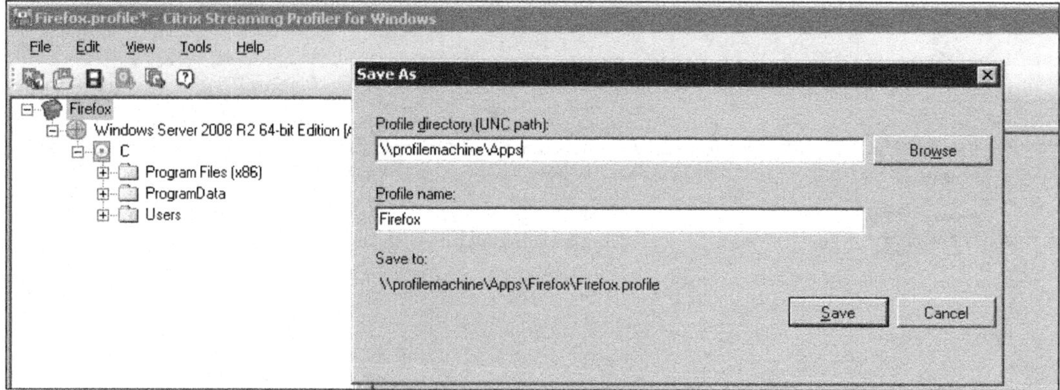


20. Repeat all the profile creation tasks to generate the profile for a different application (in this book this task will be performed on the Notepad++ software).
21. Connect to the Citrix XenApp server farm with domain administrative credentials, and run the Citrix AppCenter console (link located at **Start** | **All Programs** | **Administrative Tools** | **Citrix** | **Management Consoles**).
22. In the left-hand side menu click on your farm name link, and select the **Applications** option. Right-click on it and select the **Publish application** option, as shown in the following screenshot:

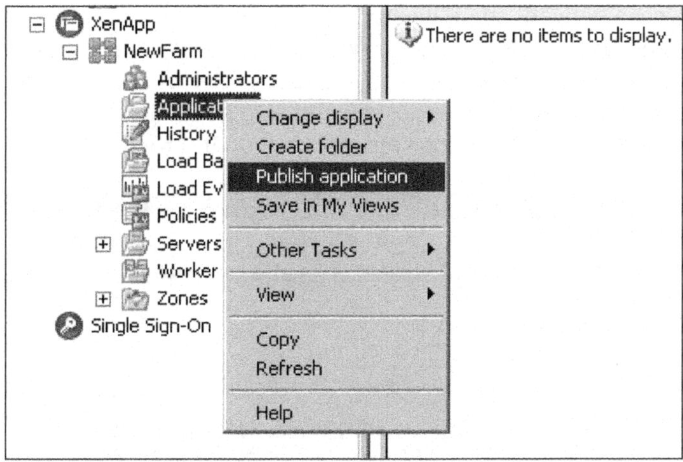


23. On the welcome screen click on the **Next** button, then insert an application's display name in the **Display Name** field and its description in the **Name** field, and then click on **Next**.

24. In the **Type** section select **Accessed from a server** as **Application type**, selecting **Streamed to server** as **Server application type**. After completing this click on the **Next** button.

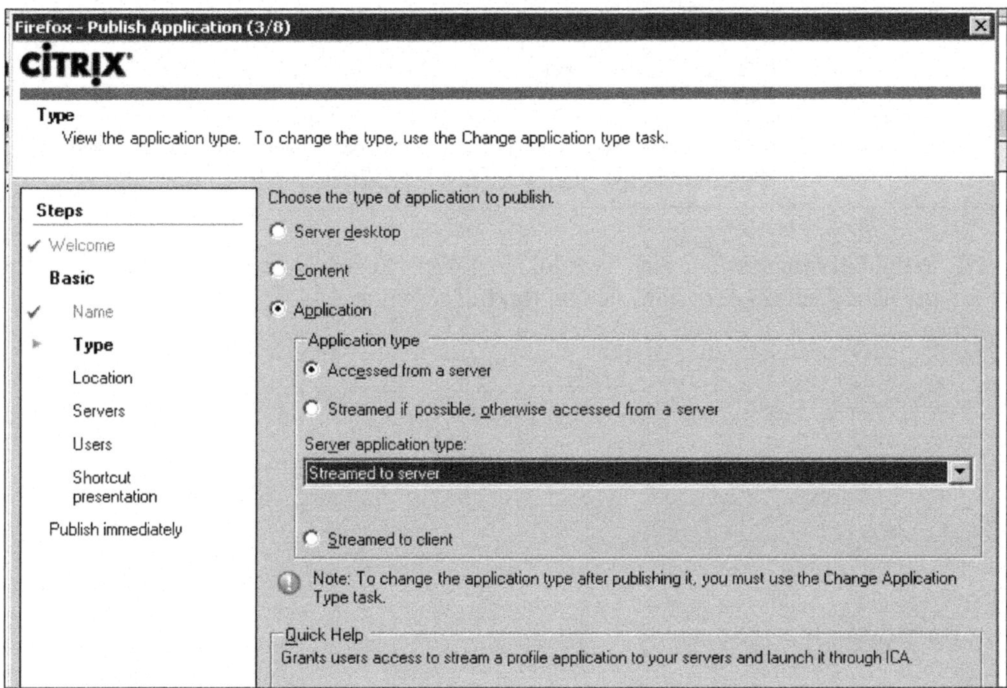

25. Browse for the network share located on the profiler server, and choose one of the existing application profiles (in this case select Firefox as the application to publish, choosing the file with the `.profile` extension). Select the application to launch from the drop-down list; if needed, you can also populate the last field with any extra command line parameter. Once finished, click on the **Next** button.

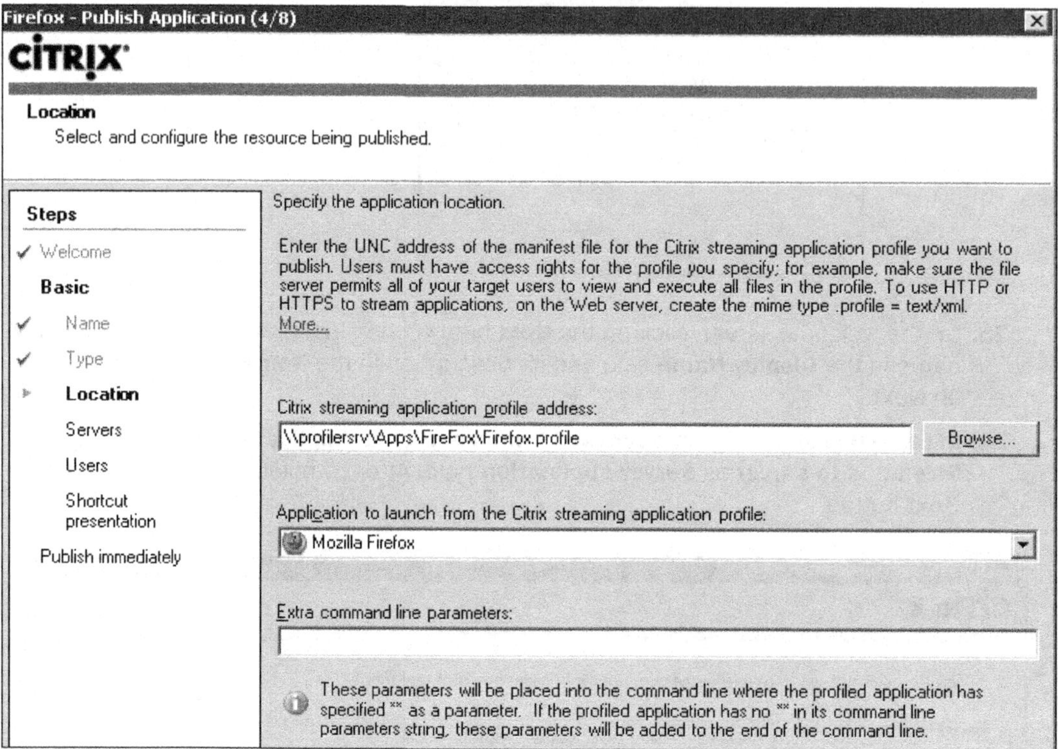


26. In the **Servers** section, click on **Add...** to select the servers on which you will run the published application, and click on **Next** to continue.

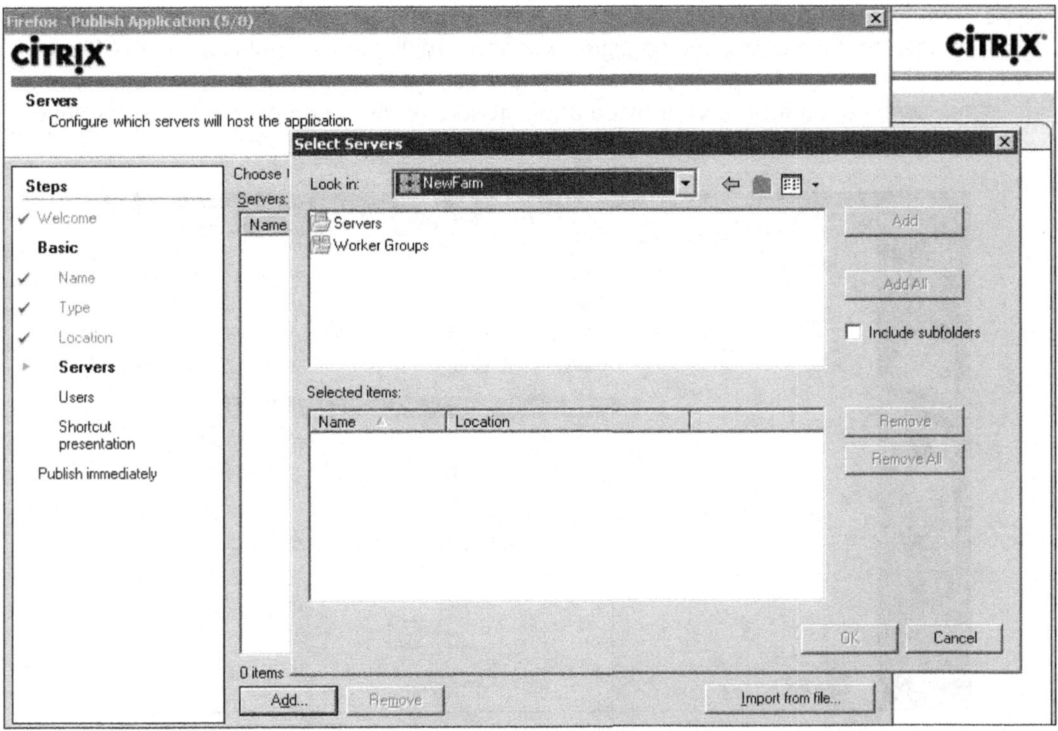


27. In the **Users** section, select the **Allow only configured users** radio button, and browse your domain for users to which you will assign permissions on the published application. After completing this, click on **Next**.
28. In the shortcut presentation area, select the application icon, and choose if you want to publish it on the client's **Start** menu or desktop, then click on **Next**.
29. In the last section choose if you want to initially disable the application or not, then click on **Finish** to complete the creation procedure.
30. Repeat the publishing procedure on the XenApp server also for the Notepad++ application profile, selecting **Streamed to client** as an application type. In case you have enabled the offline access for the application, you have to decide either pre-caching the application at login, or caching the application at the launch time.

31. Connect to a XenDesktop machine instance through the Web Interface, log in with a user enabled to use the configured XenApp applications, right-click on the Citrix Receiver icon in the Windows taskbar, and configure it to point to the XenApp farm, as seen earlier for the VM-hosted apps procedure. After completing this you will be able to run the streamed applications within your virtual desktop.

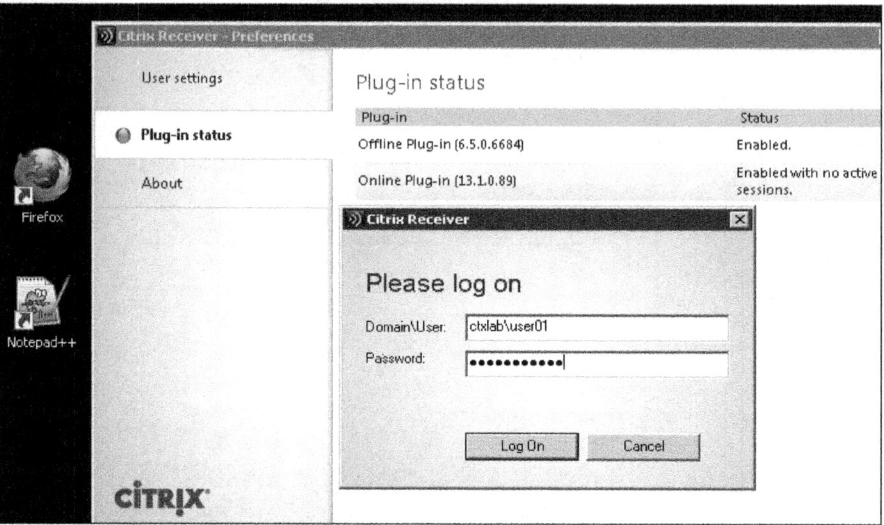


## How it works...

The use of the streamed applications with the XenApp platform permits administrators and end users working on a centralized application store profile to deliver and stream the software to the clients. With this configuration you can set up, update, and tune the applications exclusively in the central store, and then propagate the latest software version to the users without any additional operation.

As explained in the previous section, you can stream an application in two different ways:

- **Streamed to server application**: In this approach the most important part of the communication is between the XenApp farm server and the profiler machine on which the application store has been configured. So, when a user will call an application using the online or the web plugin, the application will be streamed from the profiler to the XenApp server, and then redirected to the client through the listed plugins.
- **Streamed to client application**: In this case the most critical application flow is redirected to the client machines. In fact, when a user asks for a published application, this is redirected to the client, caching some of the application files, or the entire streamed software. In this second case it will be entirely downloaded to the user's machine, making it usable even in an offline mode. For this reason, it's necessary to install the Citrix offline plugin in the presence of the streaming to client solution.

The choice depends on the architecture characteristics. In case of a lot of users and a XenApp farm with low performances you have to operate in a streaming-to-client manner; otherwise with a strong XenApp architecture you can stream the applications to server with no need of caching information on the client resources.

All of these publishing approaches permit you to have a fully isolated application environment; you can see the streamed apps as a set of bubbles that have no impact on the software running locally, even if they belong to the same software category/vendor (for instance, you could have two different versions of the same text editor). This is granted by the centralized profiles store managed by the Citrix Streaming Profiler.

Remember that the Windows Terminal Server licenses (CAL) are necessary in order to use the Citrix XenApp platform!

## There's more...

XenApp allows you to reduce the impact on your system in terms of update and maintenance activities, thanks to the Linked Streaming Profiles. This technology, in fact, changes the way of assigning an application to an existing profile, transforming it to a set of linked applications, and not to a precompiled package with the full set of software.

In this way, when you only need to update one application, you have to operate only on the specific software, and the new application version will be reflected to all the linked profiles. Without this technique, you have to update every application installed in every profile, with unnecessary efforts in terms of operations.

## See also

- The *Configuring the Citrix Access Gateway virtual appliance* recipe in *Chapter 8, XenDesktop Tuning and Security*

# Publishing applications using Microsoft App-V

An alternative to the Citrix XenApp streaming method is offered by Microsoft with its App-V platforms. This software—which is quite similar to the XenApp application profiling technique—permits you to publish the software to the end user's desktop through the use of a specific client.

In this chapter we will discuss the components and the way in which Microsoft App-V works.

To learn how to implement an App-V architecture you can refer to the book *Microsoft Application Virtualization Advanced Guide, Augusto Alvarez, Packt Publishing*.

## Getting ready

For a full version of the App-V infrastructure, you need two or more servers on which you are installing and configuring the following roles:

- **App-V Management System**: This component is the centralized management console for all the configured applications and the associated users.

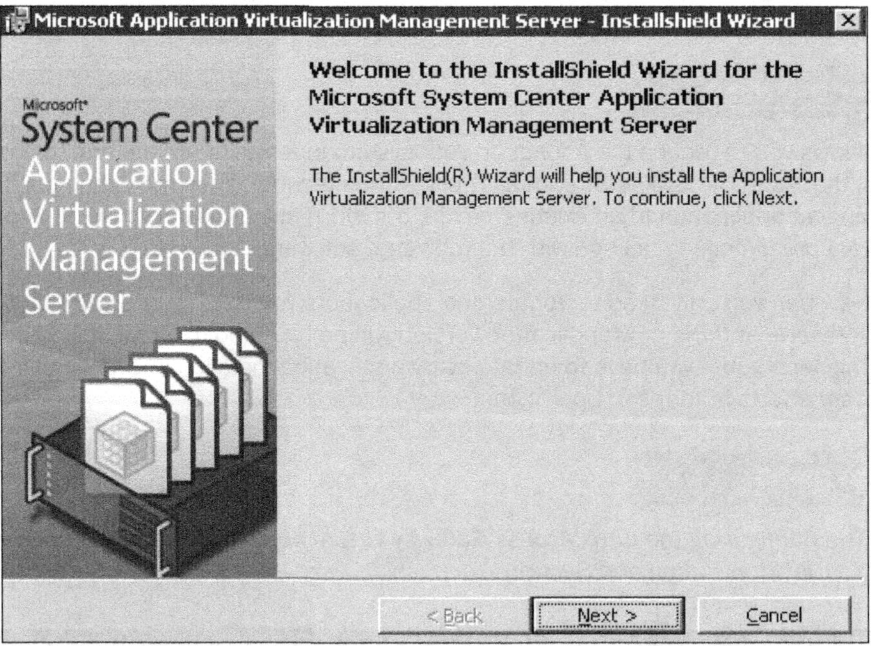


- **App-V Management Server**: This is the application broker, the core of the App-V infrastructure, which delivers the software to the clients. App-V also permits you to use the independent file streaming, which is the ability to directly stream the applications from a network share without using the management server.

IIS 7.0, .NET framework (at least 2.0), and SQL Server 2008 R2 are required in order to implement the management server.

- **App-V Sequencer**: This is the packaging software which creates the application profiles. This must be installed on a Windows 7 client machine on which the application setups are located.
- **App-V Streaming Server**: This server is used to stream the published applications to the clients.

On the XenDesktop base image template, you need to install the Microsoft Application Virtualization Desktop Client component in order to be able to contact the App-V infrastructure.

Remember that after installing the App-V client you have to update the existing XenDesktop machine instances in order to use the client on the assigned virtual desktops.

## How to do it...

The following are the necessary steps to implement the application sequencing and deployment using the Microsoft App-V platform:

1. Connect to the App-V Sequencer machine with domain administrative credentials, then click on **Start** | **All Programs** | **Microsoft Application Virtualization** | **Microsoft Application Virtualization Sequencer**.
2. On the application menu, click on **Create a New Virtual Application Package**.
3. From the **Packaging Method** section select **Create Package (default)** and click on **Next**.

4. In the **Type of Application** section select the **Standard Application (default)** option and then click on **Next**.

5. In the **Select Installer** menu, browse for a previously copied software setup on the Sequencer server and click on **Next**. The application chosen for this step is the Notepad++ text editor.
6. In the **Package Name** section assign a name to the virtual application, and if you want, you can also edit the location on which the package will be stored (the default is the virtual volume created during the App-V Sequencer installation process). After completing this click on **Next**.
7. In the **Installation** section, perform and complete the installation procedure for the selected software. After completing this, check the **I am finished installing** checkbox, and click on **Next**.

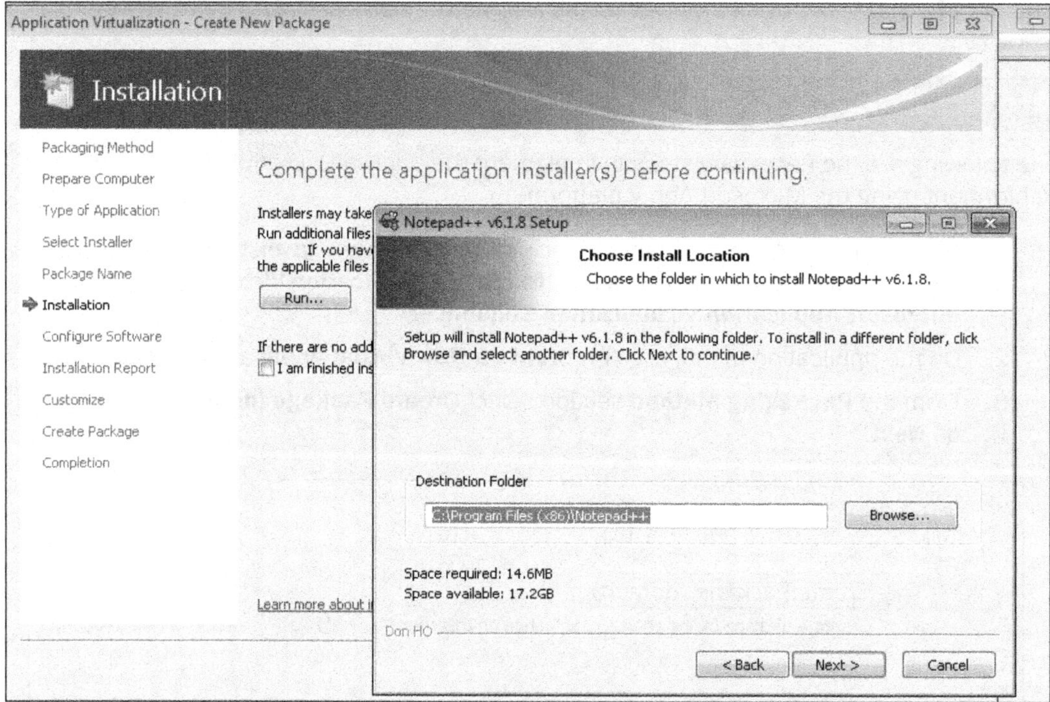


8. In the **Configure Software** section, select the earlier installed application and run it in order to complete the required configurations during the first application execution. Then click on **Next**.
9. If the **Installation Report** section notifies you with no warnings, you can continue by clicking on the **Next** button.
10. In the **Customize** section select the **Customize** option and click on **Next**.
11. In the **Edit Shortcuts** subsection, select where you want to publish the application links by clicking on the **Edit Locations** button. After completing this, click on **Next** to continue.

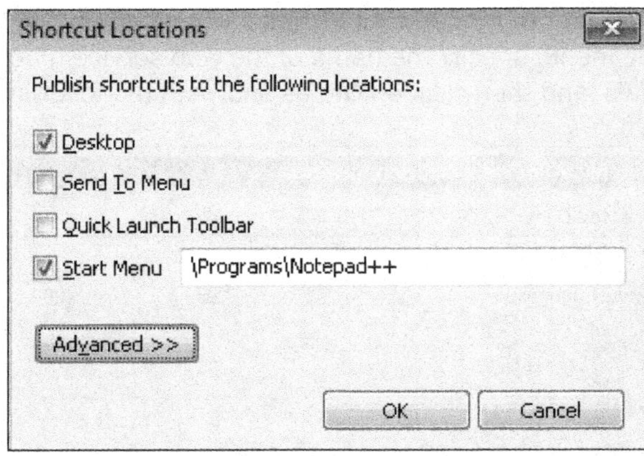


12. If you want to stream the application, you have to run it in the **Streaming** section in order to optimize its execution on the remote clients, and then click on **Next** to continue.
13. In the **Target OS** area you can choose to filter or not to filter the target operating system versions on which you want to allow the application to run. After choosing this click on **Next**.

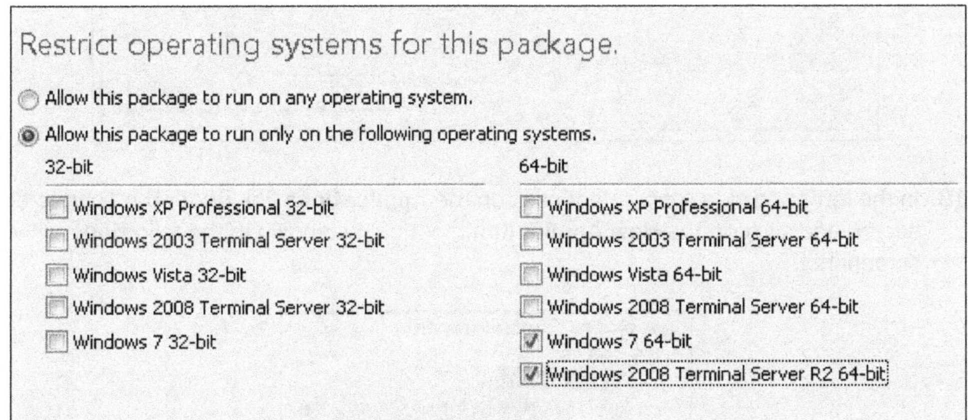


14. In the **Create Package section**, select **Save the package now**, and select the virtual volume previously used as location. In order to optimize the streaming activities for big packages (greater than 4 GB), you can check the **Compress Package** checkbox. To complete the entire procedure click on the **Create** button.
15. In the **Completion** menu click on **Close** to exit from the creation wizard.
16. Connect to the App-V Management System server with domain administrative credentials, then click on **Start** | **All Programs** | **Administrative Tools** | **Application Virtualization Management Console**.

17. Click on the **Connect to Application Virtualization System** link located in the right-hand side menu, specify the name of the web service machine and the login credentials, and then click on **OK**, as shown in the following screenshot:

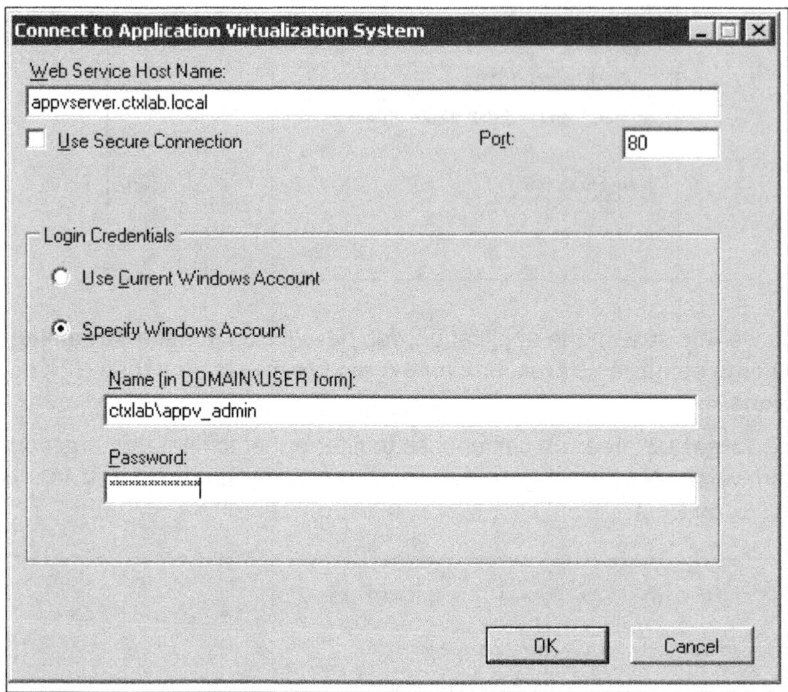


18. In the left-hand side menu, right-click on the **Applications** link under the connected server, and click on the **New Application...** option, as shown in the following screenshot:

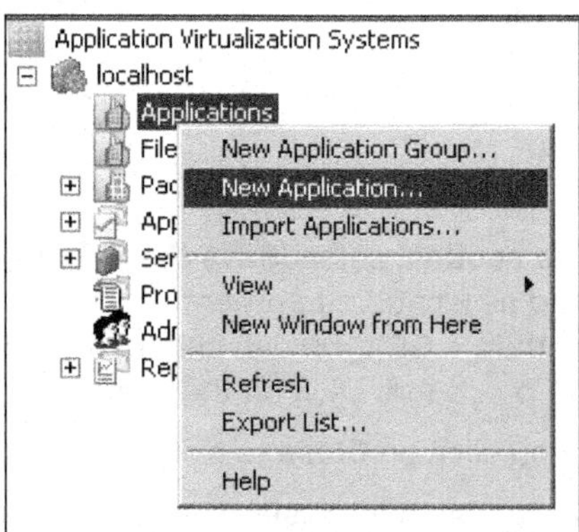


19. Populate the fields with the required information and click on **Next** to proceed:

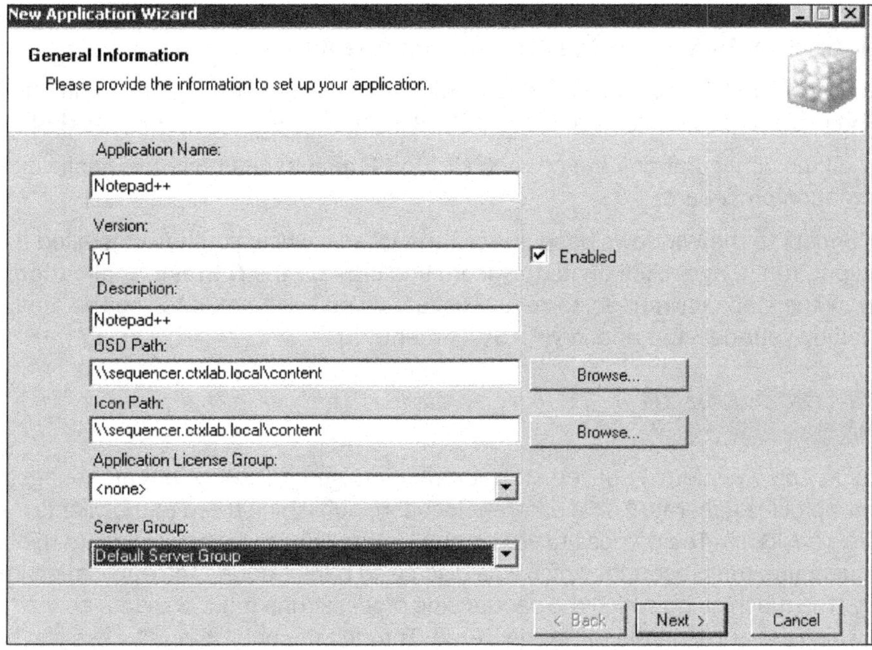


20. On the **Select Package** screen, click on the application version you want to publish, and click on **Next**.
21. Decide where to publish the software on the client machine by flagging the appropriate option, and then click on **Next**.

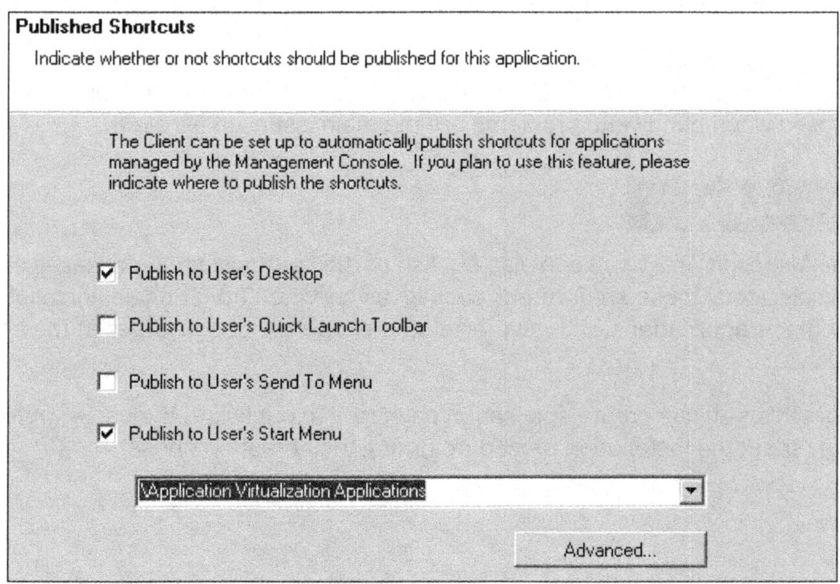

22. In the **File Associations** section you can assign a file type (extension) to the published application. After completing this click on the **Next** button.
23. In the **Access Permissions** section, select a specific domain group containing only the users who need to access the published resource, and click on **Next** to proceed.
24. If all the configurations are correct, click on **Finish** to complete the application creation procedure.
25. Connect to the Windows base image template on which you have installed the App-V client, run it, right-click on its tray icon, and click on the **Refresh Applications** option. If all the steps have been correctly executed, you will be able to see the application link on your desktop and in your **Start** menu.

## How it works...

The Microsoft App-V platform is based on a central management console that manages the application's profiles generated on a different location, publishing them to the clients installed on the user's desktops. The process to create application profiles to redistribute to the users is called **sequencing**, the procedure which was discussed earlier during the application installation monitoring. The machine on which the sequencing process runs must be same as the target clients to which the applications will be delivered. Through the publishing process you have the possibility to filter the destination operating system versions.

After generating the application sequence it's time to use the App-V Management Server; with this platform, it's now possible to load the application sequence and generate the software that will be delivered to the users. In this section you can also assign a particular file extension to the software, which means implementing the user experience also for the application virtualization, applying it when a user needs to open a certain file.

To improve the application flow from the server to the clients, App-V permits you to use the streaming technology; this is based on the same concept of the Citrix XenApp application streaming used when bandwidth problems are the main issues to fight with.

## There's more...

Through the Microsoft App-V you can also publish particular application packages called package accelerators; these are formerly packages generated from original installation media of complex applications, with all the setup procedure that converges at the end in a `.cab` archive.

Starting from this, you can create application packages to publish to the users without the necessity to repeat the installation procedure during their creation phase.

You can run the CAB generation procedure from the **Create Package Accelerator** section's **Tools** menu in the Sequencer main menu. During the creation activities you have to specify the installation files' location, the Guidance for administrators (a file in an RTF format generated by you which should contain information about the application package use), and the destination location for the archive. Once completing this step, you can use the CAB file to create the application package by selecting **Create Package Using a Package Accelerator** on the **Packaging Method** screen.

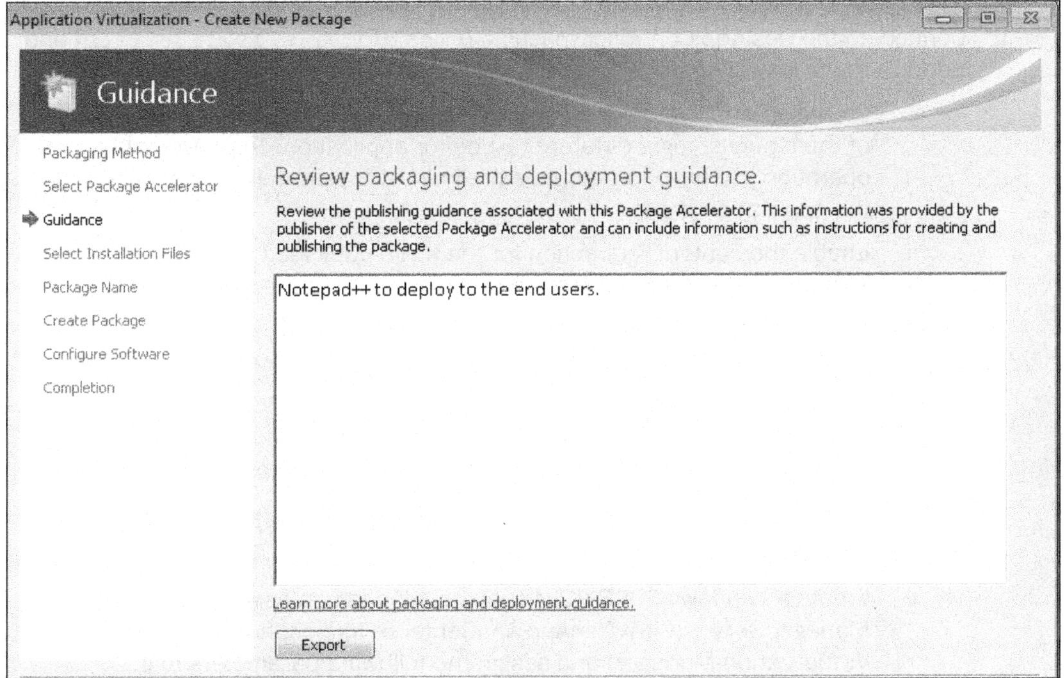


## See also

- The *Configuring XenDesktop to interact with Microsoft Hyper-V* recipe in *Chapter 2, Deploying Virtual Machines for XenDesktop*

# Chapter 7 XenDesktop lab

In this chapter we've discussed the three main supported technologies to deploy applications in a VDI environment: the VM-hosted apps architecture using Citrix XenDesktop, the streamed application profiles with Citrix XenApp, and the Microsoft App-V technology for both streamed and nonstreamed software. In this lab we will implement a software distribution using two of these three architectures. Perform the following steps:

1. Connect to the Desktop Controller machine (`vmctxddc01 - 192.168.1.60`) and perform the following operations:
    i. Create an application desktop group made up of three machines, each of them publishing a different text editor application. To perform this operation you have to execute a preliminary task required to populate the application group.
    ii. Enable the content redirection for the three published software. To perform this operation remember to execute the required preliminary tasks.
    iii. Assign all the three applications to a single domain user.
    iv. Connect to one of the available desktop machines (MCS or PVS) with the user configured for the application use, point the Citrix Receiver to the VM-hosted apps architecture, and then try to run the published software.
2. Perform an evaluation of the use of Citrix XenApp or Microsoft App-V; after deciding this, perform the following tasks:
    i. Create a Windows 2008 R2 virtual machine to use as Application Manager Server (Citrix XenApp AppCenter or Microsoft App-V Application Virtualization Manager) and assign the following parameters to it:
        - Recommended virtual hardware resources are two vCPUs, 4 GB of RAM, 50 GB of hard disk
        - `vmctxappmv01` as the hostname
        - `192.168.1.110` as the IP address
        - Join it to the `ctxlab.local` domain before configuring any software role

ii. Create a Windows 7 64-bit virtual machine to use as profiler machine (Citrix Streaming Profiler or Microsoft App-V Sequencer) and assign it the following parameters:

   - Recommended virtual hardware resources are two vCPUs, 4 GB of RAM, 50 GB of hard disk
   - `vmctxprfv01` as the hostname
   - `192.168.1.111` as the IP address
   - Join it to the `ctxlab.local` domain before configuring any software role
   - Create a network share for the folder on which the application profiles will be archived

iii. Download the Mozilla Firefox and Google Chrome web browsers on the profiler machine, and generate two profiles for them.

iv. Create the applications from the generated profiles under the Application Manager Server, and assign them to a user different from the previous one. These have to be streamed applications.

v. Connect to one of the available desktop machines (MCS or PVS) with this second user configured for the application use, and point the right client (Citrix Receiver or App-V Virtualization Client) to the configured software farm, and then try to run the published software.

> If you have selected the Microsoft App-V farm, remember to install its client on the base image template and update the related desktop instances.

# 8
# XenDesktop Tuning and Security

In this chapter we will cover:

- Configuring the XenDesktop policies
- Configuring the Citrix Access Gateway virtual appliance
- Configuring the XenDesktop logging

## Introduction

Citrix XenDesktop offers itself as a secure and performant architecture. This does not mean that it's not possible to increase and develop both the levels; Citrix platforms or different vendor systems permit you to have a deeper protection and avoid performance issues by enabling the right policies.

During this chapter we will discuss the configuration of the XenDesktop infrastructural policies and we'll use critical platforms such as Citrix Access Gateway.

## Configuring the XenDesktop policies

Now that the XenDesktop infrastructure has been configured, it's time to activate and populate the VDI policies. This is an extremely important part of the implementation process, because with these policies you will regulate the resource use and assignments, and you will also improve the general virtual desktops performance.

## Getting ready

All the policies will be applied to the deployed virtual desktop instances and the assigned users, so you need an already existing XenDesktop infrastructure on which you will enable and use the configuration rules.

## How to do it...

In this recipe we will explain the configuration for the user and machine policies offered by Citrix XenDesktop. Perform the following steps:

1. Connect to the XenDesktop Director machine with domain administrative credentials, then navigate to **Start | All Programs | Citrix** and run the Desktop Studio.
2. On the left-hand side menu expand the **HDX Policy** section and select the **Machines** link.
3. Click on the **New** button to create a new policy container, or select the default unfiltered policies and click on **Edit** to modify them. In the first case, you have to assign a descriptive name to the created policy.
4. In the **Categories** menu, click on the following sections and configure the values for the policies that will be applied to the clients, in terms of network flow optimization and resource usage monitoring:
    - **The ICA section**
        - **ICA listener connection timeout**: Insert a value in milliseconds; default is 12000.
        - **ICA listener port number**: This is the TCP/IP port number on which the ICA protocol will try to establish the connection. The default value is 1494.
    - **The Auto Client Reconnect subsection**
        - **Auto client reconnect**: (Values **Allowed** or **Prohibited**) Specify whether or not to automatically reconnect in case of a broken connection from a client.
        - **Auto client reconnect authentication**: (Values **Do not require authentication** or **Require authentication**) Decide whether to let the Citrix infrastructure ask you for the credentials each time you have to reperform the login operation.
        - **Auto client reconnect logging**: (Values **Do Not Log auto-reconnect events** or **Log auto-reconnect events**) This policy enables or disables the logging activities in the system log for the reconnection process. In case of active autoclient reconnect, you should also activate its logging.

- **End User Monitoring subsection**
    - **ICA round trip calculation**: (Values **Enabled** or **Disabled**) This decides whether or not to enable the calculation of the ICA network traffic time.
    - **ICA round trip calculation interval**: Insert the time interval in seconds for the period of the round trip calculation.
    - **ICA round trip calculations for idle connections**: (Values **Enabled** or **Disabled**) Decide whether to enable the round trip calculation for connections that are not performing traffic. Enable this policy only if necessary.
- **The Graphics subsection**
    - **Display memory limit**: Configure the maximum value in KB to assign it to the video buffer for a session.
    - **Display mode degrade preference**: (Values **Degrade color depth first** or **Degrade resolution first**) Configure a parameter to lower the resolution or the color quality in case of graphic memory overflow.
    - **Dynamic Windows Preview**: (Values **Enabled** or **Disabled**) With this policy you have the ability to turn on or turn off the high-level preview of the windows open on the screen.
    - **Image caching**: (Values **Enabled** or **Disabled**) With this parameter you can cache images on the client to obtain a faster response.
    - **Notify user when display mode is degraded**: (Values **Enabled** or **Disabled**) In case of degraded connections you can display a pop up to send a notification to the involved users.
    - **Queueing and tossing**: (Values **Enabled** or **Disabled**) By enabling this policy you can stop the processing of the images that are replaced by other pictures.

In presence of slow or WAN network connections, you should create a separate policy group which will reduce the display memory size, configure the degrade color depth policy, activate the image caching, and remove the advanced Windows graphical features.

- **The Keep Alive subsection**
    - **ICA keep alive timeout**: Insert a value in seconds to configure the keep alive timeout for the ICA connections.
    - **ICA keep alives**: (Values **Do not send ICA keep alive messages** or **Send ICA keep alive messages**) Configure whether or not to send keep-alive signals for the running sessions.

- **The Multimedia subsection**
    - **Windows Media Redirection**: (Values **Allowed** or **Prohibited**) Decide whether or not to redirect the multimedia execution on the Citrix server(s) and then stream it to the clients.
    - **Windows Media Redirection Buffer Size**: Insert a value in seconds for the buffer used to deliver multimedia contents to the clients.
    - **Windows Media Redirection Buffer Size Use**: (Values **Enabled** or **Disabled**) This policy decides whether or not to let you use the previously configured media buffer size.
- **The Multi-Stream Connections subsection**
    - **Audio UDP Port Range**: Specify a port range for the UDP connections used to stream audio data. The default range is 16500 to 16509.
    - **Multi-Port Policy**: This policy configures the traffic shaping to implement the **quality of service** (**QoS**). You have to specify from two to four ports and assign them a priority level.

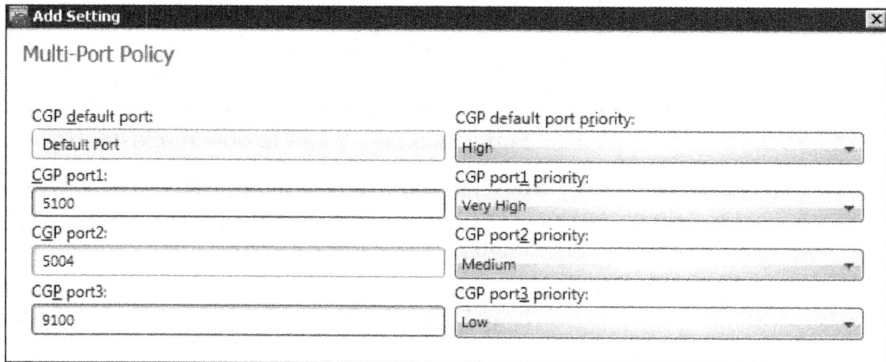


- 
    - **Multi-Stream**: (Values **Enabled** or **Disabled**) Decide whether or not to activate the previously configured multistream ports.

You have to enable this policy to activate the port configuration in the Multi-Port Policy.

- **The Session Reliability subsection**
    - **Session reliability connections**: (Values **Allowed** or **Prohibited**) By enabling this policy you allow the sessions to remain active in case of network problems.

- Session reliability port number: Specify the port used by ICA to check the reliability of incoming connections. The default port is 2598.
- **Session reliability timeout**: Specify a value in seconds used by the session reliability manager component to wait for a client reconnection.

You cannot enable the ICA keep alives policy if the policies under the **Session Reliability** subsection have been activated.

- **The Virtual Desktop Agent Settings section**
    - **Controller Registration Port**: Specify the port used by Virtual Desktop Agent on the client to register with the Desktop Controller. The default value is 80.

Changing this port number will require you to also modify the port on the controller machine by running the following command:

```
<BrokerInstallationPath>\BrokerService.exe /
VdaPort <newPort>
```

- **Controller SIDs**: Specify a single controller SID or a list of them used by Virtual Desktop Agent for registration procedures.
- **Controllers**: Specify a single or a set of Desktop Controllers in the form of FQDN, used by Virtual Desktop Agent for registration procedures.
- **Site GUID**: Specify the XenDesktop unique site identifier used by Virtual Desktop Agent for registration procedures.

In presence of more than one Desktop Controller, you should create multiple VDA policies with different controllers for a load-balanced infrastructure.

- **The CPU Usage Monitoring subsection**
    - **Enable Monitoring**: (Values **Allowed** or **Prohibited**) With this policy you can enable or disable the monitoring for the CPU usage.
    - **Monitoring Period**: Insert a value in seconds to configure the time period to run the CPU usage recalculation.
    - **Threshold**: Configure a percentage value to activate the high CPU usage alert. The default value is 95 percent.

[ Enable the CPU Usage Monitoring policies in order to better troubleshoot machine load issues. ]

5. After configuring, click on the **OK** button to save the modifications.
6. On the left-hand side menu, click on the **Users** policy link in the **HDX Policy** section.
7. Click on the **New** button to create a new policy container, or select the default unfiltered policies and click on **Edit** to modify them. In the first case, you have to assign a descriptive name to the created policy.
8. In the **Categories** menu click on the following sections and configure the associated values:
    - **The ICA section**
        - **Client clipboard redirection**: (Values **Allowed** or **Prohibited**) This policy permits you to decide whether or not to enable the use of the client clipboard in the XenDesktop session, and to perform copy and paste operations from the physical device to the remote Citrix session.

[ The active clipboard redirection could be a security issue; be sure about its activation! ]

- **The Flash Redirection subsection**
    - **Flash acceleration**: (Values **Enabled** or **Disabled**) This policy permits you to redirect the Flash rendering activities to the client. This is possible only with the legacy mode. Enable this policy to have a better user experience for the Flash contents.
    - **Flash backwards compatibility**: (Values **Enabled** or **Disabled**) With this policy you can decide whether or not to activate the compatibility of older versions of Citrix Receiver with the most recent Citrix Flash policies and features.
    - **Flash default behavior**: (Values **Enable Flash acceleration**, **Disable Flash acceleration**, or **Block Flash player**) This policy regulates the use of the Adobe Flash technology, respectively enabling the most recent Citrix for Flash features (including the client-side processing), permitting only server-side processed contents, or blocking any Flash content.
    - **Flash event logging**: (Values **Enabled** or **Disabled**) Decide whether or not to create system logs for the Adobe Flash events.

  - **Flash intelligent fallback**: (Values **Enabled** or **Disabled**) This policy, if enabled, is able to activate the server-side Flash content processing when the client side is not required.

The Flash Redirection features have been strongly improved starting from XenDesktop Version 5.5.

- **The Audio subsection**
  - **Audio over UDP Real-time transport**: (Values **Enabled** or **Disabled**) With this policy you can decide which protocols to transmit the audio packets, RTP/UDP (policy enabled) or TCP (policy disabled). The choice depends on the kind of audio traffic to transmit. UDP is better in terms of performance and bandwidth consumption.
  - **Audio quality**: (Values **Low**, **Medium**, or **High**) This parameter depends on a comparison between the quality of the network connections and the audio level, and they respectively cover the low-speed connections, optimized for speech and high-definition audio cases.
  - **Client audio redirection**: (Values **Allowed** or **Prohibited**) Allowing or prohibiting this policy permits applications to use the audio device on the client's machine(s).
  - **Client microphone redirection**: (Values **Allowed** or **Prohibited**) This policy permits you to map client microphone devices to use within a desktop session.

Try to reduce the network and load impact of the multimedia components and devices where the high user experience is not required.

- **The Bandwidth subsection**
  - **Audio redirection bandwidth limit**: Insert a value in **kilobits per second** (**Kbps**) to set the maximum bandwidth assigned to the playing and recording audio activities.
  - **Audio redirection bandwidth limit percent**: Insert a maximum percentage value to play and record audio.
  - **Client USB device redirection bandwidth limit**: Insert a value in Kbps to set the maximum bandwidth assigned to USB devices redirection.
  - **Client USB device redirection bandwidth limit percent**: Insert a maximum percentage value for USB devices redirection.

- **Clipboard redirection bandwidth limit**: Insert a value in Kbps to set the maximum bandwidth assigned to the clipboard traffic from the local client to the remote session.
- **Clipboard redirection bandwidth limit percent**: Insert a maximum percentage value for the clipboard traffic from the local client to the remote session.
- **COM port redirection bandwidth limit**: Insert a value in Kbps to set the maximum bandwidth assigned to the client COM port redirected traffic.
- **COM port redirection bandwidth limit percent**: Insert a maximum percentage value for the client COM port redirected traffic.
- **File redirection bandwidth limit**: Insert a value in Kbps to set the maximum bandwidth assigned to client drives redirection.
- **File redirection bandwidth limit percent**: Insert a maximum percentage value for client drives redirection.
- **HDX MediaStream Multimedia Acceleration bandwidth limit**: Insert a value in Kbps to set the maximum bandwidth assigned to the multimedia content redirected through the HDX MediaStream acceleration.
- **HDX MediaStream Multimedia Acceleration bandwidth limit percent**: Insert a maximum percentage value for the multimedia content redirected through the HDX MediaStream acceleration.
- **Overall session bandwidth limit**: Specify a value in Kbps for the total bandwidth assigned to the client sessions.

In presence of both bandwidth limit and bandwidth limit percent enabled policies, the most restrictive value will be used.

- **The Desktop UI subsection**
    - **Aero Redirection**: (Values **Enabled** or **Disabled**) This policy decides whether or not to activate the redirection of the Windows Aero graphical feature to the client device. If Aero has been disabled, this policy has no value.
    - **Aero Redirection Graphics Quality**: (Values **High**, **Medium**, **Low**, and **Lossless**) If Aero has been enabled, you can configure its graphics level.
    - **Desktop wallpaper**: (Values **Allowed** or **Prohibited**) Through this policy you can decide whether or not to permit the users having the desktop wallpaper in your session. Disable this policy if you want to standardize your desktop deployment.

- **Menu animation**: (Values **Allowed** or **Prohibited**) This policy permits you to decide whether or not to have the animated menu of the Microsoft operating systems. The choice depends on what kind of performances you need for your desktops.
- **View window contents while dragging**: (Values **Allowed** or **Prohibited**) This policy gives you the ability to see the entire window contents during the drag-and-drop activities between windows, if enabled. Otherwise you'll see only the window's border.

Enabling the Aero redirection will have impact only on the LAN-based connection; on WAN, Aero will not be redirected by default.

- **The File Redirection subsection**
  - **Auto connect client drives**: (Values **Enabled** or **Disabled**) With this policy the local drives of your client will or will not be automatically connected at logon time.
  - **Client drive redirection**: (Values **Allowed** or **Prohibited**) The drive redirection policy allows you to decide whether it is permitted or not to save files locally on the client machine drives.
  - **Client fixed drives**: (Values **Allowed** or **Prohibited**) This policy decides whether or not to permit you to read data from and save information to the fixed drives of your client machine.
  - **Client floppy drives**: (Values **Allowed** or **Prohibited**) This policy decides whether or not to permit you to read data from and save information to the floppy drives of your client machine. This should be allowed only in presence of an existing floppy drive, otherwise it has no value to your infrastructure.
  - **Client network drives**: (Values **Allowed** or **Prohibited**) With this policy you have the capability of mapping the remote network drives from your client.
  - **Client optical drives**: (Values **Allowed** or **Prohibited**) With this policy you can enable or disable the access to the optical client drives, such as CD-ROM or DVD-ROM.
  - **Client removable drives**: (Values **Allowed** or **Prohibited**) This policy allows or prohibits you to map, read, and save removable drives from your client, such as USB keys.
  - **Preserve client drive letters**: (Values **Enabled** or **Disabled**) Enabling this policy offers you the possibility of maintaining the client drive letters when mapping them in the remote session, whenever possible.

- **Read-only client drive access**: (Values **Enabled** or **Disabled**) Enabling this policy will not permit you to access the mapped client drivers in write mode. By default, this policy is disabled to permit the full drive access. To reduce the impact on the client security, you should enable it. You can always modify it when necessary.

These are powerful policies for regulating the access to the physical storage resources. You should configure them to be consistent with your company security policies.

- **The Multi-Stream connections subsection**
  - **Multi-Stream**: (Values **Enabled** or **Disabled**) As seen earlier for the machine section, this policy enables or disables the multistreamed traffic for specific users.
- **The Port Redirection subsection**
  - **Auto connect client COM ports**: (Values **Enabled** or **Disabled**) If enabled, this policy automatically maps the client COM ports.
  - **Auto connect client LPT ports**: (Values **Enabled** or **Disabled**) This policy, if enabled, autoconnects the client LPT ports.
  - **Client COM port redirection**: (Values **Allowed** or **Prohibited**) This policy configures the COM port redirection between the client and the remote session.
  - **Client LPT port redirection**: (Values **Allowed** or **Prohibited**) This policy configures the LPT port redirection between the client and the remote session.

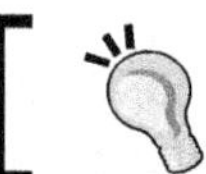

You have to enable only the necessary ports, so disable the policies for the missing COM or LPT ports.

- **The Session Limits subsection**
  - **Disconnected session timer**: (Values **Enabled** or **Disabled**) This policy enables or disables the counter used to migrate from a locked workstation to a logged off session. For security reasons, you should enable the automatic logoff of the idle sessions.
  - **Disconnected session timer interval**: Insert a value in minutes, which will be used as a counter reference value to log off locked workstations. Set this parameter based on a real inactivity time for your company employees.

- **Session connection to timer**: (Values **Enabled** or **Disabled**) This policy will or will not use a timer to measure the duration of active connections from clients to the remote sessions.

- **The Time Zone Control subsection**
  - **Use local time of client**: (Values **Use server time zone** or **Use client time zone**) With this policy you can decide whether to use the time settings from your client or from the server.

[ XenDesktop uses the user session's time zone. ]

- **The USB Devices subsection**
  - **Client USB device redirection**: (Values **Allowed** or **Prohibited**) With this important policy you can permit or prohibit USB drives redirection.
  - **Client USB device redirection rules**: Through this policy you can generate rules for specific USB devices and vendors, in order to filter or not; and if yes, what types of external devices mapping.
- **The Visual Display subsection**
  - **Max Frame Per Second**: Insert a value, in terms of frames per second, which will define the number of frames sent from the virtual desktop to the user client. This parameter could dramatically impact the network performance, so be careful about it and your network connection.
- **The Server Session Settings section**
  - **Single Sign-On**: (Values **Enabled** or **Disabled**) This policy decides whether to turn on or turn off the SSO for the user sessions.
  - **Single Sign-On central store**: Specify the SSO store server to which the user will connect for the logon operations, in the form of a UNC path.
- **The Virtual Desktop Agent Settings section**
- **The HDX3DPro subsection**
  - **EnableLossLess**: (Values **Allowed** or **Prohibited**) This policy permits or prohibits the use of a lossless codec.
  - **HDX3DPro Quality Settings**: Specify two values, **Minimum Quality** and **Maximum Quality** (from 0 to 100), as HDX 3D Pro quality levels. In the absence of a valid HDX 3D Pro license, this policy has no effect.

- **The ICA Latency Monitoring subsection**
    - **Enable Monitoring**: (Values **Allowed** or **Prohibited**) This rule will or will not monitor the ICA latency problems.
    - **Monitoring Period**: Define a value in seconds to run the ICA latency monitor.
    - **Threshold**: Insert a threshold value in milliseconds to check if the ICA latency has arrived to the highest level.
- **The Profile Load Time Monitoring subsection**
    - **Enable Monitoring**: (Values **Allowed** or **Prohibited**) With this policy you can monitor the time required to load a user profile.
    - **Threshold**: Specify a value in seconds to activate the trigger for the high profile loading time event.

These are important policies to troubleshoot performance issues in the profile loading activities, especially referred to the centralized profiles.

9. After configuring click on the **OK** button to save the modifications.
10. For both the edited policy categories (**Machines** and **Users**), click on the **Edit** button, select the **Filters** tab, and add one or more of the following filters:
    - **Access Control**: (**Mode**: **Allow** or **Deny**, **Connection Type**: **With Access Gateway** or **Without Access Gateway**) Insert the parameters for the type of connection to which you are applying the policies, using or not using Citrix Access Gateway.
    - **Branch Repeater**: (Values **Connections with Branch Repeater** or **Connections without Branch Repeater**) This policy decides whether or not to apply the policies to the connection that passes or doesn't pass through a configured Citrix Branch Repeater.
    - **Client IP Address**: (**Mode**: **Allow** or **Deny**) Specify a client IP address to which you are allowing or denying the policy application.
    - **Client Name**: (**Mode**: **Allow** or **Deny**) Specify a client name to which you are allowing or denying the policy application.
    - **Desktop Group**: (**Mode**: **Allow** or **Deny**) Select from the drop-down list an existing desktop or application group to which you are applying or not applying the configured policies.
    - **Desktop Type**: (**Mode**: **Allow** or **Deny**) This policy decides to allow or deny the policy application to the existing deployed resources (**Private Desktop** or **Shared Desktop**, **Private Applications** or **Shared Applications**).

- Organizational Unit: (Mode: Allow or Deny) Browse for an existing domain OU to which you are applying or not applying the configured policies.
- **Tag**: (**Mode**: **Allow** or **Deny**) This policy decides to allow or deny the application of the policies to specific tags applied to the desktops.
- **User or Group**: (**Mode**: **Allow** or **Deny**) Browse for existing domain users and groups to which you are applying or not applying the configured policies.

For the machine section, you'll only have the desktop group, desktop type, organizational unit, and tag categories of filters.

11. After completing this, click on the **OK** button to save the changed filters.

## How it works...

The Citrix XenDesktop policies work at two different levels of components, machines and users, and for each of them you can apply a set of filters to decide when and where to permit or not to permit the policy utilization. These configurations should be strongly oriented to the performance and security optimization, so the best practices to apply is to generate different sets of policies and specifically apply them to different kinds of virtual desktops, clients, and users. The following is the explanation of the previously applied configurations:

- **Machines policy level**: These kinds of policies apply at the machine level, trying to regulate and optimize the session management, and the multimedia resources redirection.

  With this group of settings you are able to configure the standard ICA port to listen, and the relative connection timeouts. It's possible to decide whether or not to automatically reconnect a client in case of broken connections. Enabling Auto client reconnect policy could be right in some cases, especially when you have interrupted an important working session, but on the other hand, you could not have calculated waste of resources, because the Citrix broker could run a new session in the presence of issues with the session cookies.

  With the ICA round trip policies, you can monitor and measure the response time taken by the users for the operations. This data permits you to understand the responsiveness of your Citrix infrastructure. In case it allows you to apply remediation to the configuration, especially for the policies that involve graphics components, you can size the display memory and the image caching area, or turn on or off specific Windows advanced graphical features, such as the **Dynamic Windows Preview** (**DWP**).

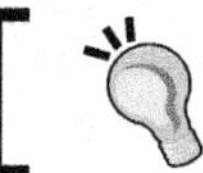

With the queuing and tossing policy active, you could have problems of lost frames when reproducing animations.

The Windows media redirection policy optimizes the reproduction of multimedia objects; by applying a correct sizing to its buffer size you should obtain evident improvements in the streaming and reproduction operations. So, you should consider disabling this policy, demanding the processing of audio and video to the clients only when you can see no particular benefits.

Another important feature offered by these policies is the QoS implementation; you can enable the multistream connection configurations and apply the traffic priority levels to them, permitting to give precedence and more bandwidth to the traffic that is considered more critical than others.

> The Multi-Stream policy for the QoS can be considered a less powerful alternative to Citrix Branch Repeater.

As the last part of this section, the **Virtual Desktop Agent Settings** section permits you to restrict the access to only pre-configured resources, such as specific Desktop Controllers.

- **Users policy level**: Combined with the machines policies we have the users policies. These policies apply settings from a user session perspective, so you can configure, for instance, processing the Adobe Flash contents, deciding whether or not to activate the compatibility with the oldest version of this software, and whether to elaborate the Flash multimedia objects on the user's clients or on the Citrix servers. Moreover, you can configure the audio settings, such as audio and microphone client redirection (in the sense of using the local device resources), the desktop settings (Aero parameters, desktop wallpapers, and so on), or the HDX protocol quality settings.

> Be careful when applying policies for the desktop graphical settings; remember to be consistent with the base image template configurations performed in *Chapter 3, Master Image Configuration and Tuning*, and *Chapter 4, User Experience – Planning and Configuring*.

To optimize the information transmission for the desktops the bandwidth policy is extremely important; by this you can assign, in the form of maximum Kbps or percentage, the values for the traffic types such as audio, USB, clipboard, COM and LPT ports, and file redirection. These configurations require a good analysis of the traffic levels and their priorities within your organization.

The last great configuration is the redirection of the client drives to the remote Citrix sessions; in fact, you can activate the mount (automatic or not) and the users rights (read only or read/write) on the client drives, removable or not, such as CD-ROM or DVD-ROM, removable USB devices, and fixed drives as the client device operating system root. This option gives you the flexibility to transfer information from the local device to the XenDesktop instance through the use of properly configured Virtual Desktop Agent.

> This last device policy could make your infrastructure more secure, thanks to the use of the USB device redirection rules; through it, in fact, you could only permit the use of USB keys approved by your company, prohibiting any other nonpolicy-compliant device.

The granularity of the policy application is granted by the configuration of the filters; by using these-you can apply the policies to specific clients, desktop or application groups, or domain users and groups. In this way you can create different policies with different configurations, and apply them to specific areas of your company, without generalizing and overriding settings.

## There's more...

To verify the effective running of the policies applied to your VDI infrastructure, there's a tool called Citrix Group Policy Modeling Wizard inside the **HDX Policy** section, which performs this task. This tool performs a simulation for the policy applications, returning a report with the current configuration. This is something similar to Microsoft Windows Domain Group Policy Results.

The simulations apply to one or all the domain controllers configured within your domain, being able to test the application for a specific user or computer object, including organizational units containing them.

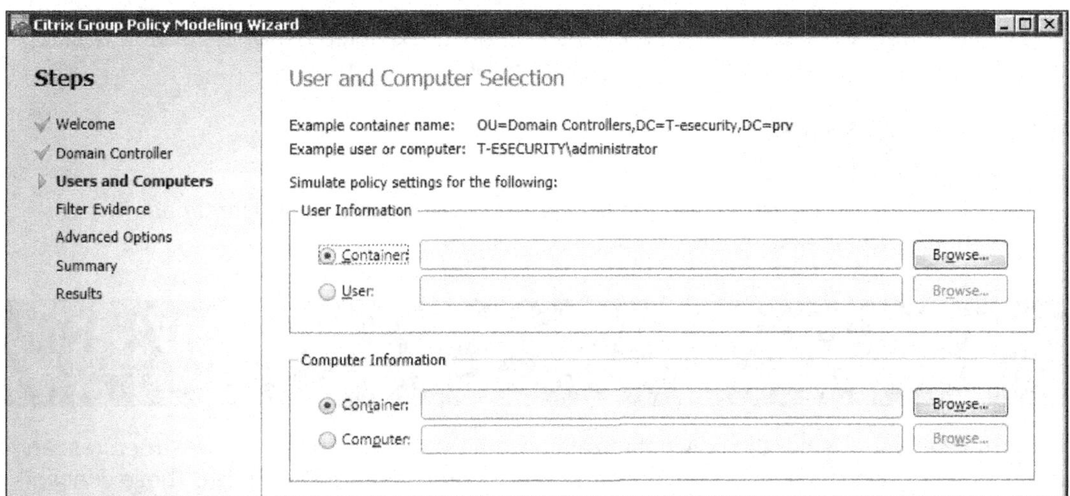


Moreover, you can apply filters based on the client IP address, the client name, the type of machine (private or shared desktop, private or shared application), or you can apply the simulation to a specific desktop group.

In the **Advanced Options** section you can simulate slow network connections and/or loopback processing (basically, a policy application only based on the computer object locations, instead of both the user and computer object positions) for a configured XenDesktop site.

After running the policy application test, you can check the results by right-clicking on the generated report name, and selecting the **View Report** option.

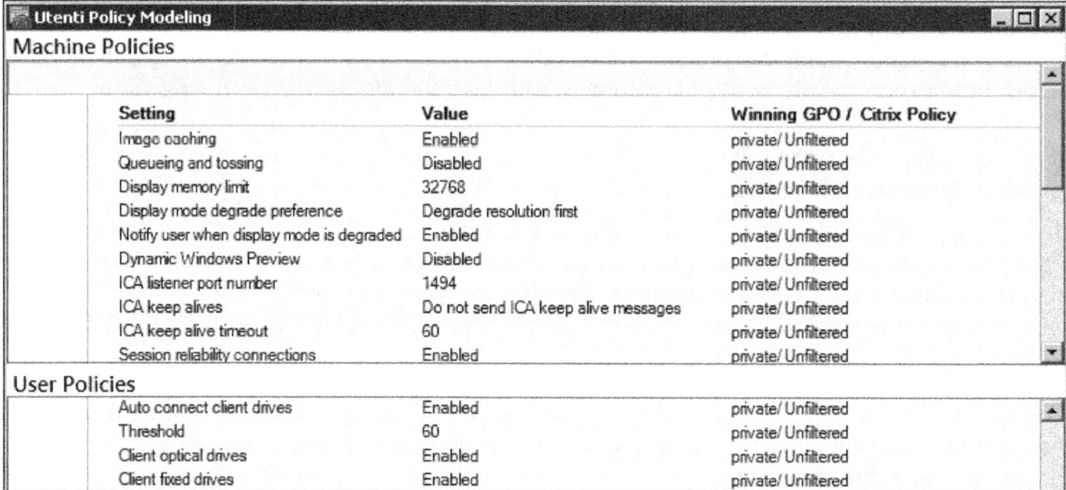


| Setting | Value | Winning GPO / Citrix Policy |
|---|---|---|
| Image caching | Enabled | private/ Unfiltered |
| Queueing and tossing | Disabled | private/ Unfiltered |
| Display memory limit | 32768 | private/ Unfiltered |
| Display mode degrade preference | Degrade resolution first | private/ Unfiltered |
| Notify user when display mode is degraded | Enabled | private/ Unfiltered |
| Dynamic Windows Preview | Disabled | private/ Unfiltered |
| ICA listener port number | 1494 | private/ Unfiltered |
| ICA keep alives | Do not send ICA keep alive messages | private/ Unfiltered |
| ICA keep alive timeout | 60 | private/ Unfiltered |
| Session reliability connections | Enabled | private/ Unfiltered |

| | | |
|---|---|---|
| Auto connect client drives | Enabled | private/ Unfiltered |
| Threshold | 60 | private/ Unfiltered |
| Client optical drives | Enabled | private/ Unfiltered |
| Client fixed drives | Enabled | private/ Unfiltered |

This tool is extremely powerful when you have to verify unexpected behaviors of your desktop instances or user rights because of the application of incorrect policies.

## See also

- The *Configuring virtual desktop policies* recipe in *Chapter 3, Master Image Configuration and Tuning*

# Configuring the Citrix Access Gateway virtual appliance

Performance tuning is not the only optimization work to perform on the IT infrastructures; an IT staff should also focus on the security features to implement and optimize. These concepts need particular care in infrastructures where access is granted to the users' resources. For the Citrix VDI architectures, Citrix NetScaler Access Gateway permits you to have a secure gateway in front of your connection manager, the Web Interface.

In this recipe, we're going to discuss how to implement the virtual appliance version of Citrix Access Gateway.

## Getting ready

In order to perform the configuration operation for Citrix Access Gateway, first of all you need to download it from your MyCitrix account by navigating to the **Download** area, selecting the **Netscaler Access Gateway** section, then selecting the **Virtual Appliances** subsection, and downloading the appropriate VPX version for your hypervisor (the supported systems are Citrix XenServer, VMware ESX/ESXi, and Microsoft Hyper-V). After downloading you have to import it into your virtual infrastructure.

When importing the virtual appliance, during the configuration steps, you should assign two different networks to the virtual appliance's virtual network cards, one pointing to the private network, and the other configured for the public network.

Moreover, you need to allocate a number of licenses equal to the number of your XenDesktop users. As we have seen in *Chapter 1, XenDesktop Installation and Configuration*, you have to generate a license file and associate it to the Access Gateway hostname virtual appliance.

## How to do it...

In this recipe we will perform the tasks to configure the Citrix Access Gateway virtual appliance. Perform the following steps:

1. Connect to the console of the configured Access Gateway virtual machine, and configure the network parameters, **IPv4 address**, **Netmask**, and **Gateway IPv4 address**. After completing this, select option number **4**, **Save and quit**.

```
Your identification has been saved in /nsconfig/ssh/ssh_host_dsa_key.
Your public key has been saved in /nsconfig/ssh/ssh_host_dsa_key.pub.
The key fingerprint is:
34:01:49:69:35:0e:7d:f9:ef:f6:56:ec:b7:3c:ec:40 root@ns
.
machdep.cpu_idle_hlt: 0 -> 1
Start daemons: syslogd Oct  7 15:14:15 <kern.info> ns syslogd: kernel boot file
is /flash/ns-10.0-70.7
inetd cron httpd monit sshd vmware_guestd .

!There is no ns.conf in the /nsconfig!

Start Netscaler software
tput: no terminal type specified and no TERM environmental variable.
No machine id



Enter NetScaler's IPv4 address []:
```

2. Open a compatible web browser and in the address bar, type the address that was previously assigned to the virtual appliance.
3. Insert the default web portal credentials (`nsroot/nsroot`) and click on the **Login** button to continue.
4. On the left-hand side menu, click on the **System** link, then click on the **Setup Wizard...** button at the bottom of the page to proceed with the necessary configurations, as shown in the following screenshot:

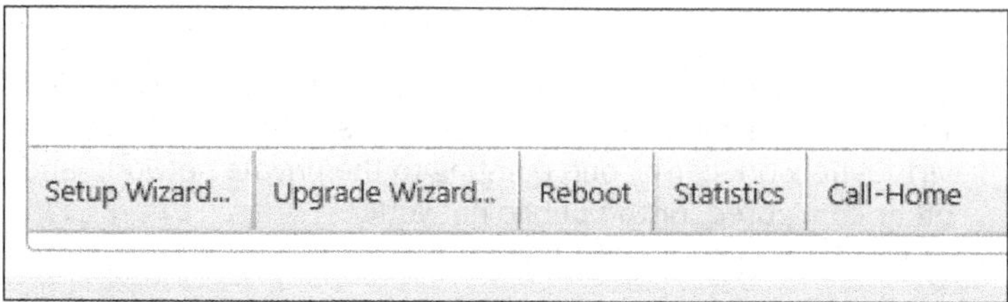


5. On the **Introduction** screen click on **Next** to continue.
6. In the **Network Config** panel confirm or change the configured network parameters assigned previously, and type in a hostname for the CAG VPX. Additionally, you can insert a mapped IP or an SNIP. After completing this click on **Next**.
7. In the **Choose Application** menu, select if configuring an existing application template by importing it, or skipping this step. After selecting the radio button for the chosen option, click on **Next** to continue.
8. In the **Summary** section, after verifying the inserted information, click on the **Finish** button to complete the configuration wizard.
9. On the left-hand side menu, expand the **System** section, and click on the **Licenses** link.
10. In the **Licenses** main menu, click on the **Manage Licenses** choice, click on the **Add...** button, and browse for the previously generated and downloaded license file. After completing this click on the **OK** button, and on the new prompted window, check the **Save configuration** checkbox, and accept to restart the virtual appliance, as shown in the following screenshot:

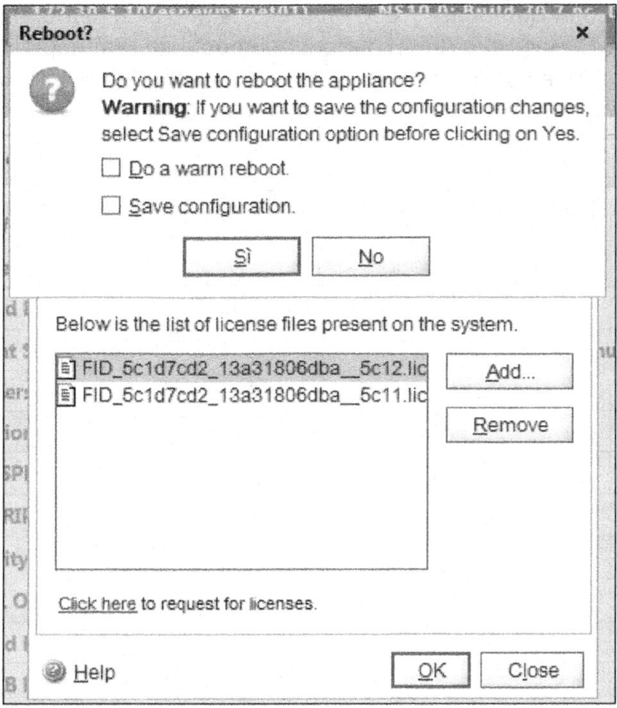


11. In the **System** menu click on the **Settings** link, then select the **Configure Basic Features** choice, and verify that the **Access Gateway** checkbox has been checked. After clicking on **OK**, click on the **Save** link to register all the changes.

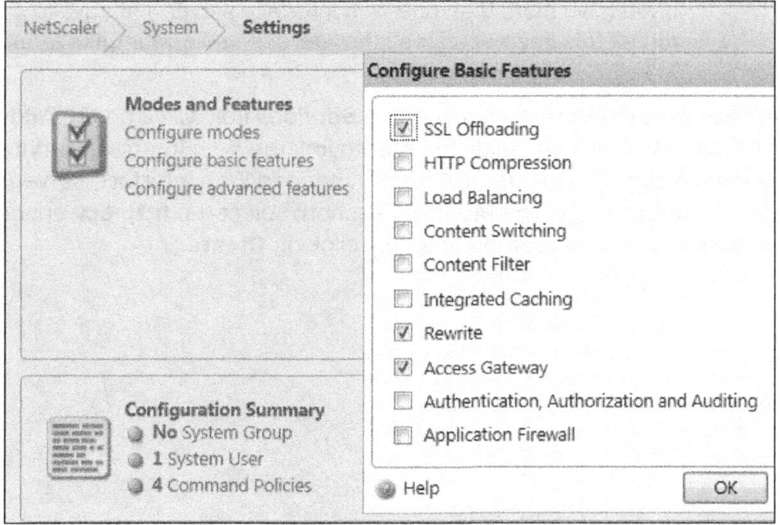

12. Expand the **Load Balancing** group on the left-hand side menu, then select the **Servers** link. Click on the **Add...** button, and populate the required fields with the Web Interface machine configured parameters. Check the **Enable after Creating** checkbox and click on the **Create** button. These steps are required to map the Web Interface server within the Access Gateway structure.

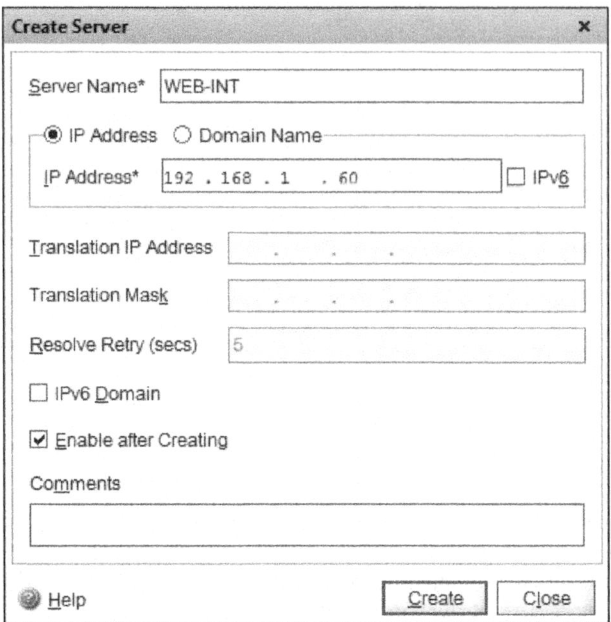


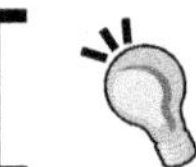

If you have more than one Web Interface server, you have to repeat this operation for all the web servers in your Citrix farm.

13. In the **Load Balancing** section select the **Services** link. Click on the **Add...** button and populate the required fields in order to link the Web Interface service, namely the **Service Name**, **Server** (the previously mapped Web Interface server(s)), **Protocol** (`HTTP`), and **Port** (`80`). In the **Monitors** section, select the **http-ecv** option and click on the **Add** button. After completing this, click on **Create**.

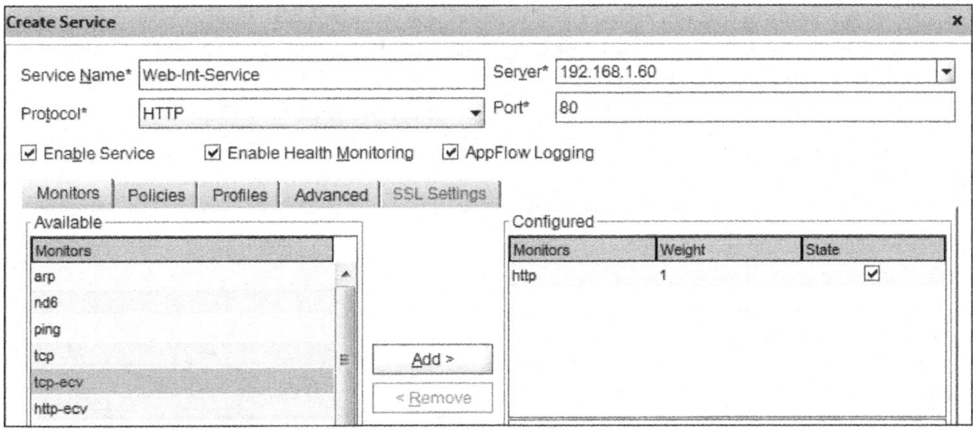


14. In presence of two or more Web Interface machines, you have to create a virtual server with a virtual address to load balance the requests. Navigate to **Load Balancing | Virtual Servers**, and use the **Add** button.
15. Specify **Name** for the load balanced cluster, select **HTTP** as **Protocol**, specify **IP address**, which will be the VIP for this configuration, and check all the previously loaded Web Interface machines that you want to put in load balancing mode. After finishing this click on the **Create** button.

[ If you have only one Web Interface server, you can skip the last task. ]

16. Expand the **SSL** section on the left-hand side menu, and click on one of the links in the **Getting Started** wizard area to generate server, client, intermediate-CA, or Root CA certificates.

[ Follow the standard procedures to generate a self-signed certificate or a CA verified certificate. In this book we will not discuss the full generation of a certificate, but remember that you need at least a Root CA certificate and a server certificate to configure the Citrix Gateway. ]

17. After generating the necessary certificates, expand the **SSL** section from the left-hand side menu, and click on **Certificates**. In this section, click on the **Install** button at the bottom of the page, then populate the required fields with the information about the server certificate; after completing this, click on the **Install** button.

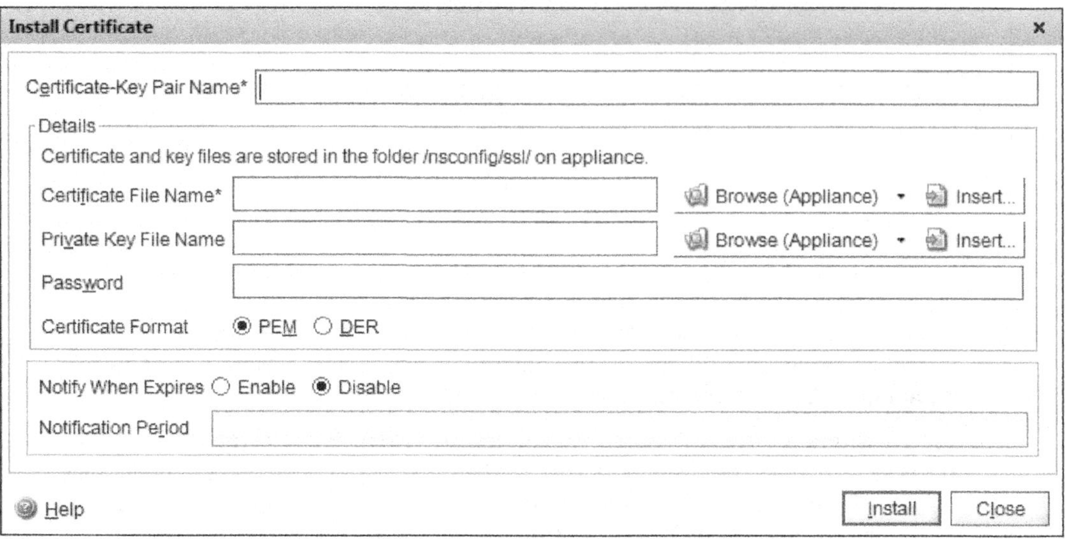


18. Expand the **Access Gateway** section on the left-hand side menu; then in the **Getting Started** section, click on the **Access Gateway** wizard link.
19. In the **Introduction** menu click on **Next** to continue.
20. Specify **IP Address** and **Virtual Server Name** in the second creation step; leave the **Port** field configured for the SSL connection (**443**), and then click on **Next**.

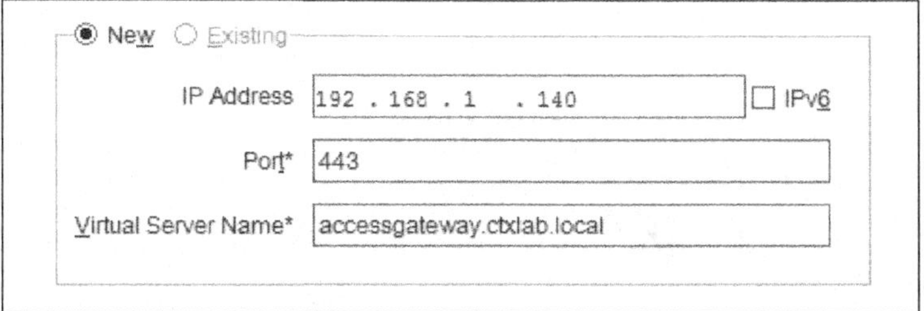


21. In **Certificate Options** select the **Use an installed certificate and private key pair** option. Choose the previously configured server certificate and click on **Next**.

22. Enter valid values in the **DNS Server** and **WINS Server IP Address** fields; select **Name Lookup Priority** (**DNS** or **WINS**), insert the number of times to retry the DNS connection, and then click on **Next**.

23. In the **Configure authentication** section, select **LDAP** as the authentication type and populate the following required fields:

    - **The Server section**
        - **IP Address**: The IP of one of your domain controller servers
        - **Port**: The port used to connect to the LDAP (default 389)
        - **Type**: Select the **AD** option (Active Directory LDAP type option)
    - **The Connection Settings section**
        - **Base DN**: Specify the DN in the form of DC = domain, DC = domain suffix (`DC=ctxlab, DC=local`)
        - **Administrator Bind DN**: Specify the full user DN path (for instance, `CN=admin-user, CN=users, DC=ctxlab, DC=local`)
        - **Administrator Password and Confirm Administrator Password**: Enter and confirm the password for the inserted administrative user

24. Click on the **Retrieve Attributes** link to check the correct LDAP configuration, then click on **Next** to proceed.

25. In the **Configure Authorization** section, select either **Allow** or **Deny** to allow or deny the connection for the configured users, and decide whether or not to redirect all the standard HTTP traffic to a secure web address. In this case, you have to enter a secure Access Gateway web address in the form of `https://<webaddress>`, and then click on **Next**.

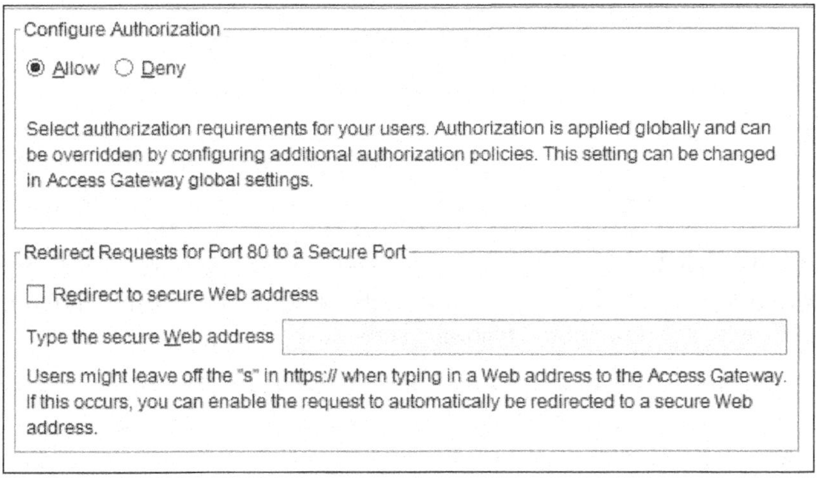

26. In the **Clientless Access** section configure what kind of access is permitted, then choose the **Allow**, **Deny**, or **Prompt** option for the **Client Access Persistent Cookie** area, and click on **Next**.

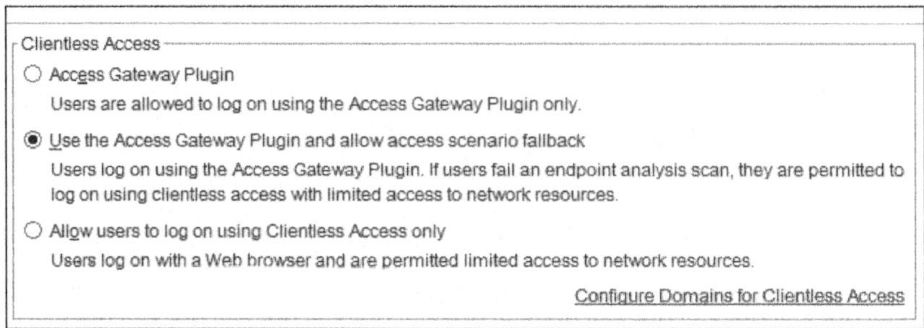


27. After reviewing all the configured parameters, click on the **Finish** button in the **Summary** tab to complete the configuration procedure.
28. On the left-hand side menu, expand the **Access Gateway** section, and click on the **Virtual Servers** link. Select the previously created virtual server and click on the **Open** button at the bottom of the page.
29. Select the **Published Applications** tab and click on the **Add** link in the **Secure Ticket Authority** section. In the pop-up menu, enter the address of your XenDesktop broker in the form of `http://DDCname/scripts/ctxsta.dll`, and click on the **OK** button. After completing this, flag the mapped server link and click on the **Activate All** link, then click on **OK**.

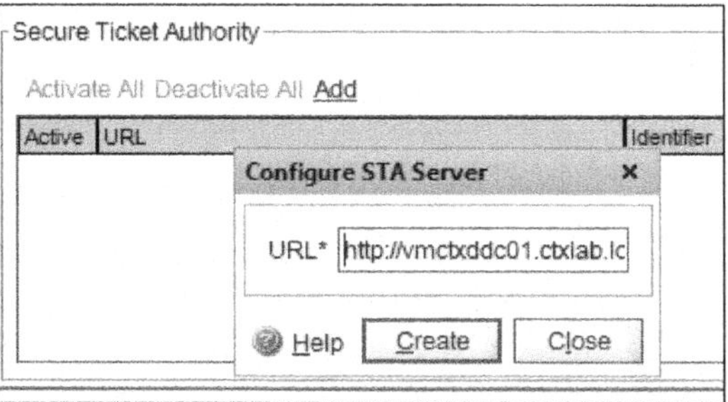


30. Select the **Policies** tab and click on the **Insert Policy** link at the bottom of the page.
31. Assign a name to the policy, and click on the **New...** button next to the **Request Profile** field, as shown in the following screenshot:

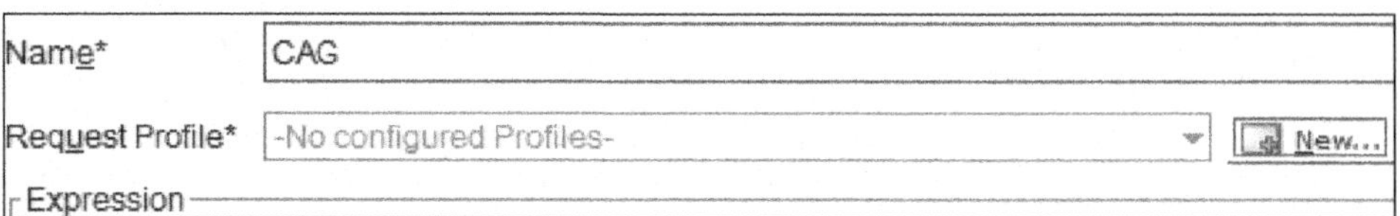

32. In the **Create Access Gateway Session Profile** window assign a name to the profile, select the **Published Applications** tab and check the first four checkboxes under the **Override Global** settings.
33. Enter the required information (**ICA Proxy**: **ON**, **Web Interface Address**: type in the configured Access Gateway website address for the Web Interface, **Web Interface Portal Mode**: **NORMAL**, and **Single Sign-On Domain**: type in the configured domain for your company, then click on the **Create** button.

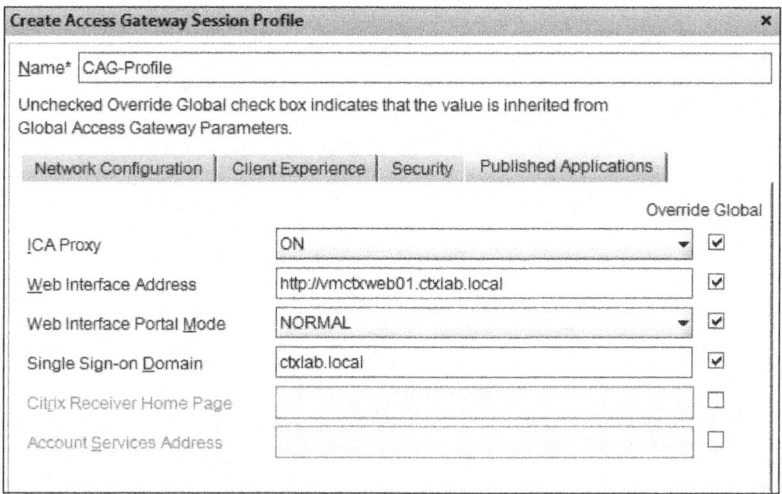


34. On the **Session Policy** screen, select **General** and **True Value** as **Named Expressions** and click on the **Add Expression** link. After completing this, click on **Create**.
35. Connect to your Web Interface machine with domain administrative credentials, click on the **Web Interface Management** link located at **Start | All Programs | Citrix**.
36. Select the **XenApp Web Sites** section (left-hand side menu), then click on the **Create Site** link on the right side of the screen.
37. In the **Path** field, type in a new web path to identify the Access Gateway site (for example, `/Citrix/AG`) and click on **Next**.
38. On the **Specify Point of Authentication** screen, select **At Access Gateway** from the drop-down list and click on **Next**.

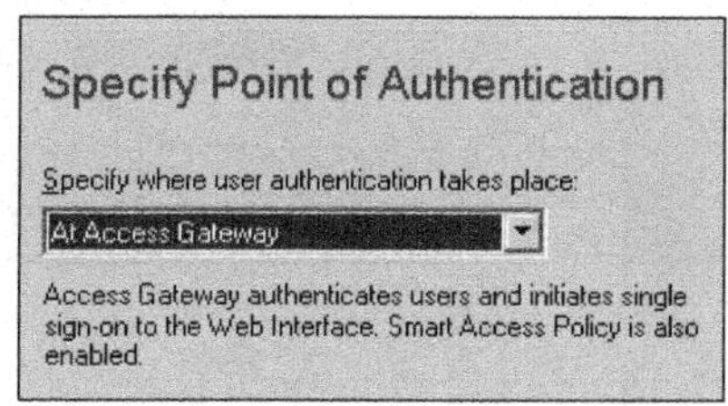

39. Specify an Authentication service URL in the form of `https://accessgatewayaddress/CitrixAuthService/AuthService.asmx`, select the **Explicit** radio button option for the **Authentication Options** menu, and click on the **Next** button.

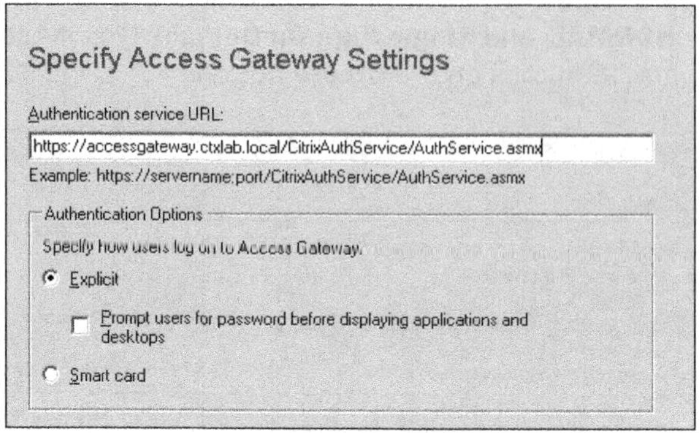


40. On the **Confirm Settings for New Site** screen, click on **Next** after reviewing the configuration information. To start the site configuration process, check the **Configure this site now** checkbox and again click on **Next** to proceed.
41. In the **Specify Server Farm** section, type in the Citrix Access Gateway VIP address configured previously, assign a name to the farm, and click on **Next**.
42. Select **Minimal Logon Screen Appearance** or **Full Logon Screen Appearance**, then click on the **Next** button.
43. Select **Published Resource Type** (**Online**, **Offline**, or **Dual Mode**) and click on **Next**. To complete the configuration, click on **Finish** on the last screen.
44. Highlight the created Citrix website, and click on the **Secure Access** link on the right-hand side menu.
45. Double-click on the default configured access method and change it from **Direct** to **Gateway direct**, then click on **OK** and click on the **Next** button to continue.

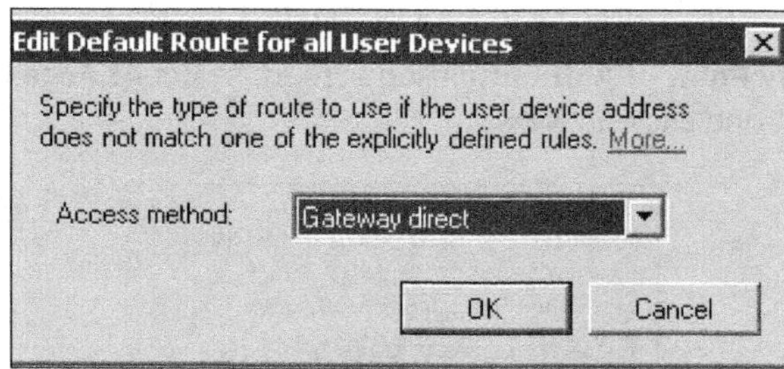

46. On the **Specify Gateway Settings** screen, enter the gateway VIP address in the form of FQDN, check the **Enable session reliability** checkbox, and eventually check the second checkbox only if you have more than one STA servers, then click on **Next**.

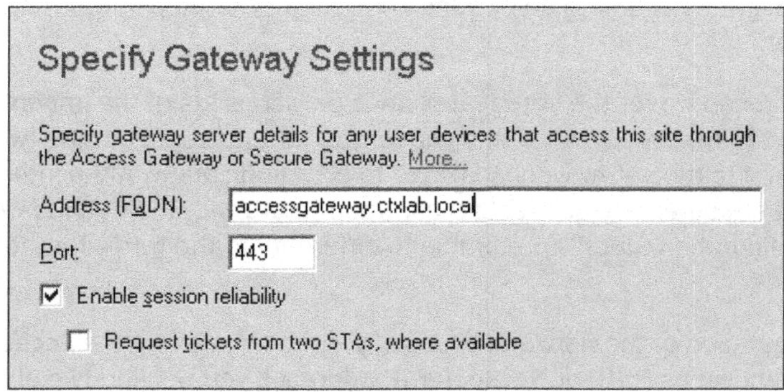


47. Specify the Secure Ticket Authority server address by clicking on the **Add** button and entering the STA URL in the form of `http(s)://XenDesktopDDCFQDN/scripts/ctxsta.dll`. Click on **OK** to close the URL screen, and then click on **Finish** to complete the procedure.
48. Open a web browser and type in the address of the configured FQDN VIP access gateway in the form of `https://AGaddress`. You'll see a logon screen on which you have to enter valid domain credentials. At this point, you will be able to connect to your published resources through the Access Gateway.

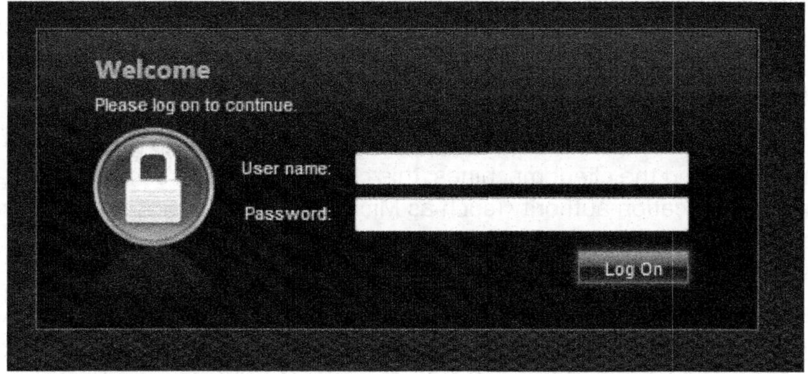

To avoid resolution errors for the Access Gateway VIP address, you should create a DNS record for it or insert a row in the host file of the Citrix Web Interface server.

## How it works...

Citrix Access Gateway, also known as NetScaler Access Gateway, is a secure gateway which permits users to connect to an existing XenDesktop/XenApp infrastructure in a protected manner.

The installation procedure for the virtual appliance only consists of the import activities under the supported hypervisor. After this phase, you have to configure the two network interfaces assigned to the gateway; one is used to communicate with the internal area of your architecture, and the other one connects the infrastructure with the outside world. This is not a mandatory configuration, but it's preferable to differentiate the traffic for the internal and the external worlds.

During the configuration of the network, especially when configuring the Access Gateway IP Address (also known as **NSIP** or **NetScaler IP address**), you will find two other kinds of network addresses - the **mapped IP address** (**MIP**), and the **subnet IP address** (**SNIP**). The first address is used to contact the backend machines, the second allows users to access the NetScaler Access Gateway from hosts located on different networks. Another important network component is given by the **virtual IP address** (**VIP**), associated to a configured virtual server, which is formerly the Access Gateway Web Interface contacted by users and systems to access the published virtual resources.

A fundamental operation is linking the Access Gateway to the existing Web Interface systems. In this way you will establish the communication between the first point of access for the users (NetScaler AG) and the Web Interface, which in this configuration has been transformed to a sort of backend authentication server. Moreover, this configuration moment permits you to implement a load-balancing policy, configuring a virtual address for the two or more Web Interface machines within your infrastructure, and using this address to redirect requests to the active server(s).

To be able to communicate with the Access Gateway, it's necessary to generate a certificate to install on the server and the client machines; this certificate can be self signed or generated from an existing certification authority (such as Microsoft CA). Remember that in order to connect the CAG with related platforms such as the Web Interface, the certificate must be at least 1024 bits in size.

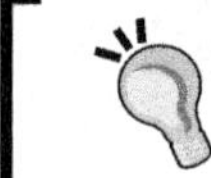

[ You should always consider generating a certificate from a valid and existing certification authority. The self-signed certificate should be used only for PoC and testing environments. ]

An important aspect is the ability to contact an LDAP server, including the Microsoft Active Directory domains; you will be able to use a single authentication method for the secure gateway, the applications, and the virtual desktop created for your infrastructure.

At this point, the critical configurations move from the CAG virtual appliance to the configured Web Interface system(s). After creating a new website and specifying the logon phase at the Access Gateway level, you have to connect this platform to the VIP address of the previously created virtual server, and register the **Secure Ticket Authority** (**STA**) to complete the linking procedure. An STA server is used to release authorization tickets when a connection request has been performed in order to access a published resource (a XenApp application or a XenDesktop virtual desktop instance).

Don't forget to save your configuration every time you make a change; it runs in a running-config manner and without explicitly registering the modifications, so you will lose any update in case of virtual appliance failure or reboot!

## There's more...

If you want, you can modify the Citrix Access Gateway GUI, by changing its default theme and applying the Citrix Receiver theme.

You have to start an SSH session with your NetScaler VPX by locating the Receiver GUI archive (`/var/netscaler/gui/vpns/customization/receivertheme` as the path and `receivertheme.tar.gz` as the filename) and extracting the archive. After completing this, run the following command in order to overwrite the old interface with the new one:

```
cp -r /var/netscaler/gui/vpns/customization/receivertheme/ns_gui/* /
netscaler/ns_gui/
```

Then execute the following command to make the change persistent across the reboots:

```
echo cp -r /var/customizations/* /netscaler/ns_gui >> /nsconfig/
rc.netscaler
```

After you have rebooted the virtual appliance, you'll be able to see the new applied Access Gateway GUI.

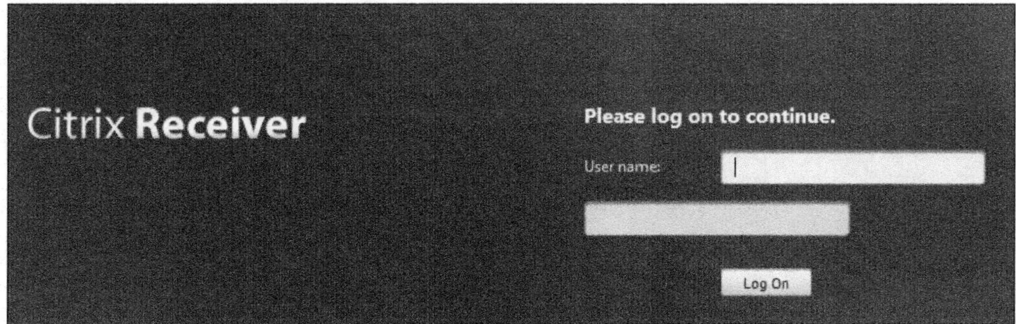

## See also

- The *Installing and configuring Web Interface* recipe in *Chapter 1, XenDesktop Installation and Configuration*

# Configuring the XenDesktop logging

Any operation performed on a system, automatic or manually executed by the users, should be registered in a log file in order to troubleshoot problems and to be able to reconstruct the activities for any kind of reason, for instance, in case of security or legal checks. In this recipe, we will discuss about the main logging activities performed by the Citrix XenDesktop machines and the way to implement them.

## Getting ready

To activate or deactivate the logging activities on the virtual desktop instances and the XenDesktop Controller server(s), you have to download the Log Enabler utility from the Citrix website; the `.zip` archive can be downloaded from `http://support.citrix.com/servlet/KbServlet/download/25517-102-691159/LogEnabler.Zip.zip`.

## How to do it...

In this recipe, we will explain how to configure and use the Citrix logger platform called Log Enabler. Perform the following steps:

1. Connect to the Citrix Desktop Director server, copy the `LogEnabler.zip` archive, and extract it.
2. Double-click on the **LogEnabler.exe** file, then select the system section for which you want to log the events. Decide if you want to overwrite existing log files by checking its checkbox, then click on the **Enable Logging** button to activate the logs or click on **Disable Logging** to turn off the system logging activities.

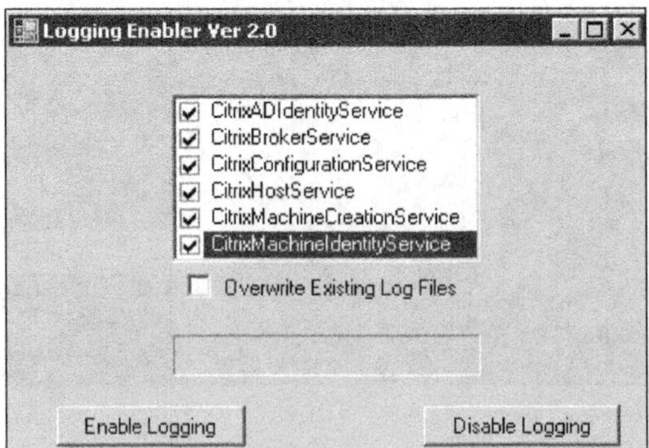

3. On the **Restart Service** pop-up screen, click on **Yes** to restart the Citrix services in order to activate the system logs.
4. After successfully restarting the services, click on **OK** to close the confirmation window.
5. Browse the `C` disk and double-click on the **XDLogs** folder generated by the Log Enabler utility, then open one of the generated log files.

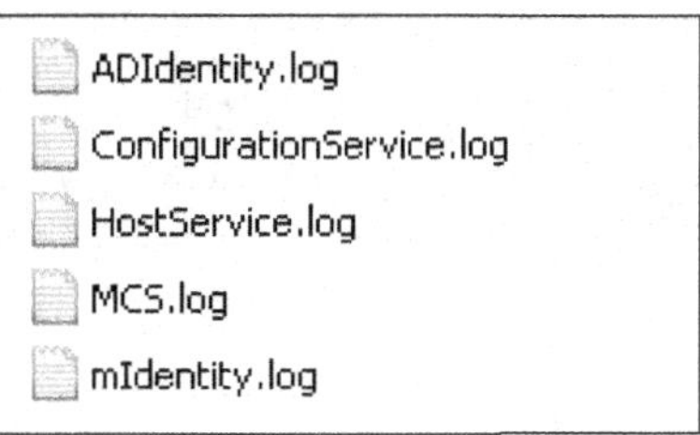


6. Connect to the Windows Desktop Image template, copy the `LogEnabler.zip` archive, and extract it.
7. Double-click on the **LogEnabler.exe** file, then select the system section for which you want to log events. Decide if you want to overwrite the existing log files by checking its checkbox, then click on the **Enable** button to activate the logs or click on **Disable** to turn off the system logging activities.

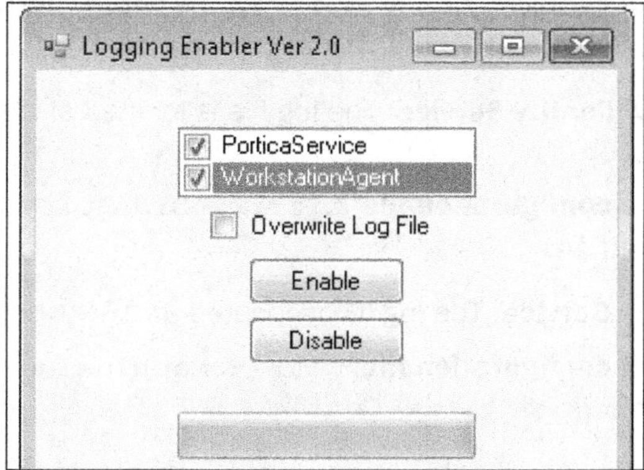


8. On the **Restart Service** pop-up screen click on **Yes** to restart the Citrix services in order to activate the system logs.
9. After successfully restarting the services, click on **OK** to close the confirmation window.

10. Browse the `C:` disk and double-click on the **XDLogs** folder generated by the Log Enabler utility, and double-click on the generated log file. This file will appear as shown in the following screenshot:

```
VDA - Blocco note
File  Modifica  Formato  Visualizza  ?
[   1] 14/10/12 22:41:33.9977 : Workstation Agent:AgentService() - entry. Agent
[   1] 14/10/12 22:41:34.0007 : Workstation Agent:AgentService() - exit
[   4] 14/10/12 22:41:34.0377 : Workstation Agent:RegistryKey.OpenSubkey success
[   4] 14/10/12 22:41:34.0387 : Workstation Agent:Win32RegistryKey.Close() for '
[   4] 14/10/12 22:41:34.0387 : Workstation Agent:Win32RegistryKey.Close() for '
[   4] 14/10/12 22:41:34.0387 : Workstation Agent:AgentService.OnStart entered
```

## How it works...

The Citrix XenDesktop logging system operates at two different levels, the first activation is performed on the Desktop Broker server, while the second works on the virtual desktop instances pointing to the installed Virtual Desktop Agent.

For the XenDesktop server components, the logs register information about the following sections:

- **Machine Creation Service**: The log file is located at `C:\XDLogs\MCS.log`
    - **Affected configuration file**: `Citrix.MachineCreation.SdkWcfEndpoint.exe.Config`
- **Active Directory Identity Service**: The log file is located at `C:\XDLogs\ADIdentitiy.log`
    - **Affected configuration file**: `Citrix.ADIdentity.SdkWcfEndpoint.exe.Config`
- **Machine Identity Service**: The log file is located at `C:\XDLogs\mIdentity.log`
    - **Affected configuration file**: `Citrix.MachineIdentity.SdkWcfEndpoint.exe.Config`
- **Citrix Host Service**: The log file is located at `C:\XDLogs\HostService.log`
    - **Affected configuration file**: `Citrix.Host.SdkWcfEndpoint.exe.Config`

For the client component, logs are registered for the following section:

- **Workstation – Virtual Desktop Agent**: The log file is located at `C:\XDLogs\VDA.log`
    - **Affected configuration file**: `WorkstationAgent.exe.config`

Be careful when configuring log overwriting; if you decide to activate this option by flagging it in the Logging Enabler menu, you will lose the entire logs generated previously, because the log file will be overwritten every time you restart the related system service.

You should consider implementing a log rotation script, in order to maintain the history of the operations performed on your XenDesktop infrastructure systems.

## There's more...

If you don't want to use the Log Enabler tool provided by Citrix, you can manually edit the previously listed configuration files, and add the following lines, which must be included in between the `<appSettings>` and `</appSettings>` tags:

```
<add key="LogToCDF" value ="1"/>
<add key="LogFileName" value ="c:\XDLogs\<logfilename.log>"/>
<add key="OverwriteLogFile" value ="<0>,<1>"/>
```

In `LogFileName` specify the location and filename for the specific log, and in the `OverwriteLogFile` row insert the `0` value if you don't want to activate the log overwriting, otherwise insert `1` if you want to regenerate the log file every time you restart the related service.

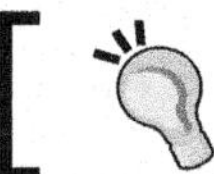

Remember to specify a different log file for every service you are going to activate the system logging.

After completing the operations you have to restart the related services for which you have activated the log registration.

## See also

- The *Installing and configuring XenDesktop Collector* recipe in *Chapter 5, Configuring Additional Architectural Components*

# Chapter 8 XenDesktop lab

In this chapter, we have implemented and optimized the security and the performance of the global VDI architecture through the activation and tuning of the Citrix policies, and then installed and configured the Citrix secure access platform, which is NetScaler Access Gateway. The last step has been to activate the system logs for the servers and the client components.

In this lab we're going to configure a set of policies useful to the user experience, and then we will activate a group of logs in order to be able to retrieve information about our lab environment. Perform the following steps to do so:

1. Connect to the Desktop Controller machine (`vmctxddc01 - 192.168.1.60`) and perform the following operations:
    i. Select a specific USB key device used within your company, and create a user policy, which only permits the mapping of this mass storage device model.
    ii. Create a set of user policies which perform the redirection of all the multimedia contents to the client, instead of the server.
    iii. Analyze the traffic priorities within your company, and create a machine policy, which is able to implement the QoS for the most important traffic flows.
    iv. Activate the logs for the Machine Creation and the Host services; be sure to never overwrite logs.
2. Connect to one of the existing virtual desktop base image templates, and perform the following tasks:
    i. Activate the system log for Virtual Desktop Agent; you will lose the log information every time you restart the template machine. This operation *must* be performed without the use of any external tool.
    ii. Verify the correct application for all the generated policies.

In case of policy application issues, access the Desktop Controller server again and run a policy application simulation to understand where the issue has occurred.

# 9

# Working with XenDesktop PowerShell

In this chapter we will cover:

- Retrieving system information – configuration service cmdlets
- Managing Active Directory accounts – AD identity cmdlets
- Managing the Citrix Desktop Controller – broker cmdlets
- Administering hosts and machines – host and machine creation cmdlets

## Introduction

At this point in the book, we have implemented a full functioning XenDesktop architecture made up of the core components plus additional features, in terms of security and performance. With hundreds or thousands of hosts to configure and machines to deploy, configuring all the components manually could be difficult. XenDesktop Version 5.6 integrates, for the very first time, a customization of Microsoft PowerShell. The Citrix team has really improved the integration and the complexity of the PoweShell commands, so the IT technicians are able to reduce the time required to perform the management tasks by the creation of PowerShell scripts, which will be used to deploy at scale the greatest part of the XenDesktop components.

Working with PowerShell instead of XenDesktop GUI will give you more flexibility in terms of the kind of operations you are executing and the way in which you are executing them, having a set of additional features to use during the infrastructure creation and configuration phases.

# Retrieving system information – configuration service cmdlets

In this recipe we will use and explain a general-purpose PowerShell cmdlet – the configuration service category. This is used to retrieve general configuration parameters and to obtain information about the implementation of the XenDesktop configuration service.

## Getting ready

No preliminary tasks are required. You have already installed the Citrix XenDesktop PowerShell SDK during the installation of Desktop Controller role machine(s).

To be sure to be able to run a PowerShell script (in the `.ps1` format), you have to enable the script execution from the PowerShell prompt by executing the following command:

```
Set-ExecutionPolicy -ExecutionPolicy RemoteSigned -Force
```

## How to do it...

In this recipe we will explain and execute the commands associated to the XenDesktop system and services configuration area. Perform the following steps to do so:

1. Connect to one of the Desktop Broker servers.
2. Click on the PowerShell icon installed on the Windows taskbar.
3. Load the Citrix PowerShell modules by typing in the following command, and then press the *Enter* key.

   ```
   Asnp Citrix*
   ```

   To execute a command, you have to press the *Enter* key after typing in the right command syntax.

4. Retrieve the configured Desktop Controller administrator by executing the command given next. If you want, you can add search filters as `-AccountSid` (searching only for the specified user SID) and `-ReadOnly` (searching for accounts only with read-only permissions).

   ```
   Get-ConfigAdministrator
   ```

5. Add a new XenDesktop farm administrator by executing the next command; optionally, you can assign the read-only permission by specifying the `-ReadOnly` parameter.

   ```
   New-ConfigAdministrator -Account <Domain\AccountName>
   ```

6. To remove an existing domain account from the XenDesktop administrators group, execute the following command:

```
Remove-ConfigAdministrator <Domain\AccountName>
```

7. To retrieve the current status of the configuration service, execute the next command; the output result will be **OK** in absence of configuration issues.

```
Get-ConfigServiceStatus
```

8. To get the connection string used by the configuration service to connect to the XenDesktop database, execute the following command:

```
Get-ConfigDBConnection
```

9. Starting from the previously received output, it's possible to configure the connection string to let the configuration service use the system database. For this command, you have to specify the `Server`, `Initial Catalog`, and `Integrated Security` parameters.

```
Set-ConfigDBConnection -DBConnection "Server=<Servername\
InstanceName>; Initial Catalog=<DatabaseName>; Integrated
Security=<True | False>"
```

10. Starting from an existing Citrix database, you can generate a SQL procedure file to recreate the database. Execute the following command to complete this task, specifying the `DatabaseName` and `ServiceGroupName` parameters.

```
Get-ConfigDBSchema -DatabaseName <DatabaseName> -ServiceGroupName
<ServiceGroupName> > Path:\FileName.sql
```

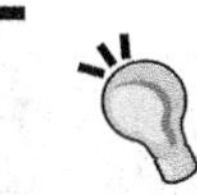

You need to configure a destination database with the same name of the source database, otherwise the script will fail!

11. To retrieve information about the active configuration service objects (`Instance`, `Service`, and `ServiceGroup`), execute the next three commands, respectively:

```
Get-ConfigRegisteredServiceInstance
Get-ConfigService
Get-ConfigServiceGroup
```

12. When necessary, you can switch a running task from one host to another by using the following PowerShell command:

```
Switch-ConfigTask -Host2 <Hostname>
```

13. To test a set of operations to check the status of the configuration service, run the following script:

```
#------------ Script - Configuration Service
#------------ Define Variables
```

```
$Server_Conn="vmddbctx01\CITRIX"
$Catalog_Conn="CitrixXenDesktopDB"
#------------
write-Host "XenDesktop - Configuration Service CmdLets"
#---------- Clear the existing Configuration Service DB connection
$Clear = Set-ConfigDBConnection -DBConnection $null
Write-Host "Clearing any previous DB connection - Status: " $Clear
#---------- Set the Configuration Service DB connection string
$New_Conn = Set-ConfigDBConnection -DBConnection "Server=$Server_
Conn; Initial Catalog=$Catalog_Conn; Integrated Security=$true"
Write-Host "Configuring the DB string connection - Status: " $New_
Conn
$Configured_String = Get-configDBConnection
Write-Host "The new configured DB connection string is: "
$Configured_String

exit
```

You have to save this script with the `.ps1` extension, in order to invoke it with PowerShell.

The preceding script produces the following screenshot:

```
Administrator: Windows PowerShell
PS C:\XD_PS_Scripts>
PS C:\XD_PS_Scripts>
PS C:\XD_PS_Scripts>
PS C:\XD_PS_Scripts>
PS C:\XD_PS_Scripts> .\Script_Recipe01.ps1
XenDesktop - Configuration Service CmdLets
Clearing any previous DB connection - Status:  DBUnconfigured
Configuring the DB string connection - Status:  OK
The new configured DB connection string is:  Server=dblocation\CITRIX; Initial Catalog=CitrixXenDesktopDB
```

## How it works...

The configuration service cmdlets of XenDesktop PowerShell permit managing the configuration service and its related information – the metadata for the entire XenDesktop infrastructure, the service instances registered within the VDI architecture, and the collections of these services, called **service groups**.

This set of commands offers the ability to retrieve the administrative user and the relative permissions (the `Get-ConfigAdministrator` command), and optionally setting new administrators for the configuration service (the `New-ConfigAdministrator` command); in this case, you can specify the level of permissions for the account, in the form of `Full` (a complete access level, no parameter is required) or `-ReadOnly` (permissions set to read-only). Based on a similar syntax, you can remove a configured administrative account by running the `Remove-ConfigAdministrator` cmdlet, filtering the existing username by account name or SID.

Moreover, it's possible to check and configure the database connection string to contact the configured XenDesktop SQL Server database. These operations are permitted by the `Get-ConfigDBConnection` (retrieve the current configuration) and `Set-ConfigDBConnection` commands (configure the database connection string); both the commands use **Database server name**, **Instance name**, **Database name**, and **Integrated security** as information fields.

In the script that we saw in the *How to do it...* section of this recipe, we have regenerated a database connection string; to be sure of being able to recreate it, first of all we have cleared any existing connection, setting it to null (verify the command associated to the `$Clear` variable). Then we have defined the `$New_Conn` variable, using the `Set-ConfigDBConnection` command. All the parameters have been defined at the top of the script, in the form of variables.

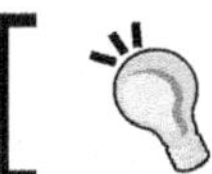

Use the `Write-Host` command to echo results on the standard output.

## There's more...

In some cases it could be useful to retrieve the state of the registered services, in order to verify their availability; you can use the `Test-ConfigServiceInstanceAvailability` cmdlet, retrieving if the service is responding or not, and its responsive time. Run the following example to test the use of this command:

```
Get-ConfigRegisteredServiceInstance | Test-ConfigServiceInstanceAvailabil
ity | more
```

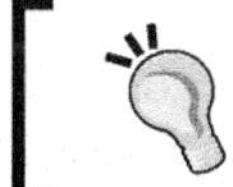

Use the `-ForceWaitForOneOfEachType` parameter to stop checking for a service category, when one of its services respond.

## See also

- The *Preparing the SQL Server database* recipe in *Chapter 1, XenDesktop Installation and Configuration*

# Managing Active Directory accounts – AD identity cmdlets

In this recipe we will discuss the utilization of the Active Directory identity cmdlets; this is a capability that permits retrieving and configuring the Active Directory objects used by Citrix XenDesktop, such as machine accounts assigned to existing desktop catalogs.

## Getting ready

No preliminary tasks are required. You have already installed the Citrix XenDesktop PowerShell SDK during the installation of Desktop Controller role machine(s).

To be sure of being able to run a PowerShell script (in the `.ps1` format), you have to enable the script execution from the PowerShell prompt by executing the following command:

```
Set-ExecutionPolicy -ExecutionPolicy RemoteSigned -Force
```

## How to do it...

The following are the steps required to manage the XenDesktop machine identity through the use of PowerShell:

1. Connect to one of the Desktop Broker servers.
2. Click on the PowerShell icon installed on the Windows taskbar.
3. Load the Citrix PowerShell modules by typing the following command, then press the *Enter* key.

   ```
   Asnp Citrix*
   ```

4. To generate a new desktop catalog and interface it with your company domain, run the next PowerShell command; the parameters involved are `-NamingScheme` and `-NamingSchemeType`.

   ```
   New-AcctIdentityPool -IdentityPoolName <PoolName> -NamingScheme
   <Machine-Name-Structure##> -Domain <ADDomainName>
   -NamingSchemeType <Numeric | Alphabetic>
   ```

5. To retrieve information on the currently existing machine catalogs, you have to use the command given next; you can use filters such as `-IdentityPoolName`, `-IdentityPoolUid`, and `-AdminAddress`, which permit you to specify the address of a particular Desktop Controller.

   ```
   Get-AcctIdentityPool
   ```

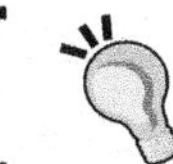

[ You can sort the output results by using the `-SortBy` parameter, specifying the file for which you want to sort the output. ]

6. To rename an existing catalog / identity pool, execute the following command:

```
Rename-AcctIdentityPool -IdentityPoolName <CurrentName>
-NewIdentityPoolName <NewName>
```

[ To modify a catalog configuration parameter, use the `Set-AcctIdentityPool` command. You can retrieve information about its use by navigating to **Get-Help Set-AcctIdentityPool -detailed | More**. ]

7. To remove a created machine catalog from your XenDesktop architecture, use the `Remove-AcctIdentityPool` cmdlet in the following way:

```
- Remove-AcctIdentityPool -IdentityPoolName <PoolName>
```

You can also use it in the following way:

```
- Remove-AcctIdentityPool -IdentityPoolUid <PoolUID>
```

8. To populate the created catalogs with domain machine accounts execute the following task:

```
New-AcctADAccount -IdentityPoolName <CatalogName> -Count
<NumberofAccounts> -StartCount <Number> -AdminAddress
<ControllerIPAddress>
```

[ You can run this command only once at a time; you cannot execute parallel account creations! ]

9. Retrieve the generated computer account data by running the next command; you can filter the information using the `-IdentityPoolName` and `-Lock` parameters:

```
Get-AcctADAccount
```

10. The next command performs the required updates on the imported Active Directory computer accounts in a catalog; optionally you can use the `-AllAccounts` and the `-AdminAddress` parameters.

```
Update-AcctADAccount -IdentityPoolName <PoolName>
```

11. Finally, you have the ability to remove computer accounts from an existing identity pool in the following way; use the `-Force` option to proceed, in case of system exceptions as well.

```
Remove-AcctADAccount -IdentityPoolName <PoolName> -ADAccountName
<ComputerAccountName> -RemovalOption <option>
```

You can reset the machine account password by running the following command:

```
Repair-AcctADAccount -ADAccountName "domain\
computerName" -Force
```

12. Execute the following script to operate on the catalog and machine accounts creation:

```
#------------ Script - Configuration Service
#------------ Define Variables
$AD_Domain="ctxlab.local"
$ID_Pool="Test-Pool-01"
$Controller_Address="192.168.1.60"

#------------ Creating and Identity Pool
write-Host "XenDesktop - Creating an Identity Pool"
$ID_Pool_Create = New-AcctIdentityPool -IdentityPoolName
$ID_Pool -NamingScheme Desk-T## -Domain $AD_Domain
-NamingSchemeType Numeric
Write-Output "Pool creation activities - Status: " $ID_Pool_Create

#---------- Verify the pool creation
$Check_Pool = Get-AcctIdentityPool -IdentityPoolName $ID_Pool |
measure

if ($Check_Pool.count -gt 0)
         {Write-Host "Identity Pool correctly created."}

   else
        {Write-Host "Identity pool not correctly generated. Please
verify."

           exit }

#---------- Creating AD computer accounts

New-AcctADAccount -IdentityPoolName $ID_Pool -Count 3 -StartCount
10 -AdminAddress $Controller_Address

exit
```

The preceding script produces the following screenshot:

```
Administrator: Windows PowerShell

XenDesktop - Creating an Identity Pool
Pool creation activities - Status:

IdentityPoolName   : Test-Pool-00
IdentityPoolUid    : d88f617e-d544-4a96-ab02-efa768696851
NamingScheme       : Desk-T##
NamingSchemeType   : Numeric
StartCount         : 1
OU                 :
Domain             :
Lock               : False

Identity Pool correctly created.
SuccessfulAccounts        : {         Desk-T10$,         Desk-T11$,         Desk-T12$}
SuccessfulAccountsCount   : 3
FailedAccountsCount       : 0
FailedAccounts            : {}
```

## How it works...

In this recipe we have discussed about the management of the XenDesktop identity pools and their objects, the Active Directory computer accounts contained within the pools. These commands could be particularly useful in case of advanced management of the pools and the computer accounts within it, in terms of changes, deletion, creation, and advanced management of the Active Directory machine accounts.

The first command collections discuss the identity pools and the four main operations that we can perform on them - the creation (`New-AcctIdentityPool`), the list of resources (`Get-AcctIdentityPool`), the renaming (`Rename-AcctIdentityPool`), and the deletion (`Remove-AcctIdentityPool`). For creating an identity pool you need to specify the name of the AD objects container, the Desktop Controller address to which the pool will refer, and the two main configurable characteristics - the naming scheme (the naming convention assigned to the AD computer accounts generated within an identity pool, in the form of `MachineName##`, where the sharp symbols specify the machine progressive numbering), and the naming scheme type (alphabetic or numeric progression). For instance, you could specify an alphabetical machine naming convention as, `Desk-T-AA`.

The `Rename-AcctIdentityPool` command permits you to rename existing pools; you only have to specify the old pool name and the new name to use as its substitution; as simple as this is the last identity pool command, `Remove-AcctIdentityPool`. Based on whether you are moving filter on the pool name or the pool UID, you can delete one or more existing pool(s).

You can remove a pool only when it has no associated machine accounts.

The second command group permits you to manage the Active Directory machine accounts, which can be grouped with the identity pools; the `New-AcctADAccount` cmdlet lets you create a computer account within your domain. Based on the naming convention defined in the pool on which the machine account is linked, you can specify the starting progressive machine number (the `-StartCount` parameter) and the number of accounts to create (the `-Count` parameter). To remove computer accounts that were created, you have to use the `Remove-AcctADAccount` command; particularly what's interesting in this cmdlet is the presence of the modality to perform the computer account deletion, with `-RemovalOption` configurable to remove the machine accounts only from the XenDesktop (the **None** option), removing them also from the Active Directory domain (the **Delete** option), or disabling the accounts in the AD domain (the **Disable** option).

Use the `-Force` parameter to remove the accounts, in case of warnings as well.

The script at the end of the recipe permits you to create an identity pool referring to the related Desktop Controller, and after verifying its correct creation, the pool will be populated with a set of three computer accounts, based on the naming convention configured for the identity pool (`Desk-T##` with numeric progression). To count the number of objects, in order to verify the pool creation, the measure command has been used, combined with the `count` property of the variable containing the number of retrieved pools (`$Check_Pool.count`).

## There's more...

With XenDesktop PowerShell, it's also possible to use existing Active Directory computer accounts to generate machine catalog accounts, importing them to the XenDesktop infrastructure, as we have seen earlier in this book for the GUI component.

You can perform this operation through the command line by using the `Add-AcctADAccount` PowerShell command with the following syntax:

```
Add-AcctADAccount -IdentityPoolName <PoolName> -ADAccountName
<ComputerName>
```

You can specify the AD computer account in all the common forms, such as `Domain\Computer Name`, `ComputerName@Domain`, or through its FQDN.

## See also

- The *Creating and configuring the machine catalog* recipe in *Chapter 6, Creating and Configuring a Desktop Environment*

# Managing the Citrix Desktop Controller – broker cmdlets

This is one of the principal PowerShell command groups for XenDesktop, because of the interaction with the Desktop Broker component. This section will be about the use of the set of commands to manage the broker, in terms of displaying configurations and setting components and parameters.

## Getting ready

No preliminary tasks are required. You have already installed the Citrix XenDesktop PowerShell SDK during the installation of Desktop Controller role machine(s).

To be sure of being able to run a PowerShell script (the `.ps1` format), you have to enable the script execution from the PowerShell prompt by executing the following command:

```
Set-ExecutionPolicy -ExecutionPolicy RemoteSigned -Force
```

## How to do it...

Let's follow the explanation of the commands included in the Desktop Controllers PowerShell command set. Perform the following steps:

1. Connect to one of the Desktop Broker servers.
2. Click on the PowerShell icon installed on the Windows taskbar.
3. Load the Citrix PowerShell modules by typing in the following command, then press the *Enter* key.

   ```
   Asnp Citrix*
   ```

4. To retrieve the configuration of the XenDesktop broker site run the following command:

   ```
   Get-Brokersite
   ```

5. To modify the parameters of an existing XenDesktop broker site, run the following command; the most important involved parameters are `-ApplicationLicenseModel`, `-AppLicenseEdition`, `-DesktopLicenseEdition`, and `-DesktopLicenseModel`.

   ```
   Set-BrokerSite -LicenseServerName <LicenseServerName> -
   LicenseServerPort <PortNumber> -AdminAddress <BrokerAddress>
   ```

6. Run the next command in order to create a desktop catalog to your infrastructure; in the case of a Provisioning Service catalog, you have to use the `-PvsAddress`, `-PvsDomain`, and `-PvsForVM` parameters.

```
New-BrokerCatalog -Name <CatalogName> -AllocationType
<Permanent | Random> -CatalogKind <TypeofCatalog> -Description
<CatalogDescription>
```

The type of catalogs for the `CatalogKind` option can be `PowerManaged`, `Unmanaged`, `ThinCloned`, `SingleImage`, `Pvd`, `Pvs`, and `PvsPvd`. With these two last catalog types you can also use the `-MachinesArePhysical` option.

7. After creating this you can retrieve information on the existing catalogs by running the command given next, filtering for information such as the allocation type (`-AllocationType`), or the catalog kind (`-CatalogKind`). Without any specific option, you will list the entire infrastructure catalogs:

```
Get-BrokerCatalog
```

8. To modify the previously configured catalog characteristics, you have to run the following command:

```
Set-BrokerCatalog -Description -MachinesArePhysical -PvsAddress -
PvsDomain -PvsForVM
```

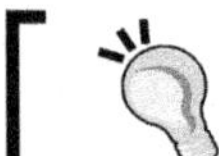

You cannot modify the allocation type and catalog kind settings!

9. To remove an existing catalog, run the following cmdlet:

```
Remove-BrokerCatalog -Name <CatalogName>
```

10. To list the entire set of existing desktops in your site, run the following command:

```
Get-BrokerDesktop
```

Later on in this recipe, we will list the most important parameters for this command.

11. To configure a desktop group in your Citrix broker execute the following cmdlet:

```
New-BrokerDesktopGroup -Name <DesktopGroupName> -DesktopKind
<Private|Shared> -Enabled <True|False> -PublishedName
<DesktopDisplayName> -SecureIcaRequired <True|False>
```

The `-AutomaticPowerOnForAssigned` parameter is usable only for the private desktops, `-ShutdownDesktopsAfterUse` can be activated only in presence of power-managed desktops.

12. After creating a broker desktop group, you can get back information by using the command given next; you can use the same filters explained in the previous explanation:

```
Get-BrokerDesktopGroup
```

13. To modify the configuration of an existing group, you have to use the `Set-BrokerDesktopGroup` cmdlet; for instance, you could put a desktop group in maintenance mode in the following way:

```
Set-BrokerDesktopGroup <GroupName> -InMaintenanceMode $true
```

To display the historical usage of the desktop groups run the following command:

```
Get-BrokerDesktopUsage -DesktopGroupName
<DesktopGroupName> -MaxRecordCount <MaxNumberofRecords>
```

14. To populate the previously configured desktop groups, you have to use the following cmdlet:

```
Add-BrokerMachinesToDesktopGroup -Catalog <CatalogName>
-DesktopGroup <DesktopGroupName> -Count <NumberofMachines>
```

After creating a desktop group machine, you can prepare it for the personal vDisk creation by running the following command:

```
Start-BrokerMachinePvdImagePrepare -InputObject
<MachineName>
```

The task will be performed the next time the machine is started.

15. To retrieve any existing private group (desktop or application desktop), run the following two PowerShell commands respectively; useful filters are `-MachineName`, `-DesktopGroupUid`, `-InMaintenanceMode`, and `-OSType`.

```
Get-BrokerPrivateDesktop
```

```
Get-BrokerPrivateAppDesktop
```

To verify the resources to which a user has access, use the `Get-BrokerResource` command, filtering for `-User <Username>` and / or `-Group <GroupName>` (AD group membership for the specified user).

16. After completing the machine creation and grouping, it's time to publish applications and to assign them to the existing virtual desktops. The first useful command permits you to create applications; for using XenDesktop without combining it with XenApp, the only allowed application type is hosted applications:

```
New-BrokerApplication -CommandLineExecutable <FullApplicationPath>
-BrowserName <InternalAppName> -DisplayName <ExternalAppName>
-Enabled <True|False> -ShortcutAddedToDesktop <True|False>
-ShortcutAddedToStartMenu <True|False> - IconFromClient
<True|False>  -Description <AppDescription>
```

You can also use resources control parameters such as `-CpuPriorityLevel` (`Low`, `BelowNormal`, `Normal`, `AboveNormal`, and `High`), `-WaitForPrinterCreation`, and `-ColorDepth` (`FourBit`, `EightBit`, `SixteenBit`, and `TwentyFourBit`).

17. To retrieve the published applications, use the following PowerShell cmdlet, combining it with filters such as `-DisplayName`, `-Enabled`, or `-BrowserName`:

```
Get-BrokerApplication
```

To rename an already published application use the following command line:

```
Rename-BrokerApplication -Application
<CurrentBrowserName> -DisplayName <NewExternalName>
-BrowserName <NewInternalName>
```

18. You can create application folders on which to catalogue and organize published software:

```
New-BrokerApplicationFolder -Name <FolderName> -Description -
AdminAddress <BrokerAddress>
```

19. An alternative to the application creation is the application copy; run the following command to make a copy of the published apps:

```
Copy-BrokerApplication -Application <BrowserName>
-ApplicationFolder <FolderName> -AdminAddress <BrokerAddress>
```

20. Use the following PowerShell cmdlet to associate one or more file extension(s) to a published application:

```
New-BrokerConfiguredFTA -ExtensionName <Extension> -ApplicationUid
<ApplicationID>
```

21. To retrieve the association between file types and software run the next command; you can use filters such as `-Uid` (specific file type by its UID) and `-ExtensionName`.

```
Get-BrokerConfiguredFTA
```

22. To remove a published application from the XenDesktop infrastructure use the following PowerShell cmdlet:

```
Remove-BrokerApplication -BrowserName <ApplicationBrowserName>
-DesktopGroup <DeskGroupName> -AdminAddress <BrokerAddress>
```

23. Once all the application configurations have been completed, you have to assign the software to an existing desktop group in the following way:

```
Add-BrokerApplication -BrowserName <ApplicationBrowserName>
-DesktopGroup <DeskGroupName>
```

24. A fundamental implementation is the access control on the XenDesktop site resources; the following is the command and related syntax to configure a rule:

```
New-BrokerAccessPolicyRule -Name <RuleName>
-IncludedUserFilterEnabled <True|False>  -IncludedUsers <Domain\
User|Group> -IncludedDesktopGroupFilterEnabled <True|False>
-IncludedDesktopGroups <DesktopGroupName> -AllowRestart
<True|False>
```

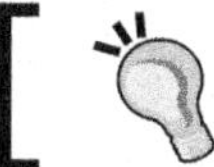

You can also use excluding filters such as `-ExcludedClientIPs`, `-ExcludedDesktopGroups`, and `-ExcludedUsers`.

25. To retrieve the configured access rules, execute the following cmdlet using the same filters explained previously for the rule creation process:

```
Get-BrokerAccessPolicyRule
```

Remove an existing access rule in the following way:

```
Remove-BrokerAccessPolicyRule -Name <RuleName>
```

26. To create a new assignment rule use the following syntax:

```
New-BrokerAssignmentPolicyRule -Name <RuleName> -DesktopGroupUid
<DesktopGroupUID> -IncludedUsers <Domain\User|Group>
-PublishedName <DesktopGroupName>
```

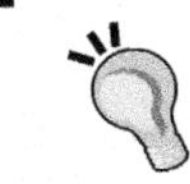

To modify and remove an assignment policy, run the `Set-BrokerAssignmentPolicyRule` cmdlet and the `Remove-BrokerAssignmentPolicyRule` command, respectively.

27. After creating that rule, you can retrieve the currently configured assignment rules by running the following command:

```
Get-BrokerAssignmentPolicyRule -Name <RuleName>
```

28. The following script operates on part of the discussed broker commands:

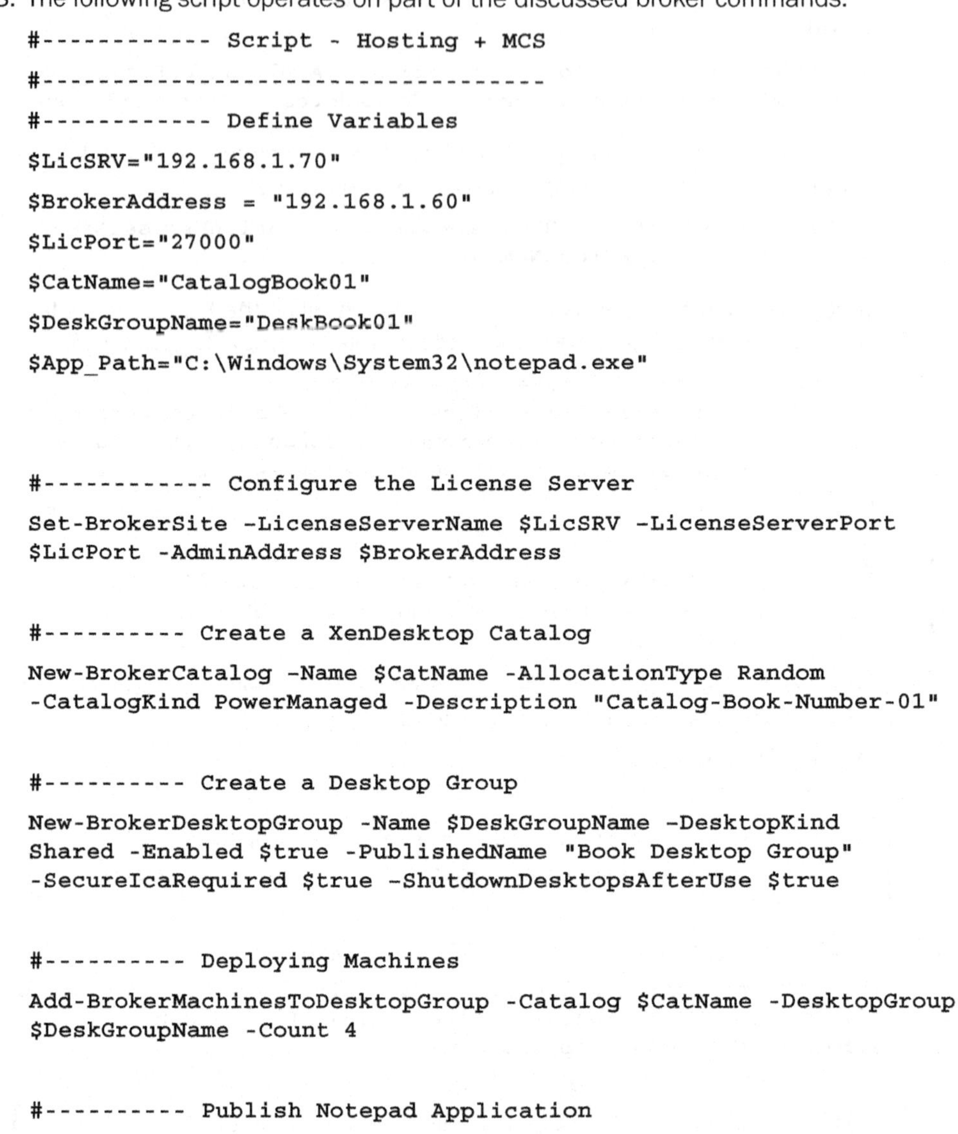

```
#------------ Script - Hosting + MCS
#----------------------------------
#------------ Define Variables
$LicSRV="192.168.1.70"
$BrokerAddress = "192.168.1.60"
$LicPort="27000"
$CatName="CatalogBook01"
$DeskGroupName="DeskBook01"
$App_Path="C:\Windows\System32\notepad.exe"



#------------ Configure the License Server
Set-BrokerSite -LicenseServerName $LicSRV -LicenseServerPort
$LicPort -AdminAddress $BrokerAddress


#---------- Create a XenDesktop Catalog
New-BrokerCatalog -Name $CatName -AllocationType Random
-CatalogKind PowerManaged -Description "Catalog-Book-Number-01"


#---------- Create a Desktop Group
New-BrokerDesktopGroup -Name $DeskGroupName -DesktopKind
Shared -Enabled $true -PublishedName "Book Desktop Group"
-SecureIcaRequired $true -ShutdownDesktopsAfterUse $true


#---------- Deploying Machines
Add-BrokerMachinesToDesktopGroup -Catalog $CatName -DesktopGroup
$DeskGroupName -Count 4


#---------- Publish Notepad Application
```

```
New-BrokerApplication -CommandLineExecutable $App_Path
-BrowserName NotepadExe -DisplayName "Windows Notepad" -Enabled
$true -ShortcutAddedToDesktop $true -ShortcutAddedToStartMenu
$false -Description "Notepad Text Editor"


#--------- Associate the .txt extension

$AppID=$(Get-BrokerApplication -BrowserName NotepadExe)

New-BrokerConfiguredFTA -ExtensionName ".txt" -ApplicationUid
$AppID.Uid -HandlerName "textfile"


#--------- Retrieve published applications

Get-BrokerApplication


#--------- Filter the resources for the Help Desk team

New-BrokerAccessPolicyRule -Name HelpDeskFilter01
-IncludedUserFilterEnabled $true -IncludedUsers "ctxlab\HDL1"
-IncludedDesktopGroupFilterEnabled $true -IncludedDesktopGroups
$DeskGroupName -AllowRestart $true


exit
```

The preceding script produces the following screenshot:

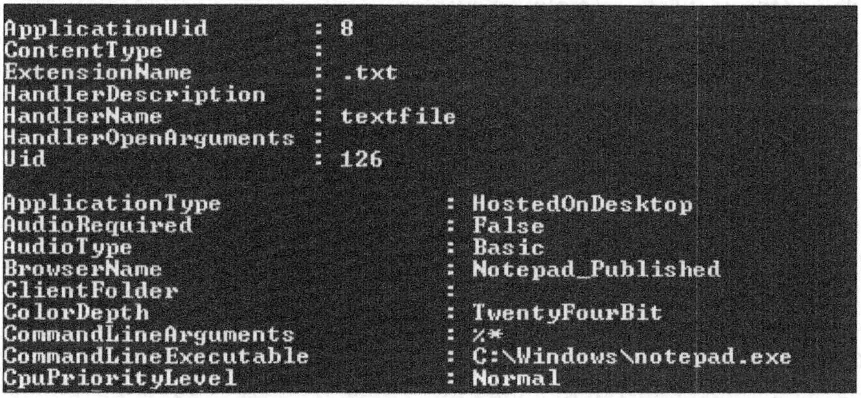

```
ApplicationUid          : 8
ContentType             :
ExtensionName           : .txt
HandlerDescription      :
HandlerName             : textfile
HandlerOpenArguments    :
Uid                     : 126

ApplicationType                  : HostedOnDesktop
AudioRequired                    : False
AudioType                        : Basic
BrowserName                      : Notepad_Published
ClientFolder                     :
ColorDepth                       : TwentyFourBit
CommandLineArguments             : %*
CommandLineExecutable            : C:\Windows\notepad.exe
CpuPriorityLevel                 : Normal
```

## How it works...

Using and configuring the broker cmdlet category has permitted to generate resource containers (catalogs and desktop groups) to which we can assign end-user resources (desktops and applications) and filtering rules (access and assignment); using this division, we can discuss the following five main PowerShell broker command subcategories:

- **The Site and Catalog subsection**: In this area we've configured the XenDesktop site and the contained catalogs, then we have retrieved information about them. The `Set-BrokerSite` configuration command permits you to define the application and desktop license model (user device or concurrent modalities) and the desktop license edition (STD = Express or VDI, ENT = Enterprise, PLT = Platinum). The `New-BrokerCatalog` command performs the creation of a machine's catalog; the `ThinCloned` catalogs and `SingleImage` catalogs are parts of the **Provisioning Services** (**PVS**) architecture. It's also possible to configure catalogs with the personal vDisk technology for both the MCS and PVS infrastructures. The `New-BrokerCatalog` command lets you create random or static assigned resource catalogs, specifying which type of catalog you want to create. Moreover, it's possible to use physical machines and assign them to the catalog object (the `-MachinesArePhysical` option); the only limitation is that you have to deploy a PVS architecture.
- **The Desktops and Desktop groups subsection**: In this subsection we've created and managed the desktop groups and the related desktops. For this second object type, the `Get-BrokerDesktop` command permits to retrieve existing desktop machines by filtering the search for information such as `-MachineName` (in the form of `Domain\ComputerName`), `-ApplicationInUse`, `-CatalogKind`, `-CatalogName`, `-DesktopCondition` (high resource usage or latency, parameters in the form of `--CPU`, `--ICALatency`, and `--UPMLogonTime`), `-DesktopGroupName` , `-DesktopKind` (a desktop can be private or shared), `-ImageOutOfDate` (a desktop not compliant with the latest base image template updates), `-InMaintenanceMode`, `-IsAssigned` (a desktop resource already assigned or not assigned to a user), `-LastConnectionTime`, `-LastConnectionUser`, `-OSType`, `-PowerState` (the current situation for the desktop, in the form of `On|Off|TurningOn|TurningOff|Suspending|Resuming|Unmanaged|Unavailable|Unknown`), `-Protocol` (for instance, HDX), and `-LastDeregistrationReason`. This option permits you to discover why a deregistration has occurred, retrieving the result data as `AgentShutdown`, `AgentSuspended`, `BrokerRegistrationLimitReached`, `AgentNotContactable`, `ContactLost`, `BrokerError`, and `DesktopRemoved`. After this we have used `New-BrokerDesktopGroup` to generate a desktop group, and then linked the existing machine with the related desktop group by using the `Add-BrokerMachinesToDesktopGroup` command (the main parameters are the desktop group name and the number of machines to deploy). To retrieve the existing group types (private – applications and desktops), the `Get-BrokerPrivateDesktop` and `Get-BrokerPrivateAppDesktop` commands have been used to execute the task.

- **The Applications subsection**: In this subsection we have created, modified, and copied hosted applications in the XenDesktop architecture using the command line. The `New-BrokerApplication` command permits you to publish existing applications that are already installed on desktops, which are part of an application desktop group, as we have seen earlier in this book. Also in this case you can specify the already discussed main application option, such as the links publication for the desktop and the **Start** menu, the visibility and the enabling of the app (the `-Visible` and `-Enabled` parameters).

  The browser name for a published application must be unique within a XenDesktop infrastructure!

  A published application can also be copied using the `Copy-BrokerApplication` cmdlet, specifying the names of the source application and the destination application. All these resources can be grouped in folders, created through the use of the `New-BrokerApplicationFolder` command. For any app you can specify the file type association (explicitly specifying it with the `-ExtensionName` or importing them from the known list of Citrix using the `-ImportedFTA` parameter) with the `New-BrokerConfiguredFTA` command. After completing the software publication, you can assign them to existing desktops through the `Add-BrokerApplication` command, associating the application browser name to the desktop group name to which you want to assign it.

- **The Access and Assignment filtering rules subsection**: This last subsection has covered the access and assignment rules configuration; in other words, using these two policy categories it has been possible to regulate the resource usage and access for the users. The `New-BrokerAccessPolicyRule` command creates an access policy rule for the existing XenDesktop resources, setting which users have the ability to access and use defined desktop resources; you have to enable the inclusion (`-IncludedApplicationFilterEnabled`, `-IncludedClientIPFilterEnabled`, `-IncludedClientNameFilterEnabled`, `-IncludedDesktopGroupFilterEnabled`, and `-IncludedDesktopKindFilterEnabled`) and exclusion (`-ExcludedClientIPFilterEnabled`, `-ExcludedClientNameFilterEnabled`, `-ExcludedDesktopGroupFilterEnabled`, and `-ExcludedDesktopKindFilterEnabled`) filters to be sure that the included (`-IncludedApplications`, `-IncludedClientIPs`, `-IncludedClientNames`, `-IncludedDesktopGroups`, and `-IncludedDesktopKinds`) and excluded (`-ExcludedClientIPs`, `-ExcludedClientNames`, `-ExcludedDesktopGroups`, and `-ExcludedDesktopKinds`) resources are managed in the right way. For the assignment policy rule, the command to use is `New-BrokerAssignmentPolicyRule`, specifying the included and/or excluded users (in this second case you have to enable the `ExcludedUserFilterEnabled` filter), and the desktop group UID to which you are applying the assignment task.

## There's more...

With the broker cmdlets group it is also possible to manage the power actions to apply to the catalog machines; you can create a new power action related to an existing desktop machine (`New-BrokerHostingPowerAction -MachineName <DesktopName> -Action <TurnOn|TurnOff|ShutDown|Reset|Restart|Suspend|Resume> -ActualPriority <PriorityValue>`) and then retrieve it (`Get-BrokerHostingPowerAction`).

The lower the priority value, the higher is its importance.

Moreover, you can create and manage a full power time scheme for a desktop group, using the creation power time cmdlet (`New-BrokerPowerTimeScheme -Name <TimeSchemeName> -DaysOfWeek <SpecificDay | WeekDays | Weekend -DesktopGroupUid <GroupUID> -DisplayName <Name> -PeakHours <PeakHoursExpression>` ) and retrieving existing configurations (`Get-BrokerPowerTimeScheme`).

The `PeakHours` expression has the following construction:

```
FromHour..ToHour | % {$_  -gt <Hour> and $_ -lt <Hour> }
```

For example, in the entire day you can set the peak hour time from 10 a.m. to 5 p.m. in the following way:

```
(0..23 | % {$_  -gt 10 and $_ -lt 17 } )
```

## See also

- The *Publishing the VM-hosted apps with XenDesktop* recipe in *Chapter 7, Deploying applications*

# Administering hosts and machines – host and machine creation cmdlets

In this recipe, we will describe how to create the connection between the hypervisor and XenDesktop servers, and the way to generate machines to assign to the end users, all by using Citrix PowerShell.

## Getting ready

No preliminary tasks are required. You have already installed the Citrix XenDesktop PowerShell SDK during the installation of Desktop Controller role machine(s).

To be sure of being able to run a PowerShell script (the `.ps1` format), you have to enable the script execution from the PowerShell prompt by executing the following command:

```
Set-ExecutionPolicy -ExecutionPolicy RemoteSigned -Force
```

## How to do it...

In this section, we will discuss the PowerShell commands used to connect XenDesktop with the supported hypervisors plus the creation of the machines from the command line. Perform the following steps:

1. Connect to one of the Desktop Broker servers.
2. Click on the PowerShell icon installed on the Windows taskbar.
3. Load the Citrix PowerShell modules by typing in the next command, then press the *Enter* key.

   ```
   Asnp Citrix*
   ```

4. To list the available hypervisor types execute the following task:

   ```
   Get-HypHypervisorPlugin -AdminAddress <BrokerAddress>
   ```

5. To list the configured properties for the XenDesktop root level location (`XDHyp:\`), execute the following command:

   ```
   Get-ChildItem XDHyp:\HostingUnits
   ```

   Please refer to the PSPath, Storage, and PersonalvDiskStorage fields to retrieve information on the storage configuration.

6. Execute the following cmdlet to add a storage resource to the XenDesktop Controller host:

   ```
   Add-HypHostingUnitStorage -LiteralPath <HostPathLocation>
   -StoragePath <StoragePath> -StorageType <OSStorage|PersonalvDiskSt
   orage> - AdminAddress <BrokerAddress>
   ```

7. To generate a snapshot for an existing VM, perform the following task:

   ```
   New-HypVMSnapshot -LiteralPath <HostPathLocation>
   -SnapshotDescription <Description>
   ```

   Use the `Get-HypVMMacAddress -LiteralPath <HostPathLocation>` command to list the MAC addresses of specified desktop VMs.

8. To provision machine instances starting from the desktop base image template, run the following command:

```
New-ProvScheme -ProvisioningSchemeName <SchemeName>
-HostingUnitName <HypervisorServer> -IdentityPoolName
<PoolName> -MasterImageVM <BaseImageTemplatePath> -VMMemoryMB
<MemoryAssigned> -VMCpuCount <NumberofCPU>
```

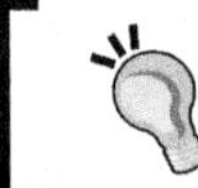

To specify the creation of instances with the personal vDisk technology, use the following option:

`-UsePersonalVDiskStorage`

9. After the creation process, retrieve the provisioning scheme information by running the following command:

```
Get-ProvScheme -ProvisioningSchemeName <SchemeName>
```

To modify the resources assigned to desktop instances in a provisioning scheme, use the `Set-ProvScheme` cmdlet. The permitted parameters are `-ProvisioningSchemeName`, `-VMCpuCount`, and `-VMMemoryMB`.

10. To update the desktop instances to the latest version of the desktop base image template, run the following cmdlet:

```
Publish-ProvMasterVmImage -ProvisioningSchemeName <SchemeName>
-MasterImageVM <BaseImageTemplatePath>
```

If you don't want to maintain the pre-update instance version to use as restore checkpoint, use the `-DoNotStoreOldImage` option.

11. To create machine instances, based on the previously configured provisioning scheme for an MCS architecture, run the following command:

```
New-ProvVM -ProvisioningSchemeName <SchemeName> -ADAccountName
"Domain\MachineAccount"
```

Use the `-FastBuild` option to make the machine creation process faster. On the other hand, you can't start up the machines until the process has been completed.

12. Retrieve the configured desktop instances using the following cmdlet:

```
Get-ProvVM -ProvisioningSchemeName <SchemeName> -VMName
<MachineName>
```

13. To remove an existing virtual desktop use the following command:

```
Remove-ProvVM -ProvisioningSchemeName <SchemeName> -VMName
<MachineName> -AdminAddress <BrokerAddress>
```

```
The next script will combine the use of part of the commands
listed in this recipe:
```

```
#----------- Script - Hosting + MCS
#----------------------------------
#----------- Define Variables
$LitPath = "XDHyp:\HostingUnits\VirtualHost01"
$StorPath = "XDHyp:\HostingUnits\VirtualHost01\DStore01.storage"
$Controller_Address="192.168.1.60"
$HostUnitName = "VirtualHost01"
$IDPool = $(Get-AcctIdentityPool -IdentityPoolName Test-Pool-00)
$BaseVMPath = "XDHyp:\HostingUnits\VirtualHost01\Win7Image01.vm"

#----------- Creating a storage location
Add-HypHostingUnitStorage -LiteralPath $LitPath -StoragePath
$StorPath -StorageType OSStorage -AdminAddress $Controller_Address

#--------- Creating a Provisioning Scheme
New-ProvScheme -ProvisioningSchemeName Deploy_01 -HostingUnitName
$HostUnitName -IdentityPoolName $IDPool.IdentityPoolName
-MasterImageVM $BaseVMPath\Snap01_Post_Upgrade.snapshot
-VMMemoryMB 4096 -VMCpuCount 2 -CleanOnBoot

#--------- List the VM configured on the Hypervisor Host
dir $LitPath\*.vm

exit
```

The preceding script produces the following screenshot:

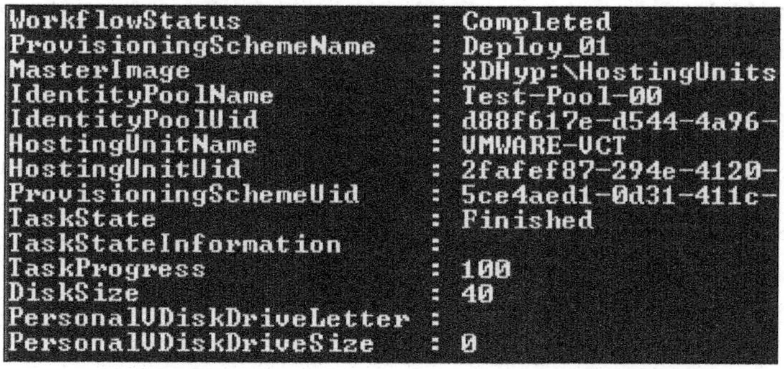

```
WorkflowStatus               : Completed
ProvisioningSchemeName       : Deploy_01
MasterImage                  : XDHyp:\HostingUnits
IdentityPoolName             : Test-Pool-00
IdentityPoolUid              : d88f617e-d544-4a96-
HostingUnitName              : VMWARE-VCT
HostingUnitUid               : 2fafef87-294e-4120-
ProvisioningSchemeUid        : 5ce4aed1-0d31-411c-
TaskState                    : Finished
TaskStateInformation         :
TaskProgress                 : 100
DiskSize                     : 40
PersonalVDiskDriveLetter     :
PersonalVDiskDriveSize       : 0
```

## How it works...

The host and machine creation cmdlet groups manage the interfacing with the hypervisor hosts, in terms of machines and storage resources, and permits to create the desktop instances to assign to the end user, starting from an existing and mapped desktop virtual machine.

The `Get-HypHypervisorPlugin` command retrieves and lists the available hypervisors on which you are deploying instances and configuring storage types. As already discussed earlier in this book, you can configure an operating system storage area or a personal vDisk storage zone. The way to map an existing storage location from the hypervisor to the XenDesktop controller is running the `Add-HypHostingUnitStorage` cmdlet; in this case, you have to specify the destination path on which the storage object will be created (`LiteralPath`) and the source storage path on the hypervisor machine(s) (`StoragePath`), and `StorageType` discussed previously. The storage types are in the form of `XDHyp:\HostingUnits\<UnitName>`.

To list all the configured storage objects, execute the following command:

```
dir XDHyp:\HostingUnits\<UnitName> \*.storage
```

Once configuring the storage area, we've discussed the **Machine Creation Service** (**MCS**) architecture; in this cmdlets collection we have the availability of commands to generate VM snapshots from which you are deploying desktop instances (`New-HypVMSnapshot`), specifying a name and a description for the generated disk snapshot. Starting from the available disk image, the `New-ProvScheme` command permits you to create a resource provisioning scheme, on which you are specifying the desktop base image, the resources to assign to the desktop instances (`-VMCpuCount` and `-VMMemoryMB` in terms of CPU and RAM), and if generating this virtual desktop in a nonpersistent mode (the `-CleanOnBoot` option), with or without the use of the personal vDisk technology (`-UsePersonalVDiskStorage`). It's possible to update the deployed instances to the latest base image update through the use of the `Publish-ProvMasterVmImage` command.

In the generated script, we have located all the main storage location (the `LitPath` and `StorPath` variables) useful to realize a provisioning scheme, then we have implemented a provisioning procedure for a desktop based on an existing base image snapshot, with two vCPUs and 4 GB of RAM for the delivered instances, which will be cleaned every time they stop and start (the `-CleanOnBoot` option).

You can navigate the local and remote storage paths configured with the XenDesktop broker machine; to list an object category (such as VM or snapshot), you can execute the following command:

```
dir XDHyp:\HostingUnits\<UnitName>\*.<category>
```

## There's more...

The discussed cmdlets also offer you the technique to preserve a virtual desktop from an accidental deletion or unauthorized use; with the machine creation cmdlets group, you have the ability to use a particular command (`Lock-ProvVM`), which permits you to lock critical desktops. This cmdlet requires the parameters such as the name of the scheme we are referring to (`-ProvisioningSchemeName`) and the ID of the virtual desktop to lock (`-VMID`).

You can retrieve the virtual machine's ID running the previously discussed `Get-ProvVM` command.

To revert the machine lock and free the desktop instance from the accidental deletion or the improper use, you have to execute the `Unlock-ProvVM` cmdlet, using the same parameter showed for the lock procedure.

## See also

- *Chapter 2, Deploying Virtual Machines for XenDesktop*

# Chapter 9 XenDesktop lab

During this chapter we have reviewed part of the topics discussed during the previous eight chapters of this book, but executing and configuring them using Citrix XenDesktop PowerShell. In this lab number nine, we will perform an infrastructural configuration of the XenDesktop components using the command line.

Connect to the Desktop Controller machine (`vmctxddc01 - 192.168.1.60`) and perform the following operations:

1. Enable the execution of the PowerShell scripts, and load the XenDesktop SDK cmdlets.
2. Configure two accounts, one as full administrator and the other with the read-only permissions.
3. Clean your existing database connection, and reconfigure it as discussed in this chapter.
4. Create a new identity pool and configure it to refer to your Active Directory domain objects.
5. Using the command line, reconfigure the connection between the XenDesktop controller and the license server machine.
6. Generate a XenDesktop catalog to randomly assign the resources and to manage the power action for its objects.

7. Create a desktop group in a way that it's possible to automatically power on desktops when assigned to the users, then deploy 10 machines referring to the catalog and desktop, created previously.
8. Locate the host storage components, create two different storage locations for the OS and personal vDisk components, and structure a provisioning scheme to maintain no historical restore points for the deployed desktops, assigning two processors and 2 GB of RAM, as virtual resources.

# 10 Configuring the XenDesktop Advanced Logon

In this chapter we will cover the following topics:

- Implementing the XenDesktop smart card authentication
- Implementing the XenDesktop strong authentication
- Implementing the Citrix SSO platform

## Introduction

The **Infrastructure Security** is an IT area that involves a lot of different technologies and implementation techniques. The same thing can be applied to the Citrix XenDesktop architectures. As seen earlier, secure connections can be realized through the use of a secure gateway located in front of the entire VDI architecture. The implementation of a strong authentication method is another important step to perform. In this chapter we will discuss the use of the Smart Card devices to perform the login phase through the use of a valid certificate, then we will discuss how to implement a strong authentication logon method, and then at the end of this chapter, we will discuss the implementation of the Citrix SSO platform.

# Implementing the XenDesktop smart card authentication

With your personal data archived on your desktop machine, the standard authentication made up of a username and password combination could not be enough to avoid privacy and security problems.

A valid solution to this situation can be given by the use of devices, such as smart cards or PKI tokens when trying to access your working resources.

Citrix XenDesktop is able to use this type of strong authentication. In this recipe we're going to see the implementation of this process in detail.

## Getting ready

In order to be able to utilize valid certificates, you need to perform the following configuration tasks:

- Use an existing Enterprise CA or install an Enterprise Certification Authority machine to generate valid certificates. You can find more details at `http://technet.microsoft.com/en-us/library/cc770357%28v=WS.10%29.aspx`.
- Configure an existing domain machine as an Enrollment agent station in order to configure the smart cards with your certificates. You can find more details at `http://technet.microsoft.com/en-us/library/cc732895.aspx`.
- Install on the Enrollment agent station the specific CSP drivers for your authentication devices vendor.
- On the Web Interface server, be sure you have installed the Client Certificate Mapping Authentication service for the IIS 7.x installed role.

You have to be a member of the Enterprise Admins group in order to generate and release certificate, on the authentication devices.

## How to do it...

In this recipe, we will explain with the help of the following steps how to authenticate users by the use of smart cards or PKI tokens with a personal certificate on board:

1. Connect to your Web Interface machine, go to **Start** | **All Programs** | **Citrix** | **Management Consoles**, and select the **Citrix Web Interface Management** link.
2. Create a new website, populate the **Name** and **Path** fields, and select **At Web Interface** as a point of authentication. After this, click on **Next** to proceed.

3. Flag the **Smart Card** option on the **Configure Authentication Method** screen in order to activate the use of the smart card devices.
4. Create a services site, assign it a name, and flag the **Smart Card** option as the authentication method, as seen previously for the website configuration.

Citrix recommends having a Web Interface site for every single configured authentication method.

5. In the **Citrix Web Interface Management** console, on the left-hand side menu, select the website configured for the smart card access, then click on the **Server Farms** option on the right-hand side.
6. Select the configured Web Interface server and click on the **Edit** button.
7. In the **Communication Settings** area, configure the **XML Service port** field as **443** (secure connection) and select **HTTPS** from the drop-down list as the **Transport type** protocol, then click on **OK**.

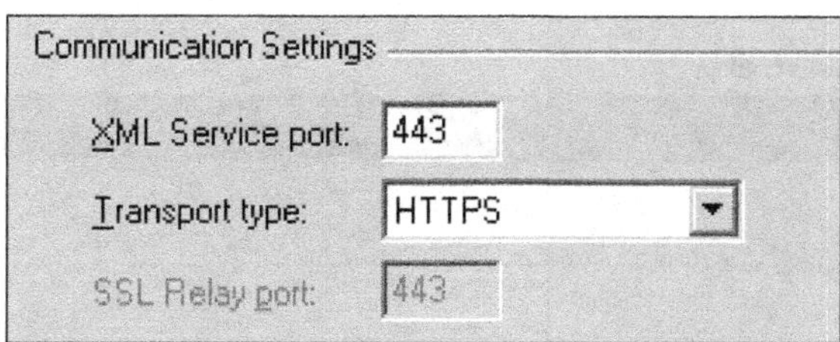


8. Repeat the previous configuration operation for the configured PNAgent service site.
9. Connect to your Enrollment station machine, go to **Start** | **Run**, and type the following command:

```
mmc.exe
```

10. Use the *Ctrl* + *M* key combination to open the Snap-in selection menu, double-click on **Certificates snap-in** from the list, select **My User account** as the certificate store, and click on **Finish**. To end the console selection, click on **OK**.

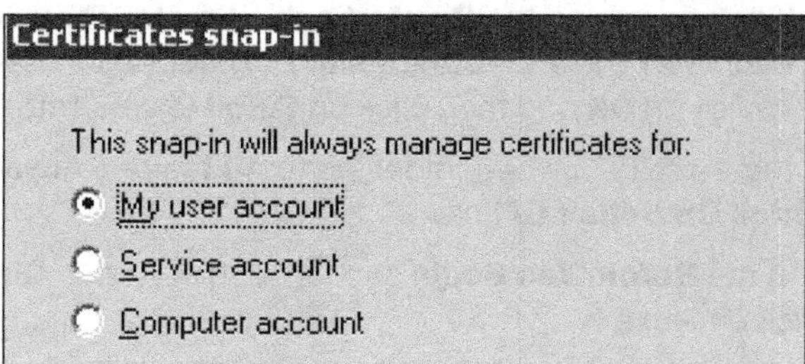

11. Go to the **Certificates** | **Current User** tree, right-click on the **Personal** folder, select **All task**, and click on the **Request new certificate...** link, as shown in the following screenshot:

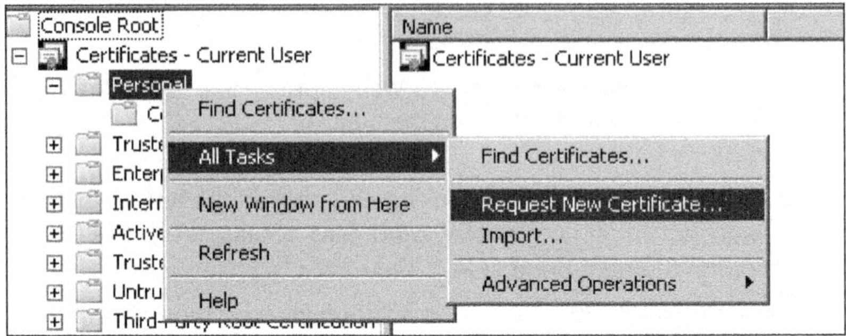


12. Click on **Next** in the **Before You Begin** section, select **Active Directory Enrollment Policy**, and click on **Next**:

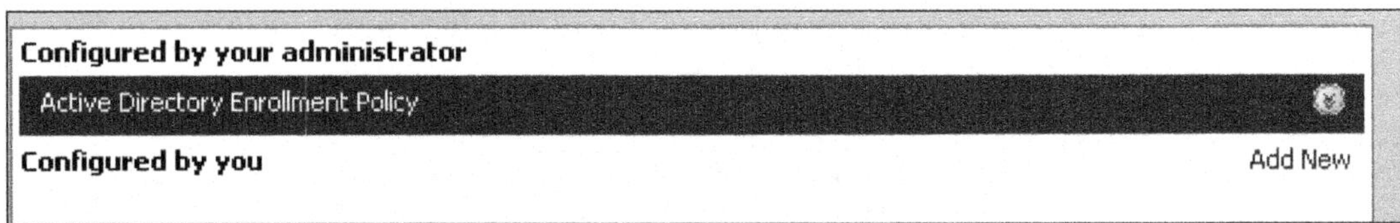


13. Flag the **Enrollment Agent** option, expand it, and click on **Properties**:

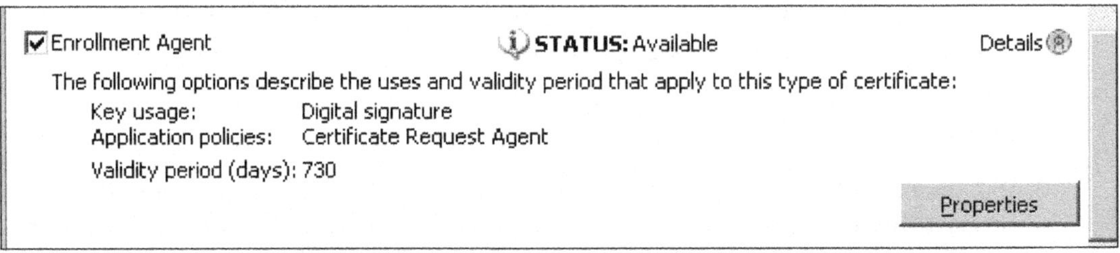


14. In the **Private Key** tab, expand the **Cryptographic Service Provider** option and verify that the **Microsoft Base Cryptographic Provider** option has been flagged. After completing this, click on **OK** and then click on **Enroll** to generate the certificate request.
15. Right-click on the `Certificates` folder, go to **All tasks** | **Advanced Operations**, and click on the **Enroll On Behalf Of** link.
16. Click on **Next** in the **Before You Begin** section, select **Active Directory Enrollment Policy**, and click on **Next**.

17. Click on **Browse...** on the **Select Enrollment Agent Certificate** screen, choose the certificate previously generated, and click on **OK**. After completing this, click on **Next** to proceed:

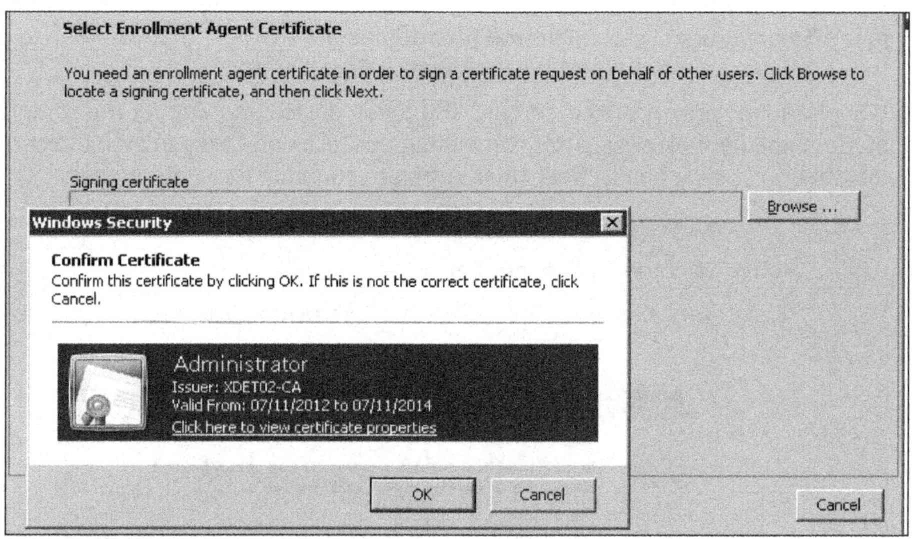


18. In the **Request Certificates** section, select the **Smartcard User** radio button, expand this section, and click on **Properties**.

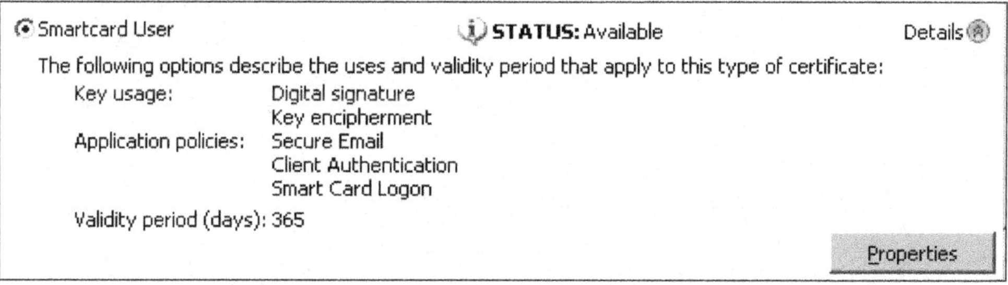


19. Expand the **Cryptographic Service Provider** section and flag your vendor-specific CSP. After completing this, click on **OK** to exit from the **Properties** menu and click on **Next** to continue:

Select cryptographic service provider (CSP):

- [ ] Microsoft Strong Cryptographic Provider (Encryption)
- [x] eToken Base Cryptographic Provider (Encryption)
- [ ] Microsoft Base Cryptographic Provider v1.0 (Encryption)

In the preceding screenshot we have selected a SafeNet eToken PKI CSP.

20. In the **Select a user** screen, browse your domain for the user that you wish to enroll the certificate for. After selecting, click on the **Enroll** button.
21. When required, insert the smart card/PKI token device and wait for the completion of the enrollment process. After completing this, click on **Close** to stop the certificate distribution or click on the **Next User** button to continue for another user:

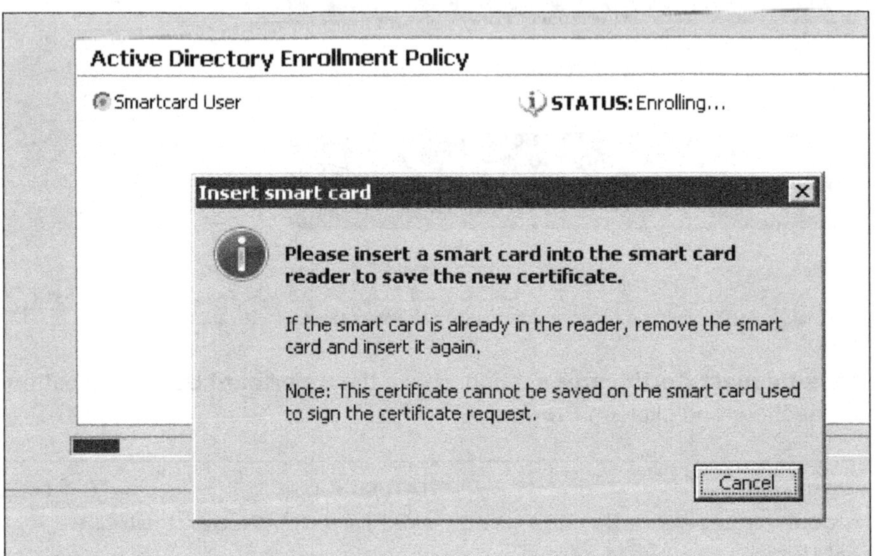


22. Connect to the Web Interface server, go to **Start** | **Administrative Tools**, and select the **Internet Information Service (IIS) Manager** link.

All the following configuration steps will be performed considering the IIS 7.x version.

23. In the **IIS** management console, select the server name in the left-hand side menu, then on the central window zone, double-click on the **Server Certificates** icon in the **IIS** section:

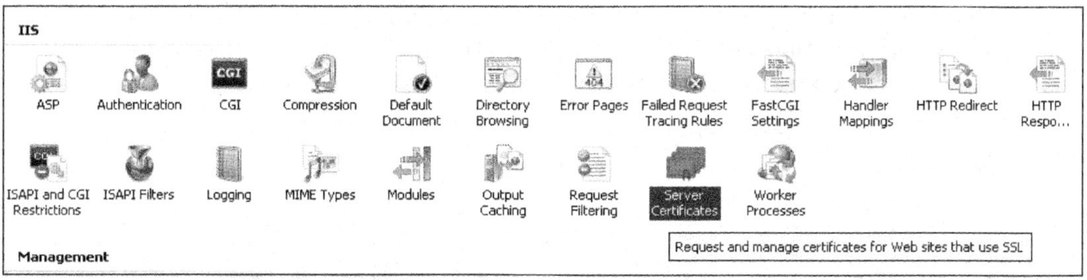


24. Click on the **Create Domain Certificate** link on the right-hand side menu, populate all the fields, and click on **Next** to continue:

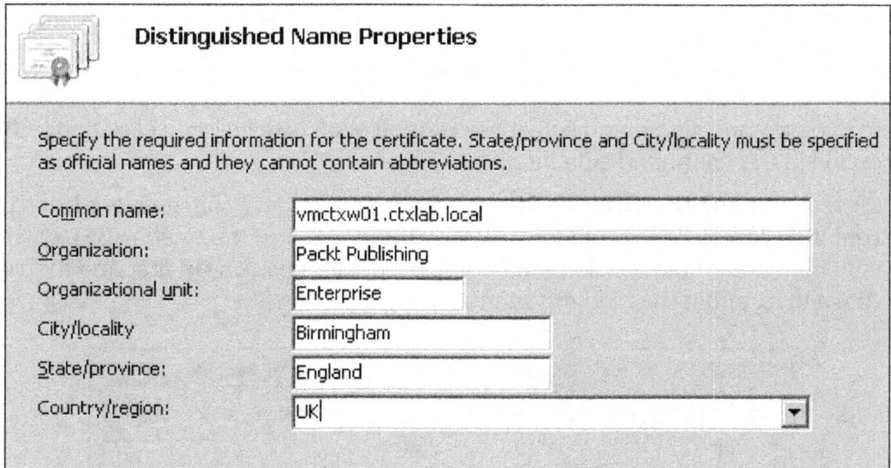

In the **Common name** field you have to insert the **Full Qualified Domain Name** (**FQDN**) of the Web Interface server.

25. In the **Online Certification Authority** section, click on the **Select** button and choose your configured Certification Authority, populate the **Friendly name** field with a value referring to your CA, and click on **Finish** to complete.

26. Click again on the server name in the left-hand side menu, double-click on the **Authentication** icon, and enable the **Active Directory Client Certificate Authentication** option by right-clicking on it and selecting **Enable**:

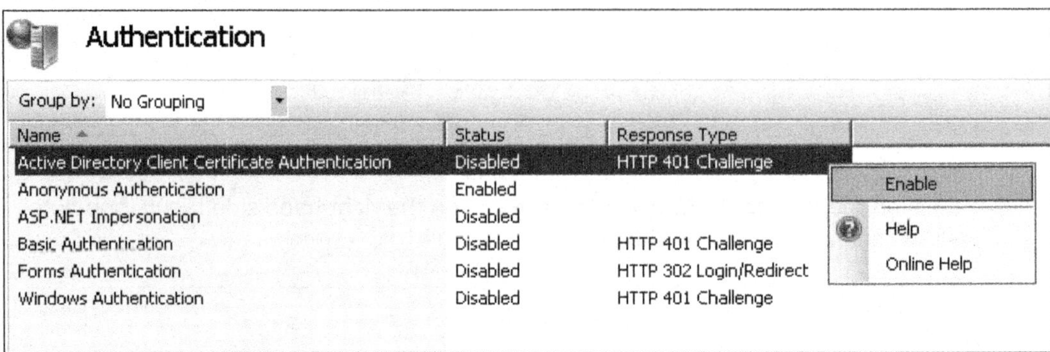


27. In the left-hand side menu select the **Default Web Site** link and click on the **Bindings** option in the right-hand side menu.

28. Click on the **Add** button in the **Site Bindings** screen, and configure the https protocol type, **IP Address** configured for your Web Interface, and the existing **SSL certificate** field from the drop-down list. After completing this, click on **OK** first and then on **Close** to exit from the bindings menu:

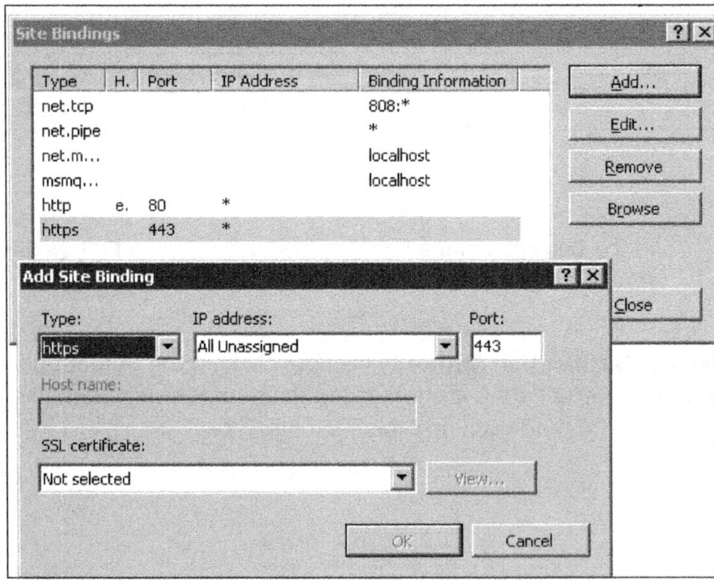


29. In the left-hand side menu expand the **Default Web Site** tree, select the **Citrix** folder, and double-click on the **SSL Settings** icon on the central part of the menu.

30. Flag the **Require SSL** option, and select the **Accept** radio button for the **Client certificates** section. Click on the **Apply** link on the right-hand side menu to confirm your choice:

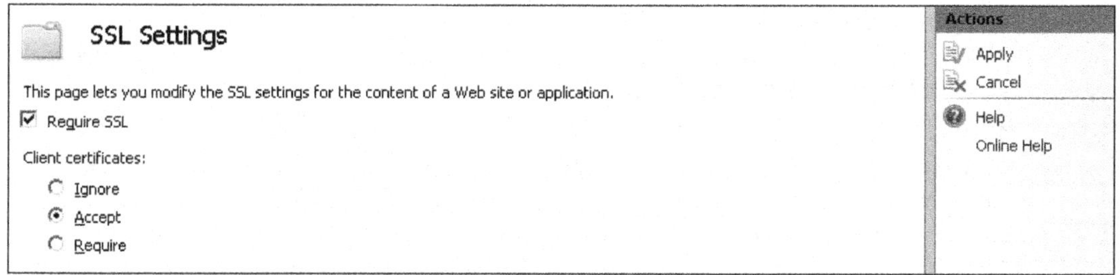


31. Add the Web Interface site to the **Trusted Site** zone of your browser, insert your smart card/PKI token in the appropriate device drive, connect to the configured Web Interface site, and insert the associated PIN if required. It's now possible to complete the authentication phase using the smart card authentication method.

In the presence of a standard physical workstation, you should install and configure the smart card reader at this level and not in XenDesktop. In case of a thin-client architecture, your only possibility is configuring the physical reader at the XenDesktop level.

## How it works...

The use of the smart cards with the XenDesktop Web Interface permits users to authenticate in a stronger and more secure way. In fact, they can access the assigned resources only through the presentation of the personal certificate installed on the physical support.

In this recipe, we have implemented the XenDesktop strong authentication by passing through three different stages:

- **Enterprise Certification Authority and Enrollment Station**: Even if this is not explicitly discussed, the first requirement to complete the strong authentication configuration is creating an Enterprise Certification Authority, based for instance, on the Microsoft CA. After this is done, we need to configure an Enrollment Station through which the generated certificate request to the Windows domain users will be assigned and then this certificate will be registered on the smart card or PKI token device. The association between the certificate and the physical device is granted by the **Cryptographic Service Provider** (**CSP**), which is based on the Microsoft native library (using a generic and compatible smart card device), or is equipped by the vendor of the token you've decided to use.

- **Web Server – IIS 7.x**: At this stage, the fundamental step is implementing the SSL for the web server machine that hosts the Web Interface site (usually the Web Interface machine itself). First of all, a domain certificate to the previously configured Certification Authority is necessary; this certificate will then be used to bind the default IIS website configuration on the SSL port (443) in order to establish a secure connection using the HTTPS protocol. Moreover, it's also necessary to enable the SSL at the web server level; we've completed navigating the SSL settings zone, enabling the secure protocol, and accepting the client certificates.
- **Web Interface**: At the Web Interface level it is possible to use the existing website (not recommended), or creating a new one only for the strong authentication type (the recommended solution). The configurations concern the XML service and Website Transport Protocol (443 and HTTPS) and the authentication method based on the smart card option.

## There's more...

It's also possible to implement the XenDesktop smart card authentication with the Web Interface by using an alternative smart card logon technique: the Pass-Through with smart card. This method is able to re-use the user credentials from the physical machine (at the first logon step) and enables reusing them without the necessity to retype information every time.

To correctly configure this option you need to insert the Web Interface site in the **Local Intranet** zone of your web browser (instead of the **Trusted Site** zone previously used for the standard smart card mode) and enable the **SSL** in the **SSL Settings** zone, but configure the **Client Certificates** section with the **Ignore** value with respect to time.

On the smart card reader client machine, open the **Local Policy** editor by clicking on **Start** | **Run** and typing the `gpedit.msc` command, import the `icaclient.adm` template located in your **Citrix Receiver** installation folder (usually `C:\Program Files (x86)\Citrix\ICA Client\Configuration`), and enable the **Smart Card** authentication policy (located at **Computer Configuration** | **Administrative Templates** | **Classic Administrative Templates (ADM)** | **Citrix Components** | **Citrix Receiver** | **User authentication**) and configure it, as shown in the following screenshot:

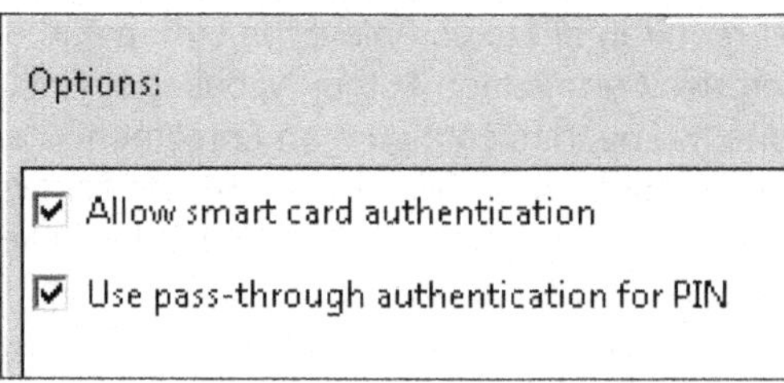

You also need to set the value for a registry key to be able to retrieve the smart card PIN in the pass-through mode:

- Registry Location: `HKLM\Software\Microsoft\WindowsNT\CurrentVersion\Winlogon\Notify`
- DWORD Key to create: `SmartCardLogonNotify`
- Value: `1`

## See also

- The *Configuring the Citrix Access Gateway virtual appliance* recipe in *Chapter 8, XenDesktop Tuning and Security*

# Implementing the XenDesktop strong authentication

An alternative method to the smart card authentication is two-factor authentication. This strong authentication type forces the user to connect to the assigned resources through the use of the password and a second authentication key. In this recipe, we're going to discuss the configuration of **RADIUS** authentication for the Citrix Web Interface. It is a strong authentication type based on the combination of a username, a password, and a pre-shared key, which can be delivered in the form of a static key or as **One Time Password** (**OTP**).

## Getting ready

In order to implement the strong authentication for the Citrix Web Interface site, you have to install a RADIUS server; this task can be accomplished by using the Microsoft RADIUS role (NPS - Network Policy Server), or by installing a Linux-based authentication server, such as FreeRADIUS or ZeroShell.

In this recipe, we will use the Windows version of the RADIUS server by installing the Network Policy Server role on a Windows 2008 R2 machine. You can find more information about the installation procedure at `http://technet.microsoft.com/it-it/library/cc725922%28v=ws.10%29.aspx`.

## How to do it...

In this section, we will explain how to configure a Windows Radius server in order to implement a multiple-factor authentication through the Citrix Web Interface:

1. Connect to the Windows RADIUS server with administrative credentials, go to **Start | Administrative Tools**, and select the **Network Policy Server** link.
2. In the left-hand side menu expand the **RADIUS Clients and Servers** folder, right-click on the **RADIUS Clients** link, and select **New**.

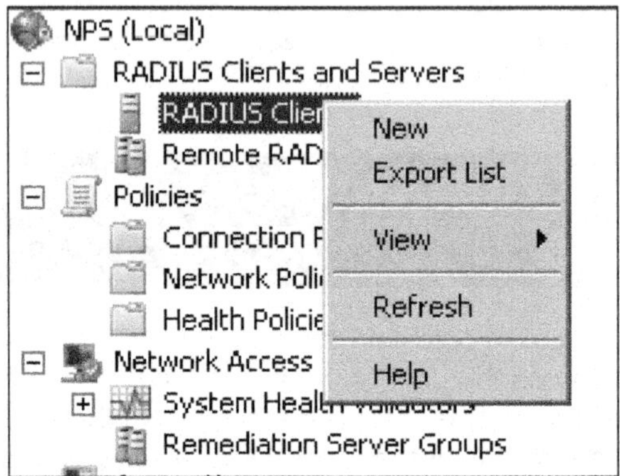


3. Assign an identification name populating the **Friendly Name** field, insert the IP address or the FQDN of your Web Interface machine, and insert a **Shared Secret** key by selecting the **Manual** radio button and typing the security code, or use a randomly generated secret code by selecting the **Generate** radio button and clicking on the **Generate** button. After completing this, click on **OK**.

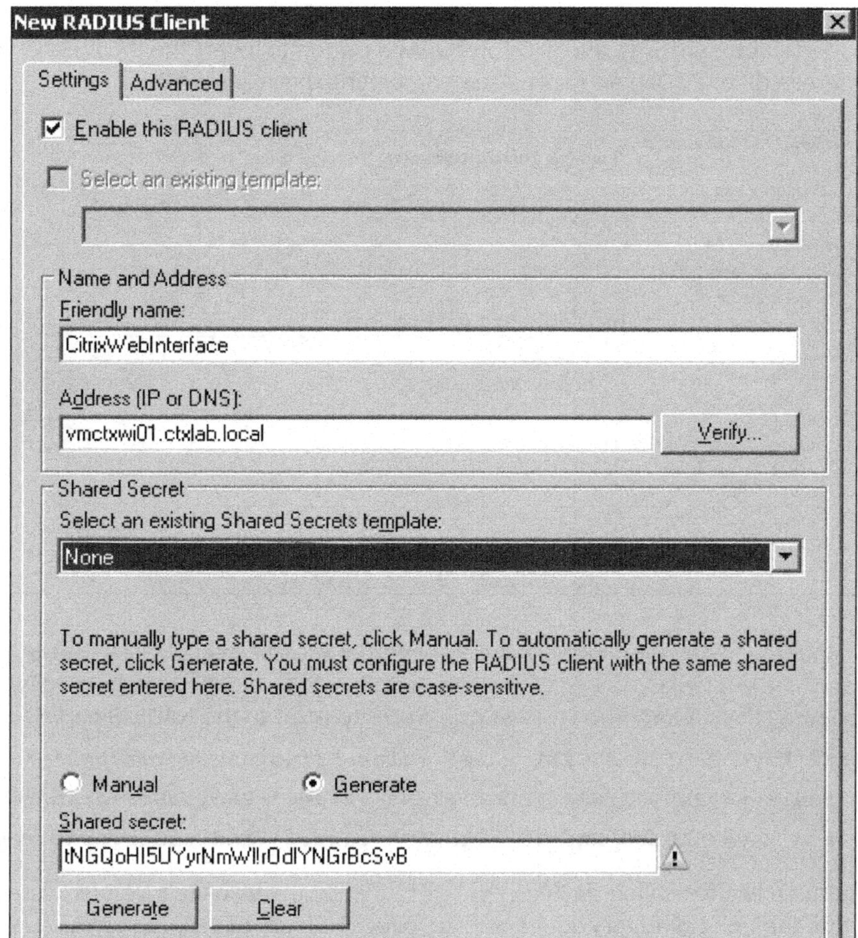

> Remember that the secret key is case sensitive, so you have to be careful when using it in the client configuration phase!

4. Connect to the Web Interface machine with administrative credentials, configure two new web and services sites as seen earlier in this chapter, and change the authentication method to **Explicit**.
5. Select the configured sites and click on the **Authentication Methods** link in the right-hand side menu.
6. On the next screen that appears, select the **Explicit** authentication method and click on the **Properties** button.

7. In the **Properties** section select the **Two-Factor Authentication** link, select **RADIUS** as **Two-factor setting**, and click on the **Add** button to insert the RADIUS server address (IP or FQDN) and port. After completing this, click on **OK**.

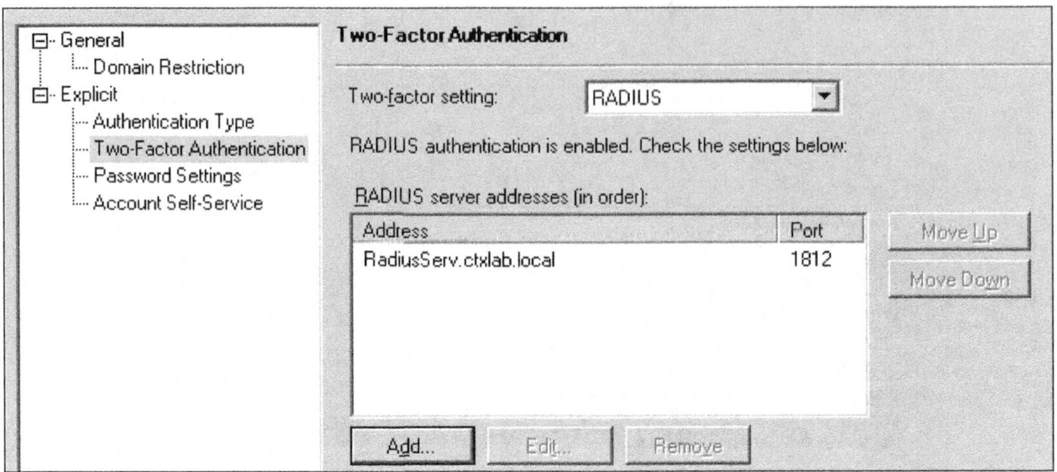


8. Locate the installation path for this configured website (usually `C:\inetpub\wwwroot\Citrix\<SiteName>`) and edit the `web.config` file by modifying the following lines in order to let the Citrix Web site point to the RADIUS server:

```
<add key="RADIUS_SECRET_PATH" value="/radius_secret.txt" />
 <add key="RADIUS_NAS_IDENTIFIER" value="<RadiusServerAddress>" />
 <add key="RADIUS_NAS_IP_ADDRESS" value="<RadiusServerAddress>" />
```

9. Create a text file called `radius_secret.txt` at the website's default installation path, the `conf` directory (`C:\inetpub\wwwroot\Citrix\<SiteName>\conf`), and populate it with the secret key generated during the RADIUS configuration phase.

> You have to assign the most restrictive permissions to the secret key file in order to avoid forbidden accesses to it.

10. Connect again to the Windows RADIUS server with administrative credentials, go to **Start** | **Administrative Tools**, and select the **Network Policy Server** link.
11. Expand the **Policies** section in the left-hand side menu, right-click on the **Network Policies** folder, and select the **New** link, as shown in the following screenshot:

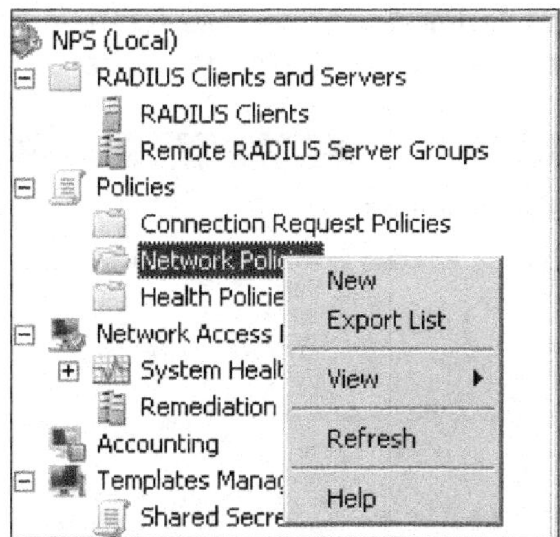


12. Assign a name to the policy in the **Policy** name field, select the **Unspecified** option for the **Type of network access server** section, and click on **Next** to continue.
13. Click on the **Add** button in the **Specify Conditions** screen, select the **User Groups** option from the list, and click on the **Add** button, as shown in the following screenshot:

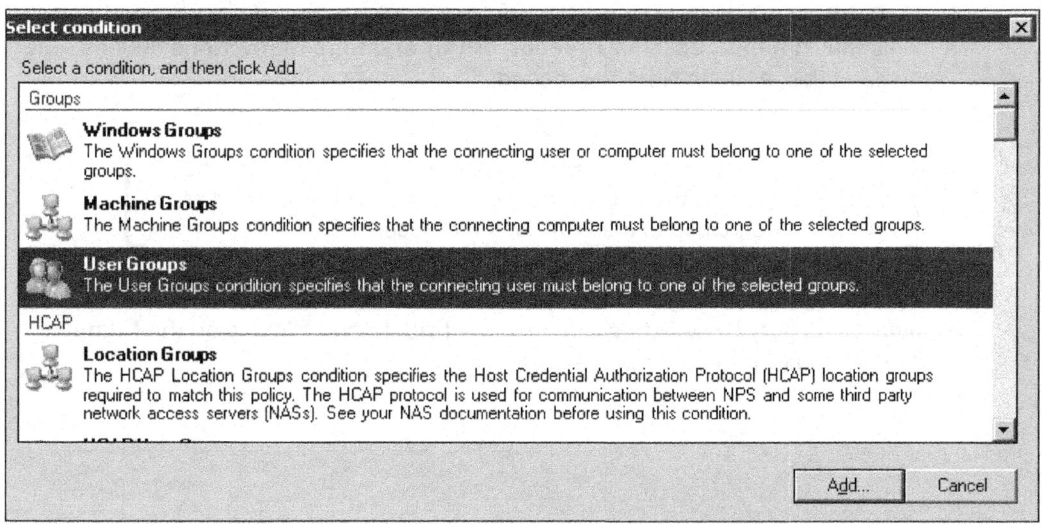


14. On the **User Groups** screen, click on the **Add Groups** button and browse for the domain group that you want to configure the strong authentication for. After completing this, click on **OK** to close the pop-up screen and click on the **Next** button to proceed with the configuration.

15. In the **Specify Access Permission** section, select the **Access granted** radio button and click on **Next**, as shown in the following screenshot:

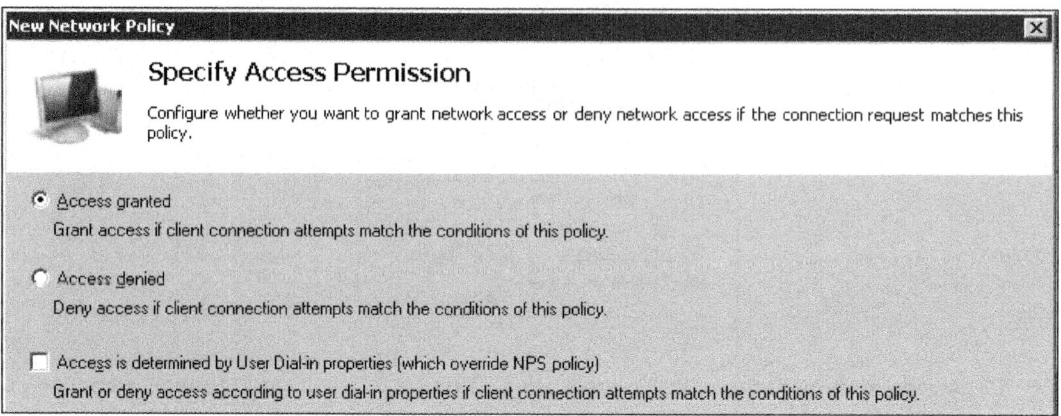


16. On the **Configure Authentication Methods** screen, clear any configured option, and only flag the **Encrypted authentication (CHAP)** and **Unencrypted authentication (PAP, SPAP)** options, and click on **Next**.
17. In the **Configure Constraints** section, you can configure specific connection options, such as **Idle Timeout**, **Session Timeout**, or **Day and time restrictions** options. After completing this, click on **Next** to proceed.

These are collateral options, which are not fundamental in order to the correct functioning of the RADIUS server combined to the Citrix Web Interface.

18. On the **Configure Settings** screen remove any configured attributes under the **Standard** category by selecting the desired attribute and clicking on the **Remove** button, as shown in the following screenshot:

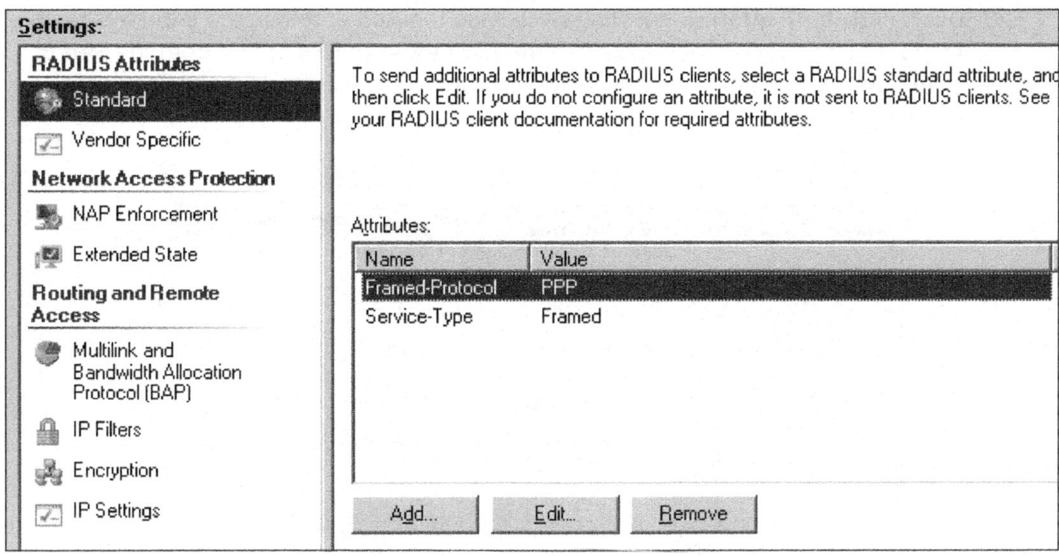


19. In the left-hand side menu select the **Vendor Specific** option, click on **Add**, choose the **Custom** option from the **Vendor** list, and select the **Vendor Specific** attributes; after completing this, click on the **Add** button:

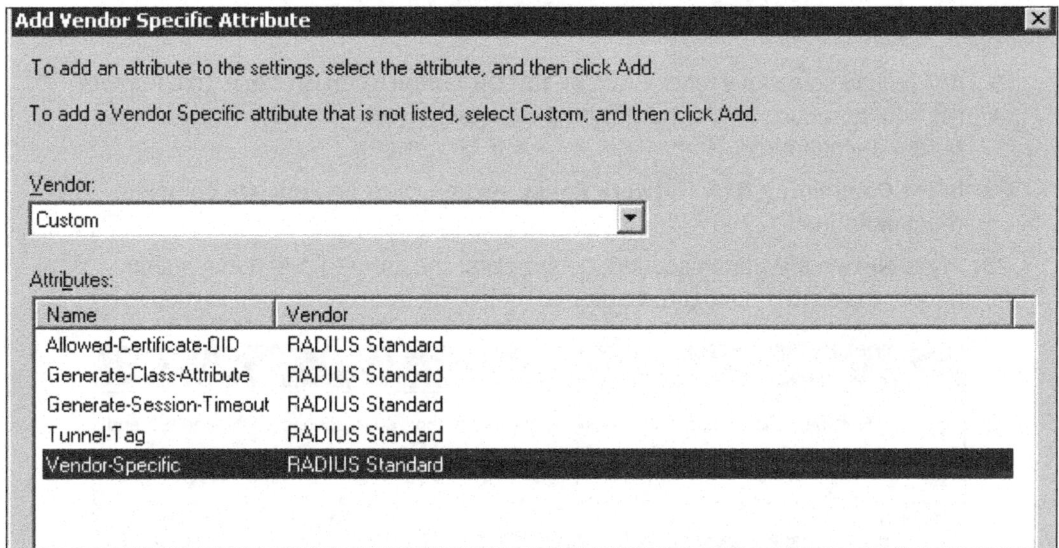

20. On the **Attribute Information** screen, click on the **Add** button in the **Vendor-Specific Attribute Information** menu, choose the **RADIUS standard** option from the **Select from list** section, and select the **Yes. It conforms** radio button, as shown in the following screenshot:

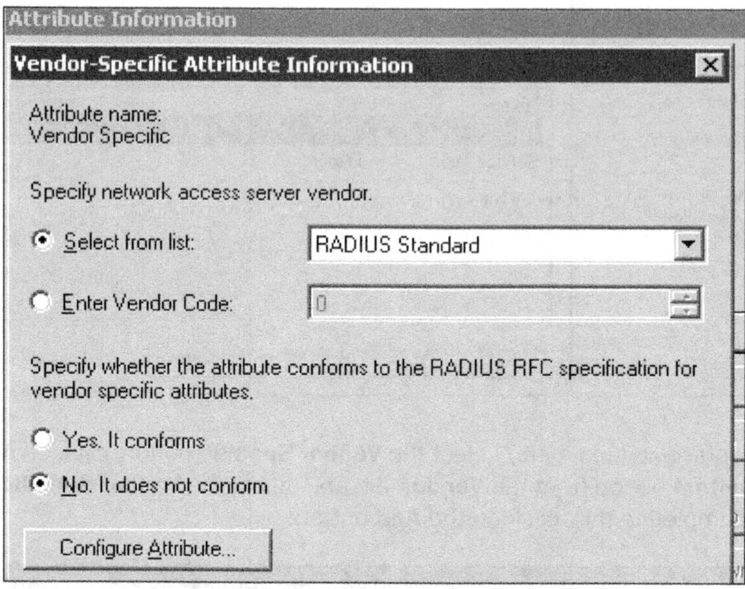


21. After these selections, click twice on the **OK** button, then on **Close** to complete the configuration. On the **Configure Settings** main screen, click on the **Next** button to continue.
22. In the **Completing New Network Policy** section, click on **Finish** to complete the procedure.
23. In the **Network Policies** section, be sure that the created rule has a higher priority than other configured rules:

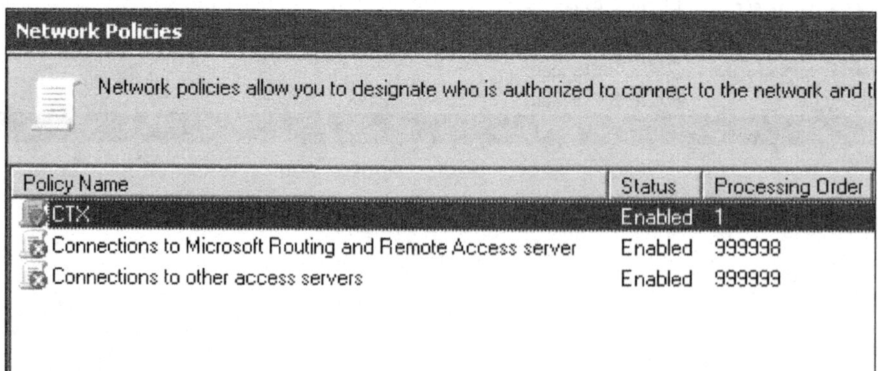

24. Connect to the Web Interface using a web browser and insert the login credentials plus the secret key configured for the RADIUS authentication in the **PASSCODE** field. At this point, you will be able to use the published resources through the RADIUS two-factor authentication:

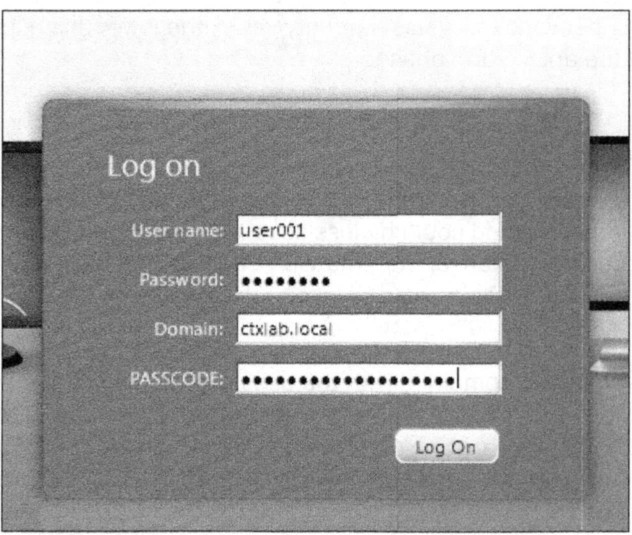


## How it works...

RADIUS is a strong authentication method based on the protocol Remote Authentication Dial In User Service, which is an AAA kind of platform (Authentication, Authorization, and Accounting) used as network resource regulator in order to manage the access to the network resources.

The first operation executed in this recipe has been the Microsoft RADIUS server configuration through the use of the **Network Policy Server** (**NPS**) role configured on the Windows 2008 R2 machine. In order to let the RADIUS communicate with the Web Interface server, this second authentication has to be configured as a client under the RADIUS server. In order to accomplish this task, it is necessary to insert the FQDN or the IP address of the Web Interface, then generate a secret key that will be used as a second authentication factor when accessing the desktops and the applications through the Web Interface.

This code should be complex in order to make it more difficult to crack; on the other hand, it should not be too long because some clients would not be able to read and use it. This generated key needs to be copied under the Web Interface website folder in the form of a text file containing the secret code. In fact, the configuration file of the Web Interface (the `web.config` file) is configured to point not only to the RADIUS server's IP address, but also to a text file that contains the generated code, which is not encrypted by default. This could be a security issue, so you have to plan a strong and valid permissions plan for this file.

After completing the Web Interface machine configuration, the last step is the configuration of a RADIUS network policy based on the RADIUS standard generic vendor. This means that it's possible to configure a generic identifier for the Citrix Web Interface (based on the generic code number 0), and on this network policy it is also possible to grant the access to the specific domain groups containing the users, who are authorized to log on using the strong authentication. Every network policy has a priority value, the lower this number is, the higher is its precedence in the application phase.

## There's more...

From a security perspective, the standard RADIUS authentication formerly based on a two-factor authentication method could be less secure than your expectations. Once the secret code is retrieved, for instance, from the Web Interface machine, the malicious activities from unauthorized people could be easier than expected.

This problem could be solved by using a third authentication factor, based on OTP. This is a temporary code that must be combined with the base secret code plus the user password, and it can be in the form of an e-mail message, proprietary token device, or an SMS on your mobile phone; the combination can be performed by separating the three access codes (so populating three different fields), or combining two of them, usually the RADIUS secret key and the OTP received code.

The market gives you a lot of technologies on which you can implement this strong authentication type, starting from a licensed platform (such as RSA, Symantec, or SafeNet) to free software (Mobile-OTP or Wright SMS2). The functioning is based on the interaction between the RADIUS server and the OTP architecture (sometimes they can be collapsed in a single one), for instance, in the form of plugins that directly interact with the RADIUS implementation.

Following is a set of product links to choose the platform to integrate with the RADIUS authentication:

- **Symantec OTP**: `https://www.symantec.com/verisign/vip-authentication-service`
- **RSA OTP**: `http://www.emc.com/security/rsa-securid.html`
- **SafeNet OTP**: `http://www.safenet-inc.com/data-protection/authentication/otp-authentication/`
- **Mobile OTP**: `http://motp.sourceforge.net/`
- **Wright SMS2**: `http://www.wrightccs.com/how-it-works/`

## See also

- The *Installing and configuring Web Interface* recipe in *Chapter 1, XenDesktop Installation and Configuration*

# Implementing the Citrix SSO platform

With the Citrix XenDesktop software and all the related components, you have the ability to access a lot of different resources in terms of virtual desktops and applications. Although for this second category, you could have the necessity to remember a lot of different access codes and/or passwords. This could be difficult in the presence of hundreds of platforms to use and to manage. To solve this situation, Citrix offers a **Single Sign On platform** (**SSO**) called **Citrix Single Sign On**, the evolution of the old Citrix Password Manager; the latest release for this platform is Version 5.0. In this recipe we're going to discuss its features and the way to implement it.

## Getting ready

You need to download the Citrix SSO from the Citrix website using the following link:

`http://www.citrix.com/downloads/single-sign-on.html`

You have to select the latest version of this software (Version 5.0); this is a `.zip` archive that needs to be extracted. In order to use the Citrix SSO platform without problems, you have to install a new Windows 2008 or Windows 2008 R2 machine.

Citrix SSO can't be installed on a Domain Controller or on a Citrix XenApp server.

You also need to create an SSO central store on which you will register the SSO user information. This can be in the form of an NTFS network share or it can be performed by extending the Active Directory domain structure.

## How to do it...

In this recipe we will explain how to configure the Citrix Single-Sign-On platform:

1. Connect to the newly installed Windows server machine and extract the SSO ZIP archive downloaded from the Citrix website.
2. Navigate to the extracted folder and locate the `Service` folder; within this directory, double-click on the `Citrix Password Manager Service.msi` file in order to install the service platform.
3. On the **Welcome** screen, click on **Next** to continue and select the **I accept the license agreement** radio button for the **License Agreement**.

4. Select an installation path on the **Destination Folder** screen; the default path is `C:\Program Files(x86)\Citrix\MetaFrame Password Manager`. After selecting the path click on **Next**.
5. From the **Select Modules** section select the components that you want to install. Based on this recipe's requirements, keep the default selected components and click on **Next**.
6. On the next screen click on the **Install** button to proceed with the service component installation. After completing, click on **Finish** to close the installation setup.
7. A screen will automatically appear to let you configure the SSO service. Click on the **Next** button to continue.
8. On the **Configure service** screen, populate the SSL **Port number** (default **443**) field, the **SSL Certificate** field to establish the secure connection with the Central Store, and the Windows account credentials, in the form of **System account** (default **NT AUTHORITY\NETWORK SERVICE**). After completing this click on **Next**:

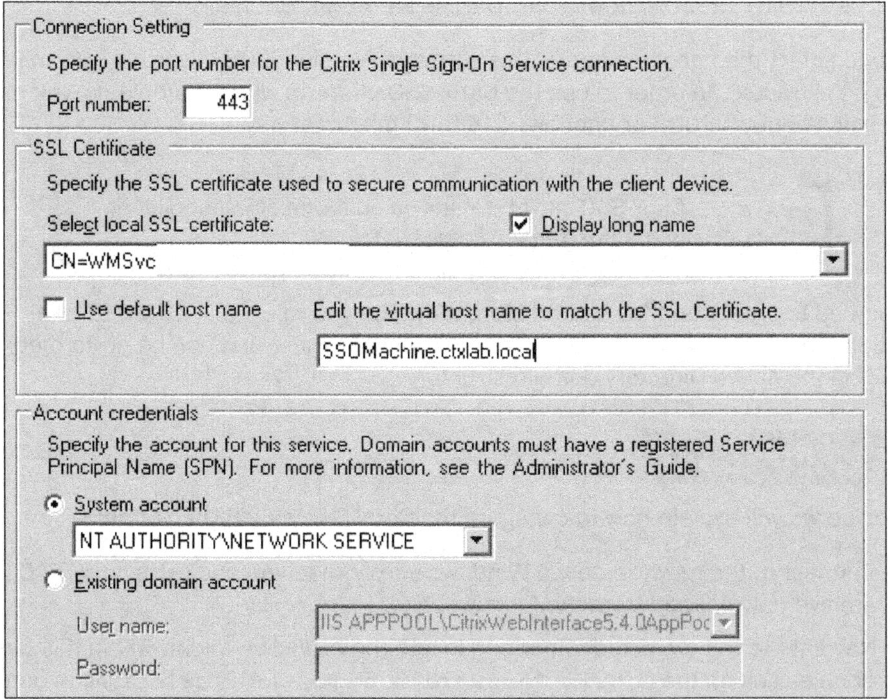


9. In the **Create signing certificate** section specify **Expiration (in months)** for the certificate to generate; the default value is 12. After completing this click on **Next**.

10. On the **Identify central store** screen select whether you are using **Active Directory** or **NTFS network share** as the central store, then click on **Next**.

In this recipe, we have decided to use the NTFS network share as a central store by specifying the network path in the form of a `\\FQDN\CitrixSync$` share.

11. In the **Configure domains** section, flag the domain that you want to use as **Central store** and click on the **Properties** button.
12. Populate the **Data Proxy Account** and **Self-Service Features Account** sections with a valid domain user and password combination. This user needs to be able to read and write the configured central store. After completing this click on **OK** and then click on **Next** to proceed.
13. On the **Confirm settings** screen, after you have reviewed all the information, click on the **Finish** button to complete the configuration procedure.
14. Return to the folder containing the extracted archive, browse the `Administration` folder, and run the `Setup.exe` installer.
15. On the **Welcome** screen click on **Next** to continue, and select the **I accept the license agreement** radio button for **License Agreement**.
16. In the **Installation Type** section flag both the **Console** and **Application Definition Tool** components, insert **Install Location** (default path `C:\Program Files (x86)\Citrix\MetaFrame Password Manager\`), and click on **Next**. On the successive screen (**Ready to Install the Application**), again click on **Next** to complete the installation.
17. After completing the installation procedure click on the **Finish** button to close the setup screen.
18. Copy the `Plugin` folder under the Citrix SSO setup location to the Windows 7 template, which is used to deploy the Desktop Instances and execute the appropriate setup for your desktop version (`\Receiver\ CitrixSSOPlugin32.exe` for the 32-bit platforms and `\Receiver\ CitrixSSOPlugin64.exe` for the 64-bit platforms). On the **Welcome** screen, click on **Next** to proceed with the installation.
19. In the **License Agreement** form select the **I accept the license agreement** radio button and click on **Next**.

20. On the **Central Store configuration** screen, select the type of store you've configured for your infrastructure and insert its address information to let the plugin retrieve it. After completing this, click on **Next**.

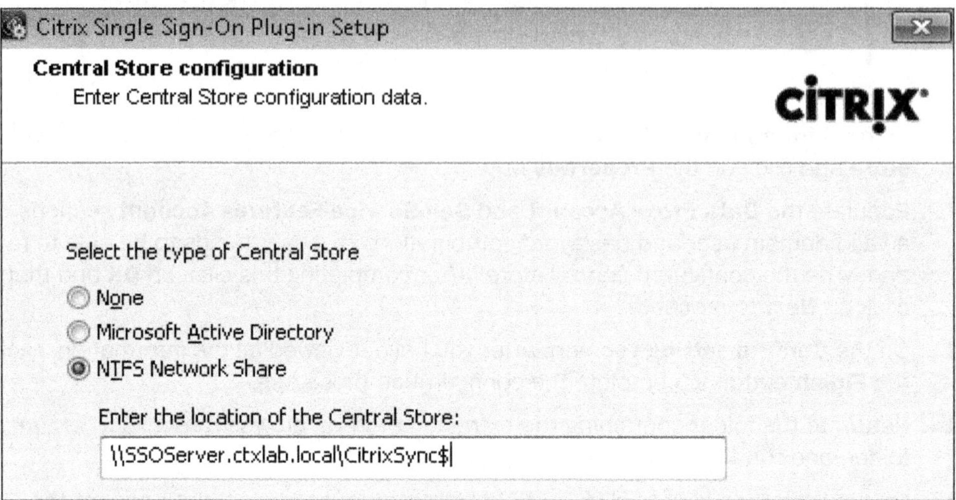


21. On the **Component Selection** screen select the part of the SSO plugin that you want to install and click on **Next** to continue:

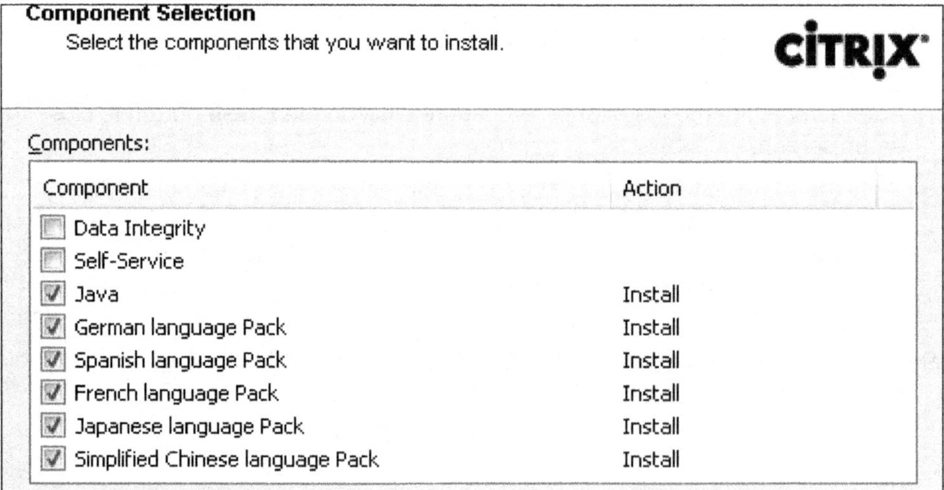

22. On the **Ready to Install** screen click on **Next** to proceed if you are sure about the selected component to install.
23. After the installation has completed, click on the **Finish** button to terminate the procedure.
24. Restart the Windows 7 template machine in order to make the system changes active.
25. Connect again to the Service and Console Windows machine, go to **Start** | **All programs** | **Citrix** | **Management Consoles**, and select the **Citrix AppCenter** link. On the **Welcome** screen click on the **Next** button to continue with the configuration.
26. On the **Identify Central Store** screen insert the location of the configured SSO store, in the form of an **Active Directory** domain or **NTFS network share** and click on **Next**.
27. In the **Select encryption method** section the only available encryption is the **Advanced Encryption Standard (AES)** option, used starting from the Citrix SSO Version 4.8, so click on **Next** to proceed.
28. On the **Preview Discovery** screen, after you have reviewed the configured information, click on **Next** to complete the operations, and at the end of the Discovery process click on the **Finish** button.
29. In the left-hand side menu, right-click on the **Application Definitions** link and click on **Create Application Definition**:

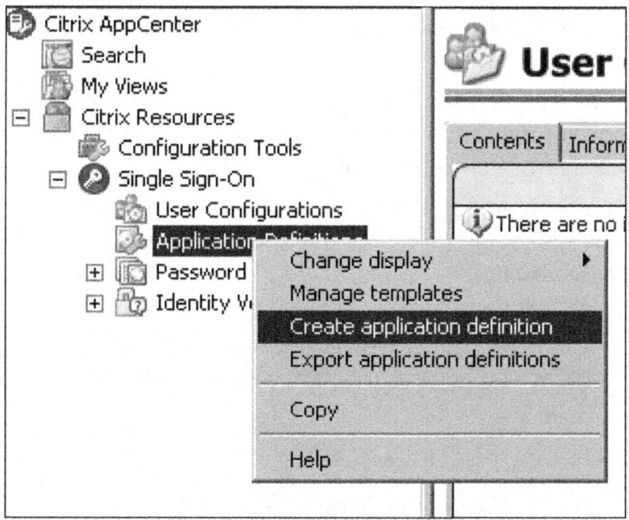

30. In the **Create Application Definition** menu select the application type you want to configure (**Windows** or **Web**); choose either by creating a new application or using a template, and click on the **Start Wizard** button.

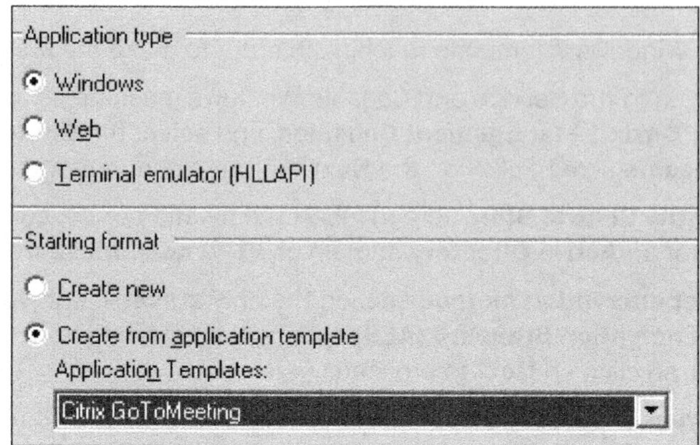

For this configuration we have selected the **Citrix GoToMeeting** Windows application template.

31. In the **Identify application** section assign a name and a description to the application and click on **Next**.
32. In the **Name Custom fields** section you can insert labels for specified custom fields. In the presence of applications from templates, these forms are grayed out, so the only task to perform is to click on **Next** to continue.
33. In **Configure advanced detection**, flag one or both the presented options depending on your company's requirements for the application password changes. After selecting click on **Next**.

Use these settings to force Single Sign-On Plug-in to ignore subsequent logon or password change forms during an application session when a logon or password change has already been processed.

- [x] Process only the first logon for this application
- [x] Process only the first password change for this application

34. On the **Configure password expiration** screen either select the **Run** script when the password expires, browsing for a customized script in the form of `.bat` or `.exe`, or **Use Citrix Single Sign-On expiration warning** and click on the **Next** button.

35. After reviewing the information on the **Confirm settings** screen, click on **Finish** to complete the application configuration.
36. In the left-hand side menu, right-click on the **User Configurations** link and click on **Add new user configuration**.
37. In the **Name user configuration** section insert a name and a description for the user or the group to configure, then browse your domain and select one of the objects. After selecting click on **Next**.
38. In **Select product edition**, choose from the drop-down list the **Single Sign-On** version on which you're currently working and click on **Next** to continue.
39. In the **Choose applications** section click on the **Add** button and select the previously configured application, assign it an application group name and description, choose whether to apply a **Domain** or **Default** password policy, and click on **OK**. To proceed click on the **Next** button.
40. In the **Configure plug-in interaction** menu, flag the desired plugin interaction options and click on the **Next** button.

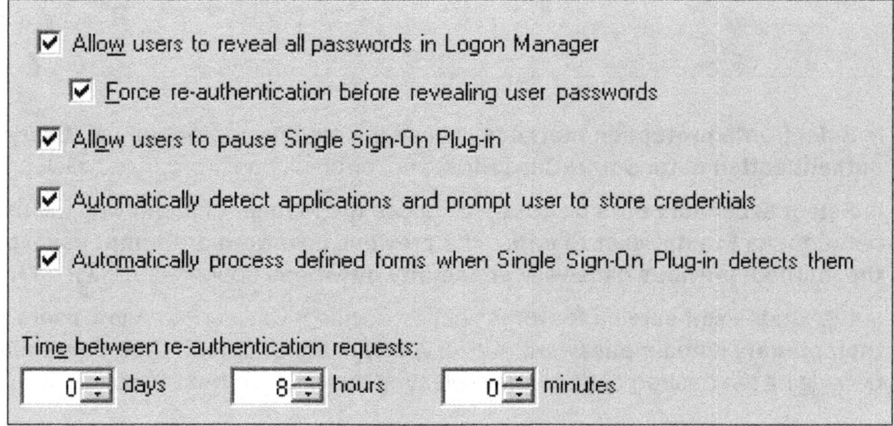

The first option flagged in the previous screenshot permits you to retrieve the password configured for the application on which it is currently enabled. To secure this procedure you have to force the SSO to re-authenticate you before showing the credentials.

41. In the **Configure licensing** section, populate the required fields with the information about your **License server address** and **Licensing model** and click on the **Next** button:

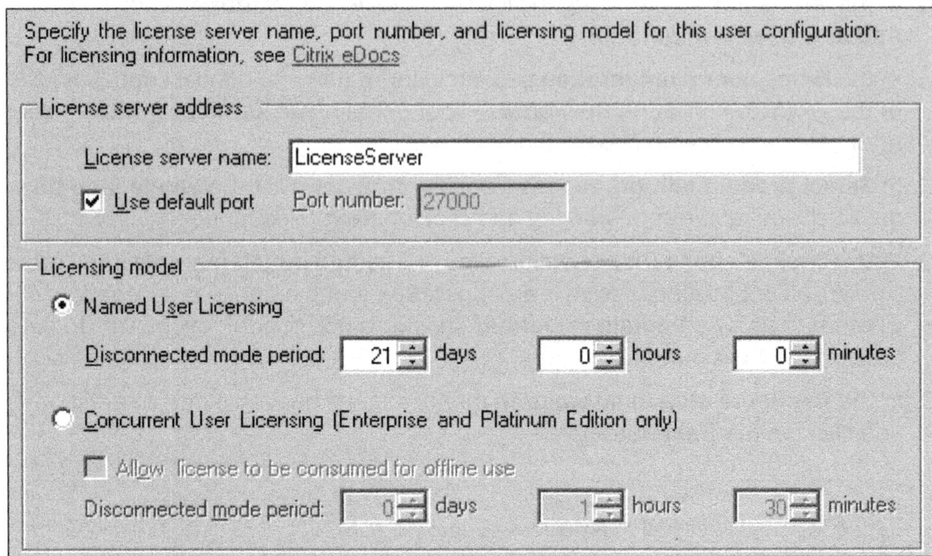


42. In **Select Data protection methods** choose the option you want to use (**User's authentication data**, **Smart Card PINs**, and/or blank passwords) and click on **Next**.
43. In **Select secondary data protection**, choose the manner of identifying the users between the **Prompt user to entire the previous password** or **Prompt user to select the method: previous password or security questions** options and click on **Next**.
44. In the **Enable self-service features** section decide if you want to **Allow users to reset their primary domain password** and/or **Allow users to unlock their domain account** by flagging the desired option. After selecting this click on **Next** to continue.

These preceding two options require the activation of the Key Management Module.

45. In the **Provisioning Module** menu decide whether you want to select **Use provisioning**. In this case you have to populate the **Service Location** field with the provisioning address. Click on the **Next** button to proceed.
46. In the **Confirm settings**, review the inserted information and click on **Finish** to complete the procedure.

These previously performed operations have to be repeated for every application configured for the SSO credentials management.

47. Connect to the client machine, right-click on **Citrix Receiver**, and select the **Single Sign-On Plug-in settings** link. From the drop-down menu select the **Manage Passwords** option. You will be prompted with a menu containing all the configured credentials.

## How it works...

The Single Sign-On is particularly useful for credential management when there are many different logins to manage for every single user.

With Version 5.0 of this component, the client part of the platform integrates itself in the Citrix Receiver, eliminating the presence of two different icons on the client machine.

The Citrix platform discussed in this recipe requires to perform operations at three different levels:

- **The store component**: This is the core of the SSO platform, which can be based on the Active Directory domain or in the form of a Microsoft NTFS hidden share. The central store contains the configured users and applications, the credentials configured for them, and the defined password policies.
- **The client plugin component**: This is a fundamental element in the SSO architecture because it intercepts the logon phase performed by the end users, delivering them to the appropriate applications in order to complete the authentication phase.
- **The user and application management**: These two categories configure the applications and their assignment to the users specifying the application category (Web or Windows) based on an already existing template or creating a new one from applications that are not already defined. These tasks are performed using the **Citrix AppCenter** console.

The user configuration is a complex part of this architecture. As seen in the previous section users have the ability, for instance, to see their protected password. This operation, which can be considered critical in terms of security, has to be regulated by using options, such as the identification of users, and performed forcing the identification of the user through the re-authentication operation.

A useful configurable option is given by the ability for the SSO to detect applications which are not yet configured, asking the user to insert the credentials that will be archived in the central store. (Automatically detect applications and prompt user to store credentials: step number 40.) The alternative option to this feature is only permitting users to manually insert the required credentials in the SSO plugin.

For the complete list of Citrix SSO 5.0 features, please refer to the official Citrix e-Docs documentation at `http://support.citrix.com/proddocs/topic/passwordmanager-5-0/pm-landing-page-version-50.html`.

## There's more

Through the use of the **Citrix AppCenter** console, it is also possible to configure the password policies assigned to your infrastructure. The link is located in its left-hand side menu, and it is called **Password Policies**. You can configure the Default and/or the Domain policies. The most important configurable parameters are the minimum and maximum password length, the Alphabetical and Numerical Character Rules (where it is possible to put a lower or upper-case character and a numeric symbol), the management of the password history and expiration, and the possibility to use a special wizard for the password change, using system-generated passwords or standard self-created access keys. All of them can be tested using the **Test Password Policy** section of this feature.

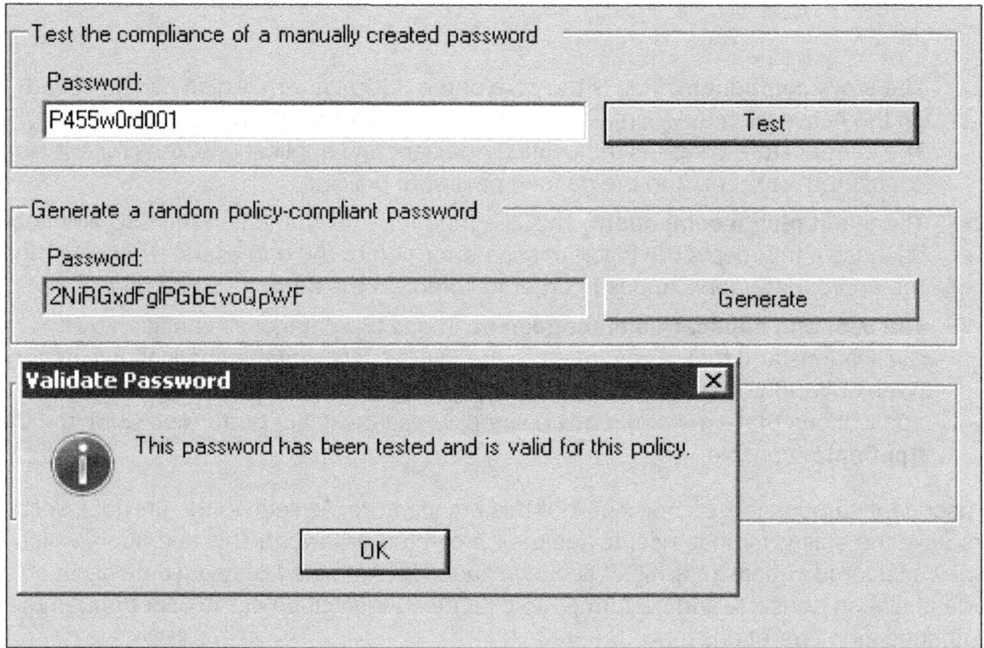


## See also

- The *Publishing the streamed apps with XenApp 6.5* recipe in *Chapter 7, Deploying Applications*

# Chapter 10 XenDesktop lab

In this last chapter we have discussed the advanced authentication methods available with the XenDesktop architecture and its collateral components.

In this laboratory, we are going to implement a set of different authentication types as discussed during this chapter:

1. Create a Windows 2008 R2 virtual machine and assign it the following parameters:
   - Recommended virtual hardware resources are two vCPUs, 4 GB of RAM, 40 GB of hard disk
   - `vmctxeca01` as the hostname
   - `192.168.1.120` as the IP address
   - Join it to the `ctxlab.local` domain before configuring any software role
   - Configure the machine as an Enterprise CA
   - Configure the machine as the Enrollment Agent station
2. Generate a valid domain certificate and enroll it on the smart cards for number three domain users selected previously.
3. Create a Windows 2008 R2 virtual machine and assign it the following parameters:
   - Recommended virtual hardware resources are two vCPUs, 4 GB of RAM, 40 GB of hard disk
   - `vmctxrad01` as the hostname
   - `192.168.1.121` as the IP address
   - Join it to the `ctxlab.local` domain before configuring any software role
   - Configure the machine as a Network Policy Server
4. Create a Windows 2008 R2 virtual machine and assign it the following parameters:
   - Recommended virtual hardware resources are two vCPUs, 4 GB of RAM, 40 GB of hard disk
   - `vmctxsso01` as the hostname
   - `192.168.1.122` as the IP address
   - Join it to the `ctxlab.local` domain before configuring any software role
   - Install on this server the Citrix SSO platform in the form of server and client components
   - Configure the central store as a Windows NTFS share

5. At the Domain Controller level, create three different groups based on already configured VDI users, and based on these domain objects, configure the following authentication methods:

    - Assign to the first group the smart card authentication mode; to perform this task you have to generate a website on the Web Interface machine and configure it to authenticate users using the smart card in the Pass-Trough mode. This group must be populated with the users for which you have already enrolled the domain certificate on the smart cards/PKI tokens. Be sure to perform all the required operations at the Web Server, Web Interface, and client levels.
    - Assign to the second group the two-factor authentication type and generate a Web Interface site based on this kind of authentication. Grant the access to this domain group and verify if all the required operations have been performed at the RADIUS server and the Web Interface website levels.
    - Assign to the third group the ability to use the Citrix SSO platform, installing the SSO plugin on the Windows 7 template. Choose a web application from the applications within your company, and configure it to store the credentials and to be assigned to the specified Active Directory domain group. Do not allow the platform to auto detect any applications, but force the users to manually insert the credentials in the client plugin.

# Index


## A

**AcctADAccount PowerShell command 282**
**AcctIdentityPool command 279**
**Active Directory accounts**
managing, AD identity cmdlets used 278, 279
**Active Directory policies**
configuring 89
working 90
**Add-BrokerApplication command 291**
**Add-BrokerMachinesToDesktopGroup command 290**
**Add-HypHostingUnitStorage cmdlet 296**
**AD identity cmdlets**
about 278
using 278, 279
working 281
**ADSI Edit Microsoft tool 131**
**advanced settings, policies sections 86**
**applications**
publishing, applications used 227-234
**App-V Management Server 228**
**App-V Management System 228**
**App-V Sequencer 229**
**App-V Streaming Server 229**
**Audio subsection 245**
**Auto Client Reconnect subsection 240**

## B

**Background Intelligent Transfer Services (BITS) 97**
**Bandwidth subsection 245, 246**
**Branch Repeater plugin**
about 148
redirector modality approach 148
transparent modality approach 148
**Branch Repeater virtual appliance**
about 140
configuring 140-146
inline mode 147
one arm mode (WCCP) 147
working 146-148
**Branch Repeater VPX.** *See* **Branch Repeater virtual appliance**
**broker cmdlets**
about 283
subcategories 290
using 283, 285
working 290

## C

**certification authority management, Merchandising Server**
export certificate signing request 139
generate self-signed certificate 139
import certificate from a certificate authority 140
import root certificate 140
manage SSL certificates 139
**Citrix Access Gateway virtual appliance**
Configure authentication section 261
configuring 255-265
working 266
**Citrix database repository 5**
**Citrix Desktop Controller**
managing, broker cmdlets used 283-287
**Citrix Desktop Director**
about 184
using 184-187
working 188, 189

**Citrix Diagnostic Facility Trace (CDF Trace) 151**
**Citrix FlexCast technique 5**
**Citrix HDX 115**
**Citrix HDX 3D Pro.** *See* **HDX 3D Pro**
**Citrix Merchandising Server.** *See* **Merchandising Server**
**Citrix Profile Management**
  about 74
  installing 74-80
  working 80
**Citrix Profile Manager**
  configuring 80
**Citrix Receiver**
  about 119
  configuring 119-122
  Preferences 119
  working 123
**Citrix Single Sign On**
  about 319
  downloading 319
**Citrix SSO platform**
  client plugin component 327
  implementing 319-327
  store component 327
  user and application management 327
**Citrix Streaming Profiler 227**
**Citrix StressPrinters software 196**
**Citrix Tool As A Service platform (TAAS) 154**
**Citrix website**
  URL 26
**Citrix XenDesktop 36**
**Citrix XenDesktop Collector.** *See* **XenDesktop Collector**
**Citrix XenDesktop Enterprise Edition 10**
**Citrix XenDesktop Express Edition 10**
**Citrix XenDesktop Platinum Edition 10**
**Citrix XenDesktop VDI Edition 10**
**Citrix XenServer**
  XenDesktop, interacting with 43
**Citrix XenServer-XenDesktop communication**
  about 43
  configuring 44-47
  working 48
**Class 201**
**client plugin component 327**
**command-line interface (CLI) 141**
**configuration service cmdlets**
  about 274, 276
  using 274
  working 277
**Configure authentication section**
  Connection Settings section 261
  Server section 261
**Copy-BrokerApplication cmdlet 291**
**CPU Usage Monitoring subsection 243**
**Cryptographic Service Provider (CSP) 307**

## D

**DDC 15, 111**
**Desktop Controller 17**
**Desktop Director.** *See* **Citrix Desktop Director**
**Desktop Director Controller.** *See* **DDC**
**Desktop Director portal 188**
**desktop experience**
  optimizing 91-95
**Desktop UI subsection 246**
**Desktop Windows Manager (DWM) service 97**
**DWORD Key 309**
**Dynamic Windows Preview (DWP) 251**

## E

**End User Monitoring subsection 241**
**Enterprise Certification Authority and Enrollment Station 307**
**ESX or ESXi servers 49**

## F

**File Redirection subsection 247**
**file system, policies sections 87**
**Flash Redirection subsection 244**
**FreeRADIUS 309**
**Full Qualified Domain Name (FQDN) 12, 44, 305**

## G

**Get-BrokerDesktop command 290**
**Get-BrokerPrivateAppDesktop command 290**
**Get-BrokerPrivateDesktop command 290**
**Get-BrokerResource command 285**
**Get-ConfigAdministrator command 277**

**Get-ConfigDBConnection command 277**
**Get-HypHypervisorPlugin command 296**
**Graphics subsection 241**

## H

**HDX 3D Pro**
about 113, 115
activating 115
download link 115
using 116
working 116
**HDX3DPro subsection 249**
**HDX Monitor**
about 117
settings and performance 118
**host and machine creation cmdlet**
about 296
using 292, 293
working 296
**hosts and machines**
administering, with host and machine creation cmdlets 292, 294

## I

**ICA Latency Monitoring subsection 250**
**ICA section 240, 244**
**Infrastructure Security 299**

## K

**Keep Alive subsection 241**

## L

**license server**
configuring 11-14
installing 10, 11
system requisites 11
working 14
**local area network (LAN) 90**
**local profile technology**
cons 107
pros 107
use cases 107
**log settings, policies sections 86**
**logs register information, for client component**
Workstation - Virtual Desktop Agent 271
**logs register information, for server components**
Active Directory Identity Service 270
Citrix Host Service 270
Machine Creation Service 270
Machine Identity Service 270

## M

**machine catalog**
configuring 160-170
creating 160
modifying 175-181
working 170-174, 182
**Machine Creation Service (MCS) architecture 296**
**Machine Creation Services.** *See* **MCS**
**machines policy level 251**
**mapped IP address (MIP) 266**
**MCS**
about 5
implementing 6
**Merchandising Server**
about 128, 139, 140
certification authority management 139
Configuration tab 135
configuring 128-137
General tab 134
Plug-ins tab 135
Rules tab 136
Schedule tab 137
working 138, 139
**Microsoft App-V**
about 227
features 234
used, for publishing applications 227-234
**Microsoft Hyper-V**
about 255
XenDesktop, interacting with 54
**Microsoft Hyper-V system**
configuring 55

**Microsoft Hyper-V-XenDesktop communication**
about 54
configuring 54
working 70
**Microsoft RADIUS role 309**
**Microsoft SQL Server 5**
**Microsoft System Center Virtual Machine Manage(SCVMM) 54**
**Mobile-OTP**
URL 318
**msiexec command**
about 14
parameters 14
**Multimedia subsection 242**
**Multi-Stream Connections subsection 242, 248**

## N

**NetScaler Access Gateway (NSIP) 266**
**Network File System (NFS) 6**
**Network Policy Server (NPS) role 317**
**New-AcctADAccount cmdlet 282**
**New-BrokerAccessPolicyRule command 291**
**New-BrokerApplication command 291**
**New-BrokerApplicationFolder command 291**
**New-BrokerAssignmentPolicyRule command 291**
**New-BrokerCatalog command 290**
**New-BrokerConfiguredFTA command 291**
**New-ConfigAdministrator command 277**
**New-ProvScheme command 296**
**NPS - Network Policy Server 309**

## O

**One Time Password (OTP) 309**
**Organizational Unit (OU) 103, 207**

## P

**performance tuning 254**
**personal vDisk technology**
about 102
cons 108
implementing 102
pros 108
use cases 108
**PID 201**
**Port Redirection subsection 248**
**Preferences, Citrix Receiver**
Application Display 122
Change Server 121
Plug-in status 120
Server Options 121
Session Options 122
User settings 120
**printer configuration**
about 194
configuration policies, Client Printers subsection 194, 195
configuration policies, for Drivers subsection 195
configuration policies, for Universal Printing subsection 196
main configuration policies 194
working 194
**printers**
configuring 190-193
**profile architecture**
implementing 102, 103
implementing, local profiles used 104
implementing, personal vDisk used 106
implementing, roaming profiles used 106
working 107
**profile handling, policies sections 86**
**Profile Load Time Monitoring subsection 250**
**Profile Management, policies sections 86**
**Prot 201**
**Provisioning Services.** *See* **PVS**
**Provisioning Services (PVS) architecture 290**
**Publish-ProvMasterVmImage command 296**
**PVS**
about 5, 6
configuring 27-34
implementing 7, 26
installing 27
working 35
**PVS ISO software**
downloading 26

## Q

**Quick Deploy option 40**

## R

**RADIUS 309, 317**
**RADIUS authentication 318**
**ReadOnly parameter 274**
**redirector modality approach 148**
**registry key 309**
**registry location 309**
**registry, policies sections 87**
**REL 201**
**Remove-AcctADAccount command 282**
**Remove-AcctIdentityPool cmdlet 279**
**Remove-ConfigAdministrator cmdlet 277**
**Rename-AcctIdentityPool command 281**
**Repeater Acceleration plugin 146**
**Reset Personal vDisk 189**
**roaming profile technology**
  cons 107
  pros 107
  use cases 107
**RSA OTP**
  URL 318

## S

**SafeNet OTP**
  URL 318
**Secure Ticket Authority (STA) 267**
**sequencing 234**
**Server Session Settings section 249**
**service groups 276**
**Session Limits subsection 248**
**Session Reliability subsection 242, 243**
**Set-BrokerDesktopGroup cmdlet 285**
**Set-BrokerSite configuration command 290**
**Set-ConfigDBConnection command 277**
**shadowing 189**
**Single Sign On platform (SSO) 319**
**SQL Server Database**
  preparing 7, 9
  working 9
**SSL VirtualCenter 51**
**SSO.** *See* **Citrix Single Sign On**
**stages, smart card authentication**
  Enterprise Certification Authority and Enrollment Station 307
  Web Interface 308
  Web Server - IIS 7.x 308
**Storage Area Network (SAN) 6**
**store component 327**
**streamed apps**
  about 226
  publishing, with XenApp 6.5 217-225
  streamed to client application 226
  streamed to server application 226
  working 226
**streamed user profiles, policies sections 87**
**subcategories, broker cmdlets**
  Access and Assignment filtering rules subsection 291
  Applications subsection 291
  Desktops and Desktop groups subsection 290
  Site and Catalog subsection 290
**Subclass 201**
**subnet IP address (SNIP) 266**
**Symantec OTP**
  URL 318
**system information**
  retrieving, configuration service cmdlets used 274, 275

## T

**Test-ConfigServiceInstanceAvailability cmdlet 277**
**Time Zone Control subsection 249**
**transparent modality approach 148**

## U

**USB devices**
  configuring 198, 200
  working 200
**USB Devices subsection 249**
**user and application management 327**
**users policy level 252**

## V

**VID 201**
**Virtual Desktop Agent**
  about 112
  installing 108-112
  installing, with personal vDisk enabled 114
  working 112

**Virtual Desktop Agent Settings section 243, 249**
**Virtual Desktop Agent (VDA) level 154**
**virtual desktop policies**
advanced settings 86
configuring 81-85
file system 87
log settings 86
profile handling 86
Profile Management 86
registry 87
streamed user profiles 87
working 86
**virtual hard disk (VHD) 221**
**virtual IP address (VIP) 266**
**Visual Display subsection 249**
**VM-hosted apps**
about 215
publishing, with XenDesktop 206-214
working 215
**VMware ESX/ESXi 255**
**VMware vCenter certificate**
importing 49
**VMware vSphere**
XenDesktop, interacting with 49
**VMware vSphere-XenDesktop communication**
about 49
configuring 49-52
working 54

## W

**Web Interface 308**
configuring 18-24
installing 18
working 24
**Web Server - IIS 7.x 308**
**Windows 2008 R2 virtual machine**
configuring, as Citrix license server 36
configuring, as Citrix Web Interface 37
configuring, as Citrix XenDesktop platform 36
configuring, as domain controller 36
configuring, as master target device 37
**Windows Automated Installation Kit (AIK) 57**
**Windows Display Driver Model (WDDM) system driver 112**
**Windows media redirection policy 252**
**Windows Radius server**
configuring 310, 312
**Windows Remote Management (WinRM) 188**
**Windows Server Update Services (WSUS) server 90**
**Wright SMS2**
URL 318

## X

**XenApp 6.5**
features 227
used, for publishing streamed apps 217-225
**XenDesktop 5.6**
about 5
license server, configuring 10
license server, installing 10
machine catalog, creating 160
Merchandising Server, configuring 128
printers, configuring 190
security 239
SQL Server Database, preparing 7-9
USB, configuring 198
used, for publishing VM-hosted apps 206-214
**XenDesktop Collector**
about 150
configuring 150-153
installing 150
working 154
**XenDesktop components**
installing 15, 16
**XenDesktop infrastructure**
about 6
creating 40-42
**XenDesktop license file 14**
**XenDesktop logging**
configuring 268, 269
working 270, 271
**XenDesktop machine catalog.** *See* **machine catalog**
**XenDesktop policies**
configuring 239, 240
effective running, verifying 253
machines policy level 251
users policy level 252
working 251

**XenDesktop policies configuration**
about 240
Audio subsection 245
Auto Client Reconnect subsection 240
Bandwidth subsection 245
CPU Usage Monitoring subsection 243
Desktop UI subsection 246
End User Monitoring subsection 241
File Redirection subsection 247
Flash Redirection subsection 244
Graphics subsection 241
HDX3DPro subsection 249
ICA Latency Monitoring subsection 250
ICA section 240, 244
Keep Alive subsection 241
Multimedia subsection 242
Multi-Stream connections subsection 248
Multi-Stream Connections subsection 242
Port Redirection subsection 248
Profile Load Time Monitoring subsection 250
Server Session Settings section 249
Session Limits subsection 248
Session Reliability subsection 242
Time Zone Control subsection 249
USB Devices subsection 249
Virtual Desktop Agent Settings section 243, 249
Visual Display subsection 249
**XenDesktop PowerShell**
Active Directory accounts, managing 278
AD identity cmdlets 278
broker cmdlets 283
Citrix Desktop Controller, managing 283
configuration service cmdlets 274
host and machine creation cmdlets 292
hosts and machines, administering 292
system information, retrieving 274
working with 273
**XenDesktop site**
configuring 40-43
configuring, for interacting with Citrix XenServer 43-47
configuring, for interacting with Microsoft Hyper-V 54-70
configuring, for interacting with VMware vSphere 49-54
**XenDesktop smart card authentication**
configuration tasks 300
implementing 300-307
stages 307
working 307
**XenDesktop strong authentication**
implementing 309-316
**XenServer 44, 48, 255**
**XenServer ISO image file**
downloading 44

## Z

**ZeroShell 309**

## Thank you for buying
# Citrix XenDesktop 5.6 Cookbook

## About Packt Publishing

Packt, pronounced 'packed', published its first book "*Mastering phpMyAdmin for Effective MySQL Management*" in April 2004 and subsequently continued to specialize in publishing highly focused books on specific technologies and solutions.

Our books and publications share the experiences of your fellow IT professionals in adapting and customizing today's systems, applications, and frameworks. Our solution-based books give you the knowledge and power to customize the software and technologies you're using to get the job done. Packt books are more specific and less general than the IT books you have seen in the past. Our unique business model allows us to bring you more focused information, giving you more of what you need to know, and less of what you don't.

Packt is a modern, yet unique publishing company, which focuses on producing quality, cutting-edge books for communities of developers, administrators, and newbies alike. For more information, please visit our website: `www.PacktPub.com`.

## About Packt Enterprise

In 2010, Packt launched two new brands, Packt Enterprise and Packt Open Source, in order to continue its focus on specialization. This book is part of the Packt Enterprise brand, home to books published on enterprise software – software created by major vendors, including (but not limited to) IBM, Microsoft and Oracle, often for use in other corporations. Its titles will offer information relevant to a range of users of this software, including administrators, developers, architects, and end users.

## Writing for Packt

We welcome all inquiries from people who are interested in authoring. Book proposals should be sent to `author@packtpub.com`. If your book idea is still at an early stage and you would like to discuss it first before writing a formal book proposal, contact us; one of our commissioning editors will get in touch with you.

We're not just looking for published authors; if you have strong technical skills but no writing experience, our experienced editors can help you develop a writing career, or simply get some additional reward for your expertise.

## Getting Started with Citrix XenApp 6.5

ISBN: 978-1-84968-666-2 Paperback: 478 pages

Design and implement Citrix farms based on XenApp 6.5

1. Use Citrix management tools to publish applications and resources on client devices with this book and eBook

2. Deploy and optimize XenApp 6.5 on Citrix XenServer, VMware ESX, and Microsoft Hyper-V virtual machines and physical servers

3. Understand new features included in XenApp 6.5 including a brand new chapter on advanced XenApp deployment covering topics such as unattended install of XenApp 6.5, using dynamic data center provisioning, and more

---

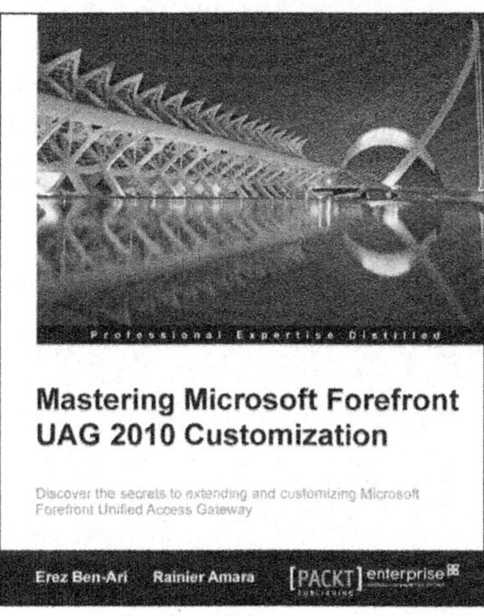


## Mastering Microsoft Forefront UAG 2010 Customization

ISBN: 978-1-84968-538-2 Paperback: 186 pages

Discover the secrets to extending and customizing Microsoft Forefront Unified Access Gateway

1. Perform UAG extension magic with high level tips and tricks only few have had knowledge of - until now!

2. Get to grips with UAG customization for endpoint detection, client components, look and feel, and much more in this book and e-book

3. An advanced, hands on guide with customization tips and code samples for extending UAG

Please check **www.PacktPub.com** for information on our titles

CPSIA information can be obtained at www.ICGtesting.com
Printed in the USA
LVOW03s1737160815

450285LV00047B/242/P

9 781849 685047